THE HERITAGE OF THE CATHEDRAL

THE LAST JUDGMENT, BOURGES CATHEDRAL

S. Michael weighs a soul; a cauldron issues from the mouth of Leviathan; Abraham holds the souls of the redeemed in his bosom; Peter guards the gate; beside
him stand a Franciscan monk and a king (Francis of Assisi and Louis IX?).
The sun and the moon, held by angels over the head of Christ, are ancient symbols of His Humanity and Divinity.

THE HERITAGE OF
The Cathedral

A STUDY OF THE INFLUENCE OF HISTORY AND
THOUGHT UPON CATHEDRAL ARCHITECTURE

By

SARTELL PRENTICE

NEW YORK
William Morrow and Company
MCMXXXVI

THE HERITAGE OF
THE CATHEDRAL

PRINTED IN THE U. S. A. BY
QUINN & BODEN COMPANY, INC.
RAHWAY, N. J.

TO MY FATHER

MAJOR SARTELL PRENTICE

1837-1905

LIEUTENANT AND CAPTAIN, XII U. S. INFANTRY (1861-1865)

MAJOR BY BREVET FOR

GALLANT AND MERITORIOUS SERVICE IN THE

BATTLE OF THE WILDERNESS AND IN THE CAMPAIGN BEFORE PETERSBURG

AND

TO MY BROTHER,

PIERREPONT ISHAM PRENTICE, M.D.,

WHO DIED SPLENDIDLY

AT THE CALL, AND IN THE SERVICE, OF HIS PROFESSION

Foreword

THIS book brings new life into the old truism that architecture mirrors life. Dr. Prentice shows how the great buildings of the world, especially the cathedrals of Italy and France, not only embody in their magnificent structure the history of their times, but also tell fascinating stories of men's beliefs, hopes, fears, work, and pleasures.

With eyes properly adjusted, we can find in their forms and decorations the tale of how men lived, how they traded; we can even find in them evidences of the persistence of ideas and of those misunderstood, vague feelings whose origins are rooted in the teeming earth of prehistoric times. The heritage of the cathedral comes from an ancestry that is long, rich, crowded, and honourable, for it is the ancestry of human thought and emotion.

A trained and careful scholar in the field of myth and early religion, a lover of the great buildings mankind has built, who knows them with the close and personal knowledge that only repeated contacts can give, Dr. Prentice is ideally fitted to introduce to his readers that ancestry, to adjust their vision to new perspectives, and give new understanding of those buildings too often visited fleetingly, seen but superficially, and then little by little forgotten. To visit them with this new insight is to make them, instead, living beings, friends, companions with a host of fascinating stories to tell. He has given us a new *Golden Bough* of architecture; and, just as Frazer leads his readers through a fascinating maze of myth, ritual, and legend that is the background of religion, so Dr. Prentice leads them in a journey, equally interesting, equally curious, through the background of human thought and work and dream that lies behind architecture.

And it is not only the bare bones of his knowledge that Dr. Prentice gives. He has the talent of projecting himself into those far times, of seeming to live in them as he writes, so that they become vital realities. With the men of the Dark Ages we follow the caravans in

their slow course into Asia, or later plough the blue Mediterranean in
unwieldy merchant ships; we wait behind the town walls for the
terrible raids of the Vikings; we feel and understand the strange
phantasmagoria of monastic life that turned dreams into visions of
angels, and nightmares into battles with an obscene Satan; farther
back still, we may even see prehistoric man piling the branches that
made his hut, and calling upon the gods of the waters to help him
with their power. So we may come to learn why churches had towers,
why the early atrium gave way to the later cloister, and what lies
behind the macabre beauty of the carvings on Moissac porch.

   There has long been need for a book with this inclusive aim, so that
all this lore, tucked away in the periodicals of learned societies or
books written only for the specialist, might be opened to all. This
book should be of the greatest interest not only to students of architecture, but also to high school and college students of history. Especially it should be a godsend to those throngs who annually fill the
Atlantic ships and sail across the ocean to see what they can of the
European world. To such travellers it will bring not only open eyes
and an alert mind, but also such an understanding of the great buildings they see as to make those buildings realities of the highest sort
—not only sights but experiences. And, finally, this book should be
of the highest value to all who wish to have an intelligent interest in
the form their own environment takes, for to them it will bring not
only a new understanding of the riches that architecture offers, but
also an abiding vision of the fascinating, spreading roots of our human
life and thought today.

                                        TALBOT FAULKNER HAMLIN

Avery Library
Columbia University
February 3rd, 1936.

Contents

PAGE

Foreword vii

Ut Gratias Reddam xiii

Introduction xv

PART ONE

THE IMPACTS OF HISTORY ON THE CATHEDRAL

CHAPTER

I. The Voices of the Cathedral 3

II. From Catacombs to Crypt 9

III. Why the Law Court Became a Church . . . 19

IV. The Origin of the Transepts 30

V. The Uncertain Transepts 43

VI. The Arches of Constantine 46

VII. The End of the Ancient World 52

VIII. The Gifts of Ignorance 56

IX. The Gifts of Fear 64

X. Gifts of Unbelief 72

XI. The Background of Romanesque Architecture:
The Treasure to Be Guarded 80

XII. The Background of Romanesque Architecture:
The Menace to the Treasure 85

XIII. The Great Gift of an Impatient Horse . . . 91

XIV. Romanesque Architecture 100

XV. The Background of Gothic Architecture: The
Way Men Lived 113

XVI. The Background of Gothic Architecture: The
Way Men Thought 122

XVII. Cargoes, Caravans, and Cathedrals 131

XVIII. Gothic Architecture 144

XIX. The Origin of the Gothic Vault 154

CHAPTER   PAGE

XX. The Origin of the Flying Buttress 160
XXI. Symbolism 163
XXII. The Romance and the Tragedy of Cathedral
  Glass 170
XXIII. Notre-Dame 181
XXIV. The Background of Rayonnant and of Flamboy-
  ant Architecture 185
XXV. Rayonnant Architecture 200
XXVI. Flamboyant Architecture 206
XXVII. The Renaissance in Italy 212
XXVIII. The Renaissance in France 223
XXIX. The End of the Road 231

PART TWO

THE ARCHÆOLOGY

XXX. What Primitive Man Contributed to Cathedral
  Architecture 235
XXXI. The Origin of the Cloister 244
XXXII. Strange Voices from the Stoup 252
XXXIII. The Origin of the Altar Rail 265
XXXIV. The Bells and the Devil 275
XXXV. The Towers of Gudea 282
XXXVI. Iconography: A Literature for the Illiterate . . 291

L'Envoi 308
Index 311

Illustrations

The Last Judgment, Bourges Cathedral . . . *Frontis.*

FACING PAGE

A Cubiculum in a Sicilian Catacomb 10

The Church of S. Maria in Trastevere 27

The Church of S. Maria Maggiore at Toscanella, Modern
  Tuscania 42

The Baptistry, Cathedral, and Campanile at Pisa, Seen from
  the Air 46

The Church of S. Pietro at Toscanella 55

Amiens Cathedral 59

The Rayonnant Church of S. Ouen at Rouen . . . 62

The Atrium of S. Ambrogio at Milan 71

The Evolution of the Spire 78

Durham Cathedral, Reflected in the River Wear . . 87

The Church of S. Beât 94

The Transept and Apse of the Abbey of Beaulieu . . 103

The Ambulatory of the Abbey of S. Benoît-sur-Loire . 106

The Cathedral of S. Madeleine at Vézelay . . . 123

The Cathedral of Lâon 126

The Choir of the Cathedral of Beauvais 135

Sainte Chapelle, Paris 138

Notre-Dame de Paris 155

The Flying Arches and Pinnacles of Notre-Dame de Paris 158

The Dome of Anthemius: Sancta Sophia, Constantinople . 167

A Twelfth-Century Window at S. Denis 174

Les Saintes Maries, a Scar of the English Wars . . 183

The Flamboyant West Front of La Trinité at Vendôme . 206

The Dome of S. Peter, Rome 215

The Church of SS. Paul and Louis, Paris . . . 218

The Madeleine, Paris 231

FACING PAGE

The Temple of Poseidon at Pæstum 235
The Cloister of Moissac 250
The Chancel Screen at Torcello 267
Gudea and His Acropolis 282
Capital from Autun 299
Bas Reliefs from the Porch of Amiens Cathedral . . . 299

Diagrams

Plan of a Typical Early Christian Basilica 27
Alexamenos Sebete Theon 31
Floor Plan of a Romanesque Church 69
Cross Section of a Romanesque Church 102
The Groin Vault over a Side Aisle 109
The Thrust and Counter-Thrust of a Gothic Vault . . 148
Cross Section of a Gothic Church 149
The Inclination of an Apse 166

Ut Gratias Reddam

THIS book owes much to my editorial son, Pierrepont Isham Prentice, whose literary criticisms, wide knowledge of history, and interpretations of historic causes and consequences play so important a part throughout these pages that only his own persistent refusal has kept his name from appearing with my own upon the title page.

I owe a debt also to my younger son, bearer of my name, who drove our car from end to end of Europe, entering with a stimulating enthusiasm into our studies of architecture and of archæology, and contributing a knowledge of Spanish without which we could not have entered so successfully into the highways and hedges of Spain in our search for her pre-Romanesque churches.

Year after year my wife, Lydia Vanderpoel, has travelled with me, not to the popular resorts and spas of Europe, but very often to little places where conveniences were counted luxuries. She has continued to show an interest when checking over manuscript with me, even when she knew each word by heart; she has corrected my spelling, an heroic undertaking, and read the printer's proof. For twelve years she has supplied much of the courage, patience, and determination that the long task has required.

I owe much to Professor Arthur Kingsley Porter, of Harvard University, whose tragic death in Irish waters brought sorrow to a far wider circle than Mr. Porter, living, could have conceived. His criticisms and comments on certain chapters, as well as his encouragements, have been most valuable.

I am greatly in debt to Professor Talbot F. Hamlin, of the School of Architecture of Columbia University, who has kindly reviewed this book from cover to cover, and called my attention to some neglected sources.

I am also indebted to Professor E. Baldwin Smith, of Princeton University; to Mr. Arthur Stanley Riggs, Editor of *Art and Archæology;* to Professor Edgar J. Goodspeed, of the University of Chicago; to Miss Margaret Bancroft, of Barnard College; and to Professor

Ernesto Buonaiuti, recently of the University of Rome, now of the University of Lausanne, for their reviews of various chapters, for their suggestions, and often for bibliographic references. Finally, and not least, I would gratefully acknowledge many courtesies from the Avery Library of Columbia University.

While drawing freely from the works of many scholars in many fields I have tried to be most scrupulous in giving credit to those by whose labors I have been enriched, yet so far as possible I have avoided the use of quotation marks, feeling that these tend to break the continuity and to distract the attention of the reader. In some parts of the book I have drawn heavily from Professor James W. Thompson's *Economic and Social History of the Middle Ages* and from his *Economic and Social History of the Later Middle Ages,* published by the D. Appleton-Century Company, but I have abbreviated the references to Thompson Vol. I or II. I have also borrowed from Frazer's *Folk Lore in the Old Testament* and his *Golden Bough* (in the one-volume edition), both published by The Macmillan Company; from *A History of Architecture,* by Russell Sturgis and A. L. Frothingham, published by Doubleday, Doran and Company; and from *Art in France* by Louis Hourticq, published by Charles Scribner's Sons, in all cases with the courteous permission of the publishers. I have also profited greatly by M. Émile Mâle's scholarly volumes, *L'Art Religieux du XIIe Siècle en France; L'Art Religieux du XIIIe Siècle en France,* and *L'Art Religieux de la Fin du Moyen Âge.* Here also, for brevity's sake, I have limited the references to Mâle, Vol. I, II, or III.

The illustrations are from photographs of the Archives Photographiques d'Art et d'Histoire, Paris; from Alinari, in Florence, Italy; from Ewing Galloway, in New York, the University Prints, Boston, from *L'Art Gothique* by Paul Leon, published by the Librairie d'Art, R. Ducher, Paris, or from the Fotographia Pontificia, Rome. The diagrams on pages 109, 148, and 149 are by T. G. Jackson, from his book *Reason in Architecture* (John Murray, London, 1906). Finally I would acknowledge the personal interest, the care and the skill which Mr. George Hiltenbeitel has given to the other drawings and diagrams.

S. P.

Introduction

SURVEYING THE ROUTE

THIS book was conceived beneath the towers of Amiens Cathedral when a wandering tourist asked me, "What is this church? Why are you going in? Is there anything to see?"

It was born shortly thereafter in Notre-Dame in Paris when two American business men of unknown names, occupations, and places of residence, having spent less than five minutes in the cathedral, started to leave it by the North Transept portal. As they passed me on their way out I called their attention to the windows under the great South Rose where four bearded giants appear, carrying four little boys —although three of them are also bearded—pick-a-back on their shoulders.

The men were amused by the naïveté of the glass until I explained that this was the Thirteenth Century way of expressing the dependence of the New Testament upon the Old; that the four giants were the four Major Prophets and the little boys were the four Evangelists.

Then one of them asked a question, and this chance encounter led to our spending an interpretative hour in the cathedral.

The great columns of the nave received a new meaning when we glimpsed behind them the shaggy hair and beard of that Mesolithic man who invented the spreading capital when he capped the tree trunk, which was the first column, with a short, rough log to keep it from piercing, instead of supporting, his heavy roof of boughs and clay.

The Basin of Holy Water became dramatic when we saw, reflected in its depths, the executioners of Xerxes scourging the waters of the Hellespont for insolently sweeping away the royal bridge, and heard in the hiss of the scourges an echo of the old belief that living water had a mind and a will of its own and could bestow blessings or curses upon men.

The stone vault overhead became more than a vault when we heard it dimly ringing the old war-cries of Northmen, Saracens, and Magyars, and understood that it came into existence to protect the church and its relics from perils of fire in those Dark Ages when savage invaders were ravaging the land.

So as we passed from portal to ambulatory and from aisle to aisle the mists cleared, the years rolled back, and a hundred generations rose from the dust to speak with us.

As I walked with these men among the aisles of Notre-Dame it occurred to me, hazily, that of the half-million tourists who annually cross from America to Europe there were few to whom the cathedral is not a closed book, and that it would be well worth while if someone should undertake for the many that which I had briefly and incompletely undertaken for these two.

Of course many books have been written on ecclesiastical architecture, but the best of these—those written for the student of architecture—are too often barred by the nature of their vocabularies from even the educated reader. Two excellent books on the architecture of Spain speak of "Carlovingian looking trefoils," of "exedræ struck on the sides of a trapezoid," and of "semi-domes carried on trompes." They tell us of the "maksura" and the "mirab" of a mosque, and of the "iconostasis" of a church; they invite us to visit an "Oriental" basilica while leaving us in ignorance as to the differences between basilicas of the Orient and of the Occident.

Then there are the guide books which take us everywhere but do not permit us to linger anywhere. They tell us of the church we see, but the very universality of the task they undertake compels them to leave unvisited the church we do not see—the church invisible which lies in and behind the stones.

Finally there are charming books of travel from whose pages we breathe in the very atmosphere of foreign lands; but, one by one, they leave us rich in impressions but not quite so rich in understanding. For instance, one very delightful volume speaks of the great church of

S. Nectaire, in Auvergne. It was dusk when the writer motored by and the twilight was fast fading into darkness; the huge bulk of the famous church, outlined in black against the evening sky, rose high on its hill-top and blotted out the stars of the horizon as the car purred along a road that was illumined only by the headlights; the author briefly regrets that the hour and the night forbade them to stop—and that, for them, was the end of S. Nectaire.

It would seem, then, that there might be real justification for an interpretation of the church in simple terms, free from technicalities, that should enable us of the laity to understand the deeper meaning, not merely of this church or of that, but of any cathedral and of any church—of Occidental origin—in whatsoever land or city we may be.

This book, consequently, is not written for archæologists or for architects; it is written for all of us who travel, whether we go by earth, or air, or sea, or only along the flickering trails of our own firesides.

The road has not always been easy to follow; there have been many alternative ways, and many places where the sign boards were confusing. Tempting by-paths have appeared to right or left, and many voices have called to us, "Lo! here," or "Lo! there." But we may neither listen nor turn aside. We must select our road and sternly follow it, or we will be lost in space.

I have many books in my library which discuss in two or more volumes aspects of ecclesiastical architecture that are limited both in time and in extent—to the architecture of the Middle Ages, of Lombardy, of the French Renaissance, or to the iconography: the art of the Church in carvings, in glass, or in frescoes. But we are here dealing with continents, not with countries; with millennia, not with centuries; with an octave of themes instead of with one. Our study will carry us from Central Asia to Western Europe, from the Azilians to the Napoleonic Era.[1]

[1] As we shall hereafter meet with the Azilians from time to time—especially when we come to consider the possible connection between their round houses and the curving east end, or apse, of the church, it may be well to introduce them here.

The Azilians (named from their camp at Mas d'Azil, forty miles from Toulouse) were one of several invading peoples (and probably the first human inhabitants of Scot-

Furthermore, this book is not the product of a typewriter, a desk, and a library. By horse, donkey, or camel; by train, motor, or canal boat, my wife and I have travelled fully fifty thousand miles, from English Durham to Arabic Petra and Sinai; from the Irish Sea to the Red Sea, the Dead Sea, and the Black Sea, that I might write of things which I had seen for myself, not borrowed from others.

We take then the pilgrim's staff and scallop shell to follow the builders from the Age of Stone to that of Steel—but not all the builders, for the architectural road early divided; one branch led through the East and those who travelled it created the Byzantine type of architecture; another turned to the West to call into being the Romanesque and the Gothic. It is from those who followed this latter road that we have, in the main, inherited, wherefore we also turn our faces towards the West.

As we pass from cycle to cycle, and from church to church, we shall discover that ecclesiastical architecture, from the Fourth to the Fourteenth Century, followed an upward, evolutionary pathway; then came a pause of a hundred years when the Church, having lost her faith and her inspiration, suffered the artist to thrust aside the architect and in the following century to bury the Church beneath a flood of Flamboyant decorations. Finally, with the Renaissance, church architecture entered a road of devolution wherein her architects, retracing all the steps of the upward march and returning to one abandoned structural form after another, ended a swift retreat of four hundred years in the purely pagan temple of the Madeleine on the Rue Royale in Paris. Thus the circle was made complete and the Church returned, in form at least, to that paganism against which nearly two thousand years before she had rebelled.

We shall further discover that the Church not merely worships a Trinity but that she is herself triune and that her architecture must be studied from a triple point of view.

First: In its form and structure the cathedral reflects the history of

land) who entered Europe about twelve thousand years ago, coming apparently from Central Asia. With them begins the Middle Stone Age (the Mesolithic) which divides the Old Stone Age (the Paleolithic) from the New Stone Age (the Neolithic).

the century in which the builders lived, and measures the velocities of the currents or cross currents which determined the course of contemporary life.

Second: The Church echoes the beliefs and fears of men who ended their days hundreds, and even thousands, of years before the rise of Antioch where "the disciples were first called Christians;" when pagan gods possessed the world, untroubled by any dim forebodings of that mightier Lord from Syrian hills who should degrade them from honoured deities to dreaded devils.

And third: We shall see the church revealing to us, through her sculptures and her glass, the mind of the Middle Ages. Through her art she will unfold to us mediæval definitions and philosophies; curious conceptions of the heavens above and of the earth beneath; superstitions, credulities, and the hopes or fears with which that Mind accepted those invisible agents of an Overworld and of an Underworld, whose activities were everywhere in evidence.

In the first part of this book, therefore, we shall follow the rise and fall, the evolution and devolution, of church architecture. We shall read the history of centuries as our fathers wrote it on the stones, and discover how intimately the lives of kings and lords, of monks and priests, of commoners and peasants, have been woven into the very structure of the churches.

But when we shall have measured all the creative forces that were contemporary with the builders we shall repeatedly detect, in the architecture, the effects of formative beliefs that were far older than the generations whose handiwork we see. Thus we shall understand the cloister only when we see it as descendant from another area of ground which, having been made dangerously holy by the visitation of some pagan god, had been enclosed by walls lest the anger of the god be unleashed against some unwarned and unwary trespasser. And the bells, clamorous when battling against the storms and solemn when tolling for the dying, arouse an echo from beyond far horizons. We hear the distant clangour of brazen gongs, beaten to drive away the devils who, having sought to destroy man's handiwork throughout his lifetime, strove to steal away his soul in the hour of his death.

In the second part of the book, therefore, we shall repeatedly see the cathedral in the crepuscule of morning where the hands of men long dead grope in mists and darkness, feeling after God.

Later we shall read, written in the carvings or in the windows, the ideas—now searching and profound, again simple and naïve—that men wove into their philosophies; we shall meet again, as we follow the chisel of the sculptor and the leads of the glazier, old pagan gods of East or West, disguised but still recognizable despite their Christian garb.

We shall learn new geographies and visit those Twilight lands where strange beasts and stranger peoples dwell; the Sciopode who runs marvellously with his single leg, which he sometimes uses as a parasol when the sun is strong; and among the people the Panotii, the Dwarfs, the Cynocephali, or the Ethiopian with his four eyes; these shall introduce us to their kin—the outlandish kind of these far outlands. Then the beasts shall become our teachers and the fox, even the dragon and the whale, shall show us how subtly Satan may seduce the souls of men. We shall laugh at the jests that amused the Middle Ages—the Baldheaded man, the Termagant wife, and the Sage who preached but failed to practise. We shall shiver at their ghost stories, tremble at their nightmares, and look with horror, through their eyes, at all women howsoever fair they be.

In our study of the church we are fortunate in our material. While time has swept away most of the examples of civil and domestic architecture that pre-date the Renaissance, there are still standing churches that represent every stage of ecclesiastical architecture, with all the steps of its development, from the basilica of Constantine's day to the Madeleine of Napoleon's Paris.

In undertaking to trace the changes that took place in the form and structure of the church between the Fourth and the Eighteenth Centuries, it will be convenient to have an outline of that development before us, even though no absolute precision may be possible. The stages of evolution were longer in some countries than they were in others; styles lingered here and hastened there.

Although the limitations of space will compel us to deal especially

with the basilicas of Italy and the churches of France, permitting us
to touch but lightly those of other countries, yet from these we shall
come to understand all churches, except the Byzantine, wherever they
may lift their walls, in the Old World or in the New, for in her architecture far more than in her theology the Church was one. Though
architectural forms were modified when they crossed frontiers, and
though the Channel, the Rhine, the Alps, and the Pyrenees formed
barriers as well as boundaries behind which each nation wrought its
own individuality into its architecture, yet the similarities among the
churches are far greater than their divergencies, and whatever we may
learn from Italy or from France we shall also learn for the architecture of every other country.

With such qualifications ecclesiastical architecture may be divided
into the following stages of development:

  I. The Period of the Basilican Church; the Fourth to the Sixth
     Century.
 II. The Period of the Carlovingian Basilican Church; the Seventh
     to the Tenth Century.
III. The Period of the Romanesque Church; the Eleventh Century.
 IV. The Period of the Transition and of the Pure Gothic; the
     Twelfth and Thirteenth Centuries.
  V. The Period of the Rayonnant Gothic; the Fourteenth Century.
 VI. The Period of the Flamboyant Gothic; the Fifteenth Century.
VII. The Period of the Renaissance and of the Classical; from the
     Sixteenth through the Eighteenth Century.

Another volume on *The Origins and Interpretations of Cathedral
Art* is now in preparation; it will treat of the iconography of the cathedral, of the thoughts and legends behind the pictures of the stained
glass, and the carvings of tympani, capitals, screens and entablatures.

"During the first 6,000 years of the world, from the immemorial pagoda of Hindustan to the Cathedral of Cologne, architecture was the great handwriting of the human race. Not only every religious symbol, but every human thought, has its page and its monument in that immense book. The human race has had no important idea that was not written in stone. Humanity has two books, two testaments: Masonry and Printing—the Bible of Stone and the Bible of Paper."

VICTOR HUGO

Part One

THE IMPACTS OF HISTORY ON THE CATHEDRAL

Chapter One

THE VOICES OF THE CATHEDRAL

IF ALL mediæval manuscripts had perished we would still be able to trace the main outlines of European history in the architecture of her churches.

Cathedrals and nations alike are the product of the common life; the men, famed or unfamed, who built the one also built the other, and as our fathers raised their churches they traced upon the walls and vaults the pathways that they trod, so that we today may read in the stones the age-old record of the compacts and conflicts by which the Present struggled from the Past.

Here have been written countless tales of war and peace; of lean years of poverty and fat years of wealth; of famines and plagues; of the rise and fall of governments; of the opening or closing of trade routes; of changes in the social order, and of the ebbs and flows of faith. Somewhere within the church, wrought into its decoration or into its very structures, is the imprint of the Babylonian, the Syrian, and the Egyptian; of the Latin, the Greek, and the Byzantine; of the Persian, the Scythian, and the Sarmatian; of Saracen and Norman; of Andalusian Moor and Castilian Spaniard; of Teuton, Celt, and Saxon. Not one of these has passed without leaving his mark upon the church.

On the pavement of the ambulatory of Toledo, where Cardinal Portocarrero lies buried, are inscribed these words:

"Hic Jacit pulvis et cineres et praeterea nihil."
("Here lie dust and ashes—and nothing more.")

In every great church such ashes lie all around; in the crypt, under the pavement, and in the walls. But once that dust spoke, and when

3

it spoke "the sun stood still over Gibeon, and the moon over the valley of Ajalon." Ferdinand and Isabella sleep in the cathedral of Granada and their great Captain, Gonsalvo de Cordova, lies near by in San Jeronimo. Roger de Loria, who won Sicily for Aragon, sleeps with his king in Santa Cruz; Columbus, after far voyagings, rests well beneath his stone canopy in Seville; and Frederick II, "Stupor Mundi," strives no more with popes or paynim from his porphyry bed in Palermo.

> "The beasts do talk in barn and byre
> On Christmas Eve, old legends know."

If this were true, and if the "Dust and Ashes" could also come forth and speak on that most Holy Night, what a vigil one might keep in the old cathedral when the sun had set and the flame of his setting had faded from the West Rose window; when the aisles were flooded with a moonlight turned into purple and crimson and gold by the alchemy of windows of jewelled glass! What a vigil one might keep when, in the hush of midnight, the great dead awoke and came up from the crypt, out from the pavements, and down from the walls, to tell again the stories of Navas de Tolosa, of Tagliacozzo and perhaps of Roncesvalles!

Cœur-de-Lion, beneath the vaults of Fontevrault, might tell how he scattered the armies of Saladin at Jaffa. The Black Prince, from the ambulatory of Canterbury, could tell how he captured a king of France at Poitiers; and who would not listen when, in the nave of Seville, the Great Admiral told of the night when, with stormy leagues of water behind him and a mutinous crew about him, he caught the gleam of fires burning along the shores of a New World, beneath the palms of San Salvador!

And not these alone; more numerous still would be the forgotten men and women whose names were writ in water, but whose feet once trod these aisles; whose fingers helped to wear down the stone of the Holy Water Basin, who knelt before these altars, prayed to these marble saints, and gathered strength or comfort from the lips of other men who, long since, became also *pulvis et cineres*.

But if the Ashes may not speak, if the Dust must continue silent, the church itself is a veritable saga, sung by the stones, and he who has ears to hear may listen as they tell the tales of centuries long dead.

The very plan of the cathedral, like some witch of old Etruria, calls ghosts from the Appian Way to fill again the nave with togaed Romans, transmuting the confessionals of the aisles into booths where shadowy merchants bargain with the *manes* of old customers. The rounded apse brings spectres from ancient *columbaria* to fill anew its benches with magistrates of vanished courts.

The Bishop's Throne, carved with the heads and claws of savage beasts, brings visions of the sands of Rome's arenas; the transepts chant a dirge for the dying Mistress of the world; the galleries speak to us of the Orient where women dwelt in strict seclusion; the altars in the depths of the apse and the scenes of Judgement carved above the western portals speak fearfully of the coming of the barbarian and of that terror of the Sclav which set all Italy aquiver when Alboin and his hordes broke through the Alpine barrier and flooded the Lombard Plain; the Black Death helped to inspire the leaping lines of Flamboyant windows and the frenzy of the *Danse Macabre,* frescoed on the walls of La Chaise Dieu.

The same pride that built the tower of Babel built also Val-de-Grâce and the smaller churches that characterize the Renaissance. Vanity, boasting itself "the image of God on earth," echoes from the walls of the Chapel of Versailles, and there are Seventeenth Century churches which assert that righteousness lies in good manners; that the sin of sins is gaucherie.

Such a cathedral as that of Chartres did not come into existence in a moment of time; it did not leap, wholly conceived, from the brain of some unknown architect of the Twelfth Century as Pallas sprang from the head of Zeus; here is no Melchisedec of stone, "without father or mother, and without descent." Through very many centuries a hundred generations have worked and planned, succeeded or failed, before the builders could raise these walls and so buttress them that they might sustain a vault of stone.

On every side the stones are speaking; they tell us of one difficulty after another conquered by the high courage and stout wills of builders who failed yet never surrendered; of the torch, falling from the hands of the fathers but caught up and carried forward by their sons. So, in the darkness, illumined by a light that never was on land or sea, we mingle with that misty row of shadow-shapes who crowd the aisles and learn, from whispering voices, the story of their labours and the cost of our inheritance. Though these visitors of the moonlight must vanish when the glow-worm shows the matin to be near, yet in the daylight the stones still carry on the tale.

Some, high overhead, tell of tragic years when the builders, ignorant of the mathematics of construction, failed to provide an adequate defence against the vault's attack; they remember how, day after day and inch by inch, the walls were driven back until the stones above crashed down, involving aisles, columns, and walls in a common ruin. They tell us of long years of heart-breaking failure before the balance of attack and defence, of thrust and counter-thrust, was so established that the entire structure stood secure.

Others from the arches speak to us of Carlovingian masons struggling with the heavy stones they had to carry on their backs as they tried to build *juxta Romanorum morem*—"according to the Roman way"—each one a Carlovingian Romulus at whom a Roman Remus would have laughed, but out of whose weakness came forth strength and beauty. There are other stones, curving diagonally with the ribs across the vault from pier to pier, that tell of Lombard masons, dwellers in a treeless and war-infested plain, who rose above their limitations and devised these curving lines that they might erect their vaults even though they had little wood for scaffoldings.

Some of the ideas realized in Chartres came from Central Italy; Byzantium also contributed; the Midi, the Rhine, and Normandy each gave something to the task. Listen, for the very stones are speaking. Here you may catch the voices of the *langue d'oc,* and there of the *langue d'oui;* the guttural notes of the Teuton sound from the Western towers, mingled with the undertones of Fourth or Fifth Century dwellers in Kalb Lauzeh, in Djeradeh, and in Kasr-il-Benat; from the compound piers of the nave come the softer voices of Northern

Italy; here speaks the Greek, and there the Latin; the Babylonian calls to us from many a capital—or again the Assyrian, the Persian, the Sarmatian, or Sythian—while from the *bénitier* and from the cloister whisperings come in a tongue that was old when Abraham was young.

Only the pilgrim of Charlemagne's day, weary and grey with dust, bearing his sins or his sickness to the healing grace of some famed relic, can make us understand the curving aisle that encircles the chancel, carrying a pilgrim's path from shrine to shrine. Only the "noble army of martyrs," whose honoured bones have been translated from the oratories of the catacombs, can interpret to us the crypt—that church which lies amid the foundations of the cathedral—and we must go back to the very beginnings of the world, or at least to the story told in Genesis, if we are to know the reason for the octagonal form of the Baptismal Font.

Thus by the magic of many voices we shall be carried from cycle to cycle; from historic to prehistoric times; from the Age of Iron to that of Bronze; from Bronze to Copper; from Copper to Stone, until at last we reach that dim aurora wherein our early ancestors lived under the tyranny of primitive taboos.

Once more we shall see our familiar sun, now shining on a world of lost beliefs, and stand before tumuli or caves where those *Inconnus* lie buried whose names are known only to their Unknown God, but whose hands—long dead—still pull the strings of action for us who dwell far beyond the space—or time—horizons of their most fantastic dreams.

No one man can interpret for us all the voices of the cathedral. For any adequate understanding we shall need, above all others, one who —like Zechariah of old—has power "to cause understanding in the seeing of God." We shall need the leadership of the architect, of the historian, and of the archæologist who, next to the prophet, will be our most necessary guide; and finally we shall have to call upon one who has looked into a past that is older than any the historian has known, who has watched—in the twilight of the dawn of human life —the efforts of primitive man as he crudely, and often cruelly, sought the favour of the Unknown God he ignorantly worshipped.

We shall travel far gathering—as the Venerable Bede once wrote—"our honey from many hives," but there is always before us the hope that we may ultimately come into a deeper understanding, not merely of the cathedral but also of the lives of those generations from whose loins we have sprung; whose labours, sacrifices, sins, and aspirations have moulded the lines of the church and are woven into its very structure.

Chapter Two

FROM CATACOMBS TO CRYPT

IN THE year 30 A.D., when Pontius Pilate was Procurator of Judea, a Jew—whom a handful of fanatics called a god—was put to death outside the walls of Jerusalem.

In 59 A.D. another Jew, one Saul of Tarsus—having been arrested in the turbulent capital of Judea—was brought to Rome, condemned after some delay, and beheaded where the Church of Tre Fontana now stands (tradition being our authority).

Less than ten years after the execution of this man Saul, a great revolt in Judea was suppressed and Jerusalem destroyed by the armies of Titus, whose Triumphal Arch still stands near the Roman Forum. Thereupon the Senate decreed a Triumph and all Rome poured out to see her legions, their Syrian prisoners and Judean spoils, pass up the Via Sacra to the Temple of Jupiter Capitolinus, where the conquerors laid down their laurel wreaths of victory before the statue of the Roman god.

This seemed to end Jerusalem and all her works. The Jew whom some men called a god, his most effective spokesman, and his city had all been destroyed, and nothing now appeared to threaten the pax Romana from that troublesome quarter of the Mediterranean.

Yet underneath the surface a new faith in a Nazarene who had been crucified steadily and increasingly made its way, gaining recruits not merely among the proletariat but in the barracks of the army and in the palaces of the Cæsars.

We read of a Roman Proconsul, of a Councillor of the Athenian Areopagus, of administrators in Asia Minor, even of members of Nero's household, who confessed the Christian faith. Clemens and Domitilla, cousins of Domitian, were enrolled among the martyrs,

9

while a rescript of Valerian complains that "Senators, Roman Knights, and ladies of quality" had forsaken the old gods and were worshipping the new.

In matters of belief Rome was tolerant, even indifferent; she was ready to admit the right of any people to worship what gods they chose, and to welcome the deities who flocked to the Imperial City in such numbers that the Christian taunt seemed justified: "Other cities worship their own gods, but the Romans worship the gods of other cities." In matters of practice, however, Rome was exacting, for her religion was imperial and governmental wherefore reverence for Roman altars was inseparable from respect for the Roman State. While welcoming all deities, Rome nevertheless demanded an equal tolerance for her own gods and an occasional offering on their altars, less as a tribute to her divinities than as an obeisance to herself.

Light through the Roman law might appear to Cæsar, to the Christian it was a summons to apostasy, and his reply, voiced by Peter to the authorities of Jerusalem, "We must obey God rather than men," challenged the Imperial theory.

To the government this nonconformist attitude involved disobedience to authority, disorder, and possible rebellion; to the average citizen it was, says Rainy, "an interference with the established ways of society—with trade interests, with family life, with popular amusements, and with accepted religious observances . . . it was a detestable infection from which no man's family was safe." To the Magistrates it was wilful suicide: "If you are so weary of your lives," said one tired Roman judge, "are there no ropes or precipices wherewith to end them?"

Tolerant and averse to persecution though Rome might be, the incalcitrant *non possumus* of Christianity seemed to force the Imperial hand and therefore, in the two hundred and fifty years that intervened between the days of Nero and those of Constantine, many persecutions, some local, others sweeping through peninsula and provinces alike, fell upon the Church and thousands suffered death in agonizing forms. Men were impaled, crucified, burned alive, sewn up in the skins of wild beasts and thrown to the dogs. Eusebius and Tertullian both

A CUBICULUM IN A SICILIAN CATACOMB

Burrowing for security, the Christians hewed their chapels among their dead, denying the victory of Death where Death's triumph seemed most in evidence, unwittingly preparing the way for the crypt of the mediæval and modern church.

testify to the suicides of young girls who took their own lives rather
than serve as handmaids dedicated to the rites of Venus and the lusts
of men. In truth, from the days of Nero on, the Church often walked
between the torturer and the executioner, and the name of Diocletian
was not forgotten when she chose the Dove for her symbol because
its feet were red, as were the feet of those who followed the pathway
that the Christians chose.

Throughout these centuries the followers of the Dove in Rome,
Naples, Sardinia, Sicily, Malta, Alexandria, Asia Minor, and North
Africa burrowed for security, seeking, in darknesses lit only by their
smoking torches, hidden sanctuaries where they might worship Christ.
Of these places of refuge the best known today are the ancient tufa
quarries—the catacombs of Rome—whither the Christians came by
night, singly or in little groups lest the sound of many footsteps should
betray their gatherings to Rome. In this maze of subterranean galleries, six hundred miles in length and sometimes seventy-five feet
underground, where between six and seven million dead were already
sleeping, or should be brought to rest, they cut their rude altars in the
rocks, carving above them the symbols of that exultant faith which
denied the victory of Death where Death's triumph seemed most in
evidence.

Today the candle-led visitor to these catacombs may see the open
graves of those who kept the perilous faith when Nero, Domitian,
Trajan, or Diocletian was on the throne. By day, by night, they lived
in dread of the fate of those, their friends and kin who, as living
torches, lit the festivities of Nero's dissipated nights; who had died
dreadfully on Roman crosses, or who, kneeling in the arena, heard
the roar of lions behind barred doors, and waited for the opening of
those gates.

So when the sun had set, when sated beasts had been driven by
their keepers to their kennels, and sated spectators by darkness to their
homes, the Brethren came to gather up the broken bodies and bear
them to the galleries of the catacombs, where they excavated for
them little chapels, or cubicula. These tombs became altars whereon
the living, praising Him who had robbed the grave of victory, shared

together that Sacrament which affirmed the unbroken unity of the
Church Militant with the Church Triumphant.

The saints for whom these cubicula were fashioned had laid down
their lives with a will in the confident expectation of a glorious immortality into which they should enter with transfigured bodies. But they
never dreamed that their rudely hewn graves should also have a
resurrection and a transfiguration; that the grey rock walls of their
cubicula should give rise to other walls of jewelled glass wherein the
stories of their lives should be endlessly retold; that above the low
roofs of their sepulchres should one day spring the soaring vaults of
great cathedrals; or that the shallow stone hollows where their bodies
lay should give birth to shrines enriched by silks, tapestries, marbles,
mosaics, by precious minerals and by very precious stones.

Yet every great church in Europe rises above the relics of some honoured saint whose holy shrine gives a deeper consecration to the aisles
and altars of the church above. Tradition tells us that S. Peter sleeps
beneath his great basilica in Rome; that S. Mark rests under the
church in Venice that bears his name; and that S. James—Spain's victorious leader in many battles for the faith—lies below the high altar
of Santiago de Compostella.

So beneath every great cathedral, from S. Ambrogio in Milan to S.
Alban's in Washington, from S. John Lateran in Rome to S. John the
Divine in New York, there lies a crypt, a lower church with aisles and
chancel, sometimes with ambulatory, transepts, and chapels, which is
really a resurrection of the cubicula of the catacombs where the early
Christians gathered to worship at a martyr's grave.

If Calvary had set men free from the fear of death, the thoughts
and feelings that illumined the cubicula translated that freedom into
exaltation. The martyrs not only revealed to the eyes of a puzzled
Rome a faith that could overcome the world; they also unveiled to
their brethren lives that had been so "hid with Christ in God" that
now these dead, having passed through the great tribulation, must
stand very near the Throne. Therefore those who still lived in the
shadow of martyrdom felt a reverence for these well-loved of God,
and a simple trust that the risen saints by whom, living, they had been

loved, could and would powerfully intercede for them at the Throne of the Most High.

For this trust in the dead as kindly intercessors there is no parallel in the pagan world where death was something sinister, turning the dead into the mysteriously menacing; wherefore the entire ancient world—Babylonian, Assyrian, Egyptian, Greek, and Roman—feared those disembodied spirits who embodied a potential threat, and sought to prevent the soul's return to the world of living men.[1]

Mourners rent their garments and cast ashes on their heads, not originally to show their grief but to disguise themselves quickly lest the soul, as it left the body, should recognize its living relatives and friends. They cremated the bodies of the dead as a practical measure of defence to make impossible the re-entrance of an exiled spirit. They dug their vaults deep, or built their tombs of massive stones, that in such prison houses the dead might be well confined. When skill was lacking for such secure incarceration, or where interment must needs be made in caves or shallow graves, men the world over buried their dead in a crouching position, with the knees drawn up and fastened to the breast, that thus manacled, they might not walk the paths of living men. Often gifts of food were offered at the sepulchre (this is still done in Yugoslavia) to keep the Silent Ones contented with their lot lest, if forced to forage in the garbage, they should visit their just resentment on the living. That their eyes might be blinded the dead were some-times buried face downward in their graves so that, in attempting to return, they might be led to burrow deeper into darkness instead of upward towards the path revealing sun.[2]

That their feet might also be confused, the bearers trod a devious way from the dwelling to the grave in the hope that the returning

---

[1] Excavations in Egypt, at Gezer in Palestine, and at Lagash in Babylonia, show that the dead were sometimes buried under the thresholds or beneath the dwellings of the living—show indeed that the aged, crippled, and infirm were often put to death in order to be so buried. This, however, was with no thought that their spirits might plead the causes of the quick in the presence of the gods. They were slain and buried that their ghosts, still responsive to the strong tribal bond and law, might guard the home from perils against which the living had no sure defence, protecting it from invasions by other spirits inclined to evil.

[2] As on a stele in the Museum of Prehistoric Antiquities in Rome.

ghost, seeking to exchange the chill of the damp earth for the dry warmth of his old hearth, might lose himself in a labyrinth of intersecting paths.

No Latin Enoch Arden, given up for dead and unexpectedly returned, might enter the door-way of his old home; an entrance must be broken for him through the roof lest he prove a ghostly revenant, seeking to trick the family into the revelation of the door-way to the house. In Egypt they made assurance doubly sure by utterly destroying the dwelling that had been visited by death so that the soul, however desirous or clever, might not be able to return to his old abode.

Indeed there was no welcome for the pagan dead either in heaven or on earth. Banished by the living, they were barred from Paradise by the gods, who—either in person or through their deceitful messenger—robbed mankind of the hope of immortality by persuading men to refuse the fruit of the Tree of Life and to eat instead of the Tree of Death.

In Egypt few might find joy beyond the gates of death; for the masses of mankind there was little hope of light in the Valley of the Shadow.[3]

To the dwellers in Babylon, whose gods were concerned neither with the dead nor for them, life ended in despair, and the kindly shade of Enkidu refused to "open the earth" for Gilgamash, the Chaldean Hercules, "lest terror and weeping overcome thee" at the sight of the final destiny of man.

In Greek thought also, few won their way to the Elysian fields. To Homer, the dead were "the fluttering images of men outworn; strength

[3] The Egyptian believed in immortality, but his faith was pale and sombre beside the triumphant expectation of the Christian who looked forward confidently to a new life wherein "none should ever hurt him or make him afraid." To the Egyptian there were no such assurances. His earthly body must be embalmed and hidden, if possible buried in impenetrable mountains of stone, for vandals seeking treasure might scatter his bones, and such injuries would fall also upon his soul. Bread and wine must forever be offered at his grave, for food was as necessary for the dead as for the living; but who could hope for remembrance from his children's children? He might provide in his will for perpetual offerings of food, and carve in stone his contracts with the priests, but wars and conquests would vitiate contracts. Nothing he could do, no utterance of any priest of Amon, could give him the assurance of S. John:—"They shall hunger no more neither thirst any more."

of body and of mind alike are gone, and their utterances are like the twittering of bats."

Nor was the hope of the future brighter to the Romans. When Æneas, seeking Anchises, descends to Hades, the dead Greeks, seeing their old enemy, rally and try to raise the battle-shout, but only thin tones, unformed and incomplete, issue from their feeble throats.

What hope might the living place in these poor dead? What trust could be reposed in the power of these fluttering shades to move the high but forgetful gods?

To us these pagan dead seem very lonely, for the fear of the living and the unconcern of the gods isolated them on every side. Driven with curses from their old homes, beaten with sticks and bruised with stones, the doors of the past were closed to them while the very fact of death seemed to reveal the anger, the injustice, or at least the indifference of the gods, and to close the gateways of the future. Although certain Oriental faiths, like the worships of Attis and of Isis, invading Rome in the declining years of paganism, brought with them dim and flickering visions of another life, yet behind these vague desires there was no substantial, historic fact. No angel stood beside an empty sepulchre; neither Attis nor Adonis rose from the dead to challenge the doubt of any Roman Thomas; and the epitaphs on pagan tombs bear witness against the gods.

"I curse the harshness of my lot," runs the writing above a boy.

"I lift up my hands against god, who took me away," cries, in stone, a Roman girl.

"The fates judged ill," when they robbed a father of his child. "The gods were angry," says a fourth.

Obviously the living could hope for nothing from the intercessions of their dead with "angry," "unjust," and "harsh" gods who "delight in death" and cheat to keep men from the thresholds of their Elyseums.

But the words of Jesus to a dying man, "This day shalt thou be with me in Paradise," opened a way through the river of Death as the Ark of the Covenant had parted the waters of the Jordan.

"I am not dead, but living beyond the stars," rings the triumphant voice of the Christian Alexander from his tomb in the catacombs. "My soul dwells in goodness," echoes Atticus from his grave. Here Lais lies "In Peace," and there Victorina "In Peace and in Christ." Often in the cubicula the soul is represented as a dove, flying swiftly to the welcoming arms of Christ.

The belief that the dead were not wandering in darkness, but were bathed in the light of the Throne of God, released the Quick from all terror of the Dead. These who were now "beyond the stars," "in Peace and in Christ," were not hostile spirits, envious of the living, but friendly ambassadors standing face to face with God. Therefore men turned to the oratories of the catacombs with the confident belief that, kneeling before those shrines, they were in the presence of guardian angels who were potent intercessors with Him who had all power in heaven and on earth.

Under Diocletian and his colleagues the cubicula of the catacombs, with their holy graves, increased with an appalling rapidity, for the Imperial triumvirate—Diocletian, Galerius, and Maximianus—were determined to stamp out, root and branch, the "pestilential superstition;" wherefore when the doors of Janus opened on the year 303 an army of executioners passed swiftly through. Bodies were broken, churches destroyed, copies of the scriptures burned—the feet of the bearers were ever at the door. Yet the faith burned high with an inextinguishable flame; the Roman hammer broke at last upon the anvil, and the Edict of Milan, in 313, confessed defeat by the legalization of Christian worship. In the year 337 an Emperor of Rome received the Sacrament of Christian baptism, and in 363 the last counter-attack of paganism collapsed when Julian "The Apostate," betrayed and defeated, died on a Persian battlefield murmuring, "Thou hast conquered, Galilean."

In 382 Gratian confiscated the temple estates, abolished the emoluments as well as the immunities of their priesthoods, and banished the altar and statue of Victory which Augustus had erected in the Senate. The old gods, upon whose altars Roman victors had once laid down their laurel wreaths, were dragged through the streets of Rome behind the chariot wheels of Theodosius; some of their images were melted down to make up the tribute which Alaric the Goth demanded when he captured Rome; those that were left were taken by the African Vandal, Genseric, together with the spoils which Titus had brought back from Jerusalem, and all were lost at sea when a storm on the Mediterranean overwhelmed Genseric's treasure ship.

"*Sic transit gloria mundi*," said the Roman; but "He hath put down the Mighty from their seat," said the Christian and the Jew.

The conversion of Constantine and the new freedom that followed the Edict of Milan, releasing all Christians from their very human fears, brought so many worshippers together, either from deep burrows or from secret closets, that their numbers far exceeded the capacities of the subterranean cubicula and compelled the erection of churches whose size and splendour challenged the pagan temples. Many, however, especially among those who had endured and survived the great persecution, believed that no prayer, wherever offered, could compare in effectiveness with one presented at those tomb-altars where lay men's most potent intercessors before the Throne of God. They clung persistently to the dark oratories of their fathers.

Therefore the tombs around the oratory were cleared away and a new church was built above the catacombs, whose pavement was sunk far enough beneath the ground to bring the tomb of the saint within its walls. Sometimes the grave, instead of lying in one of the upper galleries, was so far underground that, when the church was finished, only its roof and upper tier of windows were visible from the street. In a few instances the holy grave lay at such a depth that both church and saint were quite buried out of the sight of men. This was the origin of some of the greatest sanctuaries of Christian Rome, where nearly sixty churches owe their existence to a veneration for the dead that was more potent than the health or convenience of the living.

So great was the importance attached to the relics of the saints and martyrs that decrees of Councils, pastoral letters of bishops, and the devotion of the faithful soon joined forces to forbid the consecration of any church or altar which did not contain the body, or at least the relics, of a saint. In the Sixth Century four altars of the church at

Saintes had to remain unconsecrated because the priests were not able
to find a bone, a lock of hair, a girdle or a sandal with which to
justify their consecration.

As time passed, however, as the era of persecution drifted out of
memory, the sentiment which forbade the translation of the dead from
the cubicula of the catacombs was weakened by the inconveniences
inevitably attached to any service of worship in these underground
chapels—the lack of air, of space, and of light, the inflow of water
from rains or springs, and the difficulty of approach for the aged and
infirm.

Before the Fourth Century was far advanced the Church was able
to build basilicas wherever convenience might direct and to remove,
with due rites and ceremonies, the bodies of the martyrs to new
shrines prepared for them in crypts, excavated beneath the chancels,
which now replaced the venerated but abandoned oratories of the catacombs. Thereafter the church guarded the memory, and often bore
the name, of the saint whose body lay within its crypt, while the
altar, placed directly above the shrine, gathered a greater sanctity from
the virtues that were inherent in the very relics of the holy dead.

E. BENDANN, *Death Customs,* Chap. IV.
J. G. FRAZER, *Folk-lore in the Old Testament,* Vol. I, Chap. II.
H. O. TAYLOR, *Ancient Ideals,* Vol. I.
M. JASTROW, *Religious Belief in Babylonia and Assyria.*
H. P. SMITH, *Religion of Israel.*

Chapter Three

WHY THE LAW COURT BECAME A CHURCH

DROUGHT and famine; famine and drought. For three years no rain had fallen in the land of Israel; wells, springs, and streams had failed; grey dust and withered leaves blanketed the ground; the air was hot and breathless. Now, with some faint stirrings of hope, the people from all the villages roundabout had crossed the parched plain of Esdrælon and climbed the western slopes of Carmel where the priests of Baal were praying for rain. Early in the morning they had slain a bull for their sacrifice; they had splashed the blood upon the altar and poured it upon the ground; hour after hour, as the sun rose over Gilboa and sank behind Carmel, they had leaped and danced, gashing themselves with knives until their bodies were streaked with red, crying as they danced, "O Baal, hear us," while Elijah mocked the screaming throng of priests saying, "Call louder, for your god may be on a journey, or perchance he is asleep."

Such scenes from Israel's history give us an insight into the nature of all primitive Semitic religion—an insight without which we cannot understand the curiously complete break between the religious architecture of pagan and of Christian days.

Though the structural model for the first church was directly taken from the Latin basilica which, in turn, was derived from the secular architecture of Greece, the religious ideas which required the use of that model were drawn from the early faiths of the Semitic world where all the people must be present when sacrifice was offered.

From the first the early Fathers insisted that a Christian church must be a building wherein both priests and people might unite in public worship, and rejected the temple type of architecture which was designed to permit a pagan *sacerdos* to offer the sacrifices as the representative of an absent people. Their rejection of the pagan temple was partly due to the inherent character of Christianity, and partly to the inheritance which had been transmitted from the old Semitic world by a bequest from the ancient High Places, mediated to the Church through the Temple in Jerusalem and the synagogues of the Dispersion.

The idea of worship as a tribal act—in which each man had his part to play—was inherent in the Semitic conception of God, for the deity of the early Semites was literally the father of the tribe whose blood, flowing through their veins, created the strong tribal bond and code whence all rights and duties were derived. Into this fellowship an alien could be received only through the blood covenant wherein, drinking from the slashed vein of a member of the tribe, he mingled the god's blood with his own, for the blood of god and man was one.

Because of this interrelationship a wrong done to one member of the tribe, being an injury "to the blood," was felt by all, and the demands of justice might be satisfied, not necessarily by the punishment of the guilty but by retaliation upon any member of that other tribe who shared the offending blood.

The tribal law followed the tribal bond, and even its temporary protection could be extended only to him who, by breaking bread or eating salt with a member of the tribe, had nourished his veins from a common source.

Thus the shared meal was the creation, or the renewal, of the tribal covenant.

Into this fellowship, from which the Outlander was rigidly excluded, the domestic animals were admitted, for these were considered so closely akin to the tribe in blood that the Semite was forbidden their use as food; he partook of the flesh of his flocks and herds only in his religious rites wherein the offering of a ram or a bull, except in times of tragic need, might replace the sacrifice of a man. Sometimes, however, no substitute seemed adequate, wherefore Mesha of Moab secured the effective protection of Chemosh, his god, by offering his own son on the walls of his beleaguered city of Kir. In return for

victory given Jephthah sacrificed his daughter, and Samuel slew Agag
the Amalekite "before the Lord."

So strongly was this conception of the peculiar sanctity of the tribal
blood impressed upon the Semitic race that, very recently, a Jewish
patient in a London hospital refused the transfusion of Gentile blood
into his own veins although the refusal jeopardized his life. In primitive times such a transfusion would have involved the abandonment
of all old tribal relations, human and divine, and necessitated the
acceptance of a new people, and of new gods.

So, whenever shadows gathered and perils threatened, the people
climbed to their great High Place to prepare and offer their sacrificial
meal. The ceremony before the altar renewed the blood covenant between god and tribe, since both, partaking of a holy sacrifice, drew
into their veins anew the sacred tribal blood; it was the celebration
of a communion feast whereof the god shared as he breathed in the
ascending smoke of the burnt offering or drank of the blood that
ran into the ground, while the people divided the flesh, which must
be entirely consumed before the rising of the sun. Thus the god was
roused from his sleep, recalled from his journey, or summoned from
his pleasures. The ancient covenant was renewed and the assurance of
divine protection was secured.

The Syrian hills are silent now; the gods have fled and their worshippers are dust; yet the faith that raised these altars—the faith that
gathered the entire tribe in prayer to a god who was not a foreign
power to be appeased but a father who "in all their affliction was
afflicted"—has survived all the baalim, the Dusharas, and the Bels of
the Semitic world, and outlived the generations that called upon their
names, for Christianity struck its roots deep into these ancient faiths,
and the gathering of Christian people around our own altars to share,
in a Communion Feast, "the blood of a new covenant" carries us back
to the rituals of these forgotten altars on Syrian hills.

When at last priests, prophets, and kings united to destroy the High
Places where, since Joshua's day, Israel had sacrificed to strange gods
whose favour had been deemed essential if seed should yield its har-

vest, there was no drastic break with the past. The priests continued to offer bulls and rams to Jehovah and they offered them on the identical sacrificial rock whereon Abd Khiba of Jerusalem had sacrificed long before the walls of Jericho fell at the sound of Joshua's trumpets; the priests of Josiah's day sprinkled blood upon the altar when royal tragedies were gathering at Megiddo, even as those of the Amorites had done on the eve of that disastrous day when the sun stood still over Gibeon and the moon over Ajalon; and the smoke rose no higher from the altar of Simon the Maccabean when all Jewry was rejoicing in the death of Antiochus Epiphanes, defiler of the Temple, than it had risen more than a thousand years before from the altars of Iapahi of Gezer, when the Khabiri were overrunning the land and his younger brother had deserted to the enemy.

As in all Semitic lands, the tribes of Israel must go up to their sanctuary and assemble in its courts, for the Temple was the very dwelling place of God—indeed, from Ur of the Chaldees to Karnak of the Egyptians it had no other name. But neither in the Valley of the Tigris nor in that of the Nile, where the simplicity of tribal life had been suppressed by the growth of autocracies in countries whose kings were also gods, did the Temple become more than the "dwelling place" of deity; in Jerusalem alone did men learn to think of it as "my Father's House." Therefore, all the family of Israel, even though dispersed among the nations, must seek Jehovah's favour in Jehovah's house, for no intercessions or sacrifices of the priests could prevail with the Most High if His people were not present to fill the Temple Courts.

Until Titus drew his siege lines about Jerusalem there was no real break between the Temple and the Church. Jesus Himself often went up to the City of David and taught in the Temple, which He called "My Father's House;" there, at the cost of life itself, He went to celebrate His last Passover with the disciples.

For many years after the tragedy of Golgotha the followers of the Nazarene remained Hebrews, differing from their brethren merely in their acceptance of Jesus as the Messiah, foretold and promised by the prophets. To Jew and Christian alike, as to those earlier Semites who had worshipped the myriad baalim, the sanctuary was the residence of deity where all must go who would renew the blood covenant with their God or call upon His name. The persistence of this idea, purified and modified, sent the sons of those who had gathered on Carmel in the days of Ahab to climb the heights of Gerizim in the days of Jesus; it made the descendants of those who had filled the Court when Solomon dedicated the Temple crowd Jerusalem for the Passover when Caiaphas was High Priest. The call of the Psalmist, "Let us go into the House of the Lord," was echoed by S. Paul: "Neglect not the assembling of yourselves together." From the days of the Patriarchs to those of the Apostles the conception of worship as an act wherein priests and people must unite was universal and prescriptive throughout the Semitic world.

In Rome men thought otherwise, and Messala never could have understood the thoughts of Hur; for the Roman looked upon his god as a powerful ally with whom he had signed a contract, not as a father with whom he had sealed a covenant. Worship, to him, was a method by which the State might secure success through the goodwill of properly propitiated gods; rites and sacrifices were proffered in exchange for favours, and if the gods failed to play their expected parts new alliances might be sought with other deities. This attitude is repeatedly illustrated in Roman history. The State might cling tenaciously to the old forms; it might forbid the offering of sacrifices except on Roman altars when the first Punic War was threatening Italy, or exile those who, in 138, introduced the worship of the Sabazian Jupiter, but it could not restrain the people, made desperate by disaster, from seeking divine help wherever that help might be found. Thus in the year 493 B.C. when the old gods of agriculture failed to prevent a famine, a temple was dedicated to imported divinities who had granted fertility to the fields of Greece. In 293 B.C., when a pestilence smote the city, the Romans turned from their own too careless gods and built a temple to Æsculapius of Epidaurus, offering him sacrifices much as we, threatened by an epidemic, might engage and pay a sanitary engineer. When indifferent Roman deities suffered

Hannibal to overrun all Northern Italy, the indignant people turned to the gods and rites of Greece; when the city reeled beneath the disaster at Cannæ and the loss of eighty thousand legionaries, an Embassy was sent with gifts to the temple and oracle at Delphi. Finally, in 205 B.C., another Embassy was sent to Attalus, King of Pergamum, to bring to Rome the sacred black stone of the Magna Mater that, by her favour, the hosts of Africa might be driven from Italian shores. Thus Roman faith varied with Roman fortunes.

Nor did the Roman change his heart with his forms of government; his faith still rose and fell with his fortunes when the Empire succeeded the Republic. Augustus solemnly degraded the statue of Neptune when the Imperial fleet suffered shipwreck, and the populace stoned or overturned the altars of the gods when Germanicus died. The Hebrew might dream through seventy years of exile of the day when, having won again Jehovah's favour by deep repentance and stern obedience, he might return to the city of his fathers to reconsecrate his altars and renew the ancient blood covenant with his God; but the Roman, when threatened by disaster, went shopping among the nations, seeking other deities who might be moved to extend protection in return for honours paid before their altars.

The difference between the attitude of the Roman towards his temples and the feeling of Jew or Christian for their Holy Places was thus profound; it is reflected in the very stones of their religious architecture and explains the break between religious edifices of pagan and of Christian Rome.

Roman temples were erected as exclusively for the priests as the army camps were for the soldiers. Being intended only for the hieratic performance of a ritual and not for popular assemblies, the temples were usually small and their free space was broken up and cramped by many pillars.

Christianity, on the other hand, calling the church "The House of God," conceived religion as the intercourse of a great family within a home and therefore needed, for its worship, a large hall where all disciples could be assembled with a clear view of both priest and altar, giving the latter the place of honour. For such a house of worship the Christians could find no inspiration in the religious architecture of the pagan world. Although the Jews in the exile that followed the destruction of their temple and city by the Babylonians in 586 B.C. developed the synagogue, a building from which some scholars would derive the form of the early Christian church; yet little differences in the architecture, the historic barriers that isolated the Jew from all other peoples, and the fact that the Church early passed from Jewish-Christian to Gentile-Christian control make it far more probable that her architects found the model for their churches in the basilica which, unlike the synagogue, was familiar and esteemed throughout the entire Græco-Roman world where it served both as a law-court and a market. This rectangular edifice, with its great central nave, its flanking aisles, its galleries and curving apse, was the only structure within the boundaries of the Empire which met the essential architectural needs of Fourth Century Christianity.

Born in Greece, where an *archon basileus* sat in the *stoa basilike* to give judgement in matters affecting the State Religion, the basilica was brought to Rome by Marcus Porcius Cato in the early part of the Second Century B.C. The apse, perhaps partitioned off by curtains, was set apart as a Court of Justice, while merchants, money-lenders, and money-changers filled the aisles with their booths and counters.

Thereafter basilicas, flanking the fora and sharing their commercial life, sprang into being wherever the Romans went, and if, for centuries thereafter, Christian churches bore a strong resemblance to each other it is because, from Egypt to Britain and from Persia to Spain, Roman basilicas, like Roman roads, went everywhere and offered a universal model.

From this building the Christians drove out the "money-changers and them that bought and sold" to make a house of prayer, for its central aisle, often two hundred feet in length, could give a larger congregation an uninterrupted view of both priest and altar than could any other type of building of that day. And so it came to pass that the aisles, which had once echoed the shrill bickerings of traders, began to resound with the solemn litanies and liturgies of the Christian Church.

From the altar at the foot of the central aisle, where formerly Roman magistrates had sworn to administer impartial justice or where merchants had sealed their contracts by libations to their gods, Christian priests celebrated the most holy Sacraments of the Church.

In the semi-circular recess, or apse, which terminated the basilica, the priests took the seats of the Latin jurists, and from the curving bench of stone which followed the curving wall, where the magistrates had so long declared and delivered the Roman Law, they sang their *Jubilates*, their *Benedicites*, and their *Magnificats*. This primitive arrangement of the seats may still be seen at Torcello, in the Venetian Lagoon, where the Bishop's Throne, raised high above the pavement, is flanked by six tiers of curving stone benches.

The Bishop took the Prætor's curule chair for his throne, or *cathedra,* without even changing the motifs of its carving; so, throughout the entire Middle Ages, many episcopal thrones continued to be ornamented with the heads and claws of beasts which the games of the arena had introduced to the Roman people. Thus the curious spectacle was presented of a Christian bishop seated in the chair of the Roman magistrate, the legs of which were supported by claws whose living prototypes had torn the flesh of such as he; his hands resting on the graven heads of lions, and his fingers playing with bared fangs which once, in living ivory instead of wood or stone, had "brought deliverance to the captives, and the opening of prisons to them that were bound."

The side aisles, once occupied by the booths of Roman merchants and money-changers, now afforded additional space where the overflow of unusually large congregations might be accommodated when the central aisle was filled, while the galleries often found above these aisles—known later as *triforia* from their triple openings into the loftier nave—were set apart for purposes of which Marcus Porcius Cato never dreamed—the segregation of women. The early Church, especially where Eastern influences prevailed, looked askance upon the intermingling of the sexes in public gatherings. Consequently men and women were each assigned their own portion of the aisles, a custom that still obtains in the Greek Church. The authorities in the

THE CHURCH OF S. MARIA IN TRASTEVERE

First built seven years after the death of Constantine, this church still retains, in the main, its early form with the lintels on columns. It illustrates the starting point from which ecclesiastical architecture began its upward journey.

East, as in Egypt—and probably also in the West—soon found that more room might be gained for the increasing congregations, and the sexes more effectively separated, by employing the triforium gallery for the women and allotting the body of the church to the men.

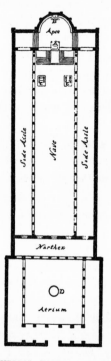

PLAN OF A TYPICAL EARLY CHRISTIAN BASILICA

A—Altar; B—Bishop's Throne; C C'—Ambos (or pulpit); D—Fountain of Ablution.

Before the portals of the church the Christians placed an open colonnaded court, or *atrium*, with a fountain of ablutions in the centre, where converts and penitents alike awaited the completion of the instruction, or the fulfilment of the penance, which should unbar the doors and admit them to the altar. This atrium, substituted for the forum which had flanked the secular basilica, eventually passed out of existence in giving birth to the cloister. So every element of the secular basilica—nave, aisles, galleries, apse, and forum—could be adapted to the needs of Christian worship.

Greek in name, it was also Greek in origin, and although not even the ruins of a Hellenic basilica have survived, yet it is reasonable to believe that such buildings were widely scattered throughout the Grecian world where they were used for popular assemblies, as markets, and as law-courts.

In the Sixth Century b.c., when the mists lift a little, something very closely resembling the basilica appears in the Bouleuterion at Olympia —a council chamber divided into two aisles by a row of columns, while an elliptical apse faced an entrance and a portico at the other end.

Nearly a thousand years earlier the elements of the basilica appeared in the Cretan Throne Room at Knosses—an aisled hall with a flight of steps leading to a rectangular apse where stood the throne of gypsum. Of this hall Glotz writes, "With its longitudinal division into three aisles, this Throne Room may well be the prototype of the 'stoa Basilike' where the King of Athens sat, and of the basilica which Rome handed down to the Middle Ages."

Possibly we can trace the elements of the basilica—aisles, columns, and apse—further still, for the throne room of this Minoan palace bears a distinct resemblance to the *megaron* of Ægean and Hellenic architecture—the great hall of the dwelling which was the centre of all social life and around which the other rooms were grouped. Homer bears witness to its size, for it was in the megaron of Penelope's dwelling that her three hundred suitors were feasting when the returned Odysseus, recognized only by his dog, drew his great bow and sped his arrows down the hall. If, indeed, the megaron be a distant ancestor of the basilica, then we may trace it back to the middle of the Third Millennium when a Thraco-Phrygian people erected the megaron dwellings of that Second City of Troy which, burned five hundred years later and buried under debris, was brought to light again in our own day by Schliemann, who thought he had discovered the splendours of Priam's Troy and the evidences of Menelaus' vengeance.

Thus throughout the centuries the basilica, with a longer history than we had dreamed, is associated with the gatherings of tribal chiefs, of magistrates, and of merchants—but not of priests. Its aisles may have rung with defiance to Xerxes of Persia, to Philip of Macedon, or to Gylippus of Syracuse; they echoed the dispassionate deliverances of Roman magistrates whose law went out over all the earth—but they never vibrated with a hymn to Zeus or with the hexameters of Delphic priestesses.

Generation after generation the basilica and the temple went their separate ways until that pregnant day when Roman Law and Christian Faith came face to face in the Prætorium of Jerusalem and a Roman magistrate condemned a Nazarene to be scourged and crucified.

Pilate might wash his hands and disclaim responsibility for "the blood of this just man," but none the less he initiated a struggle which, three hundred years later, placed a follower of the Nazarene upon the throne of Cæsar, drove the old gods from their temples, the magistrates from their seats, the merchants from their shops, and set the aisles of the basilica ringing with triumphant *Te Deums* in praise of Him whom Semites had spat upon, Greeks mocked, and Romans crucified, but who

"Deposuit potentes de seda et exaltavit humiles."

W. ROBERTSON SMITH, *Religion of the Semites.*
J. P. PETERS, *Religion of the Hebrews.*
ALLEN MARQUAND, *Greek Architecture.*
GUSTAVE GLOTZ, *Ægean Civilization,* Chap. IV.

Chapter Four

THE ORIGIN OF THE TRANSEPTS

ABOUT the time when Paul was a prisoner in Rome a boy in the palace school for pages on the Palatine Hill scrawled a rude caricature on the walls of his class-room which must have given no little pain to a certain small Greek named Alexamenos. This caricature represents a man with the head of an ass bound to a cross, his feet resting on a horizontal board. On the left, arms raised in adoration, kneels a Christian boy beneath whom these words are written, "Alexamenos worships [his] god."

Such caricatures, which mocked the Christians as much by the portrayal of the cross as by the representation of the ass, were evidently widely circulated, for Tertullian speaks of their appearance in Africa where the Christians were called *asinarii*—"Donkey-Tenders."

The contempt of the artist reflects the current conversation in the homes, in the public streets and squares of Rome, and throughout the entire Empire. Latins of the days of Alexamenos, and for centuries thereafter, could not contemplate the cross without an instinctive feeling of revulsion. Crucifixion was a punishment for barbarians and slaves; no man who could rightfully say *"civis Romanus sum"* might legally die this death, and one of the most damning charges that Cicero brought against Verres, Proconsul of Sicily, was that he had dared to crucify one over whom Rome had thrown the mantle of her citizenship.

It was inevitable that the Church, reluctant to expose the Cross to pagan jests, should substitute a symbol for the dying Saviour—a bust of Christ enclosed in a medallion above an empty cross, the symbolic Lamb, the hand of God extended in benediction, or the Labarum— the XP which were the first letters of the Greek word for "Christ."

Not until the Romans had been driven from their seats of Empire by barbarians, whose fathers had often died on Roman crosses even as Jesus had died, was the stigma so far lifted from the Cross that the Crucifixion scene began to appear in Western art. Yet long before the

Alinari

ALEXAMENOS SEBETE THEON
(Alexamenos worships [his] god)

collapse of Rome the builders had given the repellent form of the cross to the church by extending the transverse aisle which had crossed the old law-court from side to side between the nave and the apse until it projected beyond the side walls of the basilica.

Later generations, sensitive to the poetic imagery, saw in the cruciform lines thus given to the church the intentional representation of the fundamental fact of Christianity and clung to the transepts long after the need which had called them into being had disappeared, even though new uses must be found for them. But the symbol of the cross, touching and beautiful as it eventually became, was certainly not in the mind of the Fourth Century builder in whose age the cross quickened feelings of contempt rather than of reverence.

The years went by; Alexamenos lived his life keeping, we trust, his faith and died; the forgotten artist who had unwittingly conferred immortality with his scorn also went to his reward. New faces appeared, vanished, and were succeeded by still newer faces as generation followed generation on the streets of Rome—faces that grew increasingly more anxious and harassed as the Imperial sun dipped to its setting, and it is among the causes of this anxiety, rather than in the symbolism of the Church, that we must seek the origin of the transepts which gave the church the form of the cross.

This form, however, was not deliberately adopted by builders to proclaim the basic faith of Christianity; it was rather imposed upon the church as one of the consequences of the unchristian, anti-social, and uneconomic policies which undermined, and eventually overthrew, the Roman State—the ruinous usury exacted by Roman bankers, the selfishness of the great landowners, the employment of slave labour which bankrupted the independent farmers and the free artisans, and the spendthrift sybaritism which, dissipating the wealth of the capital, drained gold and silver to the East to pay for luxuries. To such economic and moral evils we owe the transformation of the rectangular into the cruciform basilica, a change which the Christians of that age, without the impact of these forces, would hardly have conceived.

The Romans were an exploiting, not a producing people. Their great prosperity sprang less from their own industry than from those military triumphs which enabled them to impose enormous tributes and taxes upon the hardier and more productive nations whom their arms subdued.

While Rome performed an inestimable service in clearing pirates from the seas, in making the Mediterranean safe for commerce, in policing all lands and waters, and in maintaining the pax Romana throughout the world, yet the price she levied ultimately brought disaster. A patrician rule benefited the few, but the increase in private fortunes so reduced the basic sources of wealth that, in the end, the wealthy shared the universal tragedy.

The prosperity of the Empire had been built upon the wealth created by a multitude of small farms whose owners, free members of the middle or working classes, planned, toiled, and saved, generation after generation, to bring waste-lands under cultivation, to increase their productivity, and to provide an inheritance of comfort with security for their children. For many centuries, however, the peasant farmers had been increasingly impoverished as the possession of the land became more and more concentrated in the hands of the few. Sicily, with an area of ten thousand square miles, was largely held by eighty-four owners of estates, and in Nero's day six proprietors held one-half the arable land in Africa. Asia, and later Gaul, underwent a similar economic revolution which dispossessed the free farmers and drove the peasants into the already overcrowded cities. This concentration of land ownership went steadily forward throughout the first three centuries of our era, and the peasant farmers were more and more impoverished by the greed of the great landowners who, stretching their possessions throughout the entire peninsula, added farm to farm and field to field—sometimes by foreclosure, but all too often by intimidation, fraud, violence, usurpation, and political influence.

The ruin of the small farmer in the West was completed by the competition of the fertile slave-tilled fields and orchards of the provinces which his sword had conquered, and by the mass of slaves which poured into Italy as the spoils of his victories.

This type of labour, however, was no more productive of real wealth in the Third Century than it was when Olmstead, journeying through our seaboard slave states in 1855, found that five slaves were required to do the farm work habitually accomplished by one free man working in the North. Yet slave labour can expel free labour if it cannot equal it, and its introduction completed the ruin of the peasant farms and depopulated entire districts. In Leontium in the course of a few years fifty-one landowners disappeared out of eighty-three; at Mutyca, one hundred and one out of one hundred and sixty-eight, and at Agyium one hundred and seventy out of two hundred and fifty lost their holdings. The majority of those thus dispossessed by servile labour were submerged in the city mobs to lead a miserable and precarious existence.

After the Antonines the supply of slave labour fell off, for the pax Romana dried the slave-stream at its source. But a new system of semi-slavery—that of the *Coloni*—was already established. Recruited from barbarians, the "undesirables," free farmers who had surrendered their freedom, and slaves who had risen slightly in the scale, the *colonus* was a serf if not a slave. Bound to the soil, bought or sold with the land, pursued as a runaway slave if he sought to escape, he must marry only within his district and bequeath his bonds to his children. So more and more the lands fell into the hands of slave-owning patricians who, now possessing the agricultural resources of the land, retired to the depths of great estates; and the fields which, properly cultivated, should have supported a teeming peasantry, were surrendered to pasturage with the exception of the few acres that were needed to supply the wants of the owner and his family. The money-lender killed out the husbandmen, the race of soldiers vanished, and the farms whereon they had once flourished were left desolate.

One result of this economic folly was the shrinkage of the population in Italy and also in the provinces. In the Fifth Century B.C. the city of Athens alone could send two hundred ships and sixty thousand soldiers against Syracuse, but Plutarch, writing in the Second Century, says that all Greece could then raise with difficulty only an army of three thousand men. In Gaul, the disasters of the Third Century A.D. so depopulated the towns that they dwindled to a fourth, a tenth, even a twentieth of their former areas; Autun, which once covered an area of five hundred square acres, shrank to one of barely twenty-five. In the Fourth Century an actual survey showed huge deserted areas in once fertile Campania.

Into such abandoned fields came the first of the barbarian invaders, carrying tools instead of swords. Successive emperors followed the example of Probus, who placed ten thousand Basternæ in Thrace, and by the Fourth Century many thousands, taken from the peoples who were attacking the confines of the Empire, had been distributed among the various provinces.[1]

If the agrarian policy followed by the great landowners was ruinous, the financial practices of the bankers who, with the owners of the great estates, controlled the Senate, was not less so, for the exhaustion of the subject nations on whose industry Rome lived was hastened by the economic ignorance of those who blindly used their capital to spread universal poverty rather than to stimulate productive industry.

The major business of Rome was usury, and the threat or force of military power was employed to compel reluctant cities to contract loans for which they had no need, and to repay when they were not able. Thus the agents of Brutus—"and Brutus was an honourable man" —imprisoned the councillors of Salamis until five of their number starved to death to compel the payment of money loaned at the illegal rate of forty-eight per cent, while Tarsus was forced to sell all her public property, to coin the sacred vessels of her temples, and to send her boys and girls, her young women and even her old men into slavery, to raise the crushing levies that Crassus had imposed.

Conditions improved somewhat when the Empire succeeded the Republic, for a remarkable series of great emperors—Augustus, Tiberius, Trajan, Hadrian, Antoninus Pius, and Marcus Aurelius—were both wise and powerful enough to check some of the worst abuses which had darkened the last days of the Republic. But evils still continued; according to Dio Cassius the revolt of Britain under Boadicea, which cost the Romans seventy thousand lives before it was suppressed, was caused by the rapacity of Seneca, the Latin moralist, who had forced a loan of nearly two million dollars on the Britons at a usurious rate of interest, and then called his loans suddenly and without notice, inflicting great suffering upon the island.

The commercial benefits of the pax Romana, together with the increased wealth which followed the extension of civilization to the barbarian world, especially to Gaul, in some measure compensated for Rome's destructive financial and agrarian policies, and the Age of the Antonines (138-180 A.D.) still gave such an appearance of prosperity

[1] Paul-Louis, *Ancient Rome at Work*, p. 255.

that Gibbon counted it among the happiest that men had known. This seeming prosperity was rudely interrupted towards the close of the Second Century by the declining production and ultimate exhaustion of the mines which for four hundred years had been equipping Roman armies for the conquest of the world. It was the mineral wealth of Spain, won for Rome by Scipio's victory over Carthage, that enabled the forces of the Republic, which had with difficulty repulsed the attacks of Pyrrhus of Epirus seventy years before, to overrun both Epirus and Macedonia. Steadily thereafter gold and silver, pouring into Rome from Spain as, centuries later, they poured into Spain from Peru, played their important part in the building of the Empire, and it is quite possible that the rule of the Cæsars might have long endured, despite the cancers of greed, slavery, usury, and of waste-thrift prodigence, had the supply of the mines, from Spain to Dacia, been maintained. Their failure precipitated the final tragedy of the ancient civilization.

For two hundred years Rome had been burning her candle at both ends; her greed had ruined her farmers and impaired the prosperity of the peoples on whose industry she throve; the selfish thrift of her aristocracy which exploited labour was joined with a reckless prodigality which squandered a pound of gold for a pound of silk and paid one hundred and sixty dollars for one of purple dyed wool. An emperor might complain that feminine vanity was draining gold from the arteries of Rome to fill the veins of the East—according to Pliny her importations of luxuries sent forty million dollars annually from Rome to the Orient—but other emperors set no stern example. Nero— who tossed his dice for twenty thousand dollars a point, paid forty thousand dollars for a drinking cup, and one hundred and sixty thousand dollars for some Oriental tissues—had no lack of patrician examples to follow; one of whom, in the days of Tiberius, paid thirty thousand *sesterce* for three mullets (the sesterce was worth about four cents). Forty years later the price had evidently fallen, for under Domitian a six-pound mullet was sold for six thousand sesterce, or one thousand sesterce a pound. Such instances were probably exceptional, since they aroused comment even in Rome; nevertheless wealth and display determined rank while the mass of the people lived in sharply contrasted simplicity which was enforced by poverty.[2]

Only the unfailing streams of gold and silver that flowed from the mines of Spain, Dalmatia, and Dacia enabled the Empire to endure the strain of such an adverse balance of trade and when, towards the end of the Second Century, the mines neared exhaustion, the collapse of the Empire could hardly be postponed. In the two generations that saw the failure of the mines, gold and silver practically disappeared from circulation, either through exportation to the East from a West which was not able to continue the supply, or else driven into hiding as the people lost confidence in a currency which was unable to withstand the drain. Harassed and almost insolvent emperors, vainly trying successive expedients to cope with their financial problems, were forced to debase the coinage, mingling at last 98.5 per cent of base metal with 1.5 per cent of silver, until under Claudius II the *antoninianus*, the only coin in circulation, became merely a piece of copper or of lead thinly covered with silver. Inevitably all gold and silver were thus driven out of circulation, for men will not pay in precious metals when they can pay in base, and the long period of demoralization in prices, with the wars and confusions which followed the inflation of the currency, drove the ancient world, which under Augustus had been a moneyed civilization comparable to our own, back to the barter stage of primitive peoples.

Taxes, wages, and salaries began to be paid less and less in coin and more in kind, and the State collected leather, meats, grain, cloth, and similar commodities from her citizens whenever it was impossible to extort gold.

At the same time the government paid its obligations partly in goods and partly in lead coins thinly plated while, in civil life, magistrates, doctors, lawyers, architects, and clerks received their compensation largely in goods instead of in cash.

No expedient availed, however, and the wealth of both government and of governed continued to decline. "Rarely in history has humanity

[2] W. S. Davis, *Influence of Wealth in Imperial Rome,* Chap. IV; Paul-Louis, *Ancient Rome at Work,* p. 266.

experienced a period of misery so continuous; rarely has despair afflicted at one time millions and millions of men bowed under the yoke of a boundless despotism and visited daily by some fresh terror," writes M. Paul-Louis; and M. Lot adds: "In the Fourth Century Rome could neither feed her citizens, provide for the upkeep of her administration, nor pay her troops; every year her people were becoming more impoverished and her burdens heavier, while her resources were becoming less."

But government must be maintained, barbarians held in check, roads kept open, and peace imposed from Spain to Persia. The demands upon the State are greater in days of stress than they are in quieter times, and heavier financial burdens must now be laid upon a poverty-stricken people than those which a prosperous nation had borne in the golden age of Marcus Aurelius. Diocletian and Constantine undertook the tremendous task of stabilizing the currency, fixing prices, and of restoring prosperity by Imperial mandate, but the success of their efforts required the full force of government and in the exercise of that force liberty perished. Thereafter the farmer, merchant, and artisan, who had followed their avocations of their own free wish and will, lay under the bondage of the law; they toiled, not with any hope of providing comfort and security for their descendants, but to fill the coffers of the State. "Revenue officers are everywhere," wrote Lactantius, "every clod in a field is measured; the number of feet in a vineyard, the number of trees, is counted; a written inventory is made of every kind of animal; men are counted by heads." The "head count" was made for the collection of a poll tax which, falling most heavily upon the poor, resulted in a lower birth-rate, a decreasing population, and consequently in a diminished return to the State.

The burdensome land tax fell principally upon the holders of modest estates, for the greater lords were often able to resist the collection of Imperial taxes by the employment of armed bands and to add their own imposts to those of the State upon an overburdened and defenceless people.

The poorer families found the burden hardly to be borne; consequently many farmers abandoned their good fields to raise what crops they might on more sterile mountain-sides where the tax would be lighter. To "coffin and confine" those who would abandon their lands in order to escape taxation the peasant farmers were forbidden to quit their fields. In like manner when the tenant farmers attempted to avoid the tax gatherer by deserting their holdings and moving to the cities Constantine made their tenancy hereditary, thus yoking them and their descendants as firmly to their farms as their landlords already had been bound. To prevent evasion of taxation by the selling of slaves these also were bound to the soil and might not be sold nor, if manumitted, might they leave the estates of their farmer owners.

When the merchant guilds which had supplied Rome with food— for sale or for free distribution—were ordered to pay the cost of transportation, whether from Egypt, Africa, or from Spain, as well as the taxes, many of their members found the burden greater than they could bear and sought to forsake their occupations. Thereupon Diocletian made membership in the guilds hereditary and compulsory, so that neither the merchants nor their sons could escape their now impoverishing tasks.

The *curiales*—members of the somewhat wealthier families—were made responsible for the collection of the taxes in the districts where they lived, and any deficiency on the part of a citizen was made good from their own estates. To prevent the curiales from retiring from their offices their positions were also made hereditary and every man who owned as much as twenty-five acres of land might be required to accept the office of a curialis for his lifetime and to transmit it to his sons when dead. If any curialis went to another city to escape the burden he became liable for service in the city where he sought refuge as well as in that from which he had fled.

This kind of semi-slavery pervaded the entire Empire. "It was a state of siege, for life or perpetuity. A man's station in society, his profession, came to be made hereditary, and the watch-word was 'Every man at his post.'" [3] The workers in the mines, in the quarries, and in the salt-pens; the armourers and smiths in the Imperial factories; muleteers, grooms, and cartwrights were all subjected to

[3] F. Lot, *The End of the Ancient World.*

military discipline and their occupations were hereditary. Gladiators, musicians of both sexes, actors, actresses, and charioteers were all chained to their professions which, although branded as "infamous," were declared compulsory and hereditary to those who were termed, in the words of the Imperial constitution, "the slaves of the peoples' pleasures." They were forbidden to leave the city and, if they did so, might be pursued like runaway slaves.

As formerly the exactions of Roman money-lenders had driven debtors to sell first their children and then themselves into slavery as the lesser evil, so now even worse scenes attended the coming of the tax gatherers. Zosimus writes: "Constantine imposed a tribute of gold and silver on all who engaged in commerce; even wretched courtesans were not exempted from the tax. As the fatal time approached all the towns were in grief and tears; the scourge and the rack were used against those whose extreme poverty could not support the tax. Mothers sold their children, and fathers prostituted their daughters, obliged to obtain, by this sorry trade, the money which the tax collectors came to snatch from them." [4]

Such burdens did not fall, however, like the rain "upon the just and upon the unjust," for the priests of the pagan faiths shared, by favour, those immunities which the powerful maintained by force; by the Edict of Milan the clergy of the Christian Church were also admitted to the ranks of the tax exempt. For the two following generations all priests, whether of the old faith or of the new, walked in the pathways of the privileged. But these ways became less crowded after the year 382 when Gratian confiscated the estates of the temples and deprived their priests of their immunities and emoluments. Thereafter only the Christian clergy could go their way untroubled by the exactions and oppressions of the tax gatherers.

[4] The result of this oppressive taxation was a flight of the taxed from the tax gatherers, the fugitives even taking refuge among the Germans and the Huns. A writer of the Fourth Century complains: "The poor are despoiled until many of them, although born of good families, flee to our enemies. They seek Roman humanity among the barbarians because they cannot bear barbarian inhumanity among the Romans." A century later, in 448, an ambassador of Theodosius II, sent to Attila, met a Roman refugee who "considered his new life among the Huns better than his old life among the Romans."

The natural result of this clerical freedom from taxation was a rush of burdened Romans towards the sacristy, clamorous for priestly ordination. In fact, so great was the pressure of the oppressed that Constantine forbade men of curial rank to apply for ordination and these laws were repeated, but feebly enforced, by later emperors. In 439 the doors to the priesthood were closed, at least legally, to those whose wealth exceeded three hundred *solidi* (about one thousand dollars).

Doubtless much of the demand for ordination which followed the conversion of Constantine was honest and sincere, but such laws as these clearly indicate that much of it was also due to a desire to escape the burden of taxation, to enjoy the exemptions of the clergy, and to share in the riches which the Imperial favour was pouring into ecclesiastical coffers. This rush of candidates for holy orders compelled the Church to make new provision for their accommodation. The apse was far too small and the clergy, even though ordained to the lower orders, might not fitly be seated with the congregation. It was to provide space for an increasing clergy that the transepts were created, sometimes by adding wings to the chancel so as to give the basilica the shape of the letter "T" but more and more frequently by extending the transverse aisle between the nave and the chancel through and beyond the side walls of the building. By means of these new wings of this now cruciform church all the priests, wherever seated, could be gathered equally near the altar which stood in the centre of the Crossing, between the aisles and the apse.[5]

---

[5] A. K. Porter (*Mediæval Architecture,* Vol. I, p. 56) declares that the transepts were not added to the church for either symbolic values or for architectural effects. The "most plausible theory," he says, is that they were adopted to provide additional room for the increasing number of the clergy. The earliest transepts—which made the church T-shaped —could only have been intended for the use of the clergy, since only the ordained might occupy the chancel. (See also Rainy, *Ancient Catholic Church,* pp. 274-279; and Thompson, Vol. I, pp. 64-70.) Perhaps a definite structural evidence supporting this derivation may be found in the churches of Syria where transepts failed to develop because the altar, which must always be kept within sight of the priests, was placed at the far end of the church—in the rear of the chancel—where it could not be seen by those who were seated in the arms of a cruciform church. In the West, on the other hand, where the altar was placed in the Crossing, transepts early made their appearance, especially in the larger metropolitan churches. They were used for the accommodation of priests until the early years of the Carlovingian era, when the altar was

Thus the popular belief that the cruciform church perpetuated the memory of a cross is true, but the cross from which the transepts sprang is not that which was raised on Calvary; it is the cross on which the economic incapacity of Rome crucified its own citizens and subjects; and our familiar church, with its aisles and transepts, bears witness through the years to the folly of a nation which, having gained the whole world, lost all that she had won because, while she had the power to rule, she lacked the will to serve.

Never creating, but only draining the wealth of her subject races, she so sapped by her exactions the vitality of her own citizens that the sons of the men who had leaped to arms to drive the Gauls from the walls of Rome, the armies of Pyrrhus from Italy, the Carthaginians from the sea, and the Germans across the Rhine, now fled to the sacristy, clothed themselves with the immunities of priests, and then watched Rome's military power decline, her frontiers shrink, and the barbarian again encamp before her gates.

So, seated in the transepts of the cathedral, we may hear the dragging footsteps of Rome's retreating legions, the melancholy sound of her crumbling walls, and the guttural voices of her conquerors shouting their *"vae victis,"* for here the very stones proclaim the fall of "Babylon" and the triumph of the Cross.

removed to the depths of the apse. The priests were then transferred to a compartment prepared for them in the long axis of the church, as in Syria, while the transepts were surrendered to other uses.

Alinari

THE CHURCH OF S. MARIA MAGGIORE AT TOSCANELLA, MODERN TUSCANIA

The transepts, whether they made the church T-shaped as here or cruciform as at Pisa, were originally added to the Western church less for the love of God than for the fear of men.

Chapter Five

THE UNCERTAIN TRANSEPTS

WITH one exception definite functions were assigned to each important member of the church—to the chancel, ambulatory, chapels, choir, and nave; only the transepts varied from age to age in the nature of the services demanded of them. Apparently first added to the basilica to accommodate the increasing number of the clergy, it is probable that they were early utilized to accommodate a choir, recruited from the minor orders of the priesthood.

This explanation answers one perplexing question that would otherwise remain unanswered and unexplained. Granted that the transepts were intended for the many clergy that flooded the Church after the Edict of Milan, what function did these clergy perform? Were they present merely as detached members of the congregation, or did they share in the performance of the liturgies?

It must be remembered that, by the Fourth Century, the liturgy of the Church had developed complicated forms and had become rather too difficult for the ordinary clergy who, however consecrated, were not always vocally gifted or musically trained, and also that the congregations had been progressively excluded from all participation in the musical portions of the service. The organization of a priestly choir had, therefore, become increasingly imperative.

Shortly after the Edict of Milan, the Council of Laodicea issued a decree which stated, "Beside the appointed singers others shall not sing in the church." The importance of the action lay more in the spirit it revealed than in its general effectiveness for, beyond the boundaries of its own jurisdiction, the action of the Council could only be accepted as a recommendation; it was not an Ecumenical Edict. In some of the great Eastern liturgies the part permitted to the people was re-

stricted to a few brief responses: the "Amens," the "Kyrie Eleisons,"
"And to thy spirit," with a few others of equal brevity. By the middle
of the Fourth Century the change had become general, if not universal; the laity had been silenced, and only the voices of the priests
might be heard in the various offices and liturgies of the Church
which now demanded, for their rendition, the voices of a large and
trained choir recruited from the ranks of the minor clergy. Schools for
the training of ordained choristers were established by the metropolitan churches—in Rome, in Lombardy, and elsewhere—and a portion of the nave was walled off to form the *Schola Cantorum,* the
"place of the singers," as in S. Clemente in Rome.

But the introduction of antiphonal singing immediately gave a practical value to the transepts for the priests, if they might not easily
sing in unison when widely scattered in the two wings of the Crossing,
in the schola cantorum, and in the chancel, could render the antiphonals of the liturgies with great effectiveness when seated in the
transepts. Whether these transepts were so used is a possibility worth
considering.

The practice of antiphonal singing must have been familiar to the
disciples even in the time of Jesus, for the Jews were wont to chant
their psalms antiphonally in their synagogues. The famous letter of
Pliny to Trajan shows that it was also known in the Church of the
First Century.

"The Christians," Pliny wrote, "are accustomed to gather on a
stated day before it is light, and to sing among themselves, alternately,
a hymn to Christ."

Tradition, doubtless embellishing but also embalming a fact, states
that Ignatius of Antioch, martyred under Trajan about 107 A.D., was
vouchsafed a vision of angels chanting antiphonally their hymns of
praise before the Throne, whereby he was divinely led to institute
the antiphon in Antioch.

At least as early as the middle of the Fourth Century the influence
of the Orient was being felt in Italy where antiphonal singing was
introduced, as by Ambrose in his Cathedral of Milan, and where the
transepts were admirably adapted for such purposes.

It is true that neither history nor tradition bears witness to this use for the transepts so that we are driven to mere conjecture as to its probability, but the argument from silence is never convincing especially when, as now, the failure of the witnesses to testify is so far from inexplicable.

The use of the transepts for a priestly choir must have been of too short duration to have left any deep impression on the Church, for the early removal of the altar from its primitive place in the Crossing to the depths of the apse forced the transference of the choir from the transepts to a new location in the long axis of the church. Then the appearance of the symbolist, with his dramatic and appealing interpretation of the transepts as the silent proclamation of the gospel of the Cross of Christ, supplanted and drove from memory the more practical, if less emotional, explanation of the transepts as having been utilized by the Church for the accommodation of a double choir. However, if the direct testimony is weak the circumstantial evidence is strong, and it is difficult to believe that the Church could have overlooked the great opportunity afforded by the transepts for the rendition of her new antiphonals.

Chapter Six

THE ARCHES OF CONSTANTINE

THE conversion of an emperor, the Edict of Milan, and the Imperial favour brought a multitude of new disciples, clamorous for baptism, sweeping towards the portals of the church and flooding her aisles.

These converts—won to Christianity by the sceptre of Constantine, not by the Sword of the Spirit—were moved more by social considerations and political sagacity than by any deep convictions or spiritual experiences, and the sudden invasion of the sanctuary by those who would be conformed to Cæsar without being consecrated to Christ severely taxed the wisdom and the discipline of the Church. Now, if ever, were miracles needed, for this worldly mass of unconverted converts must be transformed in character lest they deform the Church, and the task of making saints without the help of lions was, under the circumstances, difficult.

Since the legalization of Christianity had made confession safe, since the executioner no longer functioned to sift the sand from the steel, this transformation of character could only be effected by the memory of the illustrious martyrs, by the stimulating example of those who had been tried by fire, and above all by the spell of the Liturgy, the preaching of the Word, and the appeal of the mystic sacraments offered on the altar.

In their efforts to bring these spiritual forces to bear upon their new congregations, however, the clergy found their endeavours hampered by certain architectural elements in their churches, for when the multitudes of recent converts poured through the portals of the church their very numbers forced many of them over into the side aisles. Here the rows of closely spaced columns lining the nave not only impaired their vision of both priest and altar but, deflecting the voices

46

THE BAPTISTRY, CATHEDRAL, AND CAMPANILE AT PISA, SEEN FROM THE AIR

of the clergy, made the prayers, liturgies, scriptures, and sermons less intelligible.

For this problem the inevitable solution was the substitution of the arch for the architrave (the flat stone beam, or lintel) by which the columns of the earlier basilicas had been linked together. This architrave had compelled the builders to keep their columns close together, for there was an ever present danger that the unsupported centre of a long lintel might crack and break beneath its burden. The arch, on the other hand, permitted the wider spacing of the columns, for the weight of the masonry above glided down its curving sides to the supporting piers, much as the rain follows the slope of a slanting roof.[1]

The architraves of the secular basilica bore witness to their descent from Greece, where the arch had never found favour; and in substituting the arch for the architrave in order to open up wider vistas between side aisles and apse, the Fourth Century Christian architects unconsciously broke away from the architectural canons which bound the Roman builder, pagan and Christian alike, to the Greek tradition. The break was necessary; for the high excellence, the perfection in style and refinement in detail, which Hellenic art had attained four hundred years before Christ in such structures as the Parthenon, formed a barrier to further development since an ideal, once attained, forbids exploration and experiment. Eight hundred years later, when

[1] An examination of the floor plans of early basilicas, drawn to scale, show that the spaces between the columns are markedly greater where the arch was substituted for the architrave. For instance, the nave columns of S. Clemente, S. Maria in Cosmedin, and S. Agnese are more widely spaced by at least twenty per cent than are those of S. Pressede, S. Laurent, and S. Maria Maggiore. In the fall of 1934 I taped the distance between the bases of the columns supporting lintels in the churches of S. Pietro al Monte, S. Pressede, and S. Maria Maggiore and found them to be six feet six inches, seven feet six inches and seven feet three inches respectively. I then taped the similar distances between the columns with arches of S. Sabina, S. Maria Antiqua, and S. Maria in Aracœli, and these measured nine feet, ten feet and ten feet four inches. This gives an average distance of nine feet nine inches between columns supporting arches as against seven feet two inches between those sustaining lintels—a difference of thirty-six per cent. Thus with the space between each pair of columns widened by over two and a half feet the total additional width between the columns in a church with ten such openings, or ten bays—counting both sides of the nave aisle, would be fifty-three feet. These are the distances between the bases; those between the columns would be, of course, much greater.

Christianity was surging forward to its conquest of the world, the canons of this classic art barred the way to the expansion of a new architecture that was adapted to the triumph of a new faith. Only by breaking with these canons could the Church enter freely upon that long road which should one day lead to the great columns, the graceful pointed arches, and the lofty vaults of Amiens and Beauvais.

Had the architects of pagan Rome faced the necessity of lessening the number of columns along the sides of their naves they would have found the solution ready to their hands, for all around the Mediterranean, from Rome to Syria, Babylon, and Persia, the value of the arch was understood long before the days of Constantine. The arches of the Colosseum, the baths of Caracalla, an arcade in Spalato, and many great aqueducts still bear mute witness to the skill with which they were employed throughout the Empire and in the Imperial City itself. But the uses for which the secular basilica was employed prevented the emergence of the problem until the conversion of Constantine and the Edict of Milan transformed the old law-court and market into a Christian church. In the meantime the substitution of arches for architraves had already been made in certain churches of Central Syria, and it is quite probable that, when the overflowing congregations necessitated the reduction of the number of columns in the naves of Western churches, it was to Syria that the architects of Christian Rome turned for their inspiration.

With the arches freely and skilfully used in so many parts of the Empire, it is strange to note how hesitatingly they were introduced into the church. But the light wooden roof of the old secular basilica naturally demanded architraves on columns; and the roof of the Christian basilican church, being quite as light as that of the Roman law-court, would normally be supplied, from a structural standpoint, with beams to span its columns. The very fact that the arches displaced the architraves implies that the builders were influenced by considerations which sprang from the *use* for which the building was employed and not from any structural advantages that might be gained by the abandonment of the one or by the adoption of the other.

Sometimes the builders inserted a relieving arch in the nave wall above the lintel. The use of such arches, which transferred the burden from the beam to the column, had long been understood and their erection, since they now carried all the weight and relieved the lintels of their structural values, soon led the builders to omit the architrave between the columns and the masonry immediately above it, leaving the arches alone to span the gaps and bear the burden of the nave walls. This had already been done in tentative ways in various parts of the Roman Empire, as in the forecourt of Diocletian's palace at Spalato in Dalmatia. Like many elements in this extraordinary building, this idea may have been borrowed from the Syrian East where many Fourth Century churches, abandoning the architrave, rested the arches of their nave arcades on columns.

The fact that the arches thus entered the church is important because it gives so clear an explanation of the origin of the stilt-block— the rectangular stone standing above the capital of the column. This stone was the last survivor of the old architrave; it was the end of the ancient lintel which had formerly linked the columns together and rested upon them. When the architrave was abandoned something was needed to give a landing place to those descending arches which would otherwise have overlapped the strong core of the column and damaged, by their weight, the delicate carvings, the volutes and acanthus leaves, of Corinthian capitals. This demand became the more imperative in the Fifth and Sixth Centuries when the architects, building more splendidly, raised thicker and higher nave walls, which called for wider arches in the nave arcade to support a loftier clerestory and a heavier timber roof.[2]

This awkward square stone was later transformed by the masons of Byzantium and of Ravenna into a trapezoid whose upper surface was wide enough to support the arches while its sides sloped inward and downward to fit the core of the column.[3]

[2] T. G. Jackson, *Reason in Architecture*, p. 28.
[3] This stone (the impost block, *pulverino*, or *dosseret*, as it is called in England, Italy, and France respectively) was to serve another, and important, purpose in that barbarian age which was very near at hand when the builders—Latin, Celt, and Teuton alike— unskilled in the arts of stereotomy (the art of cutting and dressing stone), despoiled

The arch which thus hesitantly entered the church was never to give up its place. The need that called it into being—that of enabling those in the side aisles to see and hear the priests in the apse—was temporary; the arch alone was permanent.

In centuries to come the throngs who crowded the pilgrim roads compelled the builders to enlarge their churches, not to receive the faithful who lived within sight of the towers and sound of the bells, but to accommodate tens of thousands who came, many from far countries. Cathedrals and churches, rebuilt and increased in size, soon became so vast that the voice was quickly lost and preaching consequently dwindled in importance.

The Church was therefore compelled to reconstruct her services as well as her buildings, to enrich the symbolism of her liturgies, and to enact sacred dramas in her aisles, that the eye might carry those lessons to the hearts of men which the ear had become less able to receive. Wider aisles and more spacious chapels were needed to accommodate the great multitudes of the sandal-shod whose numbers at Cluny, Chartres, or Amiens might rise to eighteen thousand or even twenty thousand. Greater piers and columns were needed to carry the increased burdens, so once more the vistas of the chancel from the side aisles were obscured as in earlier centuries. These aisles, however, had lost much of their former values, for the few hundreds living in the parish could easily be accommodated in the nave.

To us, therefore, the real interest in the substitution of the arch for the architrave does not spring from our concern for the Roman of the Fourth Century who was thereby enabled to see and hear the priest in the apse better than before. Our interest centres in the historic fact that thus were born into the Western church those arches upon which the future of ecclesiastical architecture was so largely to depend. It was the arch alone which made possible the various systems of

the ancient Roman monuments, robbing them of their columns for the erection of their own churches. These pilfered columns, however, were not always of the same height; some were too short while others were too long. Therefore the impost block, varied in height and sometimes assisted by a base, was useful in bringing all columns in an arcade to the same level.

mediæval vaulting—barrel, groin, or Gothic; it is to the arch that we owe the curving aisle, with its crown of chapels, that encircles the chancel, and it is the arch which gave us those walls of jewelled glass that are the glory of Chartres, the boast of Bourges, and the pride of Le Mans.

Chapter Seven

THE END OF THE ANCIENT WORLD

A SCANT two hundred and fifty years span the gap between the Edict of Milan and the collapse of the ancient civilization in Western Europe. For that brief space of time the Church had need to labour and take no rest; first, to Christianize the Roman culture, and then to adapt the best of that culture to her own thought, law, liturgy, and architecture. Her leaders must perforce make haste to walk while they had the light, for, unforeseen and undreamed, the Lombard night was coming when she, like her Master, should be "delivered into the hands of men."

Before the brilliant period ushered in by the accession of Constantine the energies of the Church were largely consumed in the mere effort to survive; from that time onward they were spent in the administration of high responsibilities.

Under Diocletian, who abdicated his throne in 305, the Christians died in the arena because they would not bend before the gods of Rome; in 379, under Theodosius, those same gods were dragged through the dirt and dust of their own Via Sacra to grace the triumph of a Christian emperor. Bishops, forerunners of the great Innocents and Gregories, were mocked and martyred in the Third Century, but in the Fourth they barred the door, and forbade the way, to a successor of Augustus. Throughout the earlier centuries Rome, standing aloof, despised a ministry recruited from the poor, but in the Fourth Century laws were needed to keep the wealthy from serving at the altar.

In the Third Century the populace were ever swift to cry their *"Christiani ad leones,"* but in the Fourth Century their sons were offering gifts at the shrines, and entreating the intercession, of those whom the lions of their fathers had destroyed.

In the Third Century a hundred thousand Romans sat in the Circus Maximus to watch the Roman games, but in the next century that Circus was demolished to make way for the first Roman library of Christian books, and the basilica of S. Peter rose on the site of the Neronian Circus where the great apostle perished for his faith.

It is difficult to find in all history a parallel to the swift reversal of fortune which befell the Church, almost between sunrise and sunset —between the hour when the dying Galerius recalled the edicts of persecution, in 311, and that moment of the year 313 when Constantine signed the Edict of Milan.

The years that lie between the accession of Constantine and the coming of the Lombards form one of the great periods of ecclesiastical history, and the imprint of those years is deeply stamped upon the form and spirit of the Church. Conflicts with great heretics called the creeds into existence; decisions of Ecumenical Councils governed the thinking of Europe for centuries to come; such men as Gregory the Great, Jerome, Augustine, Athanasius, Arius, Ambrose of Milan, Chrysostom, Hilary of Poitiers, and Gregory of Tours would have made their mark in any age.

Architecturally, we owe to the builders of these centuries the floor plan of the church, and the arch which was to clothe that plan with beauty. All the elements of the churches they slowly built, line upon line, have been handed down through sixty generations, sometimes modified but never abandoned, to form their great bequest and our rich inheritance. The complex problems which our Latin fathers faced in those critical centuries were by them answered, not merely for their own brief day but for their sons of many generations, for us, and apparently for all time.

It may seem tragic that the leadership should have passed so soon from the Roman to the barbarian; from those who had done so much to others who were nowise prepared for their inheritance. Yet it may well be doubted whether Christian architecture could have gone further forward in Roman hands. The fact that Byzantium, although it survived the fall of the Western Empire for a thousand years, produced no greater monument than Sancta Sophia which Justinian erected; that the builders of later centuries continued to imitate the achievements of the Sixth Century, would justify the judgement that the Romans, guardians of the ancient civilization at the time of its collapse, had spent their force.

The economic confusions of the Second Century and the ruin of the Third had carried in their train the arrest, and then the decline, of all forms of ancient art, for "when poverty follows wealth, patronage fails, craft deteriorates, technique is lost, and schools die out. Lesser men, conscious perhaps of their own limitations, are content to copy the masterpiece of their greater fathers, and at last the imitating of imitations marks the approach to art's Avernus." As in art, so in architecture; the builders were becoming mere copyists, wherefore there was less of promise in the cultured Roman than in the crude barbarian who, waking or sleeping, could dream great dreams.

The failure of Latin architecture, however, was decreed even more by the heights of world power to which Rome attained in the Augustan Age than by the depths to which she fell in the Fourth Century, for, until Diocletian rent the Empire in twain, the Roman everywhere demanded uniformity—there must be one Cæsar, one rule, one law, one mode and manner of life. This instinct for regularity so standardized his architecture that, when allowances have been made for differences in building materials and racial characteristics in the various parts of the Empire, a basilica on the Tigris closely resembled one on the Guadalquivir. The Temple of Timgad, the Forum in Carthage, the Baths of Lepcis Magna, the Arch of Titus, the Aqueduct near Nîmes are echoed by the Temple in Spanish Merida, the Forum in German Trier, the Baths in English Chester, the Arch in French Orange, and the Aqueduct in Asian Smyrna.

A dull monotony pervaded the massive splendours of all Latin architecture; the old men of Latium could no longer dream dreams, nor could her young men see visions. *Roma fuit; vale.*

Neither men nor nations have here an abiding city; lives end yet life goes on, albeit never again the same. Rome passed, but on the

THE CHURCH OF S. PIETRO AT TOSCANELLA

Such wide arches, replacing lintels, gave a clearer view of the altar to the congregations that crowded into the side aisles when the conversion of Constantine made Christianity fashionable.

debris of the fallen Empire a new world arose, a broken world of rival principalities, wherein a myriad of lesser kings replaced the world-ruling Cæsar, and where countless customs succeeded the single Roman Law. In the ghastly confusion of the years, security ended, journeys became perilous, pirates infested the seas, and barbarian bands roved the land taking delight in destructions and massacres. Forests once more covered the sown fields; within the crumbling walls of ghostly towns, and in their half-deserted streets, only a few miserables vegetated. Civilization died and anarchy ruled. "If the waves of the ocean had overflowed the fields of Gaul," wrote Prosper of Aquitaine, "they would have done less damage;" and a contemporary added, "He who has bread may count himself rich."

The very violence of the age begat a hunger for order, and spurred all finer souls to energy and action. A brief reign of law, although it dissolved when Charles the Fat succeeded Charles the Great, quickened the longing for such stability as Rome, with all her faults, had given to the world. Nevertheless that spirit of individualism, which Rome had kept in shackles, found opportunity in the disorganization and complexity of society throughout the Charlemagnic Age, and the barbarian, keenly as he may have desired to build *juxta Romanorum morem*, inevitably wrought something of himself into his work. These Teutons struggled, not to postpone defeat as in the later days of Rome, but to survive and conquer; not to support and stabilize a crumbling social structure, but, throwing all the elements of civilization into the gigantic crucible of Europe, to build anew; and the church, ever sensitive to all social changes, could not but reflect in stone the defeats and victories of those who, in the swift vicissitudes of their lives, were ever passing from the throne to prison, or from prison to the throne.

The torch has fallen from the hands of Rome. It will be nearly a thousand years before the world shall again turn to Italy for leaders in the field of architecture, and then these leaders shall hark back to the ruined monuments of Cæsarian days, seeking amid the wreckage of old Rome the inspirations for that which is well called the Renaissance, since, in architecture at least, it was not so much the birth of the New, as it was the rebirth of the Old.

Chapter Eight

THE GIFTS OF IGNORANCE

TOO many years have passed since Rome, which began with a Romulus, was ending with an Augustulus; we are too far removed from those dark hours when all the civilization of the West was crumbling into an abyss. The pen of the historian may record the facts, the causes, and the consequences of the downfall of a great empire, but it cannot bring to our nostrils the tang of the smoke, to our eyes the reddened skies of night, nor to our ears the sound of fugitive feet fleeing from the sword of the invader. History is too cold and bloodless to do justice to those tragic days when the Imperial Eagles, their pinions plucked, were slowly winging their homeward way; when, from Britain to Africa, the legions of the Empire were reeling and breaking before successive barbarian blows; when the surges of Scythian or Sclav, of Goth, Hun, or Teuton, with swift and brilliant feats of arms, were sweeping over the old frontiers and lighting, with the glare of burning cities, the pathway of the retreating cohorts of dying Rome.

The Suevi seized Spanish Galicia; Jutes overran the abandoned Roman camps in Britain—camps that Boadicea had entered only when in chains; Clovis the Frank drove the last Roman from the land that Cæsar had conquered; Leovigild the Visigoth held court in Trajan's Spain; Gundobad the Burgundian triumphed where Ariovistus the German had failed; and Genseric, the Vandal, sailed from Carthage for the sack of Rome whence Scipio, the Roman, had sailed for the sack of Carthage. The great Ostrogoth, Theodoric, sat on the throne of Augustus and, last but most terrible of all, Alboin with his mixed Sclavonic and Teutonic hordes brought back to Italy terrors unknown since the days of Hannibal.

Alboin's "Long-beards"—known to us as Lombards—were the least civilized of all the Teutonic tribes, and their conquest, even more than those of Goths, Vandals, and Burgundians, was the conquest of the Roman culture. Bred in the depths of the distant North, pagans as well as barbarians, never coming into touch with Rome until her glory had departed, this last invasion brought a tribe across the Alps whose savagery was unmitigated by any of the softening influences of either Latin or Christian culture.

The scars of barbarian ferocity are deeply scored in the annals of the times where we may read, in a decadent Latin, those tales of lust, of treachery, and murder which are only varied by still other tales of murder, of treachery, and lust.

Alboin forces Rosamund, his queen, to "drink joyfully" to the memory of her father from the slain Cunimund's skull; Rosamund sacrifices her virtue to her vengeance to purchase the stroke of an assassin's sword; Gundobad the Burgundian, fearing a possible rival to his throne, burns or beheads his brothers and his sons—and then publicly bewails the fate which has robbed him of all his kin; Brunhilda, lifelong enemy of a concubine who became a queen, is dragged to death at the heels of a wild horse beneath the eyes of the concubine's son; Chlothar, angered by rebellion, chains his sons and his grandsons in their timber house, fires the building, and rides away to the music of their screams.

Among these drunken and senselessly cruel Lords of Misrule the figure of Charlemagne appears to give a brief moment of sanity to a world gone mad, and to stamp his name upon the years that lie between the Sixth and the Eleventh Centuries which we know as the "Carlovingian Era."

Except for the forty years of Charlemagne's rule these centuries mark the low ebb of European culture, an epoch which is "the chaos of all elements, the infancy of all systems, a universal confusion in which even the struggle itself is neither systematic nor permanent." [1]

The entire structure of society was shaken by the death agonies of

[1] M. Guizot.

the old world and by the birth pangs of the new. The Roman peace
was shattered by the storms of tribal warfare and by the fratricidal
strife of kings; the code of written law and statute gave way to the
unwritten law of tribal custom. In the confusion of Carlovingian centuries the Roman trade routes were abandoned and lost in jungles of
disorder, and the general debacle involved all the arts of civilization,
including the architect's skill, the engineer's science, and the mason's
craft. Nevertheless, although the air was filled with the sounds of
clashing swords and crackling flames, the building of churches went
forward, perhaps the faster for the fact that so many sons of Cain,
sitting on uneasy thrones, sought to purchase pardon for crimes and
peace with God by their benefactions to the Church.

The builders of these centuries neither desired nor attempted the
creation of a new architecture; their one ambition was to build as
Rome had done, but for this they lacked both the Roman inheritance
and the Latin skill. The Carlovingian Era is distinctly a time of architectural retrogression, but the manner of that retrogression was most
important, for the inability of the barbarians to repeat the old eventually led to the ability of their sons to create the new. We can appraise
this period best if we think of it merely as a bridge over which architecture passed from the basilica of S. Augustine to the Romanesque
church of S. Bernard, without any great achievement on the way; and
we can do better justice to the Carlovingian builder if we think of him
as a pioneer blazing a trail over which a greater than he was to pass,
or as a workman laying those deep foundations upon which later generations were to build splendidly to the glory of God and the ministry
of men.

Paradoxical as it may appear, achievement grew out of the very
failure of the Carlovingian to achieve; for the barbarian, as inexpert
with the stone-cutter's chisel as he was skilful with the weapons of
war, was forced to adopt certain makeshifts and these devices, to
which he was driven by his ignorance of mechanics and his lack of
stereotomic skill, were destined to develop into some of the supreme
achievements of mediæval cathedral architecture. To these makeshifts
we owe the beauty of the deep-set Gothic portals, the grace of the

AMIENS CATHEDRAL

The statues of prophets, Kings of Judea, and saints line the recessed portals, leading
the visitor to the figure of *le Beau Dieu d'Amiens* above the central porch.

multiple arches that rise from piers or columns of clustering shafts, and the twilight that lingers in the aisles.

The Romans, builders of such mighty structures as the Colosseum and the Pont du Gard, were rich in skilled labour and in ingenious devices for the lifting of heavy weights whereby they had been able to place huge stones in the arches or lintels above their doorways. Yet despite, or perhaps because of, their science and their skill, these, lacking depth and beauty, were rarely impressive.

The barbarians on the other hand, habitants of great forests, although they might be skilled carpenters, were indifferent masons at the best. Without the Roman facility for the handling of weights they were compelled to build their arches of such stones as a man might carry on his back or lift with the primitive tackle at his disposal. Therefore instead of the single Roman arch the Teuton mortared two arches of smaller stones side by side, placing a single arch beneath to support his double arch where the stones were joined together. Presently another arch, three stones deep, was added and now three rows of concentric, indented arches rose above the entrance to the church, each arch supported by a column on either side so placed that all these columns stood *en échelon*, each being thrust a little farther out into the porch.

The years passed and with them passed the barbarism which had called these portals into being; new centuries produced new artisans who wrought as skilfully as those of Rome. These builders of Romanesque and of Gothic days, however, seeing new possibilities of beauty in the rude makeshifts of Carlovingian masons, multiplied the arches of the door-ways until they swept over the porch in great concentric arcs, and marshalled their columns in stately procession on either hand. Then the artists covered vaults and walls with statues and bas-reliefs whereby the faiths, inspirations, legends, and philosophies of the Middle Ages spoke alike to all who entered these portals and to those who merely bent a hurried knee as they passed by.

Thus the splendours of the portals and porches of Chartres, of Amiens, of Rheims, and of all that great sorority of churches, might never have been achieved had it not been for the architectural limitations, the ignorance in technique, and the poverty in mechanical devices which compelled a ruder and less skilled people to substitute a double row of small stones for the single row of greater stones wherewith the Romans built their arches.[2]

From these funnel-shaped portals the serried arches entered and so took possession of the interior of the cathedral that the first and most enduring impression stamped upon the mind of the visitor by the aisles of a Gothic church is that of moulded arches rising one above the other. Wherever the eye turns, from Western portal to Eastern chapel, from floor to vault, these arches curve from column to column. They stand on parade in the arcades of nave, triforium, and clerestory; they surround the chancel, leap from pier to pier of the ambulatory, span the windows of aisles and apse, and canopy the decorative panellings.

As the theme in a symphony unfolds and expands, repeating itself again and again with many changes of time and rhythm yet always at heart the same, so the arches—the theme in Gothic architecture— repeat each other with infinite variety as they sweep from portal to ambulatory, rise in a great crescendo to the vault, and then sink down to the arches of the nave arcade—the chords in a mighty chorus.

Although the arch itself was a gift from Rome, these recessed and moulded arches were bequests from those barbarians who, because they were unable to handle great weights, built lesser stones into nests of expanding arches—three, four, five—each supporting, and in turn being supported by, another arch. Like the bands of a rainbow, like ripples in still waters where arc quivers within arc, these arches curve from column to column, arch upon arch, each one receiving a little slanting shadow from the wider arch above, and casting a slanting little shadow upon the narrower arch below.

They touch and transform the piers and columns into clusters of graceful shafts. Each arch of an arcade rests upon one of these encircling shafts; each greater arch that spans the vault merges into a slender colonnette which drops down the nave walls, past clerestory and triforium gallery, to become a part of the clustered column. The

[2] T. G. Jackson, *Reason in Architecture,* Chap. III.

effectiveness of these columns with their congeries of shafts is inde-
finably increased by the modulations of the shadings, for each shaft is
thrown into relief by the faint shadows it casts into the hollows—
shadows that the eye can barely see, but which deepen the little valleys
and accentuate the heights, thus repeating in the columns the chiaro-
scuro effects of the arches in the arcades.

The inherent beauty of these multiple arches and clustered columns
made any other decoration unnecessary to relieve what might otherwise have been the too great severity and simplicity of the Gothic
church. Constantly repeating, accentuating, and varying the elemental
structural lines of the cathedral, they give it that ultimate touch which
creates a unity of pure beauty, a beauty from which the hand of the
decorator might detract, but to which it could not add.

Once more "out of the carcass came forth honey," and we who have
borrowed these multiple and serried arches for our own architecture
may well stop to burn a candle to the unknown workman who, centuries ago, with aching back and cracking sinew, mortared above his
head the heaviest stones his hands could carry into an arch the Latin
would have despised, for it was this barbarian who brought to birth a
beauty the Roman could never have conceived. The graceful arcades
of all the Notre-Dames of France and England are the direct descendants of those crude arches of small stones, mortared one above
the other which carpenters, trying to be masons, raised to the glory of
God in early Carlovingian centuries.

The same lack of skill which called the Gothic portal into being
also touched and darkened the churches of the Carlovingian age and
thus prepared the way for those Romanesque and Gothic cathedrals
whose sombre aisles seem filled with mysteries which men may feel
but cannot see.

The loss in the arts of stereotomy—the diminished skill in the cutting and dressing of stone—forced the builders to erect thick walls of
"rubble"—roughly broken stone of varying shapes and sizes whose in-
terstices were filled with mortar—instead of the squared and dressed
stone which the Roman masons had cemented in regular courses to

form their enduring walls. Windows had to be reduced, both in number and in size, lest these walls of rubble, lacking the strength of dressed stone, be dangerously weakened by their insertion.[3]

The brilliant sunshine which had flooded the old basilica could not find entrance through these diminished windows; the daylight faded, the dusk of the Romanesque church began to fall, and in the growing shadows one World drew back to let another World draw near.

The Roman needed daylight for his legal or commercial transactions, and the skill of his masons enabled him to erect basilicas with many windows. Although the Carlovingian builder also would doubtless have preferred light, yet, lacking skill, he must needs content himself with small splayed windows and with darkened aisles. So it came to pass that a twilight fell upon his house of prayer wherein, like a miracle from the hand of God, those fine realities were suddenly unveiled which daylight may no more reveal than midday can disclose the stars.

Architects of succeeding ages, sensitive to the charm and responsive to the spell of this mellowing twilight, did from choice what the Carlovingian had done from sheer necessity. Although they learned to build stone vaults that could rest on walls of glass and no longer needed the thick walls of barbarian rubble for their support, yet they so veiled the light of their many windows by the use of jewelled glass that the dim half lights of Carlovingian days still clung to the aisles. Not until the coming of the Renaissance when men, impatient of all mysteries, tore out the coloured glass and filled their windows with white or yellow lights did the Church lose that gift of grace which the ignorance of barbarians had unwittingly bestowed.

The values of the gifts men bring cannot always be measured by their cost or cunning; it took two thousand fishes and seven thousand birds to supply a banquet for Vitellius, but we remember better those

[3] The builders soon found that more light might be safely admitted to their churches by either "splaying" or by "double-splaying" their windows. A "splayed" window is narrowest on the exterior face of the thick wall, and wider on the interior; a "double-splayed" window has a "wasp's-waist" in the centre of the wall, and widens from that line both towards the exterior and towards the interior of the church. In either case the window sill was given a downward slant.

THE RAYONNANT CHURCH OF S. OUEN AT ROUEN

The moulded and recessed arches, a "gift of ignorance," stand on parade in the arcades, span the windows, and surround the chancel.

that were fed with two fishes and five loaves; locusts and wild honey sustained one of whom Jesus said "none born of woman is greater than he," and a cruse of water and a cake baked on coals was the gift of an angel to Elijah.

Certainly neither Wise Men from the East, nor yet Kings from the West, ever brought finer gifts into the Church than did the barbarian whose ignorance achieved as much as art, for from him the Church received the multiple arches of her aisles, her recessed portals, and—finest gift of all—silence and twilight, the twin portals to those secret places where rests the shadow of the Almighty.

Chapter Nine

THE GIFTS OF FEAR

THE visitor to Bourges Cathedral is shown monstrous devils with faces carved on their abdomens (to indicate the controlling powers of their baser natures) as—spikes in hand—they drive the lost into the smoking mouth of that Leviathan whose jaws are the gateway to a flaming Hell; but no one associates the scene with the fury of the Northman, of the Vandal, or the Goth. On the same tympanum the stone images of these most miserable and hopeless ones, toads and frogs already dripping from their mouths, are being hurled within those teeth where Terror dwells, while little devils with their bellows blow hot the flames beneath; but the visitor never thinks of the dread that once possessed the hearts of men at the whisper of the Lombard name.

Nor do the angels, carrying tiny souls in little napkins to lay them in the already crowded bosom of a patient Abraham, remind us of Alboin and those wild Sclavonic hordes from whom, in their day, there seemed to be no place of refuge apart from the patriarchal arms.

Doubtless the Thirteenth Century artist who wrought above this portal never thought of them either, yet "Lombard," "Vandal," "Goth," cry out in every line graven by his chisel.

From the Edict of Milan in 313 until the passing of the Western Empire the Christian Church had developed under the protection of Roman laws and courts whose utterances were enforced by the Imperial favour and the secular power. In Italy, even after the fall of Rome, Arian Goths, ruling from Ravenna and professing allegiance to the Byzantine Court, had striven to continue the traditions inherited from Constantine. But Ravenna fell, and Justinian's suicidal struggle with the Ostrogoth Totila destroyed the last power capable of defending the Alpine barrier, for the victories won by Belisarius and Narses in Italy between 533 and 553 overthrew the Gothic State and left the land defenceless against the Lombards in 567. Thus the very triumphs of Rome proved the prelude to her fall, for with the coming of Alboin the last vestige of Roman power vanished from the West, together with the authority of her austere courts and the protection of her highly developed legal codes.

In the barbarian world where the Church must henceforth live there were no courts as Rome understood the term; the laws, enacted by a general assembly of the people, were simple and few; infractions of these laws might be atoned for by a money payment, the damages being assessed on a sliding scale according to the victim's status in society.

"Every wound and mutilation of each particular part of the body," says Milman, "was carefully registered in the code, and estimated according as the injured man was noble, freeman, slave, or in holy orders." But, adds Mr. Lea, "these laws could be easily brushed aside by one with power and audacity sufficient to disregard them, and it can readily be imagined how hopeless would be the application to the Court of Freemen by a cleric who would be regarded with double contempt—as a Roman by his conquerors, and as a man of peace by warriors emulous only of martial renown." [1]

The priest, therefore, dwelling among these savage tribes, could not but feel himself to be in constant danger from which there was no material power able, or willing, to protect him. His only security lay in his ability to play upon the superstitious terrors of those whom as a Christian he loved, but whom as a man he feared; and so it came about that, while the Church civilized the barbarians, these, in turn, barbarized the Church.

"Cursing," says Mr. Lea, "was the only arm of the defenceless Churchman, and if he cursed with heart and soul we can only measure the intensity of his malignity by the real intensity of his fear."

Although the early Church had not failed to warn men of the wages of sin, yet the penalties, whether they were physical or spiritual, were

[1] H. C. Lea, *Church History*, pp. 290 *et seq.*

the consequences of sin, not punishments inflicted for the injuries to the person or to the property rights of a cleric. But because of the conditions confronting the Church after the Sixth Century, tales of the miraculous power of relics to reward or punish men according to the good or evil that they visited upon the Church or upon churchmen began to be manufactured and circulated by priests and monks, for the warning of the sacrilegious and the violent.

"Thus," adds Mr. Lea, "there sprang up a luxuriant growth of miraculous interpositions of Providence to vindicate the respect due to the Church and to punish the despoiler of her goods. In fact, the manufacture of these miracles became a recognized armoury to which, for centuries, the Church was accustomed to resort. They formed part of the education of the people, who were taught to look with awe upon the priest and his church with their assortment of relics; upon the monastery with its tempting vineyards, orchards, apiaries, and fields of grain; upon the Episcopal palace and cathedral with their treasures accumulated from the piety of generations. The unarmed Churchman could ill guard, by force, the rich possessions entrusted to his care and, if he busied himself with imagining and disseminating the marvels which proved that his person and his property were the peculiar care of God, we should not too sternly judge and condemn him."

The changes that came to Europe with the barbarian invasions went to the very roots of life. They concern not only the forms of government, the codes and courts of law, the habits and relationships of men; they are also reflected in those deeper mental attitudes which lie below the threshold of consciousness and are beyond the reach of argument.

The cultures of the more enlightened and advanced nations of the Mediterranean basin had impressed a somewhat scientific and sceptic spirit upon the minds of the Southern peoples where the rural districts had been depopulated to overcrowd the cities and to pack their slums. The gods had been lost in the very multitudes of their temples, and the pipes of Pan could not be heard above the chatter of the agora or the uproar of the forum. But in the North where mists often hid the mountains, and deep forests always limited man's sight, where the stars shone down upon the sombre needles of the pines or on the shimmering leaves of the oaks of Thor; where the Night had a thousand whispers, each one new-born on the lips of a god, mystery was everywhere. The supernatural interpenetrated and explained the natural and the gods were as circumambient as was the air men breathed. Day unto day revealed their handiwork and night unto night declared their knowledge. All Transalpine Europe was a fairyland, often more grim and sombre than that of our childhood, but a fairyland none the less where the mysterious and the miraculous might be encountered at any hour and in any place. Celts and Teutons, when they became Christians, vitalized the new religion with their age-old mysticism and in their hands the worship of relics became, to borrow and translate a vivid expression from the French, "passionated."

"Every province had its holy places. The fountains where once the goddess-mothers dwelt, the menhirs of the land which had formerly been haunted by fairies, all became Christian. Each year in the Morvan the peasants came to drink at the spring which S. Martin had called into existence by a stroke of his crosier, or crept on their knees around the rock where the mule of the great bishop had left the imprint of his shoe. The saints replaced the spirits of the mountains, the valleys, and the forests. All the heights, once dedicated to Mercury, were now consecrated to S. Michael, the messenger of Heaven, who had revealed himself upon their crests. The entire land had become one vast sanctuary, as in the Celtic Age, and the deepest solitudes guarded some souvenir of some man of God." [2]

Thus the gods and goddesses, the gnomes, genii, fairies, sprites, and spirits of all kinds who had once peopled the Celtic and Teutonic lands did not vanish with the coming of Christianity; they were merely transformed into the holy souls—bishops, hermits, martyrs, and saints of the invading faith. Although these died, to whom God had given the grace of miracles, yet they had not left the world uncomforted, for the power which had flowed from their lips or hands continued to stream from their bones, even from their garments, to secure forgiveness of sins, to heal the sick, raise the dead, exorcise demons, and rout devils. All the trust which had hitherto reposed in magic amulets

[2] Mâle, Vol. I, p. 271.

and charms was now transferred to these holy relics around which "a world of hopes and desires float, moving us today as all things must upon which the thoughts and desires of men have long rested." [3]

Although the reverence for relics was not an entirely new development of the Carlovingian Age since Ambrose of Milan, in the Fourth Century, had made their possession a precondition for the consecration of a church, yet they were now given increased significance by a clergy who, walking amid many perils, spread their fame abroad thus rein. forcing the defensive legends, at first for the sake of increased protection but later because of the wealth that flowed into their treasuries from the pilgrim tide. So powerful did their fame become that the scallop shell around the neck, the holy image in the cap, worn by him who sought a shrine, were more potent protections than the safe conduct of the King, since brigands in times of peace and armies in days of war opened their ranks to let him pass who travelled for the welfare of his soul.

In such an age the greatest prize of war or of commerce was the acquisition of relics—by force, fraud, or purchase—and where the arm of an apostle, the blood of a martyr, or the bones of a saint were found or acquired, there a rich abbey sprang into existence and there a village was born. The reliquary of S. Foy created Conques in Aveyron; the Benedictine monastery of the Casa Dei called the town of La Chaise Dieu into being, and the abbey of Westminster, erected on a marsh-encircled island in the Thames, was the nucleus of an important part of London. Relics not only created towns and compelled the erection of new churches, they also profoundly modified church architecture for provision must be made for the housing of these relics, and the solutions of the problems thus presented were responsible for the most important changes in the interiors of Carlovingian basilicas.

Perhaps the most striking innovation was the introduction of the ambulatory, a curving aisle which ran behind both choir and chancel connecting the two transepts. At first the relics were attached to the wall of this aisle with small altars placed before them; later these altars

[3] Mâle, Vol. I, p. 271.

were sunk into niches cut into the walls—niches which ultimately developed into those radiating chapels which form one of the most beautiful features of Romanesque and Gothic architecture and helped to create that rounding *chevet* which distinguishes the churches of France. Born in the Carlovingian era, reaching maturity in the Ro-

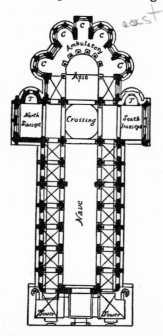

FLOOR PLAN OF A ROMANESQUE CHURCH
C—Chevet chapels; T—Transept chapels.

manesque and Gothic centuries, this curving aisle enabled pilgrims to enter by one transept and to leave by the other without retracing their steps. Until this "Pilgrim Way" was arranged, loss of life and of limb might, and sometimes did, occur when streams of pilgrims met, struggling to pass each other in crowded aisles or chapels.

Another familiar alteration in the plan of the church was the addition of two smaller apses which flanked the great main apse, an arrangement already common in Syria. Sometimes apses were placed in the centre of the transept wall; or again both devices were employed that more altars, each with its relics, might be provided for the worship of the people.

Still further provision for the housing of relics was made by the enlargement of the crypt which was now extended until it ran under the entire eastern portion of the church. This extension was made possible by the deepening of the apse and the erection of a compartment for the choir directly in front of the chancel. This choir was elevated above the pavement of the nave, sometimes by as much as ten or twelve feet, to provide room for the crypt below. Thus arose that arrangement, so usual in the cathedrals and larger churches of Europe, where the pavement reveals three levels; that of the choir, which is reached from the Crossing by a short flight of steps, while another flight of steps leads to the still higher level of the chancel.

An occasional expedient imposed by the tyranny of relics was the erection of a second great apse at the western end of the church. This scheme was not new, for Roman basilicas with the double apse were not unknown in pre-Christian days, but the device was not popular and was rarely adopted except in North Africa and to some extent in Germany; in France the double apse rarely occurs—at Albi, in a church of the little hill town of Garde Adhémar, the Cathedrals of Nevers and of Besançon, but this about exhausts the list.

In addition to the relics which hallowed the Pilgrim Way that led around the church from aisle to ambulatory and from crypt to chancel, other most venerated relics were buried in the altar which thus became the holiest of the holy. To their sanctity was added that of the daily miracle of the Mass whereby the Bread and Wine were changed into the very Body and Blood of Christ. The table, therefore, on which this miracle was wrought became far too sacred for close contact with the laity. Mediæval tales and legends are rich in stories that illustrate its searching judgements.

For instance when Godwin, Duke of Kent, having sworn his innocence to a charge of murder, choked and died in the attempt to swallow a piece of bread which his accuser, Edward the Confessor, had blessed and handed him, all men knew he had committed perjury.[4]

4 H. C. Lea, *Superstition and Force*, p. 301.

THE ATRIUM OF S. AMBROGIO AT MILAN

In such courts priests disciplined penitents, instructed converts, and satisfied the curiosity of pagans. Their removal, exposing the awkward triangular façade of the church, led to the erection of the flanking towers and of the Cloister.

If bread, when blessed by a mere layman, could be invested with such discerning powers of judgement, what unimaginable forces must enter into the Elements when they were administered by the priest! The altar therefore vanished into the depths of the chancel, doubtless to the great relief of the congregation.

With these alterations and adaptations the interior of the old secular basilica has been transformed, step by step, into a Christian church whose plan and arrangement of elements underlie the work of all church architects to our own day. Nave and aisles, choir, crossing, chancel, ambulatory, and transepts; crypt below and triforium above— not one of these is strange to us nor have they been less familiar to any generation of our fathers.

"Trust," said the Hebrew Sage, "is born of fear and the children of him who rightly fears shall have a place of refuge."

As the years passed, as the era of barbarism drifted into the background and faded from memory, the terror which the relics had once inspired gave place to confidence in their kindly efficiency. Then Fear, through Faith her offspring, began to pour out new gifts upon the church, thrusting out her walls, enlarging her aisles, and multiplying her chapels in order to provide altars for her relics and a place of refuge for her children.

Chapter Ten

GIFTS OF UNBELIEF

SOMETIMES the architecture of the church records the rise or fall of the tides of man's belief as well as the ebbs and flows of secular history, and there are stones in her aisles which declare that here died some ancient article of faith or there a new belief was born.

The new faiths of a barbarian world in the miracle-working powers of relics filled the roads with the sinners or the sick and compelled the church to extend her walls, to create new aisles, apses, and chapels, and to bind all these together by a Pilgrim Way which ran from shrine to shrine, through aisles, transepts, ambulatories, and so down into the crypt.

New unfaiths in the same age, new unbeliefs in things that once had been thought vital, moulded the exterior of the church as new faiths had moulded the interior, forcing changes in the architecture, with the atrium and the baptistry as the victims of this unbelief, while the cloister and the towers were its gifts.

When the eunuch of Ethiopia's Candace met Philip on his way to Gaza, was instructed in the faith, and received baptism from the apostle on the same afternoon, he entered into the privileges of the Church with a speed that would have amazed later generations. Had he encountered a bishop of the Third Century there would have been a very different answer to his question, "What doth hinder me to be baptized?" He would have been examined as to his theology and then sent to a priest to be enrolled in a class for catechumens and to receive instruction in the articles of the faith. According to some canons this instruction might have lasted for two, even for three years, and certainly would have taken many months.

72

Since the church was holy ground, to whose aisles and altars only those who had been baptized might be admitted, the authorities had to provide some place beyond the portals of the church where converts might be prepared for baptism. Therefore wherever possible atria, colonnaded courts similar to those which stood in front of pagan temples, were erected before the porch and portals of the church.

The atrium also permitted the church to have contact with a world which was intellectually curious, if religiously indifferent. This curiosity had led the Jews to open their synagogues to those who, while refusing circumcision, yet wished some knowledge of the Hebrew culture. With the same curiosity the pagans came also to the Church asking, in the words of the Athenians to S. Paul, "May we know what this new doctrine is, for thou bringest strange tidings to our ears?"

Although the church, unlike the synagogue, was consecrated and therefore closed to the pagan world, yet the atrium remained to afford a convenient meeting place where the gospel might be explained to the curious in the hope that some seed might fall on fertile soil.

Valuable as the atrium may have been to the early church, there were undermining forces that were older still and the atrium was eventually sacrificed in a struggle of Christian pity with parental cruelty and of orthodoxy against heresy.

The first call to that battle in which the atrium was to perish came from a source that was eloquent and imperious only because it was inarticulate and weak; it came from multitudes of unwanted babies, slain by their parents or left to die of exposure in the public squares. Of the two, exposure was the darker evil, for the stronger and more promising of these abandoned infants were rescued by speculators who brought them up and trained them to serve as slaves, prostitutes, or gladiators; thus the blood of Rome's patrician families often flowed in the veins of those who bore her burdens, satiated her lusts, or were slaughtered to make her holidays.

Though Roman laws and pagan moralists alike condemned infanticide, statutes and precepts were both evaded until the Church, at least as early as the Second Century, gave up her insistence upon adult baptism and extended the protection of her sacraments to the least among her little ones, abandoning the atrium rather than the infants who now became members of the "very body of Christ Himself." By this act the Church proclaimed that even the baby at the breast had entered into solemn covenant with that Almighty God who, ever mindful of His own, would exact an eternal penalty for wrongs inflicted upon the helpless who bore His name. But inevitably this admission of infants by baptism tended to destroy the significance of an atrium where adult catechumens had received instruction for years in order to prepare themselves for a sacrament which was now bestowed upon babes who could not tell their right hands from their left.

A second attack upon the atrium came from the heresy of Arius which, although condemned in 325 at the Council of Nicæa, proved as seductive to the speculative Oriental mind as it was repugnant to the more practical West. Had Arianism remained a problem in theology the issue involved might have been fought out at long range in the Councils of the Church, but the heresy entered the field of politics when Arian missionaries, like Ulfilas, carried the strange gospel to those barbarians who were soon to invade the West. When the Goths, Ostrogoths, Burgundians, Suevi, Vandals, and Visigoths poured over the Alps and flooded the valleys of the Po, the Rhône, and the Garonne, they brought Arianism, armed with the sword, to the very gates of Rome herself.

Although these invaders were usually tolerant, yet Arians in the East had often persecuted the followers of Athanasius, whose creed was the creed of Rome. The same exiles, proscriptions, and confiscations that had frequently terrorized the Byzantine world might, and actually did, break out in the West where Catholics suffered severely from Arian rulers both in North Africa and in Spain.

To the Bishop of Rome the outlook must, indeed, have seemed desperate, for not only in Constantinople but in Carthage, in Ravenna, Pavia, Vienne, throughout all France south of the Loire, and in Spain the followers of Ulfilas, the "Little Wolf" of Arianism, occupied the seats of the mighty. In all the Western world Clovis and his pagan Franks were the only people with whom papal Rome had to deal who were not Arians, and it was the influence of a woman rather than the eloquence of the priest which, turning the Franks to Rome, determined the creed of the West. Threatened by defeat on the field of Tolbiac, Clovis, first of the Merovingians, appealed to the God of his Christian wife, and after his victory was baptized into the orthodox faith with three thousand of his warriors. The mass baptism of Tolbiac was soon followed by another general baptism among the Suevi of Spain and, somewhat later, by that of ten thousand Anglo-Saxons. Boniface baptized his converts in Germany by the thousands in the early Eighth Century, while Charlemagne imposed the rite upon the Saxons as a penalty of defeat and an evidence of submission.

Obviously a Church which was baptizing converts *en masse* and receiving heretics on the mere recital of a creed, no longer needed an atrium where catechumens might be prepared for baptism. The environment of the church had changed since the days of Constantine and because of that change the colonnaded court before the church yielded to the cloister at its side which, offering the clergy a retreat from the invading world, met the need of an age to which the atrium no longer ministered.

The disorders that multiplied as the Dark Ages drew near, the uproar of civil strife, fratricidal struggles between Merovingian heirs, the inroads of Norse, Moslem, or Magyar invaders, all united to call into existence those quiet aisles, pools, and gardens where priests, forgetting the fretting world, might lift their thoughts to God.

So the atrium perished in parturition, giving birth to the cloister which, flanking the church instead of preceding it, was closed to the lay world and surrendered to the priest. The fountain of ablutions, which once stood in the centre of the atrium, shared its fate and vanished, only to reappear in diminished form as the Basin of Holy Water near the entrance of the church.

Thus the double assault led on the one hand by Rome's unwelcome infants and on the other by her still more unwelcome Arian invaders, undermining the belief that only those who were wise in the faith might receive the sacraments, destroyed the atrium and created the cloister.

But when the babes and the barbarians together banned the atrium they created a new difficulty, for the disappearance of the old colon-naded court, like the withdrawal of a veil, exposed the flat, triangular, and barn-like façade of the basilica to the gaze of the open street. The problem thus presented was never solved in Italy, where by preference the awkward lines of the triangular front were retained even in such Gothic cathedrals as those of Milan and Orvieto, and no attempt was made to compensate the church for the loss of the atrium. Although the detached bell tower, or campanile, served in some measure to dis-tract attention from the angular façade, yet a trip from end to end of Italy only serves to heighten the conviction that the Italian never realized the æsthetic problem that had been created by the disap-pearance of the atrium.

It was the Transalpine Teuton, instead of the Cisalpine Latin, who first saw the need and it is to him that we owe the towers which, flanking the façade, ultimately solved the problem.

Of course neither the problem nor its solution was immediately rec-ognized by the Carlovingian architects; appreciation came slowly and through much experimentation. As early as the Eighth Century the builders were placing towers on their churches, erecting them on either side of the apse, beside the North and South portals, and on the Western front. All these may still be found—for instance towers still flank the apse of Worms Cathedral in Germany, of S. Abbondio at Como, Italy; and of the abbey of Morienval in France. However, these towers like those that rise over the side portals are comparatively rare, while those which frame the Western front are almost universal. The fact that only these latter towers were so consistently retained clearly indicates that the builders had recognized both the problem and its solution, and had discovered the value of the towers as compensation for the loss of the atrium and as an architectural balance for the façade. By the Ninth Century these flanking towers had won such general favour that, for the next six hundred years at least, they were among the usual features of cathedral architecture.

Other, and more comforting, purposes followed hard upon the ap-pearance of these towers, for they were soon used to shelter the anointed bells whose notes, first ringing over the roofs of Eighth Century churches, foiled the malice of demons riding the black clouds to assail, with hails and lightning bolts, the farms and homes of men; they also drove hungry devils from the bedsides of the dying, rang the tocsins of alarms, and called the faithful to sacrament and prayer.

In the century of their birth, however, these towers gave slight promise of their high destiny, and nearly three hundred years were required to transform their low, flat-topped turrets into the great spires of Chartres and of Caen.

First, a low pyramidal cap of wood, later replaced in stone, was added to throw off the rains and snows which, falling on the exposed summits, often seeped down the walls and damaged the interiors of the churches. With the passing years this stone pyramid was first heightened and then turned into an octagon because the breadth of the sides was too great to be pleasing, and so a spire was born whose height was supposed to equal that of the tower from which it sprang. The introduction of the octagon, however, created a new difficulty for—as the most casual glance at the towers of Jumièges will show—the change from the square below to the octagon above was much too abrupt, and the loftier the spire the more displeasing the effect. Obviously some way had to be found to mask the transition between the two.

The builders of Normandy and of the Île-de-France attacked the problem by placing dormer windows on the sides of the spire and turrets at the corners where it rested upon the tower, thus continuing the essential lines of the square above the point where the octagon began. Later still these turrets were made narrower and higher, while all the perpendicular lines of the tower were emphasized by means of shafts which climbed the corners, and by supplying all openings in tower and spire alike with sharply pointed gables.

In such ways, and by such means, the eye was gently led up these perpendicular shafts, pointed gables, and narrow turrets, from foundation stone to weather-vane, and the awkward line where the transition was effected was so concealed that one may stand long before such a tower as that at Caen without even noticing that an octagon rests upon a square foundation.

Thus the story of the tower is not unlike *The Tale of the House that Jack Built,* for shafts, gables, and turrets were added to conceal the birth of an octagon spire; the spire was made octagonal because a high stone pyramid displeased the eye; this stone pyramid, because it was durable, replaced an earlier conical cap of wood; this wooden cap had been added to prevent rain or snow from falling on the exposed summits of the towers; the towers themselves sprang from the need of compensating architecturally for the loss of the atrium; the atrium vanished because barbarians were being admitted to the Church without preliminary instruction; and the baptism of the barbarians, often *en masse,* destroyed the belief on which the atrium rested, that only the wise might receive the sacraments.

The same pressure of multitudes demanding baptism which had banished the atrium also undermined the baptistry and once more the change was due to the abandonment of an old belief—the belief that only a bishop should baptize.

Although the Church recognized the validity of baptism by laymen, even by heretics if only the correct formula was precisely used, yet orderly procedure demanded that only a bishop should perform the rite except in cases of exceptional urgency.

Throughout the early centuries, when this belief in the exclusive episcopal authority was strong, every great city had its Baptistry, a vital centre of ecclesiastical life and the scene of solemn ceremonies, whither converts throughout the diocese were gathered at stated seasons to receive the touch of episcopal hands and be enrolled in the membership of the Church. But in the Carlovingian centuries, when Rome rose from her grave to conquer the world anew, not by her legions but by her missionaries, churches were so multiplied on both sides of the Alps that the applicants for baptism increased beyond the abilities of even the busiest episcopal fingers. Therefore the bishops were forced to share their baptismal functions with the parish priests and thus each church came to possess its own baptismal font while the baptistry became either an anachronism or a memory.

So far the Roman of earlier days—Marcus Porcius Cato of the Second Century, or Julius Cæsar of the First before Christ; Trajan of

THE EVOLUTION OF THE SPIRE

1. A simple pyramidal cap on the unfinished towers of Notre-Dame de la Couture at Le Mans. 2. The Problem: The octagonal spire of Montricourt on a square base. 3. The Solution: The spire of S. Pierre at Caen, where the transition is masked. 4. The spire of Caudebec, "quills upon a fretful porcupine."

the Second Century A.D., or Constantine of the Fourth—had he been permitted to rise from the Shades and survey with us the Carlovingian church would have been able to recognize, despite all changes, the off-spring of his own basilicas.

The ambulatory and the towers might seem strange to him and though he would probably fail to recognize the baptistry in the font or the fountain of ablutions in the Basin of Holy Water, he would surely discover the atrium in the cloister, and certainly nave, aisles, apse and galleries would all be familiar. But let him now speedily return to his rest for those are drawing near who never knew a Cæsar.

All along the coasts of Scandinavia and on the warmer littorals of Africa, Northmen and Saracens alike are stepping their masts, mending their sails, splicing their ropes, and trimming their oars.

Off to the East the Magyars have whetted their swords, sharpened their spears, new-shod their shaggy steeds, and turned their faces towards the West. New barbarian floods are rising; strange camp-fires shall presently throw their red reflections over Alpine snows and on the reeds and rippling flows of quiet inland water-ways; dark faces shall be seen, and fearsome ululations heard from end to end of France, for the shadows of the Dark Ages are falling upon Europe, and in these shadows the church shall be so reborn and so rebuilt that no togaed ghost of ancient Latium could again recognize, in its sombre dignity, the basilica of his own, or of his father's, day.

Chapter Eleven

THE BACKGROUND OF ROMANESQUE ARCHITECTURE
THE TREASURE TO BE GUARDED

NOT many years ago I was permitted to step out of the Twentieth Century, to enter the Eleventh Century and spend a day with its pilgrims.

We were at Assisi; all through the night, almost until cockcrow, we had listened to the sound of feet—young feet, old feet, but always tired feet—climbing the hill towards the Church of S. Francis. From the valley below, the hot night wind brought the sound of a pilgrim chorus which grew louder as the singers came nearer, then died away to break out again in a crescendo of sound beneath our windows.

The first of August is a great day in this hill-town of Umbria, for on this day—if you come to Assisi—you may release the souls of your dead from Purgatory; therefore peasants from far and near crowd the converging roads that lead to the stable where S. Francis was born and to the church where his body lies. Many of these pilgrims had come from the far Abruzzi mountains. Taking no baggage, they had left their homes just as they were, ten days, two weeks, some of them three weeks before; they had slept where night had overtaken them, and lived on the bread and water, with sometimes a little cheese, given by the charitable.

When day dawned in Assisi the pilgrims were lying all along the streets; young and old, many very old, with arms thrown out, palms up, fingers slightly curved, they were sleeping the sleep of complete exhaustion. All traffic had been halted in the city lest these sleepers be injured by the wheels of cars or carts, and the way became increasingly difficult, even for pedestrians, as we drew nearer to the church.

Inside, the crypt was literally almost paved with sleeping pilgrims and the air was close and fetid. As we slowly picked our way one of the sleepers suddenly awoke, sprang to his feet and raised a chant. Other sleepers, also waking, fell in behind him, joining in the hymn, until several hundred were passing in procession around the church, from shrine to shrine, bending, kneeling, or prostrating themselves to kiss the bars, the stones, or the steps of the holy places until they had completed the circuit of the church. Then the song died on their lips, they dropped again to the ground and in a few seconds were once more sound asleep. Hardly had one procession ended, however, than another was being formed; again we heard the song and watched another swaying line of pilgrims as it moved from altar to altar, kneeling to kiss the stones all around the church.

This was the faith, the hunger of soul, the fanatical exultation, these were the miracle-working images, of centuries earlier even than S. Francis' day. As I stood and watched, the light of the Twentieth Century dimmed and died; the sun of well-nigh a thousand years ago was bathing the Umbrian hills and throwing blue-black shadows in the streets. Assisi had become any pilgrimage town and shrine of the Eleventh Century. The Almoravides are overrunning Spain but Norman ships are driving Saracen fleets before their prows from the Western Mediterranean; Hildebrand, the monk of Cluny, is Pope in Rome; Henry of Germany, deposed and excommunicated, stands barefoot in the snows of Canossa; the stars, with the Norman lions, keep watch over the dead on the field of Hastings; Peter the Hermit is at Clermont, and the West is all astir for—with Godfrey of Bouillon, Robert of Normandy, Stephen of Blois, Raymond of Toulouse, Bohemond, Tancred, and a thousand more whose very names are battle-cries—we have shouted our *"Deus vult"* and are going to deliver the Holy Sepulchre from paynim hands.

All over Europe men were pilgrimage-bent in the Eleventh Century. The proclamation of a Jubilee where one might see, even from afar, the robe that Jesus had worn to the cross brought forty thousand pilgrims to the shrine of Aachen. The very stars of heaven seemed concerned for the guidance of these unlettered ones—even more concerned for them than for the Wise Men who once crossed desert sands seeking a King of the Jews in Bethlehem—for instead of the single star that led the Magi all the galaxy of the Milky Way was divinely marshalled into the *Chemin de S. Jacques* to guide sinners on their way to the holy tomb of S. James at Santiago. Indeed, the heavens seemed less filled with stars than were the roads with pilgrims who, driven by troubled consciences, illnesses of the body or disorders of the mind, sought the deliverances which were assured to all who should kiss, touch, or even see the holy relics.

The Church has been *enceinte* with this worship of relics from early days when it began with a pure reverence for those holy men whose stalwart faith had conquered Rome. But the triumphant Monasticism of the Eleventh Century gave birth, in the gloom of cloistered cells, to a new and frightful conception of an ever present Devil, bestial in form and mighty in wickedness. His demoniacal agents were without the man, terrifying him with mysterious sights and sounds; they were also an indwelling force, driving him to perform their service. The slightest act surrendered the reluctant soul to resistless powers of Evil.[1]

The great aqueduct, which all men knew the Devil had built at Segovia in a single night, was a proof of his power and reality; his footsteps might be seen in many places, impressed in the hard rock; gorges, called by his name, proclaimed the might of that Ruler of Hell who had riven them among the mountains. Gargoyles, leering from the eves of churches, were constant reminders of those sleepless legions which were in earth and air and water, seeking entrance into the bodies of men; from such as these there was no safety except within the protection of Holy Church.

To the mediæval mind Hell was as near as were the fires of Vesuvius, and Heaven was as real as the gleaming snows of Mt. Blanc. The visions of Dante were factual experiences; S. Dunstan was merely one of many who had seen the Devil face to face. The fear of demoniacal possession was a fixed idea of the Middle Ages when the vivid imagination of an Age of Faith, the lack of any scientific background, the nightmares of monkish cells, objectified in the carvings on the churches

[1] H. H. Milman, *Latin Christianity*, Book V, Chap. VII.

and in the legends of the times, all combined to centre the minds of men upon their unending struggle with the Powers of Darkness.

The shadows which such fears cast over the mediæval mind must be clearly understood before we can realize the relief which the mightier powers attributed to the most holy relics brought to the hearts of men. By the possession of these relics the Church was able to offer all believers a counter-working miraculous force which could break the power of Satan, absolve from sin, and heal the sick. Kings and peasants alike bowed in awe before these relics, and for their sake men everywhere, of all ranks and ages, took up the pilgrim's staff and scallop shell, gladly undertaking toilsome pilgrimages that promised deliverance from this mystery of Evil, this overpowering Satanic Will.

Perhaps, therefore, it is not strange that even crime might not be counted too high a price to pay for such possessions. The Spear which pierced the side of Christ on Calvary was earned by Innocent VIII as part payment from the Sultan Bayazid for making a virtual prisoner of Prince Djem, whose claim to the Sultanate Bayazid feared.

The Seamless Robe and three hundred thousand ducats were promised Innocent's successor, Alexander VI of the House of Borgia, if he would secure the assassination of the Prince. Although Charles VIII of France seized the prisoner from the Pope for his own ends, Djem did die shortly thereafter in the French camp between Naples and Rome, perhaps from fatigue and hardships but perhaps rather from a slow poison administered to make the Borgian reward secure.[2]

The body of S. Benedict was stolen from Italy; theft brought the bones of S. Foy to Conques; the monks of Vézelay falsely swore that they had robbed the Church of S. Maximim of the body of S. Madeleine, willing to commit perjury if only they could persuade good Christians that they really had committed theft. Tours and Poitiers quarrelled over the body of S. Martin. There were constant feuds between the monasteries, and monks stood ready to defend their relics by force of arms against prowling bands of other monks who came against each charnel treasure-house, armed with carnal weapons and most holy purposes. Sometimes, however, the clergy realized that

[2] J. A. Symonds, *Age of the Despots,* p. 415.

dangers to the soul lurked within the relics. When miracles occurred at the tomb of a recently deceased prior of Grandmont the troubled monks sent his successor to remonstrate with the bones of the new saint—"Would'st thou convert our holy solitude into a market-place and a fair?" We may hope that he who was in heaven was as pure-minded as they who were on earth, that he abated his miracles, and left the Brethren to their desired peace.

The church among the barbarians had already been remodelled to accommodate the increasing number of holy relics which prompted priests to perjury, monks to battle, and pilgrims to face the perils of dangerous roads, and while Charlemagne lived these priceless treasures were safe, even beneath timbered roofs and within wooden walls. But when the Dark Ages came, when the flames of war swept down from the fjords of Scandinavia, up from the coasts of Africa, and out from the plains of Hungary, when dangers far more threatening than the greed of predatory priests and thieving monks began to menace these most prized possessions, the churches had to be rebuilt from their foundations that vaults of stone upon stone walls might encase and protect those endangered relics which, charged with the immeasurable power of the Most High God, had been given unto men for the healing of their bodies, the forgiveness of their sins, the foiling of Satanic malice, and the salvation of their souls.

Chapter Twelve

THE BACKGROUND OF ROMANESQUE ARCHITECTURE
THE MENACE TO THE TREASURE

IN THE year 827, Euphemius, an officer in the Byzantine army stationed in Sicily, violated the walls of a Sicilian convent and carried away a nun. The offence was so flagrant that not only the island but distant Constantinople itself was stirred, and an Imperial courier was instantly dispatched to Syracuse carrying orders that Euphemius should be arrested and mutilated, both as a punishment and as a warning.

The offender, however, made his escape to the only corner of the world still open to one who had committed so great a sacrilege—to the Moslems of North Africa, where he presently persuaded the Aglabite monarch, Ziadet-Allah, to win Sicily for Islam and to add it to his own domains.

In the Holy War that followed, the Christian army was so defeated that only a pestilence, which smote the camp of the invaders before Syracuse, prevented the complete realization of the dreams of Ziadet-Allah and Euphemius. This easy victory, which led to the occupation of the greater part of the island and to rich booty in treasures and slaves, opened the eyes of the Moslems to the defenceless wealth lying at their doors, and the attack on Sicily proved only the prelude to a long series of plundering raids which for many years harried the shores, and even the inland water-ways, of Italy and France.

About the same time fishermen on the coasts of Holland abandoned their nets and fled in terror before a strange fleet of long, low boats driven by oars and carrying fair-haired, blue-eyed men who were clad in armour and wielded formidable swords or ponderous battle-axes with amazing ease. The invaders ravaged the coastal settlements, sacked the cities and retreated with their spoils before resistance could be organized.

The vision which this raid afforded of cities defenceless against swift, unheralded attacks, led these Vikings of the North, as a similar assault had led the Saracens of the South, to a century of bold and profitable ventures against the shores of Germany, Holland, France, and England. "They came," says an eye-witness, Simeon of Durham, "like stinging wasps; they roamed the country like savage wolves, robbing, biting, and killing not merely cattle but priests, monks, and nuns."

Before the end of the century other barbarians, the Magyars, appeared from the East. Mounted on light, swift, and strong horses, trained from infancy to the saddle, so skilled with bow and javelin that they could discharge their shafts with unerring accuracy even when riding at full speed, they filled the land with the terror of their name.

These successive blows fell upon a world which had only begun to recover from the barbarism that, nearly four hundred years before, had overthrown the Western Roman Empire with a fury that seemed to entail the permanent eclipse of civilization throughout the West. To the Church the inroads of the Northmen, the Magyars, and the Moslems were, for several reasons, more dangerous than those of the Goths, Burgundians, and Vandals who flooded Europe in the Fifth and Sixth Centuries.

In the first place, in neither of those centuries had the Church yet entered into extensive possession of the land beyond the Alps; her clerics were missionaries, and her churches were comparatively few and small; in the Ninth Century, on the other hand, Roman Christianity was everywhere established and its churches or monasteries—the first, richest and easiest prey of any invader—covered the land.

In the second place, many of the earlier invading tribes—the Goths in their several branches, the Burgundians, and the Vandals—were already converts to Christianity, although of the Arian type, and their ferocity was thereby in some measure mitigated. The Lombards were pagans when they entered Italy, but thirty years later they also surrendered to the influences of Latin Christianity, while the Franks accepted the Faith when Clovis was baptized in 496.

DURHAM CATHEDRAL, REFLECTED IN THE RIVER WEAR
The square flanking towers of the western façade.

The Northmen, on the other hand, were not won to Christ until the year 950, while their dragon ships first entered English waters in 787, and sailed up the Seine in 841. The Magyars, whose fury devastated both Germany and Italy and did not spare France, were not converted until 974, and the Saracens who "slew the people of God with a continual slaughter" carried the sword as the Christian missionary carried the Cross.

These invasions, whose flames and confusions imperilled the relics, gave birth to the Romanesque church, and the "fury of the Northmen," celebrated in old Liturgies, with that of the Moslem and the Magyar, form the lurid background of a new architecture. The churches that perished in these wars might be rebuilt only if their relics had been saved; if these had perished new relics must be secured before new churches might be built. Therefore some realization of the anarchy which now fell on all Western lands is essential to an understanding of the architecture of the Eleventh Century.

The weak hand of Louis the Pious could not hold the sceptre of Charles the Great, and the Treaty of Verdun in 843 wrecked the Empire that Charlemagne had fought and laboured to establish. A turbulent feudalism still further divided the fragments of the Empire; the might of the strong became the law of the land and filled all Europe with confusion, even before the cross-currents of barbarian invasions completed the chaos of all lands.

In Italy a multitude of petty princes were continually at war, each striving to establish an hereditary principality; city fought with city, and every noble aspired to sovereign rank. Two courtesans, ruling Rome, made or unmade popes. Magyars, speaking no tongue that men could understand, filled Lombardy with slaughter. Franks fought Greeks in Apulia; Saracens conquered Sicily and overran all Southern Italy up to the walls of Rome itself, where they sacked the churches of S. Peter and of S. Paul. From their fortress on the Garigliano they held all the papal territory at their mercy, plundering the land and seizing pilgrims.

Similar conditions obtained in Spain where Navarre fought with Castile, Castile with León, León with Galicia, and all the Christian North with Moslem Andalusia. Abd-er-Rahman retook Toledo, the ancient capital of the Visigoths; Almansor drove the Christians into the mountains of Asturias, capturing even far-off Coruna and defiling Santiago, the sacred city of S. James. Turning eastward, he drove the Christians out of Catalonia to the rough protection of the Pyrenees and captured Barcelona.

Yet there are basilicas still standing in Italy whose walls saw the sunlight of the Fifth Century, and churches may be visited today in Spain which were upreared by Visigothic kings in the Seventh Century, or whose walls were raised while the Carlovingians, or even the Merovingians, were on the throne in France. England is also rich in proto-Romanesque churches, but the fact that, with barely an exception, all the ecclesiastical structures of France that pre-date the middle of the Eleventh Century have been swept away indicates that that country fared far worse than its neighbours of England, Italy, or Spain. The little Baptistry of S. Jean at Poitiers; a tiny chapel at Querqueville near Cherbourg, and a few scattered crypts are practically the only survivors of these troubled centuries and they but emphasize the character of the storms that must have swept the soil of France.

The last Carlovingians died out, like the Merovingians, sluggish and divided. Hugh Capet, hardly even *primus inter pares,* came to the throne in Paris. The land was filled with private war; Fulc Nerra ruled turbulently in Anjou; France was divided into a hundred, perhaps a hundred and fifty, sovereign states, whose rivalries kept the land in desolation.

But the great enemy of order in France, from the end of the Eighth Century onward, was the Northman whose hand fell heavily on abbey, church, and convent; all "France was covered with bishops and monks flying from their ruined cloisters, their burning monasteries, their desolated churches, bearing with them the precious relics of their saints —saints who could not defend their violated sanctuaries—and so deepened the universal panic." [1]

Long before the days of the Northmen, however, the hosts of Islam poured from Spain over the Pyrenees and harried Southern France.

[1] H. H. Milman, *Latin Christianity.*

In 718 they took Narbonne; in 722 they attacked Toulouse; they entered Provence in 725, marched north and sacked the city of Autun. Six years later the great Abd-er-Rahman sacked Bordeaux, ravaged all Aquitaine, and aspired to the spoils of the city of Tours; only Charles the Hammer's hard won victory between Tours and Poitiers saved France from the grip of Cordova.

While Charles the Great lived Moslem Spain was held in check, but the Saracenic hawks of the sea continued to ravage the southern shores, and when Louis the Pious died their raiding bands penetrated the distracted country, again and again reaching the very heart of France. Nothing can more dramatically illustrate the confusion of the times than the battles that took place, not between the inhabitants defending their homes against invaders, but between Moslems raiding northward from the Mediterranean coasts and Northmen marching southward from Picardy; and also between Saracens and Magyars in the Valley of the Vaud.

The nature of the churches, the shrines and depositories of the holy relics, made these invasions trebly dangerous. Although in the Rhine Valley and in Italy—in the wealthier and more cultured parts of the Carlovingian empire—basilicas with stone walls and timbered roofs were far from rare, yet many important churches were built of wood, or at least wood entered largely into their construction. Many were unpaved, or were paved only in the chancel, while the parish churches were apt to be flimsy edifices with beaten clay floors. All were dark and damp, and all were liable to fire.[2]

Faced by such conditions the builders set themselves to the imperative task of replacing their inflammable wooden vaults with vaults of stone for the protection of those relics which were the very charters of the Church. Although few of the churches that were built north of the Pyrenees in these years have survived, yet something remains in both France and Italy, and much more in Spain, to show the humble beginnings of a new architecture as, from the Seventh Century onward, the builders learned, in small churches and over narrow naves, those

[2] Thompson, Vol. I, p. 871.

lessons which were to equip a later generation for the great achievements of the Eleventh Century.

"Surely the wrath of man shall praise Thee," sang the Psalmist; the praises of the Lord still echo, and the songs of Zion ring from the stone vaults of churches, while the "fury of the Northman," the war-cry of the Moslem, and the shrill ululations of the Magyar have long since died away. None the less, it was the wrath of man which compelled both priests and monks to build for the protection of the holy treasures committed to their care, and to proclaim the glory of God in the great monuments of the Romanesque Age.

Chapter Thirteen

THE GREAT GIFT OF AN IMPATIENT HORSE

THE visitor to France who, having stopped to see the little Tenth Century church at Querqueville in the suburbs of Cherbourg, halts his flight to Paris for a visit to the ruined abbey of Jumièges, near Rouen, cannot fail to realize that a change had come over Europe in the years that lay between the building of these two churches. Querqueville evidences the work of a people possessed of small resources, building with material close at hand, and with a labour that was not highly skilled.

Jumièges, on the other hand, testifies to a society possessing wealth to a degree not known since the days of Rome. But the traveller, while he may learn the lessons in history which the contrasts between these churches teach, will probably not appreciate the measure of the debt which tradition says he owes to a huntsman and his horse who died a thousand years ago.

According to the legend, the wealth that made Jumièges possible, and many a church besides, was the gift to Europe of a restive horse whose rider was hunting in the train of Otto the Great about the year 950. Brought to a halt while the dogs were trying to pick up a lost trail, the impatient horse, restlessly pawing the ground, brought to light the first vein of silver in the great Rammelsberg mines of the Harz mountains.

If we may believe the tale, then this chance stroking of the earth by an iron-shod hoof lifted Europe out of a semi-barbarism wherein trade was by means of barter, into a moneyed civilization where commerce could move freely and in increasing volume.

Until the opening of these mines there was little precious metal in Europe for the coining of money. Such gold as the West possessed had been steadily drained away to the East to pay for importations, and even after the rise and expansion of Islam had checked this traffic the drainage of gold continued, if not to the Levant, then to the decorations of the churches, the making of sacred vessels for the altars, or else to secret hiding places where men, because of the anarchy of the times, hoarded such gold as came into their possession. There was little mining for precious metals in the Merovingian and Carlovingian periods, and so little currency in circulation that none is listed in a minute inventory of one of Charlemagne's estates. This scarcity explains the constant raiding of the feudatories upon their neighbours, for booty in the form of plate could be melted into coin. With the opening of the Rammelsberg mines, however, silver became plentiful for the first time since the more prosperous days of Rome, and mints were established for the coining of money; thereafter goods could be sold for cash, and the seller could carry his profits in his purse instead of in bundles on his back, or in bales upon his mule.

The discovery of silver in her mountains lifted Germany into the forefront of Western nations; her population doubled, and her towns increased, in the century and a half that followed the hunting of Otto the Great, at the rate of nearly one each year. Because of the discovery of silver, governments could fortify their frontiers, consolidate their power, and centralize their administrations; commerce could also expand, since for the first time in five hundred years accumulations of capital could enlarge the fields of investment. The same discovery transformed the architecture of the churches and explains the difference between Querqueville and Jumièges, for the seeker for divine favour, as all men then were, was no longer limited in the shrines that he might visit, or the saints to whom he could appeal. Instead of driving one of his flock to a near-by sanctuary he could sell the animal in a local market, put the price in his purse, and become a pilgrim to the shrines of Bari, Lucca, Rome, or Santiago.

Until the dawn of this century pilgrims had journeyed alone or in small groups, but now they began to fill the roads and to enrich with their gifts the great shrines of Europe, while many undertook the voyage to far Jerusalem.

Inevitably church architecture felt the stimulus. Heretofore the churches had been, for the most part, small, built largely if not entirely of wood, unpaved except around the chancel, and glazed with linen sheets. But in the Eleventh Century great Romanesque churches began to rise from the ground in such numbers that a Burgundian monk thought "God had snowed churches upon the land."

The horse of Rammelsberg was fortunate in that he was born in the fulness of time; had he lived much earlier he might have pawed the earth in vain, for such churches as Jumièges demanded more than the discovery of silver for the coinage of money, or the growth of commerce for the increase of wealth.

The most pressing demand throughout the Ninth and Tenth Centuries was the repulse of the Magyars, Saracens, and Northmen—who were everywhere penetrating the Carlovingian empire, burning, killing and plundering. No law, no order, no security for merchants or for markets could anywhere obtain until these new barbarians had been driven back to the coasts from whence they came, and the land set free from their annual devastations. The accomplishment of this task was largely achieved through the institution of feudalism—that system of land tenure which bound every freeman to give military service to his overlord in return for protection and for the land he tilled; this lord, in turn, was similarly bound to some greater lord, to whom he owed service with all his tenants and retainers; so the chain reached up through all grades of society until it reached the throne, from which all rights were theoretically derived, and to which all duties were ultimately due.

Before the establishment of feudalism there were no local centres of resistance to invasion; responsibility for the defence of the realm rested solely upon the King who alone could legally erect castles or fortifications to bar the roads and rivers along which an enemy might advance. The invaders, therefore, were able to strike, pillage, and retreat before the royal levies could be mobilized and marched to the field. But in 862 Charles the Bald, confessing his inability to give protection in the face of the appalling anarchy, urged the nobles to erect castles for the defence of the country-side. This, however, with or without license, the nobles were already doing, but since they used their fortresses not only for the repulse of the invaders but also as secure retreats from which they might issue to plunder the farms and rob the roads, Charles presently withdrew his permission for the building of the castles. His cancellation of the permit, however, proved as futile as the earlier license had been needless, and the castles continued to increase, not merely along the coasts where the Northmen or the Saracens were harrying the seaport towns, but in the very heart of the land where every steep hill, every sharp cliff and bend of a river, or the meeting place of streams was fortified.

Nevertheless these robber barons, brutal and predatory though they may have been, were a necessary evil for they provided a local armed force, and a fortress from which resistance might be quickly organized. With feudal strongholds—resembling more the wooden block-houses of our frontier days than the towered castles of romance—occupying every strategic spot, and with fortified bridges thrown across all rivers up which the invaders might sail for the ravaging of the land, the Northmen were checked and the Empire freed from their long continued depredations. This is more true of France than of Germany which was better ordered and defended in this century.

The repulse of Northmen, Magyars, and Saracens was the immediate concern of the men who lived in the Dark Ages, and the discovery of silver was a primal precondition of a moneyed civilization with its greater freedom. But with equal urgency such churches as Jumièges demanded civilized minds in men, fields and farms instead of swamps and wildernesses, and secure roads for merchants and their goods. All these things, however, had vanished from the Western world with the fall of Rome, and the arts of civilization had become impossible in the new barbarian world where "men lived as beasts of prey."

"Squatted amid forests and marshes, they dwelt in family groups barricaded in their villages which were surrounded by ditches and palisades, guarded by fierce dogs, and concealed by a curtain of trees in the thick woods.

"Their existence had developed in them instincts of covetousness, grossness and brutality; a contempt for the weak and the van-

THE CHURCH OF S. BEÂT

This half barrel vault counters the outward thrust of the nave's barrel vault. In the greater churches such half barrels span the triforium gallery.

quished, and a lust for blood and the infliction of suffering. Hatreds which nothing could expiate divided them from one another. They were superstitious, ignorant, quarrelsome, and violent, like wild beasts." [1]

"All [the] guarantees with which the expiring civilization of the ancient world had surrounded the life and possessions of the individual disappeared in the anarchy let loose by the barbarians."

"Industrial economy . . . received its death blow, . . . [and] in the midst of universal disorganization trade was reduced to a simple traffic in food stuffs, or in manufactures of prime necessity, and its range of circulation was very narrow. The great home and foreign commerce, which had developed so brilliantly under the Empire, was no longer possible. . . . Trade by barter . . . reappeared, . . . money became rare, and credit disappeared. The fine Roman roads . . . deteriorated, bridges fell down, . . . everywhere insecurity reigned; . . . armed bands prowled around the country, and journeys became perilous expeditions. . . . The ports declined, the seas were infested with pirates, and maritime trade became as uncertain as land commerce." [2]

The first task was the re-creation of civilization, the re-education of men in mind, in morals, and in manners, and the only institution equipped with the materials and the motives for this gigantic undertaking was the Christian Church, heir to the Roman tradition of authority, and the embodiment of the ancient civilization as transformed by Christianity.

For the accomplishment of this purpose Rome sent out a steady stream of missionary priests who crossed the Alps, entered into the villages of these "wild beasts" where, with their lives in their hands, they organized those churches which presented to the barbarians "the only model of an ordered and stable government wherein authority was combined with liberty."

The foundations of a new civilization were thus laid, but more, much more, was needed, for the country was as savage as the people.

The motorist of today, speeding over perfect roads and through

[1] Boissonade, P., *Life and Work in Medieval Europe.*
[2] Thompson, Vol. I.

richly cultivated fields, would not recognize the land as it was a thousand years ago. Then forests, from which bands of wolves issued to attack the villages, covered Ireland, Wales, Scotland, and large parts of England; other forests, inhabited by other wolves, stretched away from the plains of Flanders to join those of the Ardennes and the Eifel. Only small clearings might be found in the Vosges, the Haardt, and in Central Germany, while the great Hercynian forest, rolling away beyond the borders of Bohemia, had hardly been touched. Two-thirds of France was forest-covered as late as the dawn of the Ninth Century, and from the Alps to the Pyrenees only occasional cultivated fields broke the tossing green of forest trees.

In addition to the woods and jungles that covered so large a part of Europe there were fens, swamps, and marshes in Eastern England, in Flanders and the Netherlands, along the coasts of Western and Southern France, and in the majority of the river valleys of all the continent.

The Church accepted the task of reclaiming the land, just as it had accepted that of reclaiming the people, and her monks, armed with axe and spade, went into the swamps and forests.

Gathered into powerful organizations, adopting the rule of labour, they set themselves to the work of clearing out the forests without wastage of trees, to the uprooting of stumps, the draining of swamps, the development of meadows, orchards, vineyards, and the cultivation of the soil. Columban worked his monks to the point of exhaustion: "Let them toil until they fall asleep upon their feet." The plough that the monk Theophilus had driven for twenty-two years was long preserved as a holy relic and as an inspiration to the Brethren, while the Benedictines wore the emblem of the pruning hook as they wore the Cross. Thus for three hundred years the monks were the methodical and persevering promoters of the first agricultural colonization of the West, and the value of their work cannot be measured alone by the productivity of their fields. They rescued the culture of the land from the scorn of a fierce, turbulent, and violent aristocracy who lived a life of pure materialism, spending their days in fighting, hunting, and in the eating of Brobdignagian meals. Despise as he might the horny hands of the serf who tilled his fields, the barbarian must reverence the guardian of the holy relics upon which he depended for divine favours today and for salvation hereafter, even though the saintly hands were as calloused as those of his own serf, and for the same reason.

To the monasteries came not only pilgrims but also merchants and traders, seeking shelter for the night, and towns sprang up around their gates.

But markets could neither draw freely from the outside world nor trade with other markets, until the roads were made safe for the journeys of merchants and for the transportation of their goods. Some steps towards greater security in travel had been taken both in Lombardy and in Gaul even as early as the Sixth Century, but these efforts, intermittent and spasmodic, ended with the invasions of the Ninth and Tenth Centuries.

The expulsion of the invaders, the deliverance of the land from their slaughters and ravages, did not wholly or finally free commerce from its bonds, for the people of France found enemies in their own household, and familiar friends who ate their bread, in whom they trusted, lifted up their heels against them. "The Vikings," they said, "came, plundered, and departed; but the barons, like the poor, are with us always." With bands of brigands in the woods and predatory nobles on the heights, all roads ran through a No-Man's Land where every step was perilous, and where neither life, purse, nor property was safe.

Once again it was the Church which led the way towards greater security in travel. She gave armed escorts to the caravans of traders and stirred up princes to guarantee their safety; later she imposed the "Truce," and then the "Peace of God," whereby all men were bound to abstain from warfare during certain seasons of the year and on appointed days of the week; she placed merchants under the safeguards of religion and threatened excommunication to any who should trouble them; she organized armed associations, "Fraternities of Peace," for the protection of traders and travellers. The Church also formed the first fraternities for the repair of roads and the building of bridges; she opened and maintained hospices among the mountains and inns along the roads, and organized the first long distance transport service by land or by river.

Little by little the Church taught the lords that more profit could be made by taxation than by confiscation, by taking a part than by taking all, and with this lesson learned efforts were made to speed the merchant on his way; brigandage was suppressed, means of communication improved, bridges opened, fairs established and markets granted special privileges.

Tariffs and taxes long remained, however, a heavy drag on trade, for the merchant had to pay tolls when he crossed the boundary that divided one fief from another; he paid for crossing a bridge; for the use of a ford, for embarking or disembarking his goods at river ports; he paid the *peage*—a tax for the right to carry his wares on his own back—and the *charriage* if he possessed a mule or a cart. In addition to these taxes on transportation there were multiple other imposts upon his person and his goods.

Such burdens were bad enough, but the merchant often found himself subjected to rules of the road which added to his costs; expensive detours were sometimes forced upon him; he might be compelled to take one road rather than another in order to extract an extra toll, or to cross a bridge for which he would pay a higher price than for the use of a more convenient ford. Anything that fell to the ground from his pack or cart became the property of the lord through whose territories he happened to be passing.

However the cities and the sovereigns struggled to bring order out of the confusion; merchants formed associations with political influence and armed forces to protect their members against arbitrary impositions; tolls, standardized and regulated, were more easily borne and the volume of commerce steadily increased.

Finally the Church gave to the merchant and his goods the secure protection of her holy ground. To this day the flower girls beneath the walls of the Madeleine in Paris, the general market before the Church of Brive, the tables of weights and measures on the walls of Friburg Cathedral, and the market crosses in the cathedral towns of Chichester, Hereford, and Winchester bear witness to a time when the sanctity of the Church was the security of the trader. Beneath her ægis the merchant set up his booth in the churchyard, displayed his goods on the flat gravestones, bargained with his customers in the porch, or sold from his tables in her aisles. The farmer's grain might be stored in the galleries and wine in the cellars, while his corn was sometimes ground or his beer brewed within the sacred walls.

Thus if the Church so profited by the new era that great Romanesque churches began to cover the land, and Querqueville gave place to Jumièges, she also helped in divers ways to make that era possible. She had transformed "wild beasts" into men; she had conquered the wilderness, built roads over mountains and plains, planted hospices amid the snows of Alpine passes, and inns beside the travelled roads; she had made travel and transportation safe; finally, she gave the merchant the privilege of selling his wares upon her holy ground where none would dare to hinder him.

Chapter Fourteen

ROMANESQUE ARCHITECTURE

THE floods of the Dark Ages, finally ebbing, deposited on the shores of the Eleventh Century not only newly discovered supplies of silver for the building of great churches, but also a new type of architecture, differing in form and appearance from all that had gone before, whereby the holy relics might be encased and protected from the hazards of fire by walls and vaults of stone.

The light and well-illumined basilica of Roman days, with its many windows, its painted wooden roof, and its walls incrusted with brilliant mosaics of many hues, is gone; gone also is the Carlovingian church with its walls of rubble, its timbered roof, and its aisles—dim in the diminished light that entered through narrow windows.

In their stead has come the Romanesque church—grim and stern, sombre with an unending twilight where the shadows hang heavy in the aisles. There rarely are windows in the clerestory now; the wooden roof has given way to a rounded vault of stone which rests heavily upon solid walls—walls whose depths must be measured in feet instead of in inches. Such windows as remain are deep, small, and splayed. Piers are more massive, aisles narrower and darker, and in the darkness monstrous beasts, and sinister devils with flaming hair, creep from monkish nightmares to take visible form as the sculptor and the architect unite their arts to create a church that shall reflect the spirit of a monastic age.

The changes wrought by Romanesque architects so altered both the outward and inward aspects of the church that one can with difficulty recognize any line of descent from S. Clemente in Rome, or S. Apollonare in Ravenna to Notre-Dame du Port in Clermont Ferrand, or to Notre-Dame le Grand in Poitiers. These changes were, however, inevitable, since they sprang from the problems which the builders of successive centuries were compelled to face.

The architects of Constantine's day were called upon to devise a church that was adequate to hold a large congregation and to secure for the worshippers an uninterrupted view of both priest and altar; the builders of Carlovingian centuries were compelled so to remodel their churches that these might accommodate the steadily increasing number of relics.

The builders of the Ninth and Tenth Centuries, on the other hand, who saw their churches swept away by the conflagrations of new barbarian invasions, were forced, as a primary necessity, to provide for the safety of their relics by the erection of churches that should be fire-proof throughout, and the stone vault by means of which they solved their fundamental problem so completely altered the structure of their edifices that only by taking thought may one detect the vital relationships between the churches of the Romanesque period and those of either pagan or Christian Rome.

To such a complete break with the architecture of the past the five centuries of cruelly savage confusion which had overshadowed all Europe since the destruction of the ancient civilization were a necessary prelude. Only the repeated strokes dealt by very dark ages could set the art of the Eleventh Century free to develop into new and untrammelled forms. The radical change which Romanesque architecture represents became possible only when the Celtic and Teutonic worlds had been carried so far forward on new, if stormy, tides that Rome, forgotten and hidden in the mists of turbulent centuries, had lost the power to impose her old standards of architectural style.

This alone, however, was not enough. Roman standards and canons could not be forgotten by the Transalpine world, nor could the ancient skill in the cutting and dressing of stone be regained, until, throughout that world, the materials had been exhausted which the Roman builders had left behind them in their amphitheatres, basilicas, porticoes, palaces, theatres, and temples. These monuments not only embodied and held before the eyes of men those models and canons which must be forgotten if a new architecture was to be born; they also provided enormous quarries from which later builders could draw stone already cut and dressed. As long as these remained, stereotomy stagnated. Why should men labour at the difficult task of hewing columns out of huge blocks of hard stone when these might be had

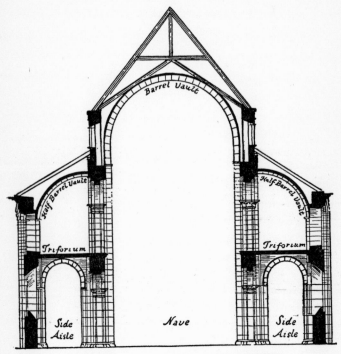

CROSS SECTION OF A ROMANESQUE CHURCH

for the taking from the edifices with which the Romans had covered their entire world? Not until these titanic remains had been quarried away could the builders of later ages be thrown back on their own resources; not until then could the art of stereotomy again come into being.[1]

By the year 1000 the barbarian centuries had accomplished their ruthless work. The minds of men had been set free from Roman archi-

[1] A. K. Porter, *Mediæval Architecture*, Vol. I, p. 165.

THE TRANSEPT AND APSE OF THE ABBEY OF BEAULIEU

With the great vault looming out of darkness overhead; with twilight in the aisles where the very "stillness crieth out that something Great is nigh," the Romanesque church is no fragile or dainty thing.

tectural standards and their hands, however unwillingly, had been
released from dependence upon stone cut by masons who were now
centuries dead. The slate had been wiped clean and a new architecture had become possible.

The men who created the new forms for the Romanesque church,
which the centuries of barbarism had made possible, were men who
had fled the world to assume the monastic vows, and their cloistered
life imposed upon them viewpoints which differed greatly from those
of the devout, but more secularly minded, priests, merchants, and artisans who were to raise the Gothic cathedrals of the following century.

When France was swept by internecine wars, when red skies at
night marked out the tracks of Scandinavian, Saracen, or Magyar
raiders, the arts of civilization retreated to the monasteries. Here the
copyists, the illuminators of manuscripts, and the goldsmiths found
their only refuge, and here the workers in stained glass, the sculptors
who carved the façades, portals, and capitals of the churches, the
artists who painted their walls and vaults, and the mosaicists who
decorated their chancels and their chapels sought, if often vainly, protection and quiet for their respective tasks.[2]

When quiet times returned once more, when Northmen, Moslems,
and Magyars no longer criss-crossed Europe with their devastations,
pilgrims began to throng the roads, compelling monks to build new
churches and to enlarge the old, even in wildernesses and waste places.

[2] Mediæval records reveal many instances of monks who were architects, builders, or
artists—men like Tutilo, a monk of S. Gall, who was "much in request for his skill
in sculpture and design" in the Tenth Century. (Helen Waddell, *The Wandering
Scholars*, p. 70.) Nevertheless, throughout the Romanesque and Gothic centuries the
architects, artists, masons, and carpenters were usually either lay brethren or laymen for
the monasteries, and laymen for the cathedrals and secular churches. Sometimes they
were serfs; Wilmar the mason must have been a bondsman, for the Earl of Surrey
gave him to Castleacre Priory for work on a new church, such also must have been
the status of "Aluric the mason" who was presented to the Cathedral of Peterborough
in 1295. The plans were often drawn by professional architects who travelled from
place to place, as their services were needed; the masons were usually itinerants drawn
from the ranks of those who practised their trade as a livelihood—and the work was
superintended, directed, and paid for by the clergy, or by overseers whom they appointed
and held responsible. (G. G. Coulton, *Art and the Reformation*, pp. 26-72; D. Knoop
and G. P. Jones, *The Mediæval Mason*, Chaps. III and IV.)

"The more famous sanctuaries attracted so many of the faithful that the aisles of churches had to be enlarged and ambulatories created; buildings were made more spacious to receive the crowds who were huddled together in the small churches of the earlier style. The imposing architecture of Vézelay and Autun, of S. Gilles and Arles, is infinitely too vast for the requirements of an ordinary abbey church. It was intended to serve worshippers far beyond the parochial limits, those itinerant congregations who came to pray to the Magdalen, to Lazarus, to S. Gilles, to S. Trophîme. Offerings enriched sanctuaries; cures and miracles paid for costly churches, for their sculptures, for their goldsmith's work, their ivories, and their precious stuffs." [3]

The gifts of these pilgrims enabled the monks to erect abbeys so vast that they were, and are, the wonders of that world which the builders had themselves abandoned; but their sombre edifices seem also to have taken the austere vows, for they bear the indelible imprint of monasticism, with its renunciation of the joys of life. One cannot stand in the semi-darkness of these aisles without feeling that the world is very far away; its laughter has been banned with its lights; austerities of monasticism seem incarnate in the very structure from crypt to vault, and the feeling grows that the monks would not have built otherwise, even if they could. Had they known how to raise the vault of Amiens they would still have built Notre-Dame du Port.

But, true as Romanesque architecture is to the spirit of monasticism, the new style would never have been evolved had there not been something more than this spiritual force acting on the minds of men. The essential innovation of the Romanesque is not the darkness that suited the monks so well, but the stone vault which the men of the Eleventh Century had not learned to erect without such massive supports that the darkness within was inevitable.

The relics were in danger in the Ninth and Tenth Centuries when the foundations of the new architecture were laid; that primary fact must continually be kept in mind. Because they were in danger the old wooden roofs must be rebuilt in stone that the churches might

[3] L. Hourticq, *Art in France*, p. 14.

be rendered as fire-proof as possible; the comparatively light and thin-walled basilica must be abandoned, and the ponderous Romanesque, more massive in all its parts, must be evolved.

It is true that even the stone vault could not entirely insure the protection of the holy relics, since above it there rose a forest of timbers to support the peaked roof of tile or lead which, especially in the North, was needed to throw off the rains of summer or the snows of winter. In any general conflagration brands, driven by the wind, might find lodgement among these timbers through some break in the protective covering and, once afire, the collapse of the heavy beams might break through the vaulting, permitting the flaming mass to find its way to the body of the church below. Many Romanesque churches were thus destroyed, but the number that have survived bear witness to the success of the monks' endeavour to protect their relics from the flames through a great structural innovation.[4]

Successful as the Romanesque builders were in overcoming the menace of fire, they did not master the new structural problems which their vault of stone itself entailed. Though they produced superb churches which in many ways are more varied and impressive than those erected a hundred or more years later, when the world was far wealthier and when architects and craftsmen were more highly skilled, yet the rôle of the Romanesque church was that of a prophet and fore-runner, a John the Baptist in stone, preparing the way for one still mightier that was to come. For more than four hundred years (including those when early and tentative steps towards stone vaulting were being taken, as in Spain) the story of Romanesque architecture is the record of a magnificent failure. In the Twelfth Century, when men solved the problem of the vault of stone, the churches were called Gothic; only in those centuries when men failed to solve that problem are they known as Romanesque.

[4] The practical value of the stone vault was tested by the great fire of 1836 when the flames that consumed the roof of Chartres Cathedral were unable to penetrate the vault and damage the church below. The demonstration was even more dramatic in the Great War when the vault of Rheims proved able to resist the fires—which destroyed the timbers of the roof—and broke only under the direct impact of German shells. It is needless to say that the tests imposed by modern artillery were far beyond the visions of the most prophetic seers of the cathedral age.

Yet structural defects have sometimes given birth to a beauty that might, possibly, not otherwise have been attained. The deafness of a Beethoven, the blindness of a Milton, the invalidism of a Stevenson, the poverty of a Spinoza, the intellectual achievements of the Jew—thrown back upon his inner life by the barriers of the Ghetto—have enriched all human life. The attic has produced more poetry and more art than has the parlour. And so in the field of architecture it is true that everything which appeals to us in the Romanesque church springs from, and is rooted in, the failure of the builders to solve a structural problem.

To that problem the heavy curving vault, which the builders of the Eleventh Century threw over both nave and choir, could not be the ultimate solution. The demands which it imposed upon the walls, calling for great strength and solidity of building, restricted the height of the church while the danger of impairing its stability by cutting into the walls to place windows in the clerestory, or any but small lights elsewhere in the edifice, made it impossible to secure adequate illumination for the aisles.

But it is these very factors which enabled the Romanesque church to appeal to the spirit in man in a way that is rarely equalled, and never excelled, by even the most aspiring of Gothic cathedrals.

The massiveness of the walls, the tremendous girth of the piers, the mighty arch of the great vault looming out of the darkness overhead enfold the worshipper as by the power of the Most High God, while in the twilight that broods upon the aisles he feels the very Shadow of the Almighty.

The stone vault that the early Romanesque architects threw across their naves—the only one they could conceive—was the rounded "barrel," or "tunnel," vault familiar to the Romans. It formed a long, continuous arch, and therefore presented to the builders the problem which is inseparable from the arch itself.

There is an ancient saying that "an arch never sleeps," and the thick stone barrel vault exerted a sleepless, unrelenting, and almost resistless outward pressure against the walls on which it rested. Therefore these walls must be stout and thick; the piers also must be heavy

Archives Photographique—Paris

THE AMBULATORY OF THE ABBEY OF S. BENOÎT-SUR-LOIRE

Built to accommodate relics, the ambulatory formed part of the Pilgrim path. Its columns swing around the curve, those on the inside close together, the outer farther apart, and the groin vault, with no keystone, is wavering and uneven.

and huge; the abbey might not soar into space as did the Gothic cathedral but the whole must be kept low, for the greater the height the weaker the resistance to the lateral thrust. Against the danger from this outward thrust the builder could marshal an equalizing inward pressure by throwing half-barrel vaults over the side aisles.

There was, however, one danger against which he could not guard; he could not keep the ground from hardening to the strength of iron under frost and ice, or from becoming soft and yielding when the thaws, rains, and freshets of spring unlocked the earth. With the weakening of the ground the whole building might settle, probably unevenly, and as it settled the supports of the barrel vault would give, a millimetre here and a centimetre there.

But neither winter nor summer affected in any way the steady, relentless drive of the ponderous vault. Clamping down on each fraction of an inch that the defence yielded, it never relinquished what it once had gained. So, as year followed year, each with its alternate frosts and thaws, with its seasonal hardening and softening of the earth, the building continued to settle, the defences continued to yield their annual tribute, until the balance was destroyed and the vault crashed down, filling the aisles with wreckage, and perhaps with broken bodies.

The great mortality among these vaults compelled the builders to throw transverse arches across their naves to give the vaults increased support. Then, since the attack continued to be stronger than the defence, the architects abandoned the barrel vault in form, if not in name, and pointed both their vaults and their transverse arches, thereby eliminating the comparatively flat central section of the vault and giving their keystones support from below instead of from the sides alone. At the same time they diverted much of the lateral pressure from the walls to the ground, for the pointing of the arches and the vault gave a downward direction to all weights and lessened the thrusts.

These last changes made the Romanesque church clearly prophetic of the Gothic, for without the pointed arch the great cathedrals of the Twelfth Century could never have been built. And the church of the Eleventh Century became still more prophetic of that of the

Twelfth when builders in Italy abandoned the barrel vault for one whose diagonal arches curved from pier to pier across the nave. Quite true, these churches continued to be Romanesque in form, for their vaults, walls, and piers remained huge, heavy, and thick; nevertheless, from the Romanesque century came all the elements, save only the flying buttresses, which were to lift the Gothic vaults high into the air, multiply and enlarge both aisles and chapels, and turn its walls of stone to glass.

Second only to the problem of strength was that of illumination, for windows could not be cut in the barrel vault that spanned the nave, nor in the half-barrel vaults above the triforium gallery, without dangerously weakening the structure; nor could any but small, splayed windows be used in the aisles beneath the gallery when these were covered with transverse barrel, or half-barrel vaults. The Romanesque builders were therefore usually forced to sacrifice all clerestory lights, and to content themselves with a single, narrow side aisle on either hand in order to permit as much light as possible to penetrate the nave from the diminished windows of the side walls.

In order to meet this problem of illumination, and to retain their clerestory windows, the later Romanesque builders attempted to "groin" their vaults.

Sacrificing intelligibility to brevity, the dictionaries tell us that the "groin vault is formed by the intersection at right angles of two barrel vaults." The illustration will interpret this definition better than words can do.

In erecting a groin vault over a square compartment, the builders raised the sides evenly, course by course, maintaining the same height, and trimming the stones to fit each other where side met side, thus giving the appearance of ribs which were unnecessary and rarely used. When the vault was properly buttressed at the corners each of its four triangular sections was locked in its place by the pressure of the adjoining sides.

The great advantage of the groin vault lay in the fact that, when used for a nave, it gave the side wall between the piers the same height as the crown of the vault and thus permitted the insertion of clerestory windows; when used for a side aisle it made those loftier windows possible which the barrel, or the half-barrel, vault prohibited.

Its most serious structural limitation was the difficulty of adapting it to any but a square compartment. Its round arches could rise neither more nor less than just one-half their span. A round arch spanning a bay forty feet wide would be exactly twenty feet high, while a round

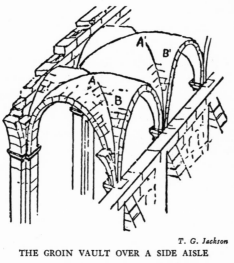

T. G. Jackson

THE GROIN VAULT OVER A SIDE AISLE

A A'—Intersection of groins; B B'—Webs.

arch over a twenty-foot space would rise only ten feet to its crown. Therefore an architect who attempted to throw a groin vault over an oblong bay which measured forty feet by twenty would find half his vaulting ten feet higher than the other half, the four divisions of his vault would be unequal both in size and height, and the lines where side met side would be wavering and uncertain.

Such vaults could be erected over an oblong bay only by depressing the longer pair of arches and the segments that rose from them, making them elliptical, and by building above the piers on the shorter side so that their arches and vault segments might start their springing at a higher point. Even at best the vault, when finished, was unsightly, and the difficulty of accurate construction, of estimating and supplying the necessary buttressing, was so great that vault after vault collapsed, while others were only saved by the timely discovery of the flying buttress; but this, like the pointed arch, does not belong to the Romanesque. They were both characteristically Gothic, and when they were introduced into the cathedral to solve a Gothic problem the day of the Romanesque was past.

Difficult as may have been the problem of vaulting the nave, choir, and aisles of a Romanesque church, that of covering the curving ambulatory was not easier.

Watch a company of marching soldiers swing around a corner; the pivot men on the inside shorten their steps while those on the outside lengthen their strides to keep the line straight. Consequently the pivot men in adjacent ranks come closer together while the end men step farther apart until the corner is turned.

The columns of an ambulatory swing around the curve in exactly the same way; those on the inside are closer together, while the outer columns are farther apart. Thus the four columns of an ambulatory bay form a trapezoid whose diagonals, if the bay be groined, will not intersect in the centre of the vault but much nearer the two inner columns. While it was possible to erect such vaults and to make them stable, yet they were exceedingly difficult to construct and, with their warped surfaces, unsightly to the point of ugliness when finished.

Throughout this period the warped surfaces and ill-balanced divisions of the ambulatory vaults restricted the height and breadth of this aisle and limited its radiating chapels. The solution of the problem had to wait the coming of the Gothic age when the builders, abandoning the attempt to run diagonal ribs across a curving aisle, placed a keystone in the centre of the vault and ran their arches from that point to the piers.

Thus in nave, side aisles, and ambulatory alike the builders faced problems for whose ultimate solution the honour has been given to another generation, to a generation that reaped where it had not sown —for the Gothic sons received from the Romanesque fathers the benefits of lessons learned in four hundred years of struggle to master the vault of stone.

The motive for that struggle was a courageous will to protect the sacred relics in disordered times. The Romanesque church was not the offspring of whim by caprice; it was a grim necessity born of war and its stone vaults are just as much the scars of conflict as are the machicolations and the *chemins-de-ronde* of the fortified churches of Royat, Agde, Albi, Les Saintes Maries, and all their kin, whose stone battlements were quarried by swords in the days of the English wars.

But when quiet times returned once more, when the ebbing tides of battle again unbarred the roads to the innumerable throngs of pilgrims who poured their gifts into monastic treasuries, the splendours of the churches which the devotion of the faithful and the labours of the monks together raised began to mould the architectural tastes of both clerics and laity.

Romanesque churches were thereafter multiplied because the wide appreciation of their inherent beauty created a demand which thrust the old basilica into the background. Not now because of any pressure of necessity, but because in the twilight of these aisles men felt more than the tongue could utter, churches began to appear which are characteristically Romanesque but which lacked that heavy vault of stone which alone explained and made intelligible the heavy and ponderous forms. The abbey churches which William the Conqueror and his wife, Matilda of Flanders, built at Caen, the abbey of Jumièges whose ruins are among the glories of France, and many others are undeniably Romanesque; yet they had to wait for a hundred years or more before their vaults of wood were replaced by Gothic vaults of stone. Preferences born of the spirit thus followed necessities born of war to create and multiply the new architecture, and for both reasons barrel and groin vaults came more and more into existence.

"The church of the Eleventh Century rises with a certain timidity; the walls betray the effort; they rest heavily upon the soil; they are sturdy and massive. The thickness of the walls and the pillars makes the free space seem confined." [5] Nevertheless the Romanesque church makes a distinct appeal. It is no fragile or dainty thing; no wind of the north may blow it down; it stands, stout and strong, incarnating

[5] Hourticq, *Art in France.*

a spirit of endurance befitting that anvil which has broken many a hammer. The dim lights of the aisles, the shadows among the vaults, the unending twilight which gives a brighter radiance and a deeper symbolism to the candles burning on the altar, all encompass the worshipper with a sense of divine mysteries already half revealed.

Romanesque architecture has not the soaring spirit of the Gothic; it lacks the beauty of great windows and the flaming lines of Flamboyant mullions; no cunning hand has twisted its rugged stone into the patterns of lace; but it imparts a feeling of quietness, of endurance, and a conviction of sure refuge.

Rest for the body, quiet for the mind, confidence for the soul—all these steal from the shadows and whisper faintly through the never broken dusk.

Chapter Fifteen

THE BACKGROUND OF GOTHIC ARCHITECTURE
THE WAY MEN LIVED

THE Twelfth and Thirteenth Centuries come to us with a challenge in each hand. Other ages may be more easily accepted and understood, but the Twelfth Century is a labyrinth, the Thirteenth Century is a problem, and the explanations of these centuries cannot be found upon the surface.

One might venture to say, perhaps, that no other centuries have given to the world so many well-remembered names; never before had Europe seen builders and architects with such exalted dreams; at no other time has the Church so rivalled in extent or power the Empire of old Rome. Only in those years have students, by the tens of thousands out of a scanty population, flocked to the universities to sit at the feet of teachers like Abélard, Bernard of Clairvaux, and Thomas Aquinas; and only in these centuries would nine great Crusades have been among the possibilities.

The ferment which wrought out a part of its vitality in Gothic architecture may well have been due in no small measure to a change in spirit as well as to the discovery of a new architectural principle. Perhaps the monks, the great builders of the Eleventh Century, would have gone on building Romanesque abbeys even if they had understood the principle of the Gothic; surely they would have felt that their churches, with their massive walls, their darkened vaults, their dim and shadowed aisles, were truer expressions of this "vale of tears" as they saw it from the narrow windows of their cells. But the question was not left to the decision of the monks for in the Twelfth Century the towns began their phenomenal rise to power and a new type of monasticism, with a harsher discipline, prevailed; these changes turned the tide of building from the country to the city, from the monks to the bishops, and from the abbey to the cathedral.

In the Eleventh Century Monasticism had been dominated by the great Order of Cluny, but when that Order, grown rich and corrupt, lost its old pre-eminence, it was succeeded by the Cistercians of Cîteaux, who were austere in the extreme.

The monks of this Order, fearing the outside world, fled to waste places where, banning all books, mosaics, mural painting, and coloured windows, they erected bare and austere abbeys which offered few opportunities for architectural development; therefore the torch of progress passed from the monks to the cathedral chapters, from the country to the city.

When Elijah dies, Elisha takes his place, and now the cathedral chapters, in the heart of the city, caught up the fallen mantle of the rural monks.

In the Tenth Century the most populous cities of Germany and of France contained no more than seven thousand or eight thousand inhabitants, and the average size of the towns was between a thousand and fifteen hundred.

In the Eleventh Century the largest Anglo-Saxon towns—London and Winchester—could not boast of more than eight thousand souls. At the close of the Twelfth Century, however, the urban populations had so increased that London had some forty-five thousand inhabitants and Paris one hundred thousand—which grew to two hundred and forty thousand by the close of the following century—while Douai, Lille, Ypres, Ghent, and Bruges had nearly or more than eighty thousand.

Thus, when the Gothic centuries began, about ten per cent of the population had flowed into the cities, giving them the financial resources, the organization, and the skilled labour necessary for great undertakings. Surrounded by stout walls, with gates, towers, and strong defences, they ranked in influence with the Crown and the Feudal lords. Within the security of their ramparts trade and commerce flourished, while labour gained skill and prestige through the formation of the guilds.

To the growth of the cities and their increase in wealth must be added the rise of a series of great pontiffs in Rome, a long period of comparative domestic peace, and the spiritual enthusiasms engendered by the earlier Crusades. All these factors united to foster a veritable renaissance which resulted in the erection of eighty great cathedrals and of nearly five hundred churches of cathedral dignity in France alone, between the years 1170 and 1270, whose replacement cost in 1840 was estimated at one thousand million dollars.[1]

And what churches they were! Again a comparison may help us to understand.

When you cross the East River, which divides Brooklyn from Manhattan, and look down from the roadway of the Bridge, the river seems very far below you; the Sound steamers and ocean freighters, the lighters, ferry boats and tugs passing beneath seem very small, and the men upon their decks are mere Lilliputians in stature. But until the year 1931 there was not a bridge in New York City, from the Narrows to Spuyten Duyvil Creek, that rose as high above the water as does the vault of Amiens above the pavement of that cathedral. In the list of the tall buildings of New York, one-third of the skyscrapers given in the *World Almanac* for 1927 are lower than the vault of the Choir of Beauvais.

When you "Walk about this Zion, tell the towers thereof," and consider her aisles and walls, you realize that the building of such palaces to God, by such a generation, is a miracle that makes small the wonder that the Abbot Haymo records when he assures us that the waters of the river at Porte-Ste.-Marie parted, even as the Red Sea and the Jordan rolled back their floods, that they who were building the Cathedral of Chartres might pass unhindered to their holy task.

Appreciation of the miracle wrought by the men of these centuries grows when you compare the churches they built with the homes from which they came, and the cities in which they lived.

But first, stand before Notre-Dame in Paris and study its deep-set

[1] One wonders what the replacement cost would be in America today, where the rate of hourly wages rose seven hundred per cent between 1840 and 1920, while the hours of the working week shrank by forty-four per cent.

portals with their multitudes of statues, medallions, bas-reliefs, and the carvings of the arches of their vaults; look up at the great gallery of the kings where stand those lords of Judah who were the ancestors of Christ, and at the countless gargoyles and chimeras that frown or leer over the city from remote and inaccessible places; then enter the cathedral and see the exquisite stained glass of the Rose Windows with the purple patterns they throw across your feet; let your eye measure the huge columns of the nave; the graceful sweep of the arches of the vault; follow the long lines of the interior, and the infinite detail wrought by men who "could do nothing in poor taste."

When we have done this with quiet care and appreciation, we will be better able to follow Mr. Tighe Hopkins as he visits the city and the homes where the masons, the sculptors, and the workers in stained glass dwelt, and realize the conditions in which these men who wrought so marvellously slept, ate, and lived.

"Old chroniclers have derived Lutetia, the name by which Paris was first known, from 'lutum,' 'mud.' The etymology is inexact, but the chroniclers thought otherwise, and the mud was always there to bear them out.

"Paris, immersed in mud, was not ashamed. The unpaved streets were without sidewalks, for this importation from England did not appear until within a few years of the Revolution, and even under the Empire the sidewalk was a rare convenience. Its sewers were uncovered until the beginning of the Seventeenth Century, and were usually dammed with refuse that the water could not carry off."[2]

The streets were mere passageways, narrow lanes reeking with abominations, strangers to cleansing winds, pure air, and sunshine, and therefore centres of infection and disease with which the medical science of the day, as primitive as was its sanitary engineering, was powerless to cope.[3]

[2] Tighe Hopkins, *An Idler in Old France*.
[3] When the plague struck Paris in the Fourteenth Century the King consulted his medical faculty as to its cause and cure. The royal physicians had no remedy to suggest, but they could inform his Majesty that the pestilence had been occasioned by a hostile conjunction between the planets Jupiter and Mars. Obviously the medical profession

There were no sanitary conveniences, even in palace, hospital, or monastery, and Paris, disobedient to the heavenly vision of ordinary cleanliness, was as pestiferous as it was unsightly. Even in the Seventeenth Century conditions had not greatly changed, although Corneille then sang of Paris as *"une île enchantée"* in a play to which, it seems ungallant to add, he gave the name of *The Liar*.

The Church was the chief sinner, for in her eyes "cleanliness was a dangerous practice, a culpable vanity, and a sin." The rule in most monasteries was two baths a year, at Christmas and at Easter. The monk was allowed to send his shirt to the laundry every fortnight, while the wearer might bathe twice a year. If a sense of duty counselled him to forego his semi-annual cleansing it was counted to him for righteousness. Two baths a year were a concession to the flesh, not an article of Faith. The rule of Cluny assigned three towels for the monks assembled at the cloister lavatory; one was reserved for the collective use of the novices; a second for those who had taken the vows, and a third for the lay brethren.

It is, however, "a popular error to believe that the upper classes were indifferent to cleanliness; the famous description of mediæval civilization as 'a thousand years without a bath' is untrue. Every castle had a well, and running water was often introduced." [4]

The common people, at least in the cities, were less ascetic than the clergy in the moral disciplines of uncleanliness, for public baths were not uncommon in Paris. These, however, afforded too many opportunities for misbehaviour, and the *bain* developed into the *bagnio,* wherefore it came under the ban of the authorities, both secular and ecclesiastical. Bathing houses were also established in the river Seine,

could not be blamed for ills whose causes were so remote, nor could the doctors, like Joshua, command the heavenly bodies to stand still.

The Church, however, had a remedy to suggest, and so an unbelievably huge candle was fashioned, carried in procession through the streets, around the walls, and then into Notre-Dame. As the vault of the cathedral was not high enough to accommodate the offering the candle was moulded into a spiral instead of standing upright as a candle should.

Disease, however, refused to burn out with the candle, the reason being that the *rues* and the river, the streets and the Seine, were polluted through and through.

[4] Thompson, Vol. II, p. 721.

but as this was little better than a sewer it is doubtful whether the bather gained or lost by his ablutions.

However, despite all that may be advanced in defence of the Middle Ages, it is doubtful if any Yseult of the Twelfth Century was more punctilious than Margaret of Navarre, who boasted, in the Sixteenth Century, that she had not washed her hands in eight days; Isabella of Spain lived her life, according to report, untroubled by the tedious implications of Saturday night, and it is quite possible that bath-tubs were as suspiciously regarded then as they were by our own Andrew Jackson who threw out those that Dolly Madison had installed in the White House on the ground that they were "objectionable to the common people." However, this is an unsavoury subject, and we will be content with the statement that the conditions in the *haut monde* and among the masses, if better than in the monasteries, still left much to be desired.

That people like this—whose streets, houses, palaces, and often persons were so indescribable—could build such cathedrals as Notre-Dame de Paris, Rheims, Amiens, Laon, and Chartres; that when they came to erect their churches they "could do nothing in poor taste;" that they could fill the graceful mullions of their windows with such exquisite stained glass, and lift high their soaring columns with their clusters of encircling shafts, is surely not the least of the wonders of which the Abbot Haymo might boast.

Still the half of the miracle of these churches has not been told.

When Nehemiah rebuilt the ruined walls of Jerusalem he tells us not only that "all the people had a mind to work," but also that every man built the stretch of the wall that was behind his own house, so that when at last all the "wall was joined together" it represented the co-operation of all the families.

In the centuries we have now under review all the people showed a "mind to work," but they showed an equal readiness to battle with their neighbours. The men of the Middle Ages wore their hearts upon their sleeves; their emotions were quick, keen, and unrestrained; hatreds flared swiftly into being, and were instantly expressed. Yet when there was a church to be built the bitterest antagonists declared a truce; injuries, rivalries, and jealousies were forgotten; the lines of caste and of class were temporarily obliterated, and all worked loyally together for the glory of God and the welfare of their souls.

If we may glimpse these hatreds in action we can better appreciate the miracle of the co-operation of the haters in the raising of these churches.

In 1228 the great lords of France, feeling that one of their number and not a woman should have the guardianship of King Louis IX during his minority and thus control the destinies of the nation, joined their forces against the Queen Mother, Blanche of Castile. Philip Hurepel, the rough uncle of the King, seemed to them the natural guardian, as he was their representative. So the Regent of Brittany—Pierre, Count of Dreux, commonly called "Mauclerc"—Enguerrand of Coucy, Hugh of Lusignan, Raymond of Toulouse, Philip Hurepel, with others entered into a formidable conspiracy against Blanche, planning the kidnapping of the boy king.

Blanche was at Orléans when this conspiracy came to a head; as she hurried to the protection of Paris word reached her that the great lords had blocked her road at Corbeil. Halting at Montleheri, the Queen sent a summons to Paris for help which was quickly answered, the citizens coming forth in such numbers that they filled the roads and frustrated the purposes of the Barons.

Now behold! A miracle at Chartres where the lion and the lamb lay down together, for the South Porch, with its great and splendid Rose Window, is the gift of that Pierre of Dreux, "Mauclerc," of whom Blanche said, "I have never found any man who sought to do me more ill than he;" while the North Porch, with its exquisite Rose Window, bears the royal fleur-de-lis and the Castles of Castile, showing that they were given by Louis, whom "Mauclerc" sought to kidnap, and by Blanche, for whom he had prepared a dungeon.

Thus the two famous Rose Windows, given by strong and enduring foes, face each other across the transepts and mingle their jewelled lights upon the pavement.

The only hatreds that might not be silenced were those of the secular clergy for the Preaching Friars, and for this there was a reason. The

Friars were responsible to the Pope alone; they were his personal militia; their travelling orders made the world their parish, and when they entered the boundaries of a bishopric they knew themselves to be independent of all episcopal control or discipline. They had received from the Pope the right to hear confession, and more and more succeeded in displacing the local clergy in the affections of the people.

As these itinerant preachers threw themselves whole-heartedly into the service of the common people, caring for the sick, even for the lepers, and were industrious in the relief of the poor, the wealth of the masses was increasingly diverted to the coffers of the Mendicant Orders. Clerical hatred grew with diminishing revenues, and envy followed hatred. Appeal after appeal to the bishops, and through the bishops to the Pope, were fruitless, and the defeated clergy found their only satisfaction in satire.

Here and there, if you look closely, you may find—carved in stone upon a porch, the capital of a column, or in the wood of the choir stalls—a hooded fox preaching to geese or being hung upon a gallows; here is one with mitre and staff; there another with a bag of money and in chains. Sometimes you may find an ass's head under a monk's hood, or a cowled head with two faces. Elsewhere, as in S. Andoche at Saulieu, blind Balaam in a monk's garb rides his wiser ass against the angel's flaming sword.[5]

Oftentimes the vengeful artist varies his models by the use of dogs, pigs, or monkeys, but he never varies the cowl. In such ways he found vent for what we today have been taught to call his "suppressed desires."

Thus for two full centuries, when the builders lived in cities that were darker and more malodorous than the worst of our city slums;

[5] At Boston an ass holds the book for a Friar-Fox as he preaches to an audience of hens whose interest is not diminished by the fact that the preacher, as he preaches, strangles a cock with his forepaws!

On a misericord of Ely a fox, in amice and stole, preaches to geese from a text held in his paws—possibly from the words of S. Paul: "God is my witness how much I long for you all." (Phil. 1:8.) (M. D. Anderson, *The Mediæval Carver*.)

Other instances of clerical rancour towards the Friars may be seen at Denbigh, Bristol, Ripon, on a choir stall of Amiens, on a moulding of the Baptistry of Parma, and on a portal of Modena.

when jealousies, hatreds, and rivalries flamed out between the Crown and the Feudatories, between noble and noble, between clergy and citizens, and between priests and friars, the French people went on building great cathedrals and churches at a rate of nearly six each year, almost one every two months.

Here is something to be explained: Is it a miracle, or is it something that we of the Twentieth Century can understand?

Perhaps we may understand, but if so it will be with difficulty, for the explanation is written in the mind of an age whose ways were not our ways and whose thoughts were not our thoughts.

Let it be fairly admitted that men of the Middle Ages were no more logical and consistent in the practice of their faith than have been the men of other centuries. There was much that was lusty and lustful, much that was passionate and brutal, to mar the record of these years. But the crime of David does not destroy for us the value of the Psalms; the passionate massacre by the great Theodosius in Thessalonica does not prevent our high appraisal of the man; the brutalities of our own Night Riders, Ku Klux Klans, and sporadic cruelties of lynching mobs do not destroy our claims to culture and civilization. Neither do the charges that might be laid against the men of the Twelfth and Thirteenth Centuries forbid our realization of the fact that the purpose of the times was that "men should be good Christians."

It is Browning who reminds us that a man is worth more to God than the sum total of all his deeds; in the final reckoning God gives high place to all great purposes, soaring dreams and aspirations, to the thwarted will for good, to the visions of the soul and the clean resolutions of the spirit, even though they died a-borning, or were defeated, failing to find expression through incalculable forces within the man himself.

So we turn from the way men lived to the way men thought, for it is only through the ideas, aspirations, and interpretations of life, as these were conceived by the Twelfth and Thirteenth Centuries, that we shall be able to estimate the quality of man's life, and thus to understand his handiwork.

Chapter Sixteen

THE BACKGROUND OF GOTHIC ARCHITECTURE
THE WAY MEN THOUGHT

ADAM of S. Victor, preaching a sermon with a chestnut for a text, made the nut's rough burr proclaim the Humanity of Christ, its wooden shell set forth the agony of His cross, and the inner kernel invite all men to partake of the sacramental Mass. To the preacher this was no mere allegory; to him the chestnut had been created to discharge this mission; it had been sent into the world by a God who had so fashioned all created things that they might declare His purposes to men.

In thus introducing the chestnut to his pulpit the great preacher interpreted to us the mind of his age, and if we are to understand his century we greatly need his interpretation, for the differences between the North Pole, where all longitudes run south, and the South Pole, where they all run north, are no greater than is the intellectual gulf which separates Anselm, Archbishop of Canterbury in 1100, from his present-day successor.

Today we start with the sciences and hope, aided by our laboratories, to understand our universe and perhaps to discover God. The Middle Ages, on the contrary, started with God, as revealed in the Scriptures, the Creeds and Councils of the Church, and then interpreted Science in the light of His revealed nature and character. Between these two points of view there is all the difference that separates the Ptolemaic from the Copernican systems of astronomy. To the mediæval mind God was the beginning and also the goal of human knowledge; that we might know Him He had given to every created thing a cryptic meaning which might be read in the light of symbolism. Sun, moon and star, day and night, the changing seasons, all things animate or

THE CATHEDRAL OF S. MADELEINE AT VÉZELAY

Twilight beneath the groin vault of the Romanesque nave; midday in the Gothic apse.

inanimate wore the prophet's mantle and spoke with the prophet's tongue.

The men of S. Victor's day may have been passionate, strong in their loves and lusts, their rebellions and their loyalties, their low desires and high devotions, yet they never questioned but that man must ever take God into his reckoning, that He was a Power with Whom the sinner must make his peace.

He who had spoken in times past by His holy prophets was speaking still, even by the chestnut in the preacher's hands.

This point of view permeates the Middle Ages, calling into being its mighty popes, its great universities, and setting in motion its nine Crusades. It unifies all disparate phenomena, explaining the Cathedral of Chartres on the one hand and Innocent III on the other; the University of Paris and the Inquisition of Toulouse; the Crusaders at Damietta and the Poor Men of Lyons. Only by a sympathetic comprehension of this point of view can we understand a people who could come from hovels to build cathedrals that must ever seem wonders in our eyes.

The remarkable Cult of Carts, though not of long duration nor very extensive in its sweep, dramatically illustrates the power of this point of view in the men and women, princes and peasants, who walked toilfully the dusty roads of Normandy dragging, like cattle, the heavy stones for the building of church or abbey, and watching, with reverent wonder, the waters "at the place called Porte-Ste.-Marie," where the waves of the sea were miraculously parted for their feet to pass.

The same point of view which bent the necks of princes to the oxen's yoke made knowledge itself the servant of religion when it created the great universities which now sprang into being from end to end of Europe. Within their walls the primary purpose of study was not the laws of nature but the mind of God. Here came thousands of pupils, some from the ends of the continent, to hear Abélard ask and answer *Cur Deus Homo:* Why Did God Become Man? To hear Thomas Aquinas discuss the relation of the Divine Wisdom to the Divine Will as both are unveiled in God's creation; to listen as Gilbert of Poitiers explained the mystery of the Trinity, as Alexander of Hales or Albertus Magnus lectured on Theology; to hear Duns Scotus argue the relation of God's Grace to Man's Free Will, or Raymond Lull, as he showed how Science confuted the beliefs of Moslems, Pagans, and Pantheists alike.

The idealistic forces of the age are not only evidenced in the costly efforts to recover the Holy Land for Christian Europe, to extirpate paganism in Livonia and heresy in Provençe; they appear in the emergence of those heretical sects which increased the spiritual ferment of the centuries. Of these the Albigenses and the Waldensians are the best known, but there were multitudes of others—their names are legion. To the heretics should be added the missionaries whom heresy called into being—the two great Orders of the Preaching Friars, the Dominicans and the more humane Franciscans. The Schoolmen and the heretics were to bring disaster upon the mediæval Church. Intellectually, the questions asked by Duns Scotus, Raymond Lull, and Roger Bacon were ultimately to summon Theology before the bar of Reason to justify its claims; while the study of the ancient Roman Law was destined to undermine the papal throne and to overthrow the mediæval ecclesiastical structure. Spiritually, the heresies of the day were to lead to Wycliffe, Huss, Luther, and Calvin, and to triumph at last in the dismemberment of the old Church.

But for the moment all these forces tended to quicken interest in spiritual things, and this heightened interest had its forceful influence upon church architecture; in truth, the Golden Age of the Gothic church coincides with this period of spiritual renaissance.

To the Middle Ages then, God, veiled by His creation, was ever present, revealing His will by symbols, oftentimes obscured and needing the interpretation of the wise. He was, however, visibly present in His vicegerents who, clothed with His authority, sat upon S. Peter's throne, bore the Apostolic keys, and possessed the awful power to loose or to bind in Heaven or on earth.

Until we understand this point of view, which was potent with the people if often opposed by kings, we cannot enter the chambers of the mediæval mind, for to it we owe that succession of great pontiffs who, without the legions of Rome, resumed the Roman sway; without armies won obedience from kings, and without a sword forced the surrender of sovereigns who had conquered at Bouvines, at Navas de Tolosa, who had even ventured to storm the walls of Rome.

Because he dared not challenge that point of view Henry II, grandson of the Conqueror and father of Cœur-de-Lion, walked with bare and bleeding feet over the flinty roads that led to Canterbury to do penance for a sin.

Because that point of view had power in the Eleventh Century an emperor of Germany must stand for three days in the snows of Canossa, with bare feet and robe of sackcloth, before the papal gates.

Because he feared it, an Archbishop of Mainz must lay aside his Office and forbear to give, or to receive, the Holy Eucharist. Because the viewpoint was mightier than the English Crown in the Twelfth Century, not all the power of the King, no guards around his ports, no threat to blind, burn, or hang a papal messenger, could bar the Pope's sentence of excommunication from the shores of England. Because of the power with which this viewpoint had endowed the hands of Rome there was no cave in the solitudes where the eye of the Pontiff could not see, no fortress impregnable to the stroke of his hand.

Germany, once mightiest of the mighty, whose sovereigns wore the Lombard's Iron Crown and carried the sceptre of the Roman Cæsars, saw her rulers crowned and deposed according to the will of Innocent; while Portugal, León, Castile, Aragon, Navarre, Poland, all heard and recognized their master's voice.

But with the passing of the Thirteenth Century the viewpoint also passed. John XXII could not appeal from his prison-palace at Avignon as had the great Innocent from the Cathedra of S. Peter; the growing corruptions of the clergy and the exchange of maledictions by rival popes robbed it of its power, and the faith which had called into being mighty pontiffs, great universities, nine Crusades, and marvellous cathedrals so changed to doubt that a Visconti could safely mock the papal decree that barred him from the altar, and an Archbishop of Milan could silence Clement II by a threat to march against him with his army.

As the eagle soars aloft with motionless wings, upborne by the very winds, so the men and events that made illustrious the Twelfth and Thirteenth Centuries rose and were sustained by the wings of a point of view; when those wings failed the Papacy crumbled, the Crusades recoiled, doubt invaded the universities, and architecture entered upon its melancholy decline.

Because it is the interpreter to us of the mind of the Middle Ages, let us look once more upon this viewpoint as it places, and prompts, the actors on the mediæval stage.

When the Thirteenth Century dawned Philip Augustus ruled in France while Innocent III wore the papal tiara. Philip was no weakling; indeed he was one of the great kings of France. He had wrested from the hands of John that château Gaillard which Cœur-de-Lion had boasted he would hold "though its walls were made of butter." He drove the English out of Normandy; shattered the combined forces of Germany and England on the field of Bouvines, and so crushed the Midi by his Albigensian Crusade that nearly all the South was brought, a few years later, under royal control. He doubled both the revenues and the territory of the State and held the feudal lords in leash.

But Philip crossed the path of Innocent and, as in ancient days, Gaul must once more yield to a new Cæsar who wore a triple crown.

Philip had married, and then repudiated, Ingeburga, sister of the King of Denmark; this was bad enough, but there was worse to follow. He darkened his offence by marrying again, this time Agnes of Meran.

Innocent was swift to act. A Council was called at Dijon where at midnight each cleric of the Council, holding a lighted torch, chanted the Miserere and recited the prayers for the dead. The Cross and its holy Image were draped in black; the relics were removed from sight; the Host was consumed. As twelve sonorous strokes of the great bell tolled the hour of midnight the torches were dashed to the ground, and in Stygian darkness the sentence was pronounced which ordered

THE CATHEDRAL OF LÂON

The long parallel lines formed by the capitals of the columns of the nave arcade, of the triforium and clerestory galleries, the string-courses of these galleries, and the stone bands around the clustered shafts emphasize the length of the cathedral.

God to take His love, His power, His mercy, and Himself from the soil of France.

The royal paroxysms of wrath and violence were vain. Innocent could not be moved by threats. The King seized the property of the Church, banished bishops, and appealed to his feudatories for support; but at last he had to yield. Agnes of Meran retired to Normandy; Ingeburga was brought from her last convent-prison; the Crown submitted to the Tiara.

Years passed; Philip Augustus and Innocent both died; another Philip—Philip the Fair—was King in France and Boniface VIII was Pope in Rome. Between these two, both strong and ambitious men, dissensions soon broke out, but when the haughty Pope launched the old terrors, threatening interdicts and excommunications, Philip merely laughed, burned the papal Bull before the eyes of all Paris, and addressed Innocent's successor as "Your very great Foolishness." Even the clergy of France rallied around the King.

The quarrel dragged along, each year adding fuel to the fire, until at last a blaze broke out in which the mediæval Papacy expired.

On the 16th of August, 1303, Boniface came to Anagni to escape the summer heat which made the Vatican an unhealthy residence. From his palace here he issued several decrees to punish those clerics of the Gallican Church who had supported the Throne of France against the Cathedra of S. Peter and then, after a few days' pause, he excommunicated Philip, releasing his subjects from all duties of allegiance but, to give the King time to return to his obedience, the publication of the sentence was withheld until the 8th of the following September.

Entirely unaware that the agents and emissaries of Philip, William de Nogaret and Sciarra Colonna—with unlimited power to draw upon the King's bankers in Florence—were near at hand, and that they were hiring bands of lawless soldiery, Boniface took no precautions for his personal safety.

The 7th of September came; the Edict of Excommunication was ready for public proclamation on the morrow; the Pontiff had retired for his siesta when suddenly the trampling of armed horses rang through the streets of Anagni and its narrow lanes echoed with the cry, "Death to Pope Boniface; long live the King of France." At the command of the startled Pope the bells of the churches tolled and the city guard sprang to arms but their commander, betraying the Pontiff, went over to his foes.

The Cardinals, whose houses were first attacked, fled through the sewers; next the Church of S. Maria, which defended the papal palace, was fired and sacked, and then Philip's long arm began to batter at the palace gates.

Deserted and alone, Boniface put on the papal tiara and the stole of S. Peter, grasped the Keys of his high office in one hand and the Cross in the other and, so arrayed, took his seat on the papal throne where he silently awaited the forcing of the last door and the entrance of his enemies. Even so had the Senators of Rome taken their seats in the Senate to await the coming of Brennus and his Goths. He had not long to wait. With a crash of falling timbers, of iron bars and hinges, the emissaries of Philip broke into his presence. Boniface was insulted, mocked, reviled, and struck; only the restraints of de Nogaret saved him from the edge of Sciarra's sword. He was seized, deprived of his attendants, placed on a vicious horse, his face towards the animal's tail, and so paraded through the streets to his prison. When at last Anagni rose and drove out the soldiery of Philip and led the Pope back to his sacked and naked palace, not a single vessel could be found from which Boniface might drink; only a chest remained which the women of Anagni filled with water that Boniface might kneel and quench his thirst.

The outrage was too much for the aged Pontiff; in a month he was dead and the Ghibellines told terrible stories of the manner of his death: he had beaten out his brains against the wall; he had smothered himself with pillows; he had died from self-administered poison—at any rate, Boniface was dead, and with him died the mediæval Papacy.

As we sit with the dying Pope, who gnaws the head of his staff in a rage of humiliation, it seems strange to recall the debasement of an earlier English king who surrendered his kingdom to a predecessor of this same Boniface to be held forever as a fief of the Roman See.

Never did the papal star shine more brightly in the heavens than when the great Innocent was on the throne; never was the point of view more powerful in the minds of men than when it clothed Gregory VII, Alexander III, and Innocent III with world power; but in Boniface's day the point of view had changed, and again "a star fell from heaven."

There is a striking parallel between the last days of the pagan Empire and those of the mediæval Papacy, for the succession of Constantine to Diocletian was hardly more swift than that of Clement V to Boniface.

If it took only eleven years to raise the Church from the persecutions of the Third Century to the securities of the Fourth, the short space of twenty-three years saw it fall from the throne of the Vatican to the prison of Avignon, from lordship over emperors to servitude in France, from world-wide freedom to Babylonian Captivity.

We do not need to dwell upon the story of the papal tragedy which darkened the reign of the crafty, ambitious, arrogant and cruel Boniface. The thunders of his excommunications and interdicts filled all Europe, his Bulls bellowed, charged, and broke their horns against the fortifications of the thrones.

The point of view had changed and when Boniface, broken by the insult of Anagni, sank into his grave he carried with him the prestige and the power of his ancient office; and with the fall of the Papacy, as with its rise to power, there rose and fell the fortunes of church architecture.

The hero of the Middle Ages is not a figure of Romance; it is not Richard Cœur-de-Lion storming the walls of Acre; it is not Godfrey of Bouillon, battering down the walls of Jerusalem; it is not Henry of England, conqueror of Normandy at Tinchebrai, who was whipped at Avranches for sacrilege against the person of a priest; it is not Abélard or Aquinas, despite the thousands who followed them and hung upon their words, nor is it Innocent III, conqueror of kings.

The hero of the Middle Ages is a Point of View; it was a Point of View which conquered the Holy City, that raised and crowded universities, that clothed Innocent with power, and created the great cathedral age. When that Point of View died all that had been upborne by its wings came fluttering to the earth; the Papacy went into eclipse; crusaders furled their banners and crept home, and the song of the builders faded into silence.

The Age of Faith was over, and with it passed the power that had moved mountains—and parted the waters at "the place called Porte-Ste.-Marie."

Chapter Seventeen

CARGOES, CARAVANS, AND CATHEDRALS

IN THE Twelfth and Thirteenth Centuries a wave of church building swept over France and England, and cathedrals, abbeys, and great
churches sprang from the ground on every hand. In France, whose
population (in 1328) was barely twelve million souls, the monks built
more than sixteen hundred abbeys in the Eleventh, Twelfth, and Thirteenth Centuries—an average of more than five each year—while the
secular clergy erected their cathedrals or important churches at a rate
of nearly six for every year between 1170 and 1270.

Across the channel the city of York had her great cathedral and
forty-four other churches, without counting her chapels, in 1377 when
her population was about eleven thousand. New York City would
need today not less than forty thousand churches to supply her population as that of York was then supplied. In England as a whole—
where the population was not over five million—the people of the
Middle Ages erected more than ten thousand churches.

This energy in building is the more remarkable since the masons
were few in number and their span of life was short (because of the
stone dust that, filling the atmosphere in which they worked, interpenetrated their lungs). In 1292 Paris, with two hundred and forty
thousand inhabitants, enrolled one hundred and four masons and
twelve stone-cutters in her guilds, while Fourteenth Century England
counted only about a dozen resident masons in such cities as York,
Oxford, and Norwich. They were more numerous in the rural districts
—because of the town walls, castles, churches, and abbeys—than in
the cities, where the houses were usually of timber or of clay, but
even in the country they were relatively few.

Bricks cannot be made without straw, nor can churches be built without money. One cannot cross Europe today and see the splendours of these cathedrals and abbeys, even in little country towns, without wondering whence the wealth that built them came; what Pactolian rivers of gold, what auriferous sands of El Dorado, had Europe discovered when she dared to launch a campaign of such ambitious magnificence?

In the year 987, when Hugh Capet reigned, there was hardly one great church in all Western Europe north of the Alps; the Romanesque Age had not yet dawned, and the majority of ecclesiastical edifices were flimsy structures, largely or wholly built of wood. But about that same year Kieff, in Southern Russia, possessed four hundred churches with gilded domes and campaniles which, towering above the city's walls, proclaimed to weary travellers their nearness to a populous and prosperous city whose commerce in the Tenth Century was so far-reaching that the citizens could build great churches.

In Western Europe, in the year 1000, there was not a single chartered city, nor any town of more than six or seven thousand people; even the capitals of kings were dark and dingy, with narrow, twisting streets and houses of wood or clay beneath whose thatched roofs there were neither windows to let in the light, nor chimneys to carry off the smoke.

In the East, on the other hand, Kieff was a busy centre of metropolitan life; Novgorod was known as "The Venice of the North;" Constantinople was still in her Golden Age; Trebizond, on the Black Sea, rivalled the magnificence of Byzantium; Khorasan was "The Garden of Asia," and Bokhara was encircled by a double line of walls whose outer circumvallation had a circuit of fifty miles, while the wide spaces between these fortifications were filled with palaces, parks, and gardens.

In the year 1000 there was little commerce in the West wherewith to build great cities or great churches, for the stream of trade that flowed across France since Phœnician days had died away as Moslem fleets swept Christian ships from the Western Mediterranean. Such trade as reached the southern shores of France was there land-locked by Saracenic corsairs so that Provence, once the richest possession of

Merovingian Gaul, became the poorest of Carlovingian France; many of her cities—Nice, Fréjus, Toulon—were held by Moslem enemies until 972, and Marseilles, after a thousand years of eminence from Grecian through Merovingian times, shrank to the insignificance of a grass-grown port and vanished from history for two hundred years.

In the East, on the other hand, merchants travelled freely from the Baltic Sea to the Caspian, the Black Sea, and the Bosphorus; while the eight markets of Kieff sent out long tentacles of trade which reached to Sweden, Iceland, even to far Greenland on the North; to Persia, India, and China on the East.

In the Eleventh Century, however, all this was changed with an abruptness so kaleidoscopic that only the Sixteenth Century can afford a parallel. Then the voyages of Columbus and of Vasco da Gama, the conquests of Pizarro and Cortez, and the discovery of gold in Peru and Mexico were to shift the trade routes from the Mediterranean to the Atlantic, ruin Genoa and Venice, give the *coup de grâce* to the Hanseatic League, confer a long hegemony on the throne of Spain, and enable the Catholic kings to dominate Italy, overawe the Pope, rule the Netherlands, defeat France at Pavia, buy the Imperial Crown, and mount the throne of England by marriage with an English Queen.

In like manner in the Eleventh Century the flood of silver from the Rammelsberg mines enabled Western Europe to outbid Constantinople, not only for the trade of Russia and the Norse Empire, but presently for that of the entire world. Year by year Byzantium declined as new markets in the West created new trade routes, along which the traffic which had hitherto flowed southward through Russia to the Bosphorus moved with greater ease and economy to and through the land of Germany, Flanders, and France. New voyages of the Normans, who drove the Saracenic rulers of the Western Mediterranean before their prows, opened those waters to Christian commerce, and finally the Crusaders, sailing eastward, conquered the Levantine ports, the termini for the traffic with the Far East, and gave the kingdoms of the world to Venice, to Genoa, to Marseilles, to the cities of Champagne and of the Low Countries. *"Les Rivières sont des routes qui marchent,*" said Etienne Boileau, Provost of Markets under Louis XI, and the commerce of the world followed the "marching roads"—the Dnieper, Volkov, and Volga in the East; the Danube in the South; the Rhine, Moselle, Weser, and Elbe in Germany; and the Rhône, Seine, Loire, and the Garonne in France.

Famous fairs sprang up along their banks, or where road crossed road between stream and stream; markets multiplied before the gates of churches, abbeys, or castles, and these gatherings of men to buy or sell drew the wealth of the East to the shores or rivers of the West. Thus when there were cargoes on the rivers or caravans on the roads, cities rose, prospered, and built their great cathedrals.

It is no mere coincidence of the Eleventh Century that the same semi-decade in which the first Western cities won their charters also saw the fall of Kieff in 1076 to the Kumans, a half-savage Asiatic tribe of Kipchak Turks, and the sack of Constantinople in 1081 by the emperor Alexius Commenus, who stormed and plundered his own capital as if it were the city of an ancient enemy. Nor is it a coincidence that Kieff could build four hundred churches in the Tenth Century, but none in the Eleventh, whereas the cities of France, which were barely geographic names in the great era of Kieff, could begin in that century the greatest church building age in history. Nor again is it a coincidence that Venice, the first seaport to feel the quickening impulse of Western trade, should build S. Mark's—the first great mediæval church in all the Occident.

All these events—the coinage of silver in the West, the decline of the commerce and cities of the East, the increase in Western trade and traffic, the rise of cities and the building of cathedrals from Italy to England—are not isolated and unrelated phenomena; each has its place in the same series, and we must follow the caravans along the trade routes of the East, and then over those of the West, if we are to understand the wave of cathedral building which created the Gothic Age in Western Europe.

The most important economic fact of the Ninth Century had been the opening of a great trade route through Russia by the Northmen, whose long Viking ships first drew near the coasts of "the five king-

THE CHOIR OF THE CATHEDRAL OF BEAUVAIS

Higher above the pavement than the Brooklyn Bridge is above the East River and loftier even than the towers of London's Tower Bridge—"Conceived in Lombardy, nested in France, springing into full flight at S. Denis, Gothic architecture reached its apogee at Beauvais."

doms of the Kuri"—which is modern Kurland—about the year 825. Because these "dragon ships" were driven by oars, the Kuri called their visitors *Rus*—"The Rowers"—a term which was eventually applied to the people, and to the land, of Russia.

Penetrating the Gulf of Finland, passing up the river Neva and through Lake Ladoga, they came to Lake Ilmen where they established a trading post which grew into the city of Novgorod, to whose doors converging rivers brought the furs, ivories, and ambers of the Arctic, and the timber, honey, wax, and furs of the Ural Mountains, while the exports of the Scandinavian world came to her through lakes and streams that led from the Baltic almost to Lake Ilmen. Still questing, these restless adventurers discovered the natural water route of the Volkov and Dnieper rivers which led from Novgorod through Kieff to the Black Sea, to Constantinople, and to Trebizond. Over this road—known as the "Varangian Route," a name that is equivalent to "Norse," or "Scandinavian"—English wool and Flemish cloths travelled to the markets of Byzantium or to the Bazaars of Trebizond and Bagdad long before Otto the Great opened the mines of Rammelsberg.[1]

It is hardly possible to overestimate the influence of the Norse upon mediæval history. They knitted North and South together into a cultural empire, possessing the intangible unity that Anglo-Saxondom has today, wherein men could travel freely from Greenland to the Caspian Sea. No international exchange of wares comparable to the commerce that they called into being had been seen since the decline of the Roman Empire.[2]

[1] The Northmen also descended the Volga River from Novgorod to Astrakhan, at the head of the Caspian, which is almost connected with the Black Sea by navigable rivers. These two cities—Astrakhan and Trebizond—were the termini of the old caravan roads which crossed the continent of Asia from India and China through Persia. Of the two, Trebizond remained the more important as long as Constantinople retained her commercial supremacy, for it was the depot for all the commerce that passed between the Greek Empire and the East; it was also a terminus of the Varangian Route, and a goal for the caravans of Bagdad—"all our merchants go there," wrote the Arabian, Istradi, in the Tenth Century. But when, because of the decline of Byzantium, the Varangian Route lost its value, the commerce of the Far East turned from Trebizond to Astrakhan; thence it ascended the longest river in Europe to Novgorod—doubtless to some early song of Volga boatmen—and so came to the markets of the West.
[2] Thompson, Vol. I, p. 281 *et seq.*

An enormous amount of Oriental goods came over these old caravan routes to Trebizond, to Astrakhan, to Constantinople, to the eight markets of Kieff, to Novgorod, and so to the West. Tartusi, an Arabian traveller, found Oriental silks, spices, and other goods, together with coins of Samarkand, in the markets of Mainz in 973, while thousands of Byzantine, Egyptian, Cufic, and Indian coins, with more than thirteen thousand that bear the stamps of Arabian sovereigns, have been found along these roads and rivers, together with English, Norman, French, Danish, and German coins. The amount and variety of all this currency bears convincing witness to the volume of the traffic.

Towards the end of the Eleventh Century this Varangian Route was virtually abandoned in favour of three new trade routes that crossed Europe farther to the west—the first, up the Rhine and over the Alpine passes to Venice; the second, down the Danube to the Euxine; while the third and last followed the Rhône to Marseilles. The purchasing power of Constantinople, declining both absolutely and relatively, had failed to keep pace with the new buying power in the West. The "dominant market"—that at which goods may be most easily sold for the greatest profit—had shifted from the Bosphorus to the Baltic, to the North Sea, to the Rhine, and to the Rhône. Therefore the tide of commerce which had heretofore flowed down the Dnieper to the Black Sea was suddenly reversed. Russian caravans no longer sought the sacked and silent markets of Kieff; they came to Novgorod from south, from east, from north, bringing the luxuries of the East, gathering up all the products of the Russian world, especially the furs, for transports to the markets of the West, where the cold climate and the unheated houses made these more of a necessity than a luxury. "We strive for a garment of marten," wrote Adam of Bremen, "as if for our soul's salvation." Nor was it only the trade of Russia that felt the influence of the new buying power of the West; all the traffic of the great Norse Empire, from Greenland to Gothland, instead of seeking the Varangian Route as heretofore, now met the reversed and west-bound current of Russian commerce and, thus reinforced, poured as through a funnel into the ports of Northern Europe, thence flowing along new trade routes that crossed Europe from the North Sea to the Mediterranean.

The Varangian Route received its first serious blow in the Tenth Century when Otto the Great defeated the Magyars in 955, thereby enabling commerce to flow freely up the Rhine from Cologne, then the seaport of Germany, and over the Alpine passes to Venice, the terminus of the sea route from Constantinople. About the same time Venice won control of the Adriatic by her victory over Croatian pirates, thereby securing, with the help of the strong Byzantine fleet which patrolled the Eastern Mediterranean, uninterrupted commercial intercourse with Byzantium. Thus the first Western trade route was opened from the North Sea through Venice to the Bosphorus.

Commerce always creates more commerce, and the traffic on the Rhine, pressing for greater opportunities, sent out strong tides towards the East which surged against the Iron Gates of the river Danube—gates which had been closed for five hundred years by barbarian invaders.

In the late Tenth Century these gates were broken down by the conversion of Hungary to Christianity, and by the Byzantine conquest of pagan Bulgaria. Thus the energies of Christian priest and soldiers opened the longest river in Europe, except the Volga, and gave the merchants of Southern Germany freedom of travel over the shortest route to Constantinople, direct contact with the Black Sea, and access to all Southeastern Europe.

Finally, in the second half of the Eleventh Century the Western Mediterranean—which had carried the commerce of the world through Cretan, Egyptian, Phœnician, Greek, Roman, and Merovingian days, was reopened to Christian merchants by the defeat of the Saracens who had closed the sea gates and controlled all Western waters since their seizure of Sicily, Sardinia, Corsica, with the shores of Southern Italy and of Provence in the Ninth Century.

As long as Moslem fleets dominated the sea from Gibraltar to Messina all the Western Mediterranean stagnated and Marseilles, Genoa, Pisa, and their sister cities were strangled in the Saracenic grip. In the early Eleventh Century, however, the Normans, whose forefathers centuries before had opened the Varangian Route, entered the Straits of Gibraltar, landed in Italy, and for their first exploit, drove the Arabs from Salerno. For years thereafter many Normans, landless younger sons or gentlemen who felt the sting of poverty, left their homes to seek fortunes in the South until one of them, Robert Guiscard, became strong enough through such reinforcements to drive the Saracens from Sicily and Southern Italy, and to unite the ports of Amalfi, Salerno, Bari, Tarentum and Palermo under a single rule. Genoa and Pisa helped in the task by defeating the Moslem fleet in the harbour of Cagliari and by the year 1070, on the eve of the Crusades, the control of all Western waters had passed into Christian hands.

While neither Guiscard nor any of his contemporaries could foresee the militant movement of the Crusades that was launched at Clermont in 1096 by Pope Urban and by Peter the Hermit, yet the freedom of the Mediterranean was the first and necessary step in that great assault upon the Islamic powers, and the Crescent had hardly vanished from Sicilian waters before the Cross was rallying its warriors in the West.

Behind this first Crusade there was more of a sincere religious purpose than there was in any later gathering of the West against the East; it was

"no vulgar war for a vulgar prize, but an alliance with the supernatural for the conquest of talismans whose possession was tantamount to omnipotence. Urban's words at Clermont have lost their meaning now, but they burned like fire into the hearts of his hearers then for he promised them glory on earth and felicity in heaven. If they triumphed, the blessings of heaven and the kingdoms of the East would be their share; if they fell, they would have the glory of dying where Christ had died, and God would not forget that He had seen them in His holy armies. They were an invincible army, marching to certain victory. In the Eleventh Century this was not a metaphor, for the Cluniac monk spoke as the mouthpiece of a God who was among them, promising triumphs—not the common triumphs which may be won by man's

SAINTE CHAPELLE, PARIS

Erected by S. Louis as a shrine for the Crown of Thorns, these walls of glass, whose huge windows stretch almost sixty-seven feet from base to peak, have only narrow pillars of stone to support them.

unaided strength, but the transcendent glory which belongs to beings of another world." [3]

The appeal of the Hermit was even more stirring than that of the Pope. Peter had made the pilgrimage to Jerusalem where he fearlessly pledged the succour of Western Christendom to the despondent Patriarch. Prostrate in the temple, he thought he heard the voice of the God of Moses and of Joshua saying, "Rise, Peter, go forth to make known the tribulations of my people; the hour is come for the delivery of my servants, for the recovery of the holy places."

Returning to Europe, Peter rode through all lands, seated on a mule, crucifix in hand, girded in a robe of the coarsest stuff. Preaching in markets and at cross-roads as well as in churches with an eloquence which moved all hearts, since it came from his own, he appealed to every passion—to valour and shame, to indignation and pity, to the pride of the warrior, the compassion of the man, the religion of the Christian, the hatred of the Unbeliever, the desire to expiate sins, and the hope of Heaven. He invoked the Holy Angels, the Saints, the Mother of God, the Lord Himself to bear witness to his truth. He called on the Holy Places—on Mt. Zion, on Calvary, on the Holy Sepulchre—to lift up their voices and implore deliverance; he made the very ivory Christ upon his crucifix cry out for succour. Miracles attended his passage, and the people fought for the hairs that dropped from his mule as for treasured relics. [4]

For two years Peter had thus been preparing the ground, and when he stood with Urban to call the Christian world to arms the response of that world had already been determined. Yet, devout as may have been the intentions of the Church and the enthusiasms of the majority, the actual results of the Crusades were more beneficial to the traffic of Europe than to its religion, and their ultimate consequences were the commercializing of the Christian West rather than the Christianizing of the Moslem East.

A triumphant Cross, when worn over armour, enabled commerce to

[3] Brookes Adams, *Law of Civilization and Decay*, p. 83.
[4] H. H. Milman, *Latin Christianity*.

sail over an opened sea from the harbours of Marseilles, Genoa, Venice, Pisa, and Amalfi to those of Tripolis, Tyre, Acre, and Alexandria. When the Fourth Crusade captured Constantinople and established Italian trading posts on the Black Sea, a great commercial crescent was completed along which the traffic of both East and West vibrated between the Baltic, the Mediterranean, the Levant, the Bosphorus, and the Black Sea. Along this crescent the raw materials of the Occident flowed freely eastward while, with equal freedom, the luxuries of the Orient sailed in the wake of Crusaders' ships to arouse Marseilles from her long slumbers and to clothe the cities of Italy with dominion, with wealth, and with splendours that still endure.

Of all the nations that enlisted in the Crusades the Italians entered the Holy War with the clearest eyes and the most realistic philosophy. The ships of Genoa, Pisa, and Venice were needed for the transportation of men and horses, for the capture of seaports, and for the maintenance of a service of supplies. The necessities of France were the opportunities of Italy, whose merchant princes, intent on profits and driving hard bargains, demanded quarters, free of taxes, in every coastal town they helped to capture. Thus *fondaci* sprang up in Syrian seaports—walled enclosures along the water-front, ruled by foreign merchants who were subject only to the authorities of their native cities. Pisa, Genoa, and Venice formed the "big three" among these Levantine powers, but they did not stand alone; Tudela, the Spanish Jew, counted twenty-eight cities that possessed quarters, or trading posts, in Alexandria in the Twelfth Century.

Men cannot, however, serve both God and Mammon, and the motives of the Crusaders grew less mixed as time went by and as the commercial opportunities of the conquest became more clearly evident. The West began to view the East with a single eye—an eye that flamed with the avariciousness of the trader, not with the rapture of the pilgrim. Richard of England might weep over lost Jerusalem from the heights of Mizpah but the "Merchants of Venice" sorrowed only for the loss of Tyre, its quays and its caravans, and the force of the Third Crusade was spent not in the rescue of the Holy Sepulchre but in the alleviation of an Italian sorrow—sorrow for the loss of coastal cities that were vital to Western trade.

By the time of the Fifth Crusade the itching palms of the West were clinging so much more tightly to their counters than to the Cross that when the Sultan of Egypt offered to deliver all the holy places of Palestine into Christian hands in exchange for his own city of Damietta the offer was refused. Without the stroke of a sword the leaders of this Crusade might have entered into possession of Bethlehem, Nazareth, Bethany, Gethsemane, Calvary, and the Holy Sepulchre; but again Barabbas was chosen instead of Christ. Cairo and Constantinople were the two richest cities west of India; and the Crusaders, already glutted with the spoils of the latter city, saw in Damietta the gateway to the plunder of the first; but the change that had come over Europe, even over the Church, since the days of Clermont, is made more clear by the fact that the voice which rejected the offer of the Sultan, which demanded Damietta and refused Jerusalem, was none other than that of Cardinal Pelagius, a Prince of the Church and the Legate of Pope Honorius III.

The temptation was doubtless great for, in addition to the riches of Cairo, the cities of the Levant spread the ancient vision before the eyes of the Crusaders, and through their gates they saw "all the kingdoms of the world and the glory of them," for the roads from those cities, piercing the great mountain barriers that bordered the sea, ran eastward and did not halt until they reached the distant lands of India and China.

Over these ancient highways from Asia, from the Persian Gulf, and from the Red Sea came the products of all the Eastern World—of India, China, the Islands of the East, from Arabia and East Africa—to be poured into the holds of Genoese or Venetian vessels for transportation to the markets of the West. Here came pearls from Ceylon, precious stones from India, spices from Sunda, perfumes from Arabia, ivories from Africa—the varieties of places and of products seem endless, while from Syria itself countless products of fields, forests, and factories flowed forth to Europe like a flood.

The trade with the East steadily increased in volume until it overflowed all Europe, even reaching to Far Iceland, and as it flowed it revolutionized the habits and standards of living. Luxuries became necessities so that, even after the Kingdom of Jerusalem had fallen and the age of the Crusades was over, the stream of commerce continued to flow, for the contacts created during the Christian occupation of Syria had broken down the barriers of race, colour, and creed. With mutual respect and understanding established, with respective financial profits at stake, Christian and Moslem sovereigns signed such treaties as that between the Sultan of Tunis, Philip III of France, and Thibaut of Navarre whereby the signatory powers pledged especial protection to the merchants of either faith when travelling in their domains. With the sea open from East to West, with all ports—African, Italian, French, and Catalan—busy and prosperous, even the papal thunders could not check the profitable traffic with the infidel.

Of all the countries of Europe, France, because of her geography, was best able to absorb and profit by this traffic, for the Rhône flows into the Mediterranean, the Loire to the Atlantic, and the Seine to the English Channel. These rivers, with many other navigable streams, converge towards their sources in the heart of the country and offer an almost interlocking system of water-ways whereby the commerce of the world could be distributed from end to end of France. Along these rivers fairs and markets multiplied, and industry blossomed like Aaron's rod, for in all the hinterlands of these streams, in all districts within reach of these markets, manufactories increased and flourished.

Thus when Suger was building his abbey of S. Denis, when Bishop Geoffrey was raising his fine tower at Chartres, when the crusading bishop Alberic de Humbert was laying the foundations of Rheims, and Evrard de Fouilloy was blessing the corner-stone of Amiens, when Notre-Dame de Paris, Soissons, Sens, Laon, and half a thousand other great churches were rising from the soil of France, the commerce of the North was pouring into French markets from the steppes of Russia, the fjords of Scandinavia, and the fishing villages of Iceland.

At the same time great fleets were bringing the wealth of the South from Egypt, Lybia, Tunis, Algiers, and Morocco, or the riches of the Orient from India, China, Sumatra, and Ceylon, to the busy ports of

Marseilles, Genoa, or Venice. From the holds of these vessels the tributes of the world were transferred to caravans or to river boats which bore them over the Alpine passes to Burgundy; down the Rhine to Flanders, or up the swift currents of the Rhône to the fairs of Nîmes, of Avignon, Beaucaire, Lyons, and Champagne. From Champagne the imports that stream into France from both North and South were scattered widely over the land; the Loire bore them to the fairs of Chinon and of Tours; the Saône carried them to Chalons, and the Seine to Rouen. Countless other towns or cities received the commerce of the world from the caravans that travelled interlacing roads or from cargoes that were borne along the marvellous network of rivers that enriched "the pleasant land of France."

Thus the kings of Sheba and of Seba offered gifts; Tarshish and the Isles brought presents; kings of the East sent gold, frankincense, and myrrh, and "God snowed churches upon the land."

BROOKES ADAMS, *Law of Civilization and Decay; New Empire.*
P. BOISSONADE, *Life and Work in the Middle Ages.*
D. KNOOP and G. P. JONES, *The Mediæval Mason,* Chap. IV.
J. W. THOMPSON, *Economic and Social History of the Middle Ages*

Chapter Eighteen

GOTHIC ARCHITECTURE

THE same centuries which launched the Crusades against the coasts of Palestine, multiplied famous universities, and raised up both powerful popes and forceful heretics, also created a new type of architecture—a type which differed from the Romanesque as radically as that, in turn, had differed from the basilican.

Italians of the Renaissance, despising this architecture as barbaric, gave it the name of a barbarian tribe and called it "Gothic." The slur, adopted by the neo-classicists of the Seventeenth Century, was finally fastened upon the churches of the Twelfth and Thirteenth Centuries during the pre-Revolutionary period in France.

Racine called Gothic art "barbarous;" Voltaire deemed it a "coarse curiosity lacking in good taste;" Molière complained that it "waged a mortal battle with refinement," while its churches were "monsters of ignorant times," and Goethe, in his *Italian Journeys,* translated the French epithets into German and added a few of his own.

About the time of the French Revolution it was proposed to free the soil of France from the artistic handicap of these "overcharged façades, with their multitudes of indecent and ridiculous figures." [1]

To the contempt of the academicians was added the antagonisms of the people who saw prelates sharing the privileges of nobles, and bishops championing the autocracies of kings. When, therefore, all passions were unchained, when blind monsters from the depths were cast up to the surface in the eruptions of the Revolution, few stood forth to

---

[1] E. B. O'Reilly, *How France Built Her Cathedrals,* p. 36; Paul Léon, *Les Monuments Historiques,* Chaps. I and II.

defend the architectural achievements of the Middle Ages from the iconoclasms of the mob.[2]

The proletariat of France, whether organized into violent governments or into howling rabbles, tore down many great churches, both Romanesque and Gothic, and desecrated many others whose priceless windows of jewelled glass were everywhere broken, whose aisles were turned into stables, and whose sculptures, the work of reverential hands through many centuries, were chipped by bullets or broken by the rifle butts of a drunken soldiery.

The church of S. Benigne at Dijon fell before the patriotic zeal of an apothecary who daily climbed a ladder to smash, with his mallet, all the stone-cutter's work within his reach. His efforts, although praiseworthy, were too slow, so the pick-axe was called upon to level the church which S. Gregorius had founded in the year 507 and which William of Volpiano rebuilt in 1002.

The cathedral at Clermont Ferrand, riddled with bullets, barely escaped destruction from the bonfires that were set blazing in the nave, while the old abbatial church of S. Martial at Limoges and the basilica of S. Martin at Tours—the oldest and the holiest shrine in France—were dismembered and destroyed.

The great Norman abbey at Jumièges, consecrated one year after the battle of Hastings, was bought by a contractor of Rouen who blew up the apse and then quarried the ruins for building stones. Cluny, grey with years, after surviving the storms of time and war from Carlovingian to Corsican days, fell before a merchant of Macon who bought it for a quarry, blew up the narthex, the transepts, and the great tower with gunpowder, and ran a road into the nave. Doubtless there are today stables, barns, and pig-sties in Burgundy built from the thousand-year-old stones of the great Benedictine abbey which sent forth Pope Urban II to preach the first Crusade, Pascal II to force the abdication of Henry IV of Germany and—greatest of all—the monk

[2] Two artists risked their lives to protect the Cathedral of Tours from the guillotine-spirit which had planned and prepared to destroy it, while the glass of S. Ouen in Rouen was only spared because a troop of Revolutionary cavalry, using the church as a barrack, objected to the wintry blasts which would have swept the aisles had the mob been permitted to break the windows.

Hildebrand who, as Pope Gregory VII, humbled a barefooted emperor waiting in sackcloth before the papal gates amid the snows of Canossa.

Only the difficulty of disposing of so great a quantity of stone prevented the destruction of Chartres, and even Notre-Dame in Paris was offered for sale. Escaping the fate of Jumièges and of Cluny by the merest chance, it was turned into a Temple of Reason where a deified prostitute sat on the altar while her sister professionals danced the *Carmagnole* beneath the grey vaults of the nave. Before long, however, the people discovered that their new goddess was too *maigre et jaune* and laughed her from her throne, whereupon the church, where an English sovereign had been crowned king of France and a Navarrese Protestant had won the throne with a mass, was converted into a hall for fêtes and finally into a warehouse.

Thus the men of the Revolution, destroying and defacing both Romanesque and Gothic cathedrals, blindly executed the sentences pronounced by Humanists and Classicists alike who had defined the architecture of the Twelfth and Thirteenth Centuries in terms of their contempt and had christened it in mockery with the name of a barbarian tribe. But we, feeling that the builders of these centuries "could do nothing in poor taste," and recognizing the fundamental differences between the Romanesque Notre-Dame in Poitiers and the Gothic Notre-Dame in Paris, must now define their work in terms of structure rather than in those of prejudice.

Gothic architecture is essentially a method of supporting a stone vault without such a sacrifice of grace, light, or height as the Romanesque entailed. Achieved by the very form of the vault itself, and by a combination of transverse and diagonal ribs, flying buttresses, and pointed arches, it derived added beauty from walls of jewelled glass, from piers of clustering shafts, and from a great increase in the height of the vault.

Perhaps we can best explain the difference between the Romanesque and the Gothic by those developments in our own day which, by turning our buildings into towers, have made canyons of our streets. Builders today raise an inner skeleton of steel which, having been nois-

ily riveted together, assumes all responsibility for that structural stability which was borne by heavy walls in Victorian years. In like manner the cathedral architect of the Twelfth Century learned to erect an
inner skeleton of stone instead of steel, in such a manner that the segments of his vault, the piers, and the vault ribs (especially when these
underlay vaults that were highly domed) received and transmitted to
the ground, either directly through the piers or indirectly through the
flying arches and their exterior supports, all the weights and thrusts
of the stone vault which had formerly fallen along the entire length
of the massive Romanesque walls. Relieved of this burden, the walls
of the Gothic church could be turned into glass, as have those of our
great commercial buildings. Thus in both mediæval and in modern
architecture the walls serve the purposes of shelter, not those of structural support.

The Gothic builder began his skeleton by throwing transverse arches,
or ribs, across his central aisle, dividing it into compartments, or bays,
which might be vaulted separately. Then he spanned each bay with
two diagonal arches that ran from corner pier to corner pier, intersecting each other at right angles at the crown of the vault. Within
this spider-web of transverse and diagonal ribs he raised the masonry
of his vault whose weight passed through the piers to the foundations
and thence to the ground, and whose lateral thrusts were transmitted
through the flying arches, which overleaped the side aisle roofs, to massive exterior buttresses. Thus an exterior articulation of flying arches
and stationary buttresses supplemented the inner skeleton of ribs and
piers.

If the Gothic builders had done no more than to shift the responsibility for the structural stability of their churches from the walls to the
piers it would have been necessary to make these so stout and strong
that they would have deformed the church, making lightness and
grace as difficult for Gothic as for Romanesque architecture.

To avoid the ponderous forms of the Romanesque and to give lightness and grace to his church the Gothic architect employed three
devices. First, he lightened the weight of his vault by diminishing its

thickness, since the panels, or "webs," unlike the masonry of the barrel vault which was sometimes nearly two feet thick, could be given a depth of only a few inches.

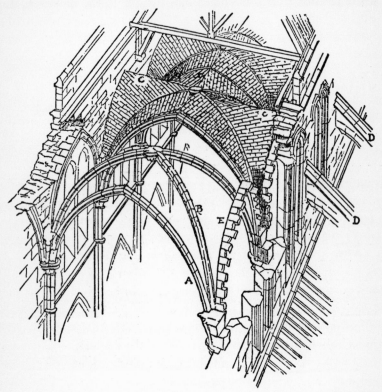

T. G. Jackson

THE THRUST AND COUNTER-THRUST OF A GOTHIC VAULT

A—transverse rib; B—diagonal, or cross, rib; C—web;
D—flying arch; E—wall rib.

Second, he brought into general use the pointed arch in which each stone, instead of being held in place mainly by pressure from the side, as in the barrel vault, was partially supported by the stones of the arch that lay below it. This form of arch, supporting the nave vault, very greatly reduced its outward thrust, while the part it played throughout the church was so important that it has been popularly, if erroneously, accepted as the defining element in Gothic architecture.

Third, he balanced thrust with thrust high up on the clerestory wall where pressure from one vaulted bay, running to the northwest, met

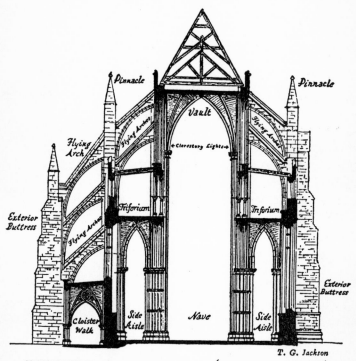

T. G. Jackson

CROSS SECTION OF A GOTHIC CHURCH (WESTMINSTER ABBEY)

that of an adjoining bay which ran towards the northeast; these two thrusts meeting on their supports, resulted in a lateral drive which could be successfully met by the flying arches for these, spanning the side-aisle roofs and impinging on the clerestory wall, received and carried the outward thrust to the stout exterior buttresses, whence it was transmitted to the ground.

Thus the fundamental difference between Romanesque and Gothic architecture lies in the fact that the monks of the Eleventh Century accepted the outward thrusts of their heavy barrel vaults as an inevitable burden upon the side walls of their churches, and built these walls massive and low to resist the strain; therefore their churches suggest a wrestler crouching to withstand the onslaught of an antagonist. Gothic architects, on the contrary, refusing to accept this thrust as unavoidable, first diverted the pressure from the walls to the piers and buttresses, and then set themselves to minimizing the strain on their skeleton by making their vaults thinner, by pointing their arches, and by balancing the thrusts that fell on the piers by the support of flying arches with their exterior buttresses, and of the side-aisle vaults. In this attempt they so far succeeded that they were able to send their vaults soaring into the air and to turn their stone walls into glass. So the crouching wrestler, his adversary thrown, stands upright, lifts his head, and stretches all his limbs.

The consequences that flowed from the adoption of the new vault were many and varied.

The barrel vault, with its simple, graceful sweep, was replaced by one which became increasingly intricate as the years went by. The early sexpartite vault gave way to the quadripartite and then to the octopartite; vaults with ridge ribs and tiercerons were followed by lierne and fan vaultings as the ribs overhead were multiplied until they became more decorative than structural. The broad rectangular piers or thick girthed columns, whose mass had been relieved in the Eleventh Century only by flat pilasters or rounded half columns to support the smaller arches of the nave arcade, were turned into clusters of graceful, encircling shafts. Some of these slender columns, replacing the pilasters and demi-columns of the Eleventh Century, supported the side-aisle vaults; others climbed the nave walls, past triforium and clerestory galleries, to receive the multiplied diagonal or transverse arches that spanned the nave.

Pointed arches also made possible wider and loftier ambulatories, where the problem of vaulting a curving aisle was solved by abandoning the attempt to run straight diagonal arches across each compartment and by substituting "broken ribs"—ribs that ran out at convenient angles from a central keystone.

They also made possible greater altitudes in aisles and chapels, as well as in naves, choirs, and chancels. The plain walls of the Romanesque church were succeeded by walls in four divisions, where triforium and clerestory galleries, with clerestory lights, rose above the arches of the aisles. The walls were turned from stone to glass, and the whole church vaulted into space.

The yard-stick will tell the tale, for while the Romanesque vault of S. Benigne was sixty-five feet in height, that of S. Sernin sixty-nine, and that of Cluny, loftiest of all Romanesque structures, ninety-eight, the first great Gothic vault at S. Denis rose ninety-five feet above the pavement; the second, at Noyon, was higher still by several feet; at Rheims the height of the vault is one hundred and twenty-six feet, at Amiens one hundred and forty-four feet; and at Beauvais it is nearly one hundred and sixty feet. The nave of S. Benigne might be superimposed upon that of S. Sernin, and both could easily be slipped into the nave of Amiens; while the Tower Bridge of London—towers and all—might be placed beneath the vault of Beauvais. The Gothic church thus began to soar at the very point where the most aspiring of Romanesque churches ended its upward flight.

Not only did the church of the Twelfth Century become lighter in form; it became lighter also in its illumination. The small, splayed windows of Romanesque days, which would have been as incongruous in a Gothic cathedral as the great windows of Bourges would have been impossible in Notre-Dame du Port, could now be abandoned for the builders, having lightened the weights of their vaults and transferred the burdens from the walls to the piers, were able to meet the demands of the new architecture for more and larger windows, finally turning the whole wall between the buttresses into glass, as at S. Ouen in Rouen, S. Chapelle in Paris, S. Etienne in Bourges, and the church in Grand Andelys.

All the elements which we have been analyzing—diagonal ribs, clustered columns, pointed arches, flying buttresses, and exterior supports—are so characteristic of the Gothic that, if the laity sometimes define this architecture in the terms of the pointed arch, there are scholars who would define it in terms of its structure; they tell us that "wherever thrust is not met by counter-thrust—there we have not Gothic."

But the architecture of the Twelfth and Thirteenth Centuries cannot be defined by any one, nor by any combination, of its elements. The whole is far greater than the sum of all its parts. We may, for convenience' sake, regard it as a skeleton of ribs, arches, piers, and buttresses; but even so might the anatomist look upon the body of dead Lazarus as a mere articulation of bones, muscles, veins, arteries, and organs. There was another Lazarus, however, who might not be so defined, wherefore Mary and Martha wept and were not comforted.

Such churches as York, Canterbury, Cologne, Chartres, Rheims, and Bourges may not be defined in terms of matter alone. They must also be defined in those of spirit; the cathedrals of the Middle Ages express the lofty rivalry of city against city to bring the best gifts to God; they reveal the zeal of countless unknown masons, carving with devout care and skill, not merely where the eyes of men might see but high up on the walls, in darkened corners beneath the vaults and eaves where only God can see.

Gothic architecture was the gift of that revived and active commerce which came by sea to all the parts of Europe and of England, or that followed continental water-ways—the Rhine, the Elbe, the Rhône, Loire, Garonne, or Seine—from city to city and from fair to fair; but not all the wealth of Europe, by itself, could have produced a single bay of Chartres, Amiens, or Rheims. No Twelfth Century builder of Lombardy, for instance, where the minds of men were dominated by political or secular interests, could have combined the elements and formulas for the countering of stresses and strains into the erection of an Italian Chartres. Gothic architecture was a supreme triumph of mathematics, yet it is not the work of the mathematician; it was a great achievement of engineering science, but it is not a masterpiece of the engineer. It may not be expressed in equations which exclude those of faith. Only the qualities of the spirit—devout, romantic, poetic and heroic—which animated the Gothic centuries, and that deep faith, more mellow and no less confident than that of the Romanesque century, could have created this architecture, for the Gothic, like the

Romanesque, was the work of men who believed profoundly in God, in His saints, and in miracles. In every line the Gothic church reveals the lofty idealism of the Age, its asceticism, its disdain for the visible, and its absolute conviction that faith in the Unseen is the greatest power in the world.

Chapter Nineteen

THE ORIGIN OF THE GOTHIC VAULT

A MOST interesting chapter might be written on the part that accident has played in human history, not the least enthralling being the rôle that chance has played in architecture. One illustration concerns us here, for it was because there were no trees on the Lombard Plain, which had been deforested even before the fall of Rome, that a new type of vault was discovered which was destined to revolutionize architecture and to lead, in another century and another land, to the supreme achievements of the Gothic.

Timber was essential to Romanesque architecture, for an enormous quantity of beams and planks was required for the scaffolding, and for the centring—a wooden form, or mould, upon which the builders rested the stones of their vault until the masonry was self-sustaining, and the mortar had hardened, when scaffolding and centring could be removed.

The demand for timber was all the greater because planks, of which great quantities were needed, had to be cut out by hand—a method which was tedious, difficult, and wasteful; the builder had to "go into the forest, cut down a tree, trim it, and then with an adze hack away first one side of the trunk and then the other; result—a plank; one tree, one plank," and a multitude of chips.[1]

The problem then of erecting a barrel vault pressed heavily upon the architects of Lombardy, who had to import all their timber since forests were unknown on their alluvial plain. But such importation was not easy, for timber, which could not be carried on the backs of mules and required some form of wheeled conveyance, demanded roads instead of trails.

[1] Bond, *Introduction to English Church Architecture*, p. 288.

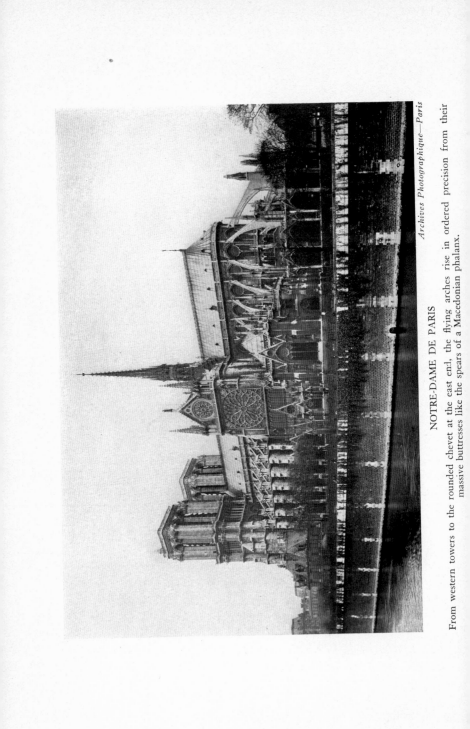

NOTRE-DAME DE PARIS

From western towers to the rounded chevet at the east end, the flying arches rise in ordered precision from their massive buttresses like the spears of a Macedonian phalanx.

The roads, however, were not only bad but were also rarely safe since the almost constant wars between the city-states interrupted all peaceful commerce for long periods of time. Such conditions demanded some method of erecting stone vaults with a minimum of scaffolding.

The problem was not new and the answer was slow in coming, but at last some Italian builder of the Eleventh Century found the solution when he threw diagonal ribs across an aisle, thereby dividing its vault into four triangular compartments. Such cross-ribbed vaults appear in the Milanese churches of S. Ambrogio, S. Eustorgio, and S. Nazaro; they were also adopted by the architects of S. Stefano Rotondo in Bologna, and of S. Flaviano at Montefiascone, north of Rome.

In these new vaults a very light scaffolding sufficed for the erection of the ribs, and when these were in place a *cerce*—two curved boards made to slide along each other so that they could be lengthened or shortened at will—was suspended from them. This *cerce* served as a "centering" by means of which the stones of each compartment of the vault could be mortared into place in turn, the *cerce* being moved to another compartment when the first was finished.

The builders, by adopting this type of vault, were enabled to effect a very great economy in scaffolding, and that this was their purpose is suggested by the fact that wherever wood was plentiful—at the foot of the well-timbered Alps and in the neighbourhood of the Apennines—barrel and groin vaults continued to be preferred; in Bologna, however, where wood was scarce, and in Milan, where its cost must have been prohibitive, the architects turned gladly to the new diagonal ribbed vault.

That they had no structural purpose in mind is evidenced by the absence of any structural advantage in these early proto-Gothic experiments.

All these churches remained Romanesque in structure; their vaults were excessively thick—between sixteen and twenty inches, and the diagonal ribs played no part in their stability since no attempt was made to take advantage of the concentration of the thrusts which had been achieved by the very form of the vault, or to balance them by counter-thrusts. The walls, as at S. Ambrogio (Milan) were forty inches thick and quite stout enough to carry the weight, and resist the thrusts, even of a barrel vault. Furthermore, the early cross-ribbed vault was often erected where a groin would have done at least as well—under towers, in porches, side aisles, chapels, and crypts.

Nor did the builders have any æsthetic ends in view, as the ribs themselves testify; those at Aversa, for instance, are out of centre, enormously heavy, and very clumsy, while at Moissac they are over twenty-six inches in breadth, awkward and uncouth.

The force of logic, therefore, seems to support Mr. Porter's interpretation of the origin of these vaults—that they were invented to effect an economy in wood.

The Lombard builders thus made one of the two great discoveries upon which Gothic architecture rests when they devised a method for the erection of a stone vault with a minimum of scaffolding at a minimum of expense. They failed, however, to realize that their diagonal ribs outlined a form of vault which logically and structurally accomplished a concentration of its thrusts at certain points; that by counterbalancing these thrusts at such points their vaults could be made lighter, their walls given over to more and larger windows, and the entire church made loftier in all its parts. These discoveries, which were really those of Gothic architecture, had to await the dawn of another century.

It is one of the tragedies of architecture that the builders of Lombardy, having come within sight of this discovery, should have failed to realize its possibilities and turned back upon their path. But the reasons for the failure of the Italians to anticipate the French in the erection of Gothic churches are many and clear.

In the first place, "Gothic architecture is essentially a style based on stone work, and for its proper expression stone is absolutely essential." [2] But while the alluvial plain of Lombardy provided its cities generously with clay for brick, it offered very little stone.

Then the great struggle between the Empire and the Papacy, which from 1076 on turned Lombardy into a huge battle-field, diverted the

[2] Sturgis and Frothingham, *History of Architecture*, Vol. IV, p. 97.

THE ORIGIN OF THE GOTHIC VAULT 157

attention of men from architecture, while the Lombard's natural distrust of the Pope, in whom they saw a dangerous neighbour—sometimes an arch enemy—prevented the growth of that religious mysticism and enthusiasm which was, at this time, strongly influencing the rest of Europe. The dominant interests in Lombardy were political and practical; trade, commerce, political intrigues, and commercial rivalries so filled men's minds that the new vault on diagonal ribs was discovered only to be abandoned by its creators and rescued by strangers.

Fortunately for the future of architecture Italy was not only the *point d'appui* for all ambitious pilgrims whose eyes were fixed on Palestine; it was a Holy Land in itself. Half the world was trudging the roads that led to Lucca, Rome, or Bari with their famous shrines.

That these pilgrims brought back, each to his own country, the knowledge of the new Lombard device is evidenced by the fact that, almost simultaneously, diagonal ribbed vaults began to appear not only in France but also in England and in Germany. The coincidental appearance of cross-ribbed vaulting over so wide an area, and in so many countries, logically implies some common foreign source of origin. Nevertheless it was neither in England nor in Germany but in the Île-de-France that the builders caught the first glimmer of the dawn of Gothic architecture, for in the early years of the Twelfth Century vaults on diagonal ribs began to appear from Provence to Brittany—under a tower at Acy-en-Multien, in a side aisle at Rhuis, in a porch at Moissac, in a crypt at Saintes, in the Choir of Viffort, then over the naves of Airenes and Bellefontaine, and finally, in more heroic stature, at S. Denis.

The new architecture, however, entered France with no beat of drums, or sound of trumpet, to herald its coming. Indeed the opening years of the Twelfth Century were far too crowded with momentous events to enable men to turn their eyes aside to watch the doings of country masons.

When the Crusaders were overseas, when the Seljukes were being crushed at Antioch and the Fatimites at Ascalon, when Godfrey of Bouillon, refusing a crown where Jesus had worn thorns, was being proclaimed "Defender and Baron of the Holy Sepulchre," who could give heed to what the builders were doing beneath a tower of the little church at Acy-en-Multien?

And there were other things much nearer home. The English, to whom Robert of Normandy, going on Crusade, had pledged his duchy, were overseas occupying Rouen and moving down the Seine. Who cared what the architects were doing in a side aisle at Rhuis?

Nearer still, Bouchard, Lord of Montmorency, was battling with the King for S. Denis; you could almost hear the clash of arms from the city walls when the King defeated his unruly vassal. Did it matter what the builders were doing in a porch at Moissac?

The air was full of interesting rumours: King Philip was dying in Paris; Louis was being crowned in Orléans; Pope Pascal was coming to France; a village priest and serfs were aiding the new king to capture Le Puisset—were, indeed, the first to break through the walls; Louis was marching to "wash Flanders in much blood" for the murder of William the Good, slain at his prayers in a church of Bruges. Who could give heed to what the builders were doing in a crypt at Saintes?

Nevertheless these unknown builders and unremembered architects, when they raised their diagonal ribs at Acy-en-Multien, Rhuis, Moissac, and Saintes, were doing that which was far more important than the trouncing of Bouchard, the capture of Le Puisset, the voyaging of a pope, or the "washing of Flanders."

A new freedom was in the air; the towns were winning charters and gaining freedom from their overlords, be they counts or bishops; the guilds were increasing their rights and powers, even the serfs were securing larger measures of protected rights. And for the church a new freedom was moving north from Lombardy. Hitherto bound to the ground by the weight of her ponderous barrel vault, dwelling in darkness lest windows should weaken walls, the church of the Twelfth Century was about to be freed from her shackles and rise to exalted heights on wings that had been feathered on the plains of Lombardy. But those wings must strengthen their sinews in many a practice flight, and the builders must gain courage and experience. Therefore, throughout the first half of the Twelfth Century the architects of France were testing the new vault in country churches; they were

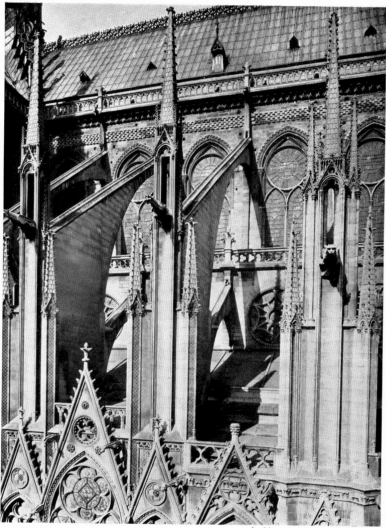

THE FLYING ARCHES AND PINNACLES OF NOTRE-DAME DE PARIS

These carry the lateral thrust of the Gothic vault down to the ground. The gargoyles, with their demoniac heads whose gaping mouths carried off the rain water, reminded all passers-by of those ever-present ministers of Hell from whom there was no safety except within the walls of Holy Church.

experimenting with it in crypts, porches, aisles, and chapels; they were learning to erect it over oblong as well as over square bays in the choirs and naves of unimportant churches. Little by little they learned that, having lightened the weight of their vault by diminishing its thickness, and having concentrated all its thrusts, they could counter these thrusts without calling for support from their walls, and thereby be enabled to meet the demand for more and for larger windows.

Thus the new architecture, conceived in Lombardy, nested in France, fluttering timidly at Viffort, sprang suddenly into full flight at S. Denis. Rising ever higher as it passed to Noyon, Chartres, Amiens, and Rheims, it reached its apogee in the Cathedral of Beauvais. Then, grown old, it began to circle downward, through Rayonnant and Flamboyant churches, coming ever closer to the earth.

Dum vivimus, vivamus; certainly Gothic architecture, while it lived, lived richly. Soaring to undreamed heights, it brought back to earth a glory that age cannot wither, nor custom stale; for such as this there is no dying.

A. K. PORTER, *The Construction of Lombard and Gothic Vaults; Mediæval Architecture,* Vol. I, Chap. V.

Chapter Twenty

THE ORIGIN OF THE FLYING BUTTRESS

LITTLE is left of the old Parisian Church of S. Julien-le-Pauvre, a withered and wrinkled octocentenarian on the left bank of the Seine with which time has dealt severely; still it is well worth visiting, not only for its venerable self but also for the view it offers of Notre-Dame who stretches her giant limbs before us from Western towers to Eastern apse. Along the flank and over the rounded chapels of the chevet flying arches sweep, like sheaves of spears, rising and falling in graceful curves from their massive buttresses.

We know their purpose; the builder placed these arches here that they might transfer the outward thrusts of a Gothic vault to their exterior supports. But when we wish to know their history and origin, they take us from the north to the south of France—from Normandy, where Duke William and Matilda his wife built their abbey churches in the city of Caen, to S. Sernin in Toulouse where half-barrel vaults over the aisles abut the thrusts of the barrel vault which spans the nave.

Never did father conceive so strange a son; never was son so unlike a father, but the fact remains that the dark and sombre vault which covers the side aisles of S. Sernin is parent to the light and graceful flying arches that sweep over the aisles or chapels of Notre-Dame. Here, in the little park which has replaced S. Julien's cloister, we may—in such peace and quiet as children, their nurses, and park politicians will permit—follow these arches in their wandering course from the Île-de-France to Normandy, and thence southward to the land of their nativity in old *langue d'oc*.

When William the Conqueror built the Abbaye-aux-Hommes at Caen (in order to purchase peace with the Church for his offence in marrying his cousin, Matilda of Flanders) he vaulted the nave in wood.

About the end of the first quarter of the Twelfth Century this wooden vault was replaced by the existing Gothic vault which demanded a change in the system of buttressing, for the walls which had been adequate to uphold the original vault could not be expected to sustain a vault of stone.

Looking to the southward, the Twelfth Century architects of Normandy saw half-barrel vaults over the side aisles of S. Sernin bracing the stone vault of the nave; but when they did more than look, when they copied from the South and threw half-barrel vaults across the side aisles of William's Norman church, they endangered his entire structure.

The problem of buttressing a barrel vault is quite different from that of buttressing a Gothic vault; that which serves in the one case disserves in the other.

The barrel vault exerts a continuous outward pressure along its whole extent, which may be safely resisted by the equally continuous inward pressure of a half-barrel vault; thus the two counterbalance each other.

But the Gothic vault concentrates all its weights and thrusts at definite points where they may be met and countered by the support of the exterior buttresses through the flying arches. Thus the nave walls which lie between the piers are not called upon to sustain any pressure from the vault at all.

If, then, the architect throws a half-barrel vault across his side aisles, and a Gothic vault across his nave, he will find that his aisle vaults are discharging a continuous inward pressure against the nave walls between the piers for which his Gothic vault provides no balancing counter-thrust.

This is exactly what the Norman builders did in the Twelfth Century when they rebuilt William's wooden vault in stone, and nothing but the great strength of the walls which the earlier builders had raised saved the old Abbaye from collapse.

The fault was corrected a few years later, in the Abbaye-aux-Dames, when a Gothic vault was placed over Matilda's church. Here the dangerous inward thrust of the half-barrel vault was avoided by cutting out that part of the side-aisle vault which lay between the piers, thus leaving only those sections of the buttressing vault which met the outward thrust of the nave vault above the piers. The result was the reduction of the half-barrel vault to a series of quarter-round arches which were braced on the one side by the stout exterior walls, and on the other side by the lateral thrust of the nave vaulting.

It should be added that in both cases, in William's church and in Matilda's, the buttressing of the nave vault was out of sight, hidden away above the roofs of the side aisles.

But the quarter-round arches by which the vault of Matilda's church was supported were really flying buttresses.

The full application of the newly discovered principle was left to the architects of the Île-de-France. They took the concealed flying arches of the Norman churches from their hiding places above the triforium galleries, placed them outside, instead of inside, the church and grounded them in stationary buttresses.

One thing more: when these exterior buttresses, rising solidly from the ground, have sent forth their flying arches, they rise still higher to end in graceful pinnacles which bristle with curving crotchets or with stone fleur-de-lis. These pinnacles, however, are not idle decorations; they have serious work to do and are not here just to please the eye.

Place the tip of the index finger of one hand against the top of the same finger on the other hand, and then press; now shift the pressure downward to the second joint of the index finger and again press. You will find that the resistance has grown stronger and can be overcome only by a much greater effort.

That is a fairly accurate illustration of the structural effect of these pinnacles. Without them the pressure of the arches would fall at the top of the buttress where the resistance would be least effective; with them, the lateral thrust falls much nearer the centre of the buttress and is diverted from a side to a downward direction. In other words, the pinnacle is placed on top of the buttress to "ground the thrust" of the flying arch.

Chapter Twenty-one

SYMBOLISM

"IF MEN should hold their peace," said Jesus as He entered Jerusalem, "the stones would immediately cry out."

In the Thirteenth Century all men knew that God, in creating, had made every created thing a symbol of His purposes. He had commissioned the eagle, bearing his young upon his wings, to declare the strength of the Everlasting Arms; the pelican, feeding her young from her own veins, to proclaim the sacrifice of Christ; the lion, breathing life into his dead cubs, to pledge our resurrection, and the fox, to warn us of the wiles of Satan. The falling leaves of autumn, the bursting buds of spring, the birds of the air, beasts of the fields, and creatures of the woods, all joined their voices in a chorused Litany.

If the entire universe thus spoke in celestial strains it was inevitable that the church, raised by men to the glory of God, should be no less eloquent, that from weather-vane to crypt, from Western portal to Eastern chapel, every stone in the cathedral should have a message for him whose eyes are open and whose ears can hear. Thus the triple portals of the Western front speak to us of the three great mysteries—the love of the Father, the sacrifice of the Son, and the guidance of the Holy Spirit—by which we who were afar have been brought near. The double door-ways of the central portal, divided by a statue of the Christ, remind us of the dual nature of Him who was both Son of God and Son of Man. The north side of the church, the side of the cold and the dark where no man would willingly be buried, tells us that we were born under a Law that is impotent to save, but the porch on that cheerless side, dedicated to Mary, comforts with the promise of redemption through a Child whom a virgin bore.

Although this symbolism did not create, although every part of the church came into being to meet some practical need, yet the mind of man speedily poured itself into every nook and cranny of the building and took possession in the name of God.

It is easy for us to smile at the credulities of the Middle Ages, at men who could really believe that the hart, disgorging floods of water from his mouth, drowned out the dragon from his hiding place among the rocks and then cut him to pieces with his sharp hoofs that he might symbolize the descent of man's Redeemer into Hell; but if they were credulous, so too are we, as our mediums and fortune-tellers testify. They may have believed too much but we, like them, believe too much and, unlike them, believe too little. If they never doubted the existence and baneful activities of devils, witches, and all their kin, neither did they doubt the reality of God, in whom they believed very simply and very deeply.

Led by men of brilliant intellectual abilities, they developed a profound philosophy whereby they interpreted their world in terms of God, instead of defining God in terms of a material Universe. In the spread of that philosophy of Faith to the common people, the stones of the cathedral had their important part.

We have already seen that the transepts were probably added to the basilica to accommodate the rush of burdened Romans who wished to join the ranks of the tax-exempt clergy; but that prosaic explanation was long since swept into oblivion by the Symbolists who fastened upon the world the conviction that the cruciform church came into being to proclaim the fundamental fact of Christianity—the Cross of Calvary.

So the Symbolists offer their own interpretation of the "inclination of the apse." If the walls of the chancel are not in the same straight line with those of the choir and the nave, if they bend to the right or to the left, this inclination, they say, is to symbolize the supreme moment when Jesus, crying, "It is finished," dropped His head upon His breast. In reality the walls were deflected for a much more practical purpose; they were "inclined" to prevent the foreshortening of the church.

When you travel by train the telegraph poles that are near you stand wide apart; as these recede into the background, however, they seem to merge together, and the consciousness of the intervening spaces is lost until the train rounds a curve; then the poles again disengage themselves and you once more become conscious of the distances between them. In like manner, when you enter a church, the columns of the nave that are near at hand stand far apart, but as your eye travels down the aisles towards the chancel the columns seem to run together and the sense of distance is lessened, if not lost. The same thing is true of the walls; these also coalesce as they recede, and are thereby deprived of their real values. If, however, the architect bends the chancel walls slightly so that the eye may pass from point to point along their surfaces, then—as with the telegraph poles when the train rounds the curve—the sense of distance and of depth is again restored. Not, then, to symbolize the falling of a dying head upon the breast, but to do justice to his own handiwork, did the architect "incline" his apse, for only so could he prevent the foreshortening of his church and bring out the full dignity and impressiveness of its depth.

A similar example of a symbolic meaning given to a purely practical development is found in the Symbolists' explanation of the round and octagonal forms which were adopted by the early Church for the baptistry, and so perpetuated in the baptismal fonts for a thousand years after the baptistry became an anachronism that M. Saintenoy found thirty-two per cent of all the fonts he visited were round and sixty-seven per cent octagonal. These forms were originally adopted because they gave the font the place of honour beneath the dome and in the centre of the building, making it possible to gather the entire congregation around a central font to witness the administration of the Sacrament. Partly for convenience and partly for symmetry the font itself was made circular or octagonal, and thus conformed to the lines of the baptistry.

These practical explanations, however, were again too prosaic for the Symbolists, who early stepped upon the field with their own curious interpretations. If the baptistry was round it was because this, the form of the endless circle, fitly represents the endless and eternal quality which underlies that Sacrament wherein God pledges the gift of eternal life to him who is baptized. So Guillaume Durandus explained to the Thirteenth Century: "Some [baptistries] are made in the form of a circle, because we reach forth to the crown of eternity which shall encircle our brows."

THE INCLINATION OF AN APSE

If the baptistry was octagonal, it was because the Lord God, having toiled through the six hard days of Creation, had rested on the seventh day; therefore the eighth was the perfect day when the task was finished and the Labourer rested. So the number "8" became the symbol of completion and of perfection, and when wrought into the font or the baptistry proclaimed the absolute efficiency of the covenant there established between man and his Maker.

"We know for a fact," wrote the translators of Guillaume, "that the reason assigned for the octagonal form, if not by S. Ambrose, [340-

THE DOME OF ANTHEMIUS: SANCTA SOPHIA, CONSTANTINOPLE

Its stability depended upon the skill of the builder, and on the relics of the saints, buried in each twelfth layer of the stones.

397 A.D.] then by a contemporary, was that the number '8' was symbolic of regeneration, for the Creation was completed in seven days, so the next ensuing number may well have been significant of the new." [1]

By the Thirteenth Century, Symbolism, come into its own, possessed the entire church until every step and every stone had acquired its cryptic meaning.

If the light, dim when we first enter the church, increases steadily as we ascend the aisles and draw nearer to the altar (whose five crosses remind us of the five wounds whereby Christ redeemed the world, and whose myriad candles scatter the shadows) it is because the darkness always breaks as, step by step, we draw closer to Him Who is "the Light of the world, in Whom is no darkness at all."

The chancel, containing the altar, is smaller than either the choir or the nave because those who live virgin lives, though holiest in the sight of God, are few in number. The choir, larger than the chancel but smaller than the nave, represents those who now live in the self-discipline of chastity; while the nave, largest division of the church and farthest from the altar, symbolizes the married.

The sacristy, robing room of the priests, speaks of the womb of the Virgin where Christ put on the garments of humanity; the circular stairways, winding upward in the depths of the walls, symbolizes that hidden wisdom that comes only to those who climb, through prayer and meditation, to celestial things.

The windows are the holy scriptures, since they repel all winds and storms, but admit the light to strengthen the faithful; there are four walls, because there are four Evangelists; the church has three dimensions: height—to represent her courage; length—to declare her fortitude; and breadth—to symbolize her charity.

The tiles of the roof, which prevent rain, snow, or sleet from entering, stand for the soldiers who guard the holy places from the assaults of paynim, heretics, and schismatics.

The portals signify obedience, for Jesus said, "If thou wilt enter into life, keep the commandments."

[1] *Catholic Encyclopedia*, Vol. XIV, p. 376; and Mâle, Vol. II, p. 12.

The stones of the church are held together by cement, which is made of lime, sand, and water; the sand represents our good works; the lime is charity which binds together the grains of sand; and the water is the Holy Spirit by Whom the love for God is shed abroad in our hearts.

The cock on the weather-vane deserves his exalted place, partly because at his voice all ghosts and witches, with every evil and uneasy spirit, must "shrink and haste away," as Horatio well knew; and also because, watching through hours of darkness, catching the first faint glimmer of the dawn, flagellating himself with his wings and waking a sleeping city with his lusty crow, he symbolizes the faithful preacher, with his vigils and scourgings, his belief in a dawn that shall end the night of sin, and his ringing call to men: "Awake, thou that sleepest, for Christ is giving light." [2]

"Nature speaks a varied language," sang Bryant in his *Thanatopsis;* so also did the church. From the weather-vane above to the crypt below, from portico to altar, from the gestures of the beggars at the portal to the genuflections of the priests in the chancel, all the essentials of the faith, the commands of God, the ideals of the soul, and the duties of life entered the hearts of men through the gateways of their eyes.

We may smile, perhaps, as we turn the pages of the *Rationale Divinorum Officiorum,* or those of the still earlier Eleventh Century

---

[2] If the Cross atop the spire at last displaced the cock it was because devils, as well as deities, love a shining mark, and this lofty perch proved too attractive to bolts of lightning, launched by those envious hosts of Hell who summon the storms and ride upon the clouds.

Of course devils could be thwarted and their malice foiled, as all good Christians knew, by the stout ringing of the holy bells, especially when these were inscribed with the name and image of S. Barbara of Heliopolis. But there were demons (doubtless spawned in the darker depths of Hell) who dared to challenge, and sometimes with success, the exorcising clangour of the bells. The surest protection from the dread thunderbolts of such as these was that Cross, the mere sight of which the Lord of the Lost himself never could abide. Thus, in 1315, the bishop of London led a solemn procession to old S. Paul's where a new Cross, well gilded and containing relics of the saints, was placed upon the spire "in order that the omnipotent God, and the glorious merits of the saints, might deign to protect it from dangers of storms."

Sometimes, however, relics reinforced and saved the cock.

In 1763 workmen, repairing the spire of Salisbury Cathedral, found a cavity in the capstone containing a box within which lay a piece of crumbling silk or linen, doubtless a relic intended to avert the lightning.

Melitonis Clavis Sanctae Scripturae, but there may well be a twist of envy to the smile. (Did not we also once dwell in Arcady?) Surely the church was then speaking deeper and wiser things to the eyes of man than do the raucous clangours of machinery to our ears today.

Chapter Twenty-two

THE ROMANCE AND THE TRAGEDY OF CATHEDRAL GLASS

THE sun, streaming through the windows of Chartres Cathedral, of Bourges, or of Poitiers, receives, as it comes, the colour of the ruby, the amethyst, the sapphire, or the emerald in colours so rich that men have called the windows "jewelled glass." Indeed it is more than possible that the early mediæval glazier not only intended to imitate jewels but also, realizing better than we can today the dense ignorance of his generation, meant that his glass should be accepted as veritable precious stones. So also did his forbears who, for hundreds of years before the birth of Christ, made quantities of glass beads that imitated jewels for the purposes of barter with barbarian tribes.

S. John probably drew upon his memories of such jewels of glass when, exiled on Patmos, he saw a holy city, not made by hands, descending to earth from Heaven. Its walls of gold and gates of pearls, its golden streets converging on the dazzling Throne which stood beneath an emerald arch and beside a crystal sea, recall Oriental romances with their palaces of red gold inset with emeralds and rubies; their alabaster couches inlaid with jewels and canopied with pearls, and their silken carpets embroidered with precious stones—tellers of tales and dreamers of dreams alike paying thus their unconscious tribute to the glazier's deceptive art.

Both the romancers and the seers also remind us that we have never adequately recognized our debt to the men who, greatly adventuring age after age, sought "something for nothing." Nevertheless it was the trade of Argonauts that developed the glazier's skill, for that art grew with the enterprise of maritime merchants who passed the Pillars of Hercules, dared the storms of the Bay of Biscay and the fog banks of the Baltic, in their search for that Ultima Thule where they dwelt who thought all gold that glittered, and who found those Blessed Isles where pastes of coloured glass were valued as jewels of great price.

Amid the ruins of the "Burnt City," buried seven cities deep, which Schliemann uncovered on the Plains of Troy and identified with the Ilium of Priam, Hector, and Cassandra, a few of these glass beads were found, the scantiness of the find indicating that there was no local manufacture but that these beads were brought by traders who gave them in exchange for other wares. And these beads, "sapphires," "rubies," "pearls," and "emeralds," are found in three-quarters of the ancient world, their profusion and wide distribution suggesting that they were brought by itinerant merchants like the Phœnicians, who gave these "priceless" jewels in exchange for commodities of greater intrinsic worth.

Pliny tells us that the discovery of glass was due to one of those happy accidents which have contributed so much to human progress. According to his tale the crew of a merchant ship, landing on a beach of fine, white sand near the mouth of the river Belus in Syria, used natron from the ship's cargo to prop their kettle over a fire kindled on the sands. Presently, to their surprise, they saw a stream of molten glass running down the beach from their camp-fire; the natron, acting as a flux (*i.e.,* a substance that promotes the fusion of minerals) had caused the silica in the sand to melt in the heat of the fire.

But glass is much older than Pliny's tale would indicate; it was known to the Egyptians from the remotest period, and glass blowing is represented in tombs that date from thousands of years before our era, when the Nile-dwellers buried their dead with glass scarabs deliberately made to imitate rubies, emeralds, and sapphires.[1]

As long ago as 2300 B.C. the Chinese were using astronomical instruments, which implies a knowledge of glass of an extreme purity of manufacture. But, if we may believe the legends, glass is older than Troy or Tyre, older than Mycenæ or Thebes, older than Chung-tu, Loh-yang, or any other city of ancient China, for it was first fashioned

---

[1] G. Maspero, *Egyptian Archæology*, p. 253.

when the angry heavens rained down fire upon the Tower of Babel so that the builders, already cursed by the confusion of tongues, were still further confounded when they found their well-baked bricks vitrified and turned into brittle glass.

This art of making glass, whenever and however it originated, was passed on from generation to generation, and window glass, although not of a very perfect quality, has been found at Herculaneum and also amid the ruins of Roman villas in England. When, therefore, cathedral windows began to blaze with jewelled glass in the days of Charlemagne it was not a new art that was then created for the service of God and of His Holy Church, but one that was already thousands of years old.

Almost no ecclesiastical coloured glass has survived to our day that is older than the Twelfth Century, but that such windows existed earlier is evidenced by the monastic chronicles of Benigne de Dijon, who tells us that a chapel window in his monastery was filled with coloured glass in the year 1052, adding that this glass had been transferred from an older church which existed in the time of Louis the Pious, the son of Charlemagne.

The abbot Gozbert, who ruled his abbey of Turgensee from 982 to 1001, wrote an undated letter to thank Count Arnold of Voraburg for windows of coloured glass, presented to the monastery.

He also sent certain boys to Voraburg to receive instruction in the art of glass colouring, "so honourable to you and so necessary to us."

These boys had much more to learn than the mere chemistry of colouring glass, for pieces of glass no more make a window than so many thousands of brick can make a house. The designing of the window and the fitting of each small piece of glass into an elaborate mosaic were equally important. Probably they had already watched the master-workman of Voraburg draw his design, set each small fragment of glass in its appointed place, and then transfer his completed window from the abbey workshop to the aisle of the abbot Gozbert's church. Doubtless his method was the same as that which the monk Theophilus described in his famous book, written about the year 1200, in which he devoted a chapter to the "construction of windows." (*De Componendis Fenestris.*)

First this master-workman made a wooden panel of the exact shape and size of the window he wished to build. This he covered with finely scraped chalk, moistened to a paste and spread evenly over the entire surface, on which he sketched out his design, indicating on each segment of the plan, by letters or numerals, the colour he purposed to employ. Upon this pattern the pieces of glass were laid down.

Each piece was cut to fit its place, not by a diamond point which was not invented until the Sixteenth Century, but by a hot iron which determined the approximate line along which the glass would break at a quick turn of the craftsman's wrist. The rough edges which remained were laboriously chipped away with a notched iron, known as the "glozing-iron," until each piece could slip smoothly into its proper place. Then strips of pliable lead, grooved on both sides like a recumbent letter "H," were brought into play, with the grooves filled with cement. The glass was then pressed into the leads and thus rendered both air- and water-tight. These leads were then soldered to one another, and strands of copper wire were also soldered in at intervals. When the window was completed the glazier's workmen lifted it from the wooden panel and carried it into the church, where iron bars had already been set into the stone-work of the embrasures. The loose ends of the copper wires were twisted around the iron bars to hold the window firmly in its place, and "the golden-haired sun began to shine upon the pavement through a window of coloured glass."

Visitors often regret these black lines of lead that wind in and out among the pieces of coloured glass, but they are really essential to the beauty of the window. Not only do they serve as the artist's crayon, to outline the figures and draw the picture; they are to the whole what shadows are to sunlight. Unbroken, unrelieved sunlight is almost unbearable; light is pleasing only when we see it in contrast to shadows, to shadows that are purple, green, violet, or blue, but which are rarely really black. So these dark lines of lead are the price the window pays for the beauty of its glass—they offer the contrast that beauty needs.

And they serve another vital purpose. Every colour has its complement—a colour which, being mixed with it, will produce white—and every colour throws around itself a halo of its complement. Since green and red are complementary, red poppies in a lawn will throw a haze of green over the grass, intensifying its colour, while the grass, in turn, will throw a veil of red over the poppies and add to their brilliance. But a green field thick with yellow buttercups will be dulled in colour, for the yellow will cast an indigo shade over the green, while the green will suffuse the yellow with red; both colours thus lose in depth, brilliance, and transparency.

When, therefore, the various colours of the glass must needs be brought so close together, the dark lines of lead serve an important purpose in holding the colours apart, in preventing their overflowing one another and thus giving the separate pieces either too great, or too slight, a value. These lines of lead enabled the glazier to give each smallest section of his window its desired worth.

The earliest ecclesiastical glass that has come down to us is known as "pot-metal" because it has been coloured through and through—blue, green, yellow, violet, or ruby, all of many shades—in the pot wherein it was made.

Another way of colouring glass was discovered in the Fourteenth Century when some workman carelessly dropped a bit of silver upon the glass as it was entering the furnace. When the work of "firing" was finished, and the glass removed, the workmen were amazed to discover a new and very beautiful yellow among the other colours. This accident led to the discovery that white glass coated with silver and then baked in the kiln would take a pure transparent stain of yellow, varying from the palest lemon to the deepest orange. Moreover, this stain, although on the glass—instead of in it (as in the case of pot-metal glass)—is indelible and can be removed only by removing the surface of the glass itself.

This yellow stain had one great advantage; it could be floated over wide areas, or again the glass might be merely touched with it. An angel's halo, a background for an entire figure, or the tiny pearls in a bishop's mitre could all be represented with equal ease and accuracy.

A TWELFTH-CENTURY WINDOW AT S. DENIS

ABOVE: Christ unveils the face of Moses, symbolizing the Synagogue ("What Moses veiled that Christ revealed"). BELOW: Christ, with the Seven Spirits of Grace, crowns the Church with one hand and unveils the Synagogue with the other.

Red glass, called "ruby," was originally made in the pot where it was coloured through and through, but this process yielded to that of "flashing" at an early date—and here we have a new word that needs some explanation.

If the glass-maker had before him a pot of molten white glass with another pot of fluid red glass alongside he could dip his blowpipe first into the one and then into the other; when he blew out this glass he had a bubble of white glass evenly coated with the red. This process is known as "flashing," and glass so coloured is called "flashed glass."

Although red glass was thus made at an early date, it was not until the Fourteenth Century that this method was generally applied to other colours. Then the glaziers began to create a brilliant purple by coating red with blue, or a splendid orange by placing red on yellow; or a rich green by putting blue on yellow. In the Fifteenth Century as many as six layers of colour were sometimes "flashed" onto the same glass.

Still another way of producing effects, when flashed glass was used, was by "abrasion." Suppose the artist in glass wished to create a Virgin in her orthodox blue robe with the blue flashed upon white glass. By carefully grinding through the layer of blue until he reached the white the artist could etch white lilies in her girdle or on her breast. Again, by combining silver stain with flashing and abrasion, he could create a background of white daisies, yellow buttercups, and bluebells amid green grass; he could even represent the yellow eye of the daisy and the green of its calyx.

It is quite probable, as M. Mâle believes, that the splendid designs and brilliant hues of these earlier windows were taken from those of the age-old tapestries of Sassanide kings of Persia, who had inherited their decorative art from still more ancient Babylon. If we will hold, he says, one of these old tissues before the window of a Romanesque church—in imagination if not in fact—we will receive an illusion of stained glass, for they share the same designs, the same glowing colours, and the same ornamentation in the borders.

The very fact that the pieces of glass were small played an important part in early windows, for the tiny flecks of many colours, bound together yet held apart by the lines of lead, possessed a brilliancy of beauty that was impossible in later centuries when the glaziers used larger panes of painted glass.

Fortunately the early manufacture of pot-metal glass was quite imperfect; it was not possible to secure the same thickness for the pieces or to give them an even smoothness of surface. By these irregularities the rays of light were so diffused that the colours often mingled in the air, somewhere between the window and the eye. For instance, the great Rose Window in the North Transept of Notre-Dame in Paris produces an effect of splendid purple. There is, however, no purple glass in that window; its colours are predominantly red and blue, but the refractions of the rays of light, as they pass through the uneven pieces of glass, cause the red and the blue to intermingle in the air so that they fall upon the eye in a royal purple. This gives us another glimpse into the difficulties of the glazier's task; it was not enough that he should place a red colour beside a blue; he must also consider the angles in the surface of his glass, whether they will so deflect the rays of light as to make, or to mar, the effects he had wished and planned.

It is partly because of the difficulties and handicaps that beset the worker in glass throughout the Twelfth and Thirteenth Centuries that his glass so far exceeds in beauty that of later generations. Craft is not craftiness, and genius is more than ingenuity. When, in later years, men turned from the old pot-metal glass to painted glass; when the colours were mixed on the artist's palette instead of in the furnace, and were transferred to the surface of the window instead of being interfused with all its texture, then cathedral windows gained in subtilty but lost the charm of the old naïveté and simplicity. The facile brush of the painter might move more easily and surely across the glass than could the leads of the early glazier; the artist could give a depth and a perspective to his drawings that had been impossible to the worker in glass throughout the Twelfth and Thirteenth Centuries; he could make his figures far more real and lifelike than the Byzantine images of the old masters, with their staring eyes, awkward postures, and ill-shaped heads; but nothing could compensate for the loss of the rich colour, the gorgeous designs, and the soft lights of the windows of jewelled glass.

In fact, the very beauty of the early glass contributed to its ruin, for the austere Cistercians deemed it too richly sumptuous for the House of God and therefore banned it; the secular cleric coveted the space occupied by its pure designs for medallions whose figures should preach sermons; and finally the painter, envious of the glazier, cast out the little jewels of ruby, sapphire, turquoise, and emerald, and filled the windows with larger panes that were better suited to his brush.

Change does not always mean decay, and these mutations were not all productive of loss, for the austerities of the Cistercians, whose influence upon the architecture we have already seen, created a new beauty that was peculiarly their own to replace the banished splendours of the jewelled glass.

In the year 1134 the General Chapter of the Order issued a decree that thereafter all windows in Cistercian churches must be clear and uncoloured. Fifty years later, in 1284, a much more Draconian edict went forth commanding the removal of all stained glass from every church under Cistercian jurisdiction within two years; abbots, priors, and cellarers who should fail in obedience were to fast on bread and water on all Fridays until the edict was obeyed and the objectionable windows destroyed.

As a result the Cistercians turned to windows of a cool, refreshing, silvery green, or sometimes of a light shade of brown, which are known as *grisaille*. With mosaics of such colours they sketched out a pattern, the various parts of which were leaded into their respective places to form an almost infinite variety of elaborate and very beautiful designs. Then the background was blocked out by countless little criss-cross lines—technically known as "cross-hatching." These grisaille windows had the further advantage of admitting more light to a church which the windows of jewelled glass sometimes made almost too sombre.

The early "storied-windows" are exceedingly beautiful, and their medallions merge harmoniously with the old designs that surround and interpenetrate them, but the figures introduced into the medallions forced the glazier to call upon the painter who, once given an inch, steadily added ell to ell. The glazier's need of the painter was due to the fact that the more minute details of his work, the fingers of a hand, for instance, if separately leaded in, would afford so many lodging places for wind-blown dust and dirt that the glass would soon become obscured and ultimately blotted out. Therefore paint must be used for the folds of mantles, for the hair, hands, feet, for smaller details, and certain backgrounds. So long as the painter appeared merely to aid the glazier he helped and did no harm, but more and more his brush swept across the glass until at last the relations were reversed and the glazier became the lowly assistant to the painter. By the Sixteenth Century the old pot-metal glass had all but disappeared, and the windows received their colours from the painter's brush.

Paint is, indeed, the sinister villain of the tragedy of cathedral glass, partly because its painted pictures and white or yellow lights broke the spell of the old jewelled windows; partly because it obscured the glass and dimmed its translucency; but principally because, unable to stand the tests of time and of varying temperatures, it ultimately began to flake away, leaving the scars of empty places in the pictures.

With his eyes blinded by the lures of paint, the artist forgot that he was working on a church, not on a canvas; the temptations of his palette led him to neglect the architectural effects for the sake of his picture, and his forgetfulness, his failure to subordinate his work to the architectural whole, broke the charm of the old church.

In earlier centuries the cathedral had enfolded the worshipper, had —for the moment—called him apart from the world and surrounded him with a twilight that was interpenetrated and illuminated with great mysteries. But by the Sixteenth Century white lights or yellow dominated windows whereon the eye gazed as on the paintings in a gallery. Instead of helping him to forget the world the windows called him forth; here he saw, in perspective, the same lakes, mountains, fields, streams, and trees, the same crowds of people, from which he had sought escape when he passed through the portals of the church.

The restfulness of the old was gone, and in its place was only the suggestion of action, of stir and bustle, of noise and tumult.

Furthermore the light streaming through these windows was no longer clear and radiant; it was no longer ruby-red, sapphire, turquoise, purple, or gold because of the very quality of the glass itself. The light is dulled and dead because the paint, from which alone all colours are now derived, has destroyed the translucency of the glass. There are windows in the Cathedral of Brussels that bear witness to the terrible decline that had taken place within a century.

The greatest disadvantage of painted glass, however, came from the impermanence of the paint, and this was due to the processes by which the pigments were prepared for the palette.

The artist made his tints by grinding the coloured pot-metal glass to an impalpable powder which he then mixed with oil-fat or with gum and water. When these paints, laid upon the glass, were baked in the kiln, the oil-fat, or the gum and water, were evaporated, leaving the powdered glass adhering, more or less firmly, wherever it had been applied. But the powdered glass in the paint must melt at a lower temperature than that which would melt the window glass, otherwise the heat of the kiln would destroy the window in the effort to fuse the powdered glass. So the pigments were mixed with some substance like borax which acted as a flux to cause them to flow and melt at a lower temperature than that which would affect the glass. But this flux, whatever it may have been, inevitably made the paint softer than the glass and more susceptible to changes in the atmosphere, since it could not expand and contract as freely as did the glass itself. The result was that, in the course of time, the softer paints tended to scale off, leaving garments that had once been rich and splendid threadbare and moth-eaten, and the faces of many of the saints unrecognizable even to their own mothers.

Pot-metal glass and enamel paint—these are the Dr. Jekylls and Mr. Hydes of the story of cathedral glass, and it is a curious, if tragic, fact that although the most beautiful windows we possess date from the Gothic centuries, yet it was the Gothic architect who made possible the ultimate triumph of the painter, and thus brought about the decadence of the glazier's art to which his church stands eternally in debt.

In the Romanesque church the windows were comparatively few and small; of structural necessity stone-work occupied by far the greater part of the wall space, so that the painter had ample scope for the exercise of his art—to fresco the wall or to hang his paintings. But when the Gothic architect so concentrated the weight of his vault on certain points of his structure that practically the entire wall could be turned over to the glazier, then the painter began to contest the windows with the workers in glass. Thereafter the old mosaics of jewelled glass were more and more driven into retreat until, by the end of the Sixteenth Century, the exquisite pot-metal glass had practically disappeared, and the brush of the painter possessed the field. Dr. Jekyll had vanished and only Mr. Hyde remained.

So it came to pass that when the days of the Renaissance were fully come, they proved to be the Ides of March for an ancient and wondrous art.

Lewis F. Day, *Stained and Painted Glass Windows.*
N. H. J. Westlake, *History of Design in Painted Glass.*
Alfred Werck, *Stained Glass.*
C. H. Sherrill, *Stained Glass Tours in France.*

Chapter Twenty-three

NOTRE-DAME

THE portal of Chartres is flanked on either hand by the statues of the great figures of the Old Testament and of the New; through that funnel-like entrance the visitor passes—as if conducted by the prophets, the kings, and the evangelists—into the presence of a Christ who sits enthroned in glory on the tympanum, the space above the central door.

There is something significant in the arrangement of the portal. It tells us that it is by the Old Testament that we have access to the New; that the men of ages past who foresaw and awaited the coming of the Christ, who "died in faith, not having received the promises but having seen them afar off, were persuaded of them and embraced them," are our proper "schoolmasters to bring us to Christ." And it also seems to say that He Whom an earlier and a later theology presented to men as their only necessary, or even possible, Intercessor before the Throne of God, must be Himself approached through the mediations and intercessions of the saints and prophets of ages past.

One finds few churches of the Middle Ages that are dedicated to the "Son of Man," but there are very many dedicated to the Virgin, to "Our Lady"—Notre-Dame. All abbey-churches of the great Cistercian Order bore her name and belonged to her; it is Notre-Dame in Paris, Notre-Dame in Chartres, Notre-Dame in Chalons, in Noyon, Airaines, Etampes, Amiens, Rheims, Rouen, Evreux, Mantes, S. Lo— Notre-Dame all.

And many churches also were dedicated to the saints; at Toulouse one church is dedicated to S. Sernin and another to S. Etienne; the church at Conques belongs to S. Foy; S. Martial intercedes for his people at Limoges. S. Nectaire, S. Hilaire, S. Savin, S. Julien, S. Trophîme, S. Front, S. Benigne, Mary Magdalen, Martha, Lazarus, these and countless others had their churches where men came to pray to them, each according to his need.

But what have the ages done to Christ? What has happened that He should have been displaced; that Mary and the saints should have been substituted for Him as man's intercessor before the Throne?

That men desperately felt the need of mediation is evidenced by the crowds who thronged the pilgrimage roads, not only to the shrines of their own country but to the distant altars of S. James at Santiago de Compostella in Western Spain and to far off Bari in Southern Italy, where a fountain of perfumed oil, ever flowing from beneath the tomb of the great S. Nicholas, never failed to cure the sick, however desperate the illness. Why these pilgrimages? Why these appeals to Mary and the Saints instead of Christ?

Because, in the effort to honour and glorify Jesus, men had stripped Him of His humanity and, exalting Him to the Throne, had clothed Him with the awful attributes of Deity. Enthroned with God, He also "dwelt in clouds and in thick darknesses." His ways could no longer be our ways, nor His thoughts our thoughts, for He had become man's judge, instead of his friend and elder brother.

Thus men saw Him at Bealieu, at Chartres, and at Autun, seated on a Throne of blinding light and encircled by an aureole of radiant glory; beneath His feet the graves yield up their Dead; before His footstool S. Michael weighs the souls, and at His left the great gullet of Leviathan, symbol of the horrors of Hell, yawns to receive the Lost. What else than this dread dragon was Job describing when he wrote:

"Who has entered into his jaws? Who will open the gates of his mouth? Around his teeth dwells terror, smoke streameth from his nostrils. His breath kindleth the coals. He maketh the sea to boil like a cauldron, and his path in the sea is a flame of fire."

Portal after portal showed to living men the devils, who had received the souls of those who had been weighed in the balance and found wanting, dragging the Lost away in chains, prodding them with spikes and casting them into those jaws of dread, while an impassive Jesus sat above and judged and watched.

LES SAINTES MARIES, A SCAR OF THE ENGLISH WARS

Organized for war as well as for worship, such churches reflect the anarchy that was
unleashed in France by the disasters of the Hundred Years' War.

What wonder that men, seeing this awesome Christ seated in the midst of that blinding glory, distant and unmoved amid a scene of terror that turned their hearts to water, should have clamoured with all their souls for some intercessor who should be holy and therefore have access to the Throne, but who should also be more human and less terribly divine. Therefore they turned to the saints, but above all to "Notre-Dame," Our Lady.

"She was," says M. Mâle, "the advocate of desperate causes. All the treasures of the pity of God were in her hands. She was all woman, regarding neither good nor evil, but pardoning all for love. Satan might be the king of logicians, but she could meet and put his scholasticism to flight with a charming grace and a finesse that were characteristically French. She would disguise herself and appear at rendezvous where Satan least expected her. She was present when S. Michael weighed the souls of men in his balances, and she knew how to make the scales tip to the kindlier side. The Book of the Miracles of Our Lady is the record of her grace. She saves those whom human and divine justice have alike condemned. Shipwrecked sailors float ashore over the stormiest waves, sustained by her mantle; her holy images shut the mouths of lions and save her pilgrims in the desert." [1]

The story of the monk Theophilus, who had bartered his soul to the Devil for the glory of this world, for whose sake the Holy Virgin faced and victoriously fought the fiend, may be read twice in the carvings of Notre-Dame in Paris, in a bas-relief at Lyons, and in the glass of Laon, Beauvais, Troyes, and Le Mans.

So the tales, carved in stone or painted in the glass, are multiplied in the churches that men built. What wonder that they honoured "Our Lady," crowned her, worshipped, and adored her, or went on long pilgrimages that they might lay their sins in the hollows of her most merciful hands.

And there were also the saints to whom men in trouble or in need of mercy might turn for help; each one had his own peculiar *métier* for the field of man's need was all so parcelled out that there was

[1] Mâle, Vol. II, Chap. III.

always some saint with especial skill for every phase of man's extremity.

In case of fever he could invoke S. Geneviève of Paris; for all troubles of the throat there was S. Blaise; S. Hubert healed those who were in danger of hydrophobia; it was only necessary to take a key which had been blessed in one of his chapels, heat it in the fire and lay it on the wound. Apollinus, whose jaws had been broken by his executioners, cured all troubles with the teeth; S. Sebastian, S. Adrian, and S. Roche protected cities against the plague. Children who wore around their necks ribbons bearing the name of S. Amable of Riom would never fear the darkness or the night. Those who were passing through the Valley of the Shadow, whose hearts quailed at the thought of Death, found strength, quietness, and peace through the power of S. Servais. S. Christopher guarded men from any danger of sudden death; he who was about to undertake a journey needed but to stop at the church and bend a knee before his image to be assured of a safe return.

The kindly interests of the saints were extended to man's possessions as well as to himself. S. Corneille looked after his cattle, S. Gall cared for his chickens, S. Antoine protected his pigs, and S. Saturninus guarded his sheep, while S. Médard kept the frosts from his vines.

"In all the difficult hours of his life, in the midst of anxieties or sorrows of the soul, the name of some helping saint was always present to his mind. The traveller lost in the darkness, far wandering from his road, prayed to S. Julien; desperate causes were laid before S. Jude; chevaliers about to engage in mortal combat laid the justice of their cause before S. Drausin. Prisoners, buried in the dungeons of deep towers, appealed confidently to S. Leonard." [2]

And so it came about that the people of mediæval Europe, fearing God and having exalted the Son of Man until He was far beyond their reach, raised their cathedrals to Notre-Dame and their great churches to that hierarchy of saints who, having themselves experienced the weakness of our frail flesh, and having won the right to stand before the glory of the Throne, could and would intercede for those who offered them a candle and a prayer.

[2] Mâle, Vol. II, Chap. IV.

Chapter Twenty-four

THE BACKGROUND OF RAYONNANT AND OF FLAMBOYANT ARCHITECTURE

TOWARDS the end of the Thirteenth Century the wave of enthusiasm which had led to the erection of nearly six hundred great churches in France alone in the short space of one hundred years was severely checked by assaults that, coming both from within and from without, not only impaired the will and the ability of men to build, but also left their mark upon the works of architecture or of art that were attempted in those troubled years.

The negations of Scholastic philosophy assailed the minds of men and generated a speculative agnosticism; the corruptions of the clergy, which the pages of Boccaccio reveal, destroyed faith alike in the Church and in her hierarchy.

The Hundred Years' War absorbed the national energies of both France and England, while the grinding taxation of State and Church not only consumed and diverted to secular ends the wealth preceding generations had lavished upon great building programmes but also fell upon peoples impoverished by war throughout a long era in which the steadily decreasing production of the silver mines, with fitful debasements of the coinage, brought constant alternations of falling and rising prices.

Finally, upon this overburdened and distracted world there fell the cataclysmic pestilence of the Black Death.

Of all these assaults that upon the mind, although without fanfare of trumpets or beat of drums, was by no means the least dangerous, for the study of Greek philosophy, imported from the Moslem schools of Spain, awakened a slowly growing scepticism which gained steadily in velocity and in volume. Although the Schools treated religion with

185

courtesy, yet they reduced it to the debatable syllogisms of philosophy, and emasculated its morality by robbing it of the stern sanctions of Mt. Sinai. Ultimately the whole Scholastic system became a universal, if tacit, revolt against Authority and prepared the way, by an inner intellectual attack, for the "new paganism" of the Renaissance which accepted the negations of unbelief as essential attributes of culture.

Side by side with the intellectual attack of Scholasticism other forces, recruited from within the Church, moved to an assault which sent the Papacy into the Babylonian Captivity, and then shattered the last remnants of ecclesiastical authority by the factional strife of the Great Schism.

Boniface VIII, broken by the insult of Anagni, died and was soon succeeded by Clement V, who bought the support of the French cardinals in the Conclave that elected him by promising Philip his reconciliation with the Church on his own terms—the condemnation of the memory of Boniface and the right to tax the churches of France. Clement died and in 1316 the son of a cobbler of Cahors—John, Bishop of Porto—taking office under the name of John XXII, removed the papal Court to Avignon, initiating what is known as the Babylonian Captivity.

When the Pope bargained away his residence in Rome for a palace in Avignon he gained a throne but lost a kingdom. No pontiff living on the Rhône, pliant and suppliant to France and ruling a Court which Petrarch, an eye-witness, called profligate, luxurious, and immoral, could appeal to the popular imagination as had the great Innocent, seated upon S. Peter's throne above the waters of the Tiber.

Sixty years later Catherine of Siena brought Pope Gregory XI back to Rome; but when he died two years later rival Conclaves elected rival popes, thereby inaugurating that Great Schism which "rent anew the seamless robe of Christ" by the establishment of two, sometimes even three, "Keepers of the Apostolic Keys" who thundered their mutual excommunications across the continent of Europe for half a century.

The disorganization of the Church, begun by the Captivity and increased by the Great Schism, spread from the head through all the members. The misuse of wealth, the greed, corruption, and immorality within the Church, the loss of inspiration among the monastic orders which no longer bore their ancient fruit, destroyed man's age-old refuge in the authority of his once venerated priests. In England, France, and Italy men saw their spiritual fathers not only often married but also engaged in most unclerical pursuits.

An abbot of Canterbury practised piracy—when not intoning the chants of Matins, Vespers, or Complines. A former prior of the knights of S. John lived pleasantly on extorted tributes from the cities of Italy, or on ransoms from prisoners taken on her roads, until he was hanged by another cleric in armour, Cardinal Albornoz, whom the Pope dispatched against him.

"Never had the clergy been more corrupt, more ignorant, never had the Christian religion been so openly the object of scorn and derision. The Papacy lost both moral and political power in the disorders of the Schism; the clergy obeyed no discipline, canonical or ethical; monks and priests vied with each other in corruption; benefices were everywhere obtained by simony, . . . and abbots and bishops, neglecting their spiritual duties, thought only of plunder." [1] In such words Arthur Kingsley Porter sums up the character of an age in which the priesthood sank to its lowest level since the great Cluniac reform under Hildebrand.

No pope had ever advanced loftier pretensions, or spoken in more imperious terms, than did Boniface VIII, yet even in his day the papal sun was setting and the popes who returned from the Rhône to the Tiber, with dreams of empire faded to a memory, were forced to content themselves with a scramble for a place among the petty Italian States where confusions, only less than those which afflicted France, had reigned throughout the long papal absences in Avignon.

Heavily as the hand of man may have rested upon his fellows that of God in the Fourteenth Century was heavier still, as a little unknown village in China began to teach once more the oft-repeated lesson that, for good or ill, all human life is bound together, that no man can live or die alone.

[1] Arthur Kingsley Porter, *Mediæval Architecture,* Vol. II.

In the year 1333 a pestilence broke out in the village of Tche, probably the Bubonic Plague, although men called it "The Black Death." Quickly spreading throughout all China, where the almost incredible number of five million are said to have perished, it crossed the Himalayas and entered India, in some parts of which nine-tenths of the people died. Soon all Asia was suffering and villages, towns, cities, even provinces were depopulated.

Following the westward routes of trade the plague swept over Asia Minor, Syria, and Egypt. It came by ship from the Crimea to Constantinople and thence to Genoa, ravaging all Italy in 1347 and 1348. It crossed the Alps and visited Switzerland, Germany, Poland, and Hungary. In January of the latter year a smitten ship sailed slowly into the harbour of Marseilles, and a few days later the pestilence appeared in that city and in Avignon. Spreading westward, it crossed the Pyrenees and overran Spain; northward, it traversed France to the English Channel, and in August, 1348, the plague broke out in Melcomb and in Weymouth, England.

According to Boissonade, two-thirds of the population of Central Italy, from one- to two-thirds of the inhabitants of Lombardy, Northern Spain, France, England, the Low Countries, and a half to two-thirds of those living in Scandinavia and the East European countries perished. The towns were attacked with especial severity. Venice lost two-thirds of her inhabitants; Bologna, four-fifths; Florence buried from eighty thousand to one hundred thousand dead. There were three hundred deaths a day in Saragossa; at Avignon four hundred; at Paris, eight hundred. It may well be, however, that "the horror and desolation wrought by the epidemic are reflected in the wild exaggerations of contemporary chroniclers." Thompson believes that an estimated death-rate of twenty-five per cent would more nearly approximate the truth, but "we must admit," he adds, "that the Black Death caused the greatest mortality known to history." [2]

Boccaccio has left us a vivid picture of the streets of Florence in the grip of the plague, portraying scenes of terror which appeared throughout all Europe as the Death travelled from land to land—

2 Thompson, Vol. II, p. 381.

scenes that are curiously paralleled in the pages of Thucydides, for the people of Athens reacted to the panic of fear four hundred and thirty years before Christ just as they did in Florence eighteen hundred years after the last plague-stricken Athenian had closed his eyes.

In the fifty-third Chapter of the *Fourth Book of the Peloponnesian War,* Thucydides wrote:

"The plague first introduced into the city a greater lawlessness. Where men had hitherto practised concealment they now showed a more careless daring. They resolved to get out of life the pleasures that could be had speedily, regarding their bodies and their wealth alike as transitory. The pleasure of the moment, with all that led to it, came to be regarded as honourable and expedient. No fear of gods or man restrained them for, seeing that all men were perishing alike, they judged that piety and impiety came to the same thing."

The same spirit ruled in Florence where, Boccaccio tells us, all authority, human and divine, broke down under the horrors of the plague. The ordinary ties of humanity, even of family affection, snapped under the strain. Brother forsook brother, sister abandoned sister; the husband fled from his wife, the wife from her husband. Parents forgot their children and left them unvisited and untended. If the servants stayed with their masters, it was to plunder them when dead, if not while dying.

In the country, and among the poor, thousands died alone and untended. In the city death was often unannounced until some house began to pollute the air; the dead, therefore, were brought out of the houses and laid before the doors where the bearers of the city gathered them up, often piling one corpse upon another on the same litter. Strangers took possession of abandoned houses, and beggars dwelt in palaces unrebuked. As the consecrated ground of the churches could not hold the myriad dead, vast trenches were opened wherein the bodies were piled, again one upon another, until they neared the top when they were covered with a little earth which the rains would presently wash away. Guy de Chauliac, physician to Pope Clement VI, wrote of the plague in Avignon where the purple-spotted corpses

were thrown into the swiftly flowing Rhône, which had been hallowed by the papal blessing in order to receive the dead, until Clement opened a new cemetery into whose trenches the bodies were
hastily cast.

"The contagion was so great that not only by remaining with
the sick, but even by looking at them, the people seemed to take it.
Many died without any to serve them, and were buried without
a priest to pray over their graves. A father did not visit his son,
nor the son his father. Charity was dead. The mortality was so
great that it hardly left a fourth of the population. Even the doctors dared not visit the sick for fear of infection. As for me, to
avoid infamy I did not dare to absent myself, but still I was in
continual fear." [3]

The event justified the fear, for de Chauliac died of the plague; the
Holy Father, however, more cautious if less courageous, isolated himself in one room and survived the pestilence.

As in Florence and in Avignon, so it was wherever the Black
Death passed; everywhere Terror and Inhumanity went as its grim
acolytes. There were some who met death bravely but there were
others, as Boccaccio tells us, who sought forgetfulness in drunken
revels and debaucheries, men and women alike, of high or low estate,
until the foundations of orderly society seemed to be crumbling everywhere. This was largely due to the fact that the Church, having lost
her hold on heaven, had also lost her hold on earth. In similar times
of stress past generations had rallied to the altar finding strength, inspiration, and comfort in a spiritual and courageous clergy. In the
Fourteenth Century the age-old message of Christianity had been
well-nigh forgotten by a priesthood whose manner of life had forfeited respect. There is an interpretative contrast between Gregory
the Great in the Sixth Century, and Clement VI in the Fourteenth,
both of whom survived pestilences that were long remembered.

Gregory daily visited the plague-stricken, led intercessory processions from church to church, and celebrated Mass at an altar where

[3] Thompson, Vol. II, p. 379.

eighty died in the aisles in a single hour; Clement, on the other hand, hid from the plague in a single room of his palace while thousands died, unshriven, untended, and uncomforted beneath his windows.

Among the victims of the plague were many whom neither the State nor the Church could spare, for they could not be replaced; "For two hundred years [these] governments had been slowly and painfully developing their administrative machinery and training up a skilled class of officials. . . . Suddenly thousands of this technically trained class were cut down, [crippling the governments] beyond anything that we can imagine. The hundred and one every-day activities of an ordered society were arrested. The machinery of Government nearly stopped. In this emergency . . . thousands of ignorant, incompetent, and dishonest men were hastily thrust into public office. . . . The result was appalling waste, great maladministration, and peculation. . . .

"The Church was no better off. . . . It, too, had to keep functioning, and to do so impressed into service all sorts and conditions of men; in the universal terror it could not be over careful in its selections. And many intruded themselves into lucrative church livings for the material nature of the preferment."

Manners declined as well as minds and morals: "In the sense of honour, in the amenities of courtesy, in the feelings of responsibility either to the individual or to society, . . . in reverence for the mysteries of life the generations of these [Fourteenth and Fifteenth] Centuries were immeasurably inferior to their predecessors. No class of society was exempt from the taint. Neither clergy nor laity, king nor courtier; neither baron nor priest, nor bourgeois measured up to the character of these men in the preceding period. Europe between 1300 and 1600 was, perhaps, the most callous age in the history of mankind." [4]

The World had travelled far since the days when men could be moved to emulation by the story of S. Martin dividing his cloak with a beggar; of S. Christopher carrying a little child across a swollen stream, or of the *jongleur* of Lucca, playing his heart out before the compassionate image of the Santa Volta.

[4] Thompson, Vol. II, pp. 9, 384-5.

To all other factors that were sapping the loyalties of the people must be added the heavy burdens of ecclesiastical taxation. In the middle of the Twelfth Century the income of the Church had far exceeded that of all the princes of Europe taken together, but in the Fourteenth Century, "The Church was rich in lands, but land values had diminished . . ." and the ancient stream of manorial revenues had shrunken to a rivulet. From England to Italy the secular powers had assumed the right to tax the clerical revenues, thereby forcing the Church to invent new forms of taxation in spheres where the State could not enter.[5]

For the collection of these taxes special agents were appointed who went from church to church, from abbot to bishop. Since the assessed did not always have the money in hand with which to pay, and because the Pope often needed to anticipate his mortgaged income, "bankers" accompanied the assessors to lend, on truly Roman terms of interest, the money required to meet the tax, and then collected both principal and interest.

To facilitate their work these "bankers" were given the power to excommunicate, and the debtor, even though he were John Peckham, Archbishop of Canterbury, found himself facing the loss of all churchly privileges on earth as well as his hopes of heaven if he failed to pay.

Heavy as was the burden of ecclesiastical taxation, that of France was even heavier and more obstructive to any programme of church building, however modest. Philip the Fair was ambitious, and the ambitions of kings are costly. To meet the expenses of his dreams Philip taxed France as that country had never been taxed before; to reinforce his levies he plundered the Jews, destroyed the wealthy order of the Knights Templars to his own great profit, sold freedom to serfs and privileges to towns; he debased the coinage to facilitate the payment of his debts, and then restored it to its former value, to increase the purchasing power of his royal income and establish a more

[5] Thompson, Vol. II, p. 286 *et seq.*; Legarde, *Latin Church in the Middle Ages,* Chap. IX; Lindsey, *History of the Reformation in Germany,* p. 7 *et seq.* In addition to these taxes, which were many and formidable, there were also profitable appeals to the papal Court, as well as Absolutions, Indulgences, and Dispensations, sold for cash by the priests and paid for by the people.

favourable basis for the contraction of new debts. Further opportunities for financial gain were offered in Champagne where Philip had acquired, by marriage, a dominant, if disastrous, influence.

Champagne had long been the most prosperous land in Central Europe. Lying mid-way between the Mediterranean and the North Sea, penetrated by a veritable network of navigable rivers—the Rhône, Saone, Seine, Marne, Moselle, and Meuse—which gave her an almost unbroken all-water route from sea to sea, the commerce of North and South brought riches to her doors. To her famous fairs came merchants from all lands, for these formed the focal point for the trade between Italy and Flanders, the most commercialized areas of the continent.

Seeing in these fairs obvious sources of new revenues Philip began to multiply his taxes, unfortunately to such an extent that his exactions forced merchants to avoid Champagne and to seek other avenues of communication between Italy and Flanders; whereupon the fairs gasped a little and then died.

The ambitions of France—although we can now see that they made war inevitable—had long looked beyond the routes of trade to their termini, to Flanders—the goal of a world trade that came from Russia through the Baltic; from Constantinople and Southeastern Europe by the Danube and through Germany; from the Levant and Italy by way of the Alpine passes and the Rhine, as well as from the Mediterranean by way of the Rhône Valley.

At first by favours and then by force successive kings of France sought to bring the Flemish cities—Ghent, Bruges, Lille, Antwerp—under their control. But success here would have been disastrous to Flanders, whose wealth had been largely created by the trade in wool with England, where the best wool in the world was grown for their looms; and ruinous to England, whose prosperity was equally dependent upon the maintenance of an open market in the Low Countries.

French ambitions menaced England in the south as well as in the north for Italian merchants, to escape Philip's clutching hand in Champagne, were landing their cargoes at Narbonne and transhipping them down the Garonne to Bordeaux. By following this route of trade these merchants could avoid the royal taxes, the long sail around the Iberian peninsula, and dangers from Barbary pirates.

But ever since the year 1158 both Guienne and Gascony had been possessed by England. If, now, these districts could be held by France, then all their trade would add to the income of the Crown. If the risks were great, so also was the temptation. No city in either France or England could compare with Bordeaux; no province in all Europe could rival the wines of Gascony; her soil was rich, her pastures bountiful, her horses famous, while the whale which still appears on the seal of Bayonne reminds us that great wealth was gained by the fishing fleets in the Bay of Biscay.

Thereafter it took more than one hundred years of war to determine whether the river Garonne, the pastures, horses, vines, and wines of Gascony, with the fish of the Bay of Biscay, should belong to England or to France.[6]

The Court of Battle is the most expensive to which litigants can appeal, and the costs imposed fell heavily on both France and England.

"From the viewpoint of duration the Hundred Years' War was worse than all others in history. In some parts, except for a few slight interruptions, it lasted for a hundred and twelve years, and even in the regions least affected it hardly lasted less than eighty to a hundred years. . . . It was an endless and terribly monotonous succession of massacres, burnings, pillages, and extortions, accompanied by the destruction of harvests and of cattle, assaults and calamities of every description. The people enjoyed scarcely any rest, [but] lived in precarious safety amidst almost constantly renewed agitations and fears."[7]

[6] In truth France, in seeking control of Flanders and of Gascony, with their trade routes, was attempting to rob a last year's bird-nest, for the pack mule had given away to the cargo ship (the *carrack*) and commerce, to escape Philip's royal greed, had left the land and taken to the sea. Early in the Fourteenth Century Genoa and Venice established a regular packet service between the Mediterranean and the English Channel, and thereafter their ships carried the imports of the Far East, of the Levant, of Mediterranean ports and Islands, to the quays of Southampton, London, Bruges and Antwerp.

[7] Thompson, Vol. II, p. 124.

The general debacle in France gave opportunity to the Free Companies, and to other more or less organized and disciplined bands of brigands, in whose ranks all classes from escaped criminals to monks and priests enlisted. Their cruelties intensified the sufferings of the people, and darkened the shadows that rested on the harried land. The outbreak of the peasantry, known as the *Jacquerrie,* wove another scarlet thread through the confused patchwork, and all France seemed to have dissolved in a cauldron of disorder where banditry, war, famine, and plague, like unholy witches of Endor, stirred the bitter brew. Petrarch, following where war had passed, wrote:

"I could not believe that this was the same France that I had seen so rich and flourishing. Nothing presented itself to my eyes but a fearful solitude, an utter poverty, land uncultivated, houses in ruins. Even the neighbourhood of Paris showed everywhere marks of desolation and conflagration. The streets are deserted, the roads overgrown with weeds; the whole is a vast solitude."

Poverty-stricken as France was, the war must be carried on and the whips of Philip's tax gatherers turned to scorpions in the hands of their successors, for in addition to the armies that must be paid, the waste, graft, and the extravagances of the Court, the nobility, and the State officials imposed ever increasing financial burdens and led to frequent changes in the values of the currency—there were twenty-four debasements or restorations in thirteen years under Philip VI. Still larger sums had to be raised after Poitiers to ransom King John, three princes, and hundreds of knights. The evils of the war fell heavily upon the churches, for the soldiery of every army established themselves in abbeys or cathedrals which they plundered and gutted. The Mendicant Orders suffered even more than the secular clergy, for their buildings were usually situated outside the cities and were demolished, either to provide material for defensive fortifications or to prevent their offering protection to an enemy.

Although the smouldering ruins of churches and abbeys, marking the swathes where the scythes of war had passed, called pitifully for succour from the builders, yet merciless taxations and destructions

stripped the people of the means to build, even if the will had survived the decline of the Church and the corruptions of the clergy.

Nevertheless the war itself called some churches into being. Writing
of the year 1358 Jean de Vinette says:

> "In this year many villages which possessed no fortification
> made veritable strongholds of their churches; moats were dug
> around the sacred edifices, and the towers were supplied with
> stones and with engines of war to defend the town in case it
> should be attacked by brigands, as often happened."

Of these churches Albi is the best known, but Royat, Agde, and
Les Saintes Maries in the Bouche du Rhône are even more effective
witnesses to the anarchy of the times.

Although England, protected by the great moat of her Channel,
was spared the ravages that desolated France, yet she also suffered
severely. Pirates from every land swarmed in all Northern waters;
English commerce was swept from the seas. No truce that obtained
on land gave respite to the sailor, and even in times of theoretic peace
French ships paraded in English waters with the bodies of English
sailors dangling from their masts and spars. Every town along the
Channel, as far as Bristol, was stormed and sacked; the dwellers on
the coast fled inland, leaving their fields to the brambles and the
thorns, and their towns to the little red lizards who sunned themselves on the sea-walls with none to frighten them.

The expenses of the war drained the income of the Crown, and
the attempt to collect the costs from the conquered districts across the
Channel failed to relieve the land, which had only a fraction of the
wealth and one-third the population of France. These burdens were
the heavier because the Church in England, while holding one-third
the land and enjoying twice the revenue of the State, bore no adequate
proportion of the costs. The results, perhaps not surprising, were the
revolt of Lollardry against the Church, and the uprising of the peasants
under Wat Tyler against the Crown.

Piers Ploughman sang in bitter verses the misery of the people, and

Green, in his *History of the English People,* passed judgement on these years;

> "The Hundred years that follow the brief sunshine of Crecy [1346] are years of the deepest gloom; no age in our history is so sad and sombre as the age we traverse between the third Edward and Joan of Arc."

Speaking again of the times of the Good Parliament (1376) when a long list of abuses was revealed, and a hundred and sixty petitions presented against the oppressive and arbitrary taxation, Green adds:

> "It was a time of shame and suffering such as England had never known. Her conquests had been lost, her shores insulted, her fleets annihilated, her commerce swept from the seas; while within she was exhausted by the long and costly war as well as by the ravages of the pestilence."

All these wars, pestilences, famines, poverties, and confusions which had made this a tragic century for England, France—and in only lesser measure for Italy—fell with a paralyzing effect on architecture and upon art, and the ornamentation of the churches show new conceptions that become ghastly when they touch the theme of death.

Throughout the Thirteenth Century death, clothed with kindliness, had been portrayed with a gentle hand and veiled in a poetry of faith and trust. In the Fourteenth Century, however, art became less serene, less exalted. This was largely due to the fact that the Church, having lost her spiritual hold upon the masses, forfeited their love, and alienated their hearts, had been appealing to their fears in order to preserve incomes that were threatened by man's decreasing loyalties. Therefore when the preaching Friars, the travelling militia of the Church, went out to thunder forth the terrors of Death and of Judgement, they found their arrows feathered and barbed by the great pestilence. Because of the visions of the Friars, and the poison with which the plague had tipped their shafts, a new conception of death began to take form in the effigies—half skeleton, half mummy—which appeared on the tombs of the early Fourteenth Century. Somewhat later this conception entered the channels of literature in the tale of the Three Quick and the Three Dead.

As told by the pen of Baudoin de Conde, three young gentlemen of high degree were halted by three Dead, just emerged from their graves in a near-by cemetery; their shrouds lay loosely on their bony shoulders and, flapping in the breeze, revealed their skeleton forms. The young men trembled like the leaves of the trees above their heads as the three Dead—Pope, Cardinal, and Papal Notary when living— spoke in unison:

"In us you see yourselves, for as we are so you shall be. In the hour of death riches and power are nothing; only good deeds count." Like many another subject this of Death was presented in the churches in dramatic form.

A document from the archives of Caudebec, described but unfortunately not copied by the Abbé Miette at the time of the French Revolution, together with a Latin Poem of the early Fourteenth Century, enable us to be present at the scene.

After a sermon on the brevity of life and the certainty of Judgement, delivered in a hushed and crowded church, a long procession began to move down the darkened aisle. Pope, king, bishop, knight, soldier, student; the young and old; the wise and foolish; rich and poor, man and maid follow each other in a parade of melancholy. Each laments the approaching hour of death, yet moves steadily forward until a hideous figure steps from the deeper shadows cast by the piers to drag the living into the darkness from which it has emerged.

From such representations on the tombs, from the moralities of the literature, and from the dramas in the churches the *Danse Macabre* took form. It appeared first on the walls of cemeteries, and then on those of churches—a weird and grim portrayal of life as really a dance of death in which all ranks must join hands. You may still see this *Danse Macabre* at Kermaria in Brittany, and in the frescoes of La Chaise Dieu near Le Puy, while many other representations have been lost. But behind the fading colours of "God's Chair" we cannot fail to feel the horrors that Boccaccio describes, or to hear the sinister cry ringing through the silent streets, "Bring out your dead." We see the hot and fetid streets of Florence where the living are as pallid as the dead who lie, awaiting the carters, on their own doorsteps; we see the litters where corpse is piled on corpse, their arms pendulous and swaying; the swine in the piazzas, rooting among the garments of the stricken and themselves dying of the contagion; we hear the song of drunken revellers, singing the only requiems for the dead.

Few examples of the *Danse Macabre* have survived to bear witness to the tragedies with which the Black Death sowed the fields of Europe, but the memories of those tragedies burned too deep to be forgotten; they still speak to us from the stripped, stark figure of the Duke de Brézé on his tomb in Rouen; in those of Henry II and Catherine de' Medici at S. Denis, in the effigy of a skeleton, still clad with some shreds of flesh, at Bar-le-Duc; and in the *Pleurants* that surround the tomb of Philip the Bold, once Duke of Burgundy, but now a spectacle for tourists in the Museum of Dijon.

If we had lost the historical records of these centuries and had nothing but the architecture and the art to guide us, we could still form some estimate of the course of events, for the chill precision of Rayonnant architecture would tell us that the world had lost its faith; the æsthetic worldliness of Flamboyant churches would speak to us of a generation which, despairing of life, sought its satisfactions in the gratification of the senses—while the art repeatedly reveals either a pagan joyousness in the fleshly and the sensuous, or else an equally pagan rebellion, unillumined by any Christian hope of resurrection, in the face of death.

Chapter Twenty-five

RAYONNANT ARCHITECTURE

CLINGING to the sides of the baptismal font in the church of S. John Lateran the mediæval pilgrim saw the petrified leprous scales, mute witnesses to the measureless mercies of God who, the legend said, had here healed the emperor Constantine of his leprosy.

In the Basin of Holy Water in the church of S. Paul-Serge at Narbonne he who followed the *Chemin de S. Jacques* over the Pyrenees to the great shrine in Galicia could see the frog which had been turned to stone because, despite all priestly admonitions, he had continued to interrupt the ceremonies of the Mass with his persistent croakings.

In the *Bénitier* of S. Ouen, in Rouen, the traveller of today may see something that is more beautiful, if less evidential of the miraculous, than the scales of Rome or the Bactrian of Narbonne, for here, as rarely elsewhere in Europe, the entire length and height of a great church is reflected in the still depths of the holy water. As you look down into this Basin coloured lights stream towards you down the aisles, or across the aisles, from windows of stained glass that are filled with exquisite traceries; the great piers, inverted, descend from their bases, straight, true, and tall as Norway pines; far below the stone vault looms out of mists and shadows, and when a breath disturbs the image the whole church trembles and becomes alive.

It would be well for the pilgrim if he could leave S. Ouen with this image in his memory, for when he lifts his eyes the church, although still so beautiful that it is hard to voice a criticism, becomes suddenly cold and hard; it appears as the realization of a draughtsman's dream but not a prophet's; its merits are those of a finished architectural drawing. Without the benediction of the Blessed Water,

S. Ouen fails to stir the pulse and quicken the breath as Chartres does, for Chartres was "born not of water but of the Spirit."

In this great Rouennais church of S. Ouen you miss the spiritual enthusiasm of the "cult of carts;" the passionate devotions, the prayers, hymns, and confessions of the thousands of men and women, some of high and some of low degree, who yoked themselves together to draw the stones for the walls of Chartres; you miss the echo of Suger's voice at S. Denis:

"I sought the advice of many wise men and the prayers of many holy monks, fearing lest my act might be displeasing to God and the holy martyrs. We hurried on the work at great expense, fearing lest God should justly complain of us 'thine eyes did see my substance being yet imperfect.'"

Although you cannot criticize S. Ouen, yet you feel that the architect worked over his mathematical formulæ without feeling the need, or asking the prayers, "of many holy monks;" and that the oxen of Laon, who freely dedicated their strength to the glory of God, had neither descendants nor disciples in the city of Rouen when S. Ouen was built. Everything is here except the life and the soul that shine through the walls and windows of Chartres, of Laon, of Notre-Dame of Paris, and of S. Denis.

The essential characteristic, the dominant quality, which pervades the architecture of the Fourteenth Century is the unbroken straight line, as illustrated by the piers which rise from floor to vault with the minimum of interruption from the horizontal lines.

In England this type of architecture was called "Perpendicular;" in France, where the word *rayon* means the spoke of a wheel, it was known as Rayonnant, the name being taken from the mullions of the Rose Windows which ran out in unbroken straight lines from a "hub," or central panel. The term was transferred from the windows to the churches themselves when the architects adopted the uninterrupted perpendicular line for the interior of their edifices.

Baring Gould says of Rayonnant architecture:

"Beautiful, the very flower of Gothic, it may be, yet it was a style that lent itself to be employed by second or third rate architects with respectable results. The compass nipped genius. Any dull man who had a pair of dividers, Caen stone, and unlimited means at his command could design [a church] which would be perfectly correct, and show no spark of invention."

The architects of the Fourteenth Century, wishing to simplify their architecture, reduced their structures to the form of an equation in which so much thrust should be equal to so much counter-thrust. Therefore all the inert elements, everything that served no logical or structural purpose, was abandoned.

The triforium which, having long since ceased to serve its ancient purpose of separating the sexes in public worship, now discharged no useful function, broke the perpendicular line and was therefore abandoned. For a similar reason the clerestory gallery disappeared. The capitals of the columns could be diminished, since they were no longer needed to provide landing places for the arches of the nave arcade which were now being absorbed in the piers themselves.

The erection of a church no longer called for inspiration or for genius since all the formulæ had been worked out; equations of stresses and strains had been calculated and the building of a cathedral had become a question of logic, of science, a problem for the geometrician rather than the vision of a creator in stone. The clever mechanism which now began to pervade Gothic architecture played no small part in calling the Italian Renaissance into being, for in Italy the builders of palaces and churches were not first enrolled in the ranks of the architects. They were decorative artists, goldsmiths, sculptors, painters, workers in metal before they became builders. The model for the Duomo in Florence was designed by a group of Florentine painters and goldsmiths in 1367. Brunelleschi, who built the Pitti Palace and designed the dome of the cathedral, studied the goldsmith's art and competed with Ghiberti for the bronze doors of the Baptistry. Michelangelo, the architect of S. Peter's in 1545, painted the vault of the Sistine Chapel, and carved the statue of Moses for S. Pietro in Vinculi. Bramante first studied painting, and Raphael was the chief architect for Leo X. Such artists rebelled against an architecture of geometry; they wanted many things which the great expanse of windows and the lofty arcades of Rayonnant and Flamboyant centuries denied; they wanted walls where Gaddo Gaddi could create, in mosaics, the Coronation of the Virgin; where Ghirlandajo could paint his frescoes of the life of Mary; where Leonardo da Vinci could hang his beautiful Annunciation. They wanted domes whereon Correggio could present his vision of Christ in glory, and ceilings that Michelangelo could decorate with the story of Man's Creation, Fall, and Christ's Redemption. Structural geometry is not art, and certainly the adoption of its formulæ entailed even more losses than those which stirred the Italians to revolt—losses which the French themselves failed to appreciate or to foresee.

When the builders of the Fourteenth Century in France discovered that walls of masonry were not necessary for the support of their vaults, and therefore substituted walls of glass for walls of stone, they unwittingly sacrificed that solid background which, framing the windows as at Chartres, had supplied a needed contrast of light and shadow, had thrown into sharper relief the jewelled windows, and given greater values to the colours of their glass.

When they discovered that lighter columns might be used instead of massive piers they lost the dignity, the sense of enduring strength, that were inseparable from the mighty arcades of Romanesque and the earlier Gothic churches. The girth of these great piers, the huge span of their circumference that made them seem like Atlas—able to sustain the world upon their shoulders—the shadows they cast upon the pavement, all united to endow the church with the sense of dominion, of power, and glory. Compared with Notre-Dame in Paris, with Chartres, or Amiens, the columns of the nave of S. Ouen, despite their structural efficiency, seem utterly inadequate.

The builders of the Fourteenth Century were deeply impressed by the daring heights to which the architects of the two preceding centuries had ventured to raise their lofty vaults. Wishing to surpass their fathers and to create an impression of height without the labour and expense of achieving it—the vault of S. Ouen is fourteen feet lower

than that of Chartres and forty-one feet lower than the vault of Amiens
—they sought to eliminate as far as possible all that could break the
soaring perpendicular line and thus obtain, by an optical illusion, the
effect which an earlier age had secured by sincerity in building. Therefore the triforium gallery became increasingly rare, the clerestory gallery vanished, and the nave walls, instead of rising in four divisions
with triforium and clerestory galleries, with clerestory lights superimposed upon the nave arcade, now rose in a new unity of design
from floor to vault.

The capitals of the columns, because they too formed long horizontal
lines when seen in perspective, were made smaller and less important
until they also vanished in the following century; the shafts of the
clustered columns became more slender, rose almost without interruption from their bases to the clerestory where they received the arches
of the vault.

By thus emphasizing the perpendicular lines at the expense of the
horizontal the architects were able to counterfeit height without the
cost of coining it.

But the clever geometricians who built these churches failed to
realize that they inevitably foreshortened their churches when they
robbed them of those parallel lines which, converging on the chancel
from both sides of the nave and choir, gave depth to the interior. The
long horizontal lines formed by the capitals on Gothic piers, by the
double railings of triforium and clerestory galleries, and by the straight
mouldings that followed the nave walls into the apse, had lent depth
and dignity to the cathedrals of the Twelfth and Thirteenth Centuries.
Because of the loss of these convergent lines the Rayonnant church,
although it may appear loftier than one of the preceding centuries
while being actually lower, seems more shallow even when it is longer.
S. Ouen, four hundred and fifty-three feet in length—twenty-five feet
longer than Chartres—fails to give the sense of depth which the older
church impressively conveys.

S. Ouen is the only important church that was built in France in
the Rayonnant period. Throughout the Fourteenth Century the interest of the builder was usually centred on the erection of a porch, a

nave, a choir, chapel, window, tower, or spire—with little or no concern for the original architectural design of the whole church. The
result was a startling disharmony which increased from year to year
as the lack of co-operation was inherited and carried further by successive generations.

So the century ends with a loss of spirituality and with a widening
line of cleavage between the artist and the architect, the prophet and
the draughtsman, the priest and the builder, the monk and the
mason. Church architecture has reached its zenith; following centuries
shall write the melancholy story of its decline, at first slow and slight
but gaining momentum as Faith decays, and as Reason challenges the
simpler enthusiasms of more naïve days. The deeply religious civilizations of the Twelfth and Thirteenth Centuries collapsed in the
confusions of the Fourteenth, and when the Fifteenth Century begins
to build we shall miss something we have never missed before; we
shall meet with something we have never encountered since Christianity began. Hereafter architects and artists, lacking that which all
their forefathers had possessed, shall raise churches sometimes possessing a touch of royal splendour, of beauty, and of artistry, but which
shall be more and more secular in spirit and in inspiration. "The silver
cord is loosened and the golden bowl is broken." So now, as the
Gothic draws near its end, we enter upon a pathway that shall lead
us through the nervous, restless fashions of the Flamboyant and the
Baroque extravagances of the Renaissance to the pure paganism of the
Classical.

There shall be many beautiful fragments scattered along the way;
here and there something shall shine forth like the pale rays of
phosphorescent lights, but—like the phosphorescence—they spring
from a decay.

Step by step, like the figures in a *Danse Macabre,* we are moving
towards the end.

Chapter Twenty-six

FLAMBOYANT ARCHITECTURE

FLAMBOYANT architecture, like the Rayonnant, receives its name in France from the mullions of the windows which now assume the form of leaping, twisting flames.

The field of architecture has been quite changed since S. Pierre of Beauvais was built. All the structural problems have been solved, all the builder's formulæ have been worked out; only in the field of decoration was experiment, ingenuity, and skill required, and it was in this field that the architects of the Fifteenth Century found their opportunity.

Architecture now became a decorative art, and it is by its decoration, rather than by its structural principles, that the church of the Flamboyant century is distinguished from that of the early Gothic.

The change is evidenced by the arches, for the round arch of Romanesque days and the pointed arch of the Gothic are alike often supplanted by the *ogee* arch which first describes a concave, then a convex curve, and finally ends in a pinnacle which may rise, as in Notre-Dame de l'Epine at Chalons-sur-Marne, clear across the face of the Rose Window, and reach the base of the last stages of the towers. The towers themselves are now supplied with corner buttresses from which flying arches leap over to the base of the spire; sometimes buttresses are also interspersed between the corner buttresses, so that eight flying arches—decorative if not structural—are crowded together on that comparatively small landing place. The spire itself is supplied with a multitude of projecting crotchets which resemble nothing so much as "the quills upon the fretful porcupine." Above the niches on the exterior walls rise thin and elongated canopies whose traceries are interwoven and twisted until the stone seems to have been threaded

Libr. d'Arch. R. Ducher, Paris

THE FLAMBOYANT WEST FRONT OF LA TRINITÉ AT VENDÔME

A flood of chisels fell upon the land to create a restless architecture. The "ogee" arch
is constantly repeated; the twisting stone tracery, especially the mullions of the windows,
seems to crackle like flames.

through a needle and then drawn in and out by the fingers of some lace-maker of Valenciennes.

Inside the church the capitals of the columns, already shrunken, disappear; the mouldings of the nave arches vanish in the columns and are there absorbed. The shafts may rise in spirals around the core of the column. Vaults are lower, for the aspiration that sent them soaring heavenward is gone. The old transverse and diagonal ribs are buried in an increasing multitude of short members that run from rib to rib, making elaborate geometric patterns against the background of the vault; a longitudinal rib runs along the whole length of the vault, from east to west, with many short, interpenetrating ribs, forming a confusion of intricate lines; the keystones become pendant and hang down from the vault, sometimes for many feet, and all these ribs with their keystones are carved by the chisel into more imitations of twisted lace.

The pier, when it nears the vault, often breaks into a myriad of ribs that run out like the spreading of an opening fan. These vaultings, Fan and Lierne, that turned the stone vault into a mere field for decoration, were imported into France from England.

To the Flamboyant architect the Gothic church was a mere blank page upon which he might write, using his chisel for a pen. He covered every available blank space, within and without, with his arabesques, rosettes, garlands, and flower-like chains; he treated his stone like thread, and wove patterns of lace upon the walls.

One reason for the failure of Flamboyant architecture, inherited from the Rayonnant age, was the growing separation between the architect and the artist.

If, in earlier years, the architect had placed a gable above his porch his purpose had been structural; he had placed it there to protect the statuary and the carvings of the porch from injury by storm, snow, sleet, or rain. But when, as at Amiens, this gable is pierced by a trefoil opening, or when—as at Rouen—it becomes a mere tracery of open voids affording no protection whatsoever; when, as at Amiens again, the gable is transferred to the interior of the church and erected over the choir stalls, it is quite evident that its original function has been forgotten, and that the artist is working independently of the architect. The Rayonnant porches of Rouen and the choir stalls of Amiens indicate that the decorator and the builder have begun to separate; each is doing his work in diminishing collaboration with the other, so that the decree of separation granted the artist in the Fourteenth Century becomes one of absolute divorce in the Fifteenth.

The Flamboyant church is adorned with intricate carvings and ornaments that form a veritable lace-work in stone, that present a marvel of the last perfection of technique in stone-cutting, yet there is often something coarse and vulgar in the pendants, something objectionable in the florid ornamentation, something weak that mars the best of Flamboyant interiors, and commonplace, if not depraved, in the tracery. Often there is also a desperate poverty of invention, characterized by neither beauty nor originality, in the designs.[1]

In all the leaping, dancing lines of Flamboyant architecture there has seemed to be something exuberant, careless, joyous, a note of apparent gaiety which has led to the feeling that only a happy people could build as joyously, sometimes as flippantly, as many of the Fifteenth Century churches imply.

It has been said that Flamboyant architecture is the concrete expression of the relief, felt from end to end of France, for the termination of the Hundred Years' War, for deliverance from the English yoke.

There was, however, little to make men glad in France throughout these years. True, victory had come at last and the English armies had been called home, but the land was utterly exhausted and the people impoverished long before the retreating English sails sank below the northern horizons.

The population had been many times decimated by war, famine, and pestilence, and the century which had opened with Agincourt was to end in the insane commitment of France, already drained and spent by more than a century of battlings, to costly adventures across the Alps which were to lead to Pavia, to new invasions, and to the disastrous Peace of Crespy.

[1] A. K. Porter, *Medieval Architecture*, Vol. II, Chap. X.

All these wars, threats of wars, and the prices they entailed necessitated heavy drains upon the nation, and the burdensome taxes from both State and Church fell principally upon the peasantry who complained to Charles VIII in 1483:

"During the past thirty-four years troops have been ever passing through France, and living on the poor people. When the poor man has managed, by the sale of the coat on his back, after hard toil, to pay his *taille,* and hopes to live out the year on the little he has left, then come fresh troops to his cottage, eating him up. In Normandy multitudes have died of hunger. From want of beasts, men and women have to yoke themselves to the carts, and others are compelled to work at night for fear lest, if seen in the daytime, they will be seized for not having paid their *taille*. The king should have pity on his poor people and relieve them of said *tailles* and charges." [2]

It would seem, therefore, that there was little to justify the explanation of Flamboyant architecture as the expression of a lighthearted people.

However, this architecture did not originate on the soil of France. Born in England in the preceding century (where it is termed "Decorated") and imported into France, it flourished especially in those districts which were under the English rule. But England in the Fourteenth Century was a confused and troubled land. The century, opening with the deposition of one king, ended with the overthrow and murder of another. It saw the great victories of Crécy and of Poitiers, but it also saw the sunken pits of Bannockburn which were as fatal to the English as the canal at Courtrai had been to the chivalry of France only a few years before. It brought in its train naval defeats that cost England the control of the sea, and military disasters that stripped her of Normandy, Anjou, Poitou, and all Aquitaine except the two cities of Bordeaux and Bayonne.

At home, increasing taxation to support armies in Spain, France, Wales, Ireland and Scotland produced the misery that echoes through

[2] Arthur Hassall, *The French People,* p. 140.

the stinging verses of *Piers Ploughman*, and that erupted in the destructions and massacres of the "Peasants' Revolt."

The Black Death came to carry away nearly half the total population so that the living were too few to bury the dead. Wages and food prices rose while rents declined; successive famines stalked the land as the harvests rotted on the ground, fields went untilled, and cattle roamed at will through the acres of corn and wheat, since herdsmen and husbandmen alike were dead.

Apparently some other explanation must be sought for the rise of Decorated architecture in England, or for the appearance of the Flamboyant in France, than that they were the expressions of exuberance.

Among the anomalies that history records is the tendency of men, when they feel themselves too much buffeted by fortune—the sport of elements they cannot control—to seek forgetfulness in dissipation. Thucydides relates this of the Greeks when Athens was gripped by the plague, and Boccaccio reports it when the Black Death struck Florence.

Flamboyant architecture may be best understood as the reaction of men against the disasters of the age; it is an expression of despair, not of exultation.

The breakdown of all spiritual leadership, with the resulting despair of the future, threw the emphasis on the present. If men were to die tomorrow, they could at least eat, drink, and be merry today.

Flamboyant architecture is the natural expression of this spirit; it is born of despair, its gaiety is forced. Behind these leaping, flame-like mullions there is no leaping of the heart; in these slender window-bars of stone that now advance and then retreat, you seem to hear the crackling of skeleton castanets. The dancing of the mullions is an echo of the *Danse Macabre*.

De gustibus non disputandum est. Questions of taste may not be submitted to argument or to arbitration. If you like the Flamboyant you like it and that ends the matter. But there are those to whom this architecture, ingenious, skilful, and beautiful in its details as it often is, is none the less decadent. The beauty of the pure lines of the Gothic is quite lost, sacrificed to a too busy chisel; the church has become a mere palimpsest, whose deeper meaning is buried by the Fifteenth Century artist under a mass of superficial decorations. It is a restless architecture, devoid of quiet or peace. The eye, hurried on from point to point, finds no landing place; one longs for the quiet pasture fields of Chartres, for the restful shadows of Notre-Dame, and for the peaceful days before the flood of chisels fell upon the land.

Chapter Twenty-seven

THE RENAISSANCE IN ITALY

IT IS hardly possible to explain, or even to define, the Renaissance—
that mysterious intellectual upheaval of the Fifteenth Century which,
born in Italy and thence communicated to the rest of Europe, revolutionized man's relationship to life and to the world about him. We
may watch its course, study its factors, and mark its effects in the
fields of art, literature, science, and architecture, but all our explanations fail; indeed the best interpreters of the Renaissance do not agree
even as to its parents, or the place and hour of its birth.

The fall of Constantinople to the Ottomans in 1453 and the flight
of Byzantine scholars to the West, with their libraries of classical literature, undoubtedly were powerful influences in the Revival of Learning; the voyages of Columbus, of Vasco da Gama, and of Magellan
gave an added impetus; new doors were opened to the imagination
by the discoveries of Copernicus; the printing presses of Aldus Manutius, the Stephani, and of Froben spread the knowledge of the ancient
classics throughout all Europe, and the invention of gunpowder conferred a new equality upon men. But the Renaissance was not due to
any one of these things, nor may it be explained by any combination
of them.

The compass that Columbus used had been known for many hundreds of years before the *Santa Maria* and her consorts sailed from
Palos; the telescope of Galileo was described by Roger Bacon in
1250; the paper that Manutius used for the spread of knowledge was
being made of cotton in the year 1000, when Hugh Capet was newly
dead. But all the equipment of the most modern laboratory would
not have produced a Renaissance in the gregarious type of society
that characterized the Middle Ages.

Prior to the Fourteenth Century life had been fairly standardized and a man's beliefs, the rules governing his conduct, his social status, even his thoughts, were determined for him, not merely by the Church but by the State, by his guild, by the whole society of which he was a part.

With the advent of the Fifteenth Century there came a quick *volte face.* As if by intellectual volcanic action old bonds were snapped; the individual, for centuries submerged, found himself abruptly tossed up and deposited upon the mountains. His thoughts, his judgements, his reactions, instead of being lost in those of the mass, became individualized and important. An intellectual intoxication took possession of Italy which, fifty years later, crossed the Alps and spread to France, Germany, the Netherlands, and England.

Wherever the Renaissance went it stirred men to question established authorities; to ask what ordination had lifted the old standards of art, literature, religion, science, or government beyond the reach of critical interrogation. Their insatiable curiosity, peering into every corner of the universe and demanding answers to all riddles, spared neither princes, pontiffs, the stars of heaven, nor the Ultima Thule of their fathers. They hurled themselves against each puzzling sphinx with the furious ardour of S. George.

It was natural that Italy should be the cradle of the Renaissance, the scene of its first and greatest triumphs. The fleets of Pisa, Genoa, and Venice had long held the carrying trade of the Western world, not only with the Orient, but also through the Straits of Gibraltar to London, Bruges, Antwerp, and Ghent. Florence was the banker for all Europe, as the word *florin* applied to the coins of England, France, Germany, Bohemia, Hungary and other countries attests. Milan, Rome, Naples, and lesser cities of the peninsula, sharing in the general prosperity, possessed the wealth necessary to great undertakings and to the luxury of life.

More important still was the encouragement Italy gave to the individual, an encouragement that sprang from the political and economic conditions in the dismembered peninsula, for here as nowhere else in Europe "there was no absorption of the great vassals in monarchies, no feudal aid or tenure of the land, no tendency to centralize the whole intellectual activity of the race in any one capital; no suppression of the individual by strongly biased public opinion, by immutable law, or by the weight of a social hierarchy. Everything tended to the free emergence of personal aims and passions." "Despotism . . . was democratic; it recruited its ranks from all classes, and erected its thrones on the sovereignty of the people it oppressed. The impulse to the free play of ambitions which this state of things communicated was enormous. Capacity might raise the meanest monk to the Chair of S. Peter, the meanest soldier to the Duchy of Milan.

"The rapid mutations of government teach men to care for themselves, and to depend upon themselves alone in the battle with the world; while the necessity for craft and policy in the conduct of affairs sharpens intelligence. . . . What is the wonder if Italy, under these circumstances, produced original characters and many-sided intellects in great profusion." [1]

Finally the Italian, living in daily contact with the monuments of a splendid past, could never forget the glories of that ancient Empire whose law once ran from the Guadalquivir to the Tigris; and Rienzi, calling and quickening dead majesties from the ruins of old Rome until the city was on fire with his visions, was still—although a century dead—the exponent of the heart and soul of his people.

All these forces—the fall of Constantinople, the westward flight of Eastern scholars, and the archæological discoveries amid the ruins of the ancient world—set the tides of Italian thought running towards the rediscovery of the art, the literature, and the architecture of the days when Augustus built his Temple to Jupiter, Nero his Golden House, Caracalla his Baths, and Antoninus his Temple to the Sun.

Men who had long felt the repressions of both Church and State were inevitably drawn by the individualism of life in Greece, where men eagerly inquired into each strange doctrine, were frankly free to appraise each new philosophy, and to welcome every fresh venture into the world of thought. They were equally attracted by the liberties of Rome where men might believe or teach as they liked and sacri-

[1] Symonds, *Age of the Despots*, Chap. III.

THE DOME OF S. PETER, ROME

Four hundred and thirty-five feet high and one hundred and thirty-eight feet across,
made stable by ingeniously concealed artifices.

fice where they pleased to gods of their own choosing, so long as they did not undermine the State, disturb the pax Romana, or refuse a handful of rice to the deities who were the guardians of Rome's political authority.

Thus the Renaissance was primarily an attempt to return to an idealized past. Of course there could be no real return. Too much had happened between the fall of Ravenna to the Herulian Odoacer in 476, and the loss of Byzantium to the Ottoman Mohammed in 1453; too many inheritances from the North or East had been intermingled with the Latin blood to make such a return possible. The men of the Renaissance were not, and could not be, Romans of the Augustan Age—but they could aspire none the less, and their aspirations brought forth fruit in many fields. First in that of art which, long dominated by the Church and patronized mainly by the clergy, had hitherto been restricted to themes taken from the Bible or from the Golden Legend—the Lives of the Saints. Now, however, emancipated by the Renaissance, the artists who but yesterday had been portraying the choirs of angels or the noble armies of the saints and martyrs, discovered beauty in the human form and turned to the study of the nude. Their Virgins, saints, and angels became humanized, and the earthly feminine appeared upborne on angelic wings. Literature also, heretofore imprisoned within the same boundaries that had confined the field of art, took a most unchurchly departure from the Fourteenth Century onward, in the hands of Petrarch, Boccaccio, Marguerite d'Angoulême, the monk Rabelais, and those who followed in their train. Philosophy, recently the faithful handmaid of Theology, also felt the call of whispering winds and boldly trimmed her sails towards seas that had never been charted by the Church. Finally Architecture, whose leaders had hitherto been clerics, now found her patrons among the princes. In all these fields the leadership passed from the ecclesiastical to the secular world—a world which, rejecting the Gothic as barbarous, sought the secret of correct and civilized architecture amid the splendours of old Rome.

But this admiration of the Past, although it might infuse something of the pagan joy of life—while life was young—into the literature and the art—could not restore to the architects or artisans of the Renaissance the Latin skill which had raised the dome of the Pantheon, the Baths of Diocletian, or the Pont du Gard. The Romans who reared these mighty structures had been builders, not artists, whereas the builders of the Renaissance were artists before they became architects. Many of them had been painters before they planned cathedrals, and the skill of the painter is, in part at least, measured by his ability to create illusions. He must give a feeling of distance on a flat surface; an impression of light and shadow where there is neither shadow nor light; a sense of movement where nothing ever moves. It was not unnatural for a man so trained to avoid the cost and labour of carving a stone ceiling for the cathedral of Milan when he could more easily secure the same effect by painting that fine Gothic vault in imitation of carved stone; he would see cleverness, not falsity, in using his brush on the flat wall behind the altar of S. Satiro, in the same city, to convey the impression of a curving apse. Neither would the artist feel himself a forger when he moulded stucco in imitation of carved stone. No Northern architect would have done these things, any more than he would have raised huge pilasters or columns which, purely decorative, appeared to perform a structural service while discharging none; nor would he have employed false façades to give an undeserved dignity to his churches. The Italian, on the other hand, trained in fields where illusion is a test of art, could not understand the attitude of the Northern builder who charged him with ignorance in the field of mathematics, and of incompetency in that of scientific construction. The Southerner could not understand why the Northerner should labour over difficulties that might easily be avoided, or why the skill with which he met those difficulties should be called makeshift and subterfuge beyond the Alps. Therefore he gave back to his critics all the scorn that the artist may feel for the engineer.

Perhaps we shall understand the Italian better if we remember that, to him, architecture was an art rather than a problem in the science of construction. Frothingham warns us that:

"In judging Italian construction it must be remembered that certain unscientific aids to stability were almost always used, so that the fact that a building is still standing is no proof that it ought to stand on its constructive merits. The Italians were quite shameless in this and saw no harm in it. It was the general habit to use heavy iron chains within the circuit of the masonry of a dome to tie it together and prevent its spreading. By 'faking' a centripetal coherence it was possible to raise domes on lofty drums. Such methods were always distasteful to Northern builders, who rarely allowed themselves to use forms that were not structurally sound. Had the Italians not sinned against this constructive ideal-ism we should never have had such domes as those of Florence, of S. Peter's in Rome, or of S. Paul's in London." [2]

The dome of which Frothingham speaks is, of course, the outstand-ing feature of Renaissance architecture. One cannot stand before Brunelleschi's dome in Florence, or Michelangelo's in Rome, without a feeling of amazement that is akin to awe, yet when we remember the concealed subterfuges—the oaken beams, iron trusses, and heavy iron chains—upon which their stability depends, we must recall with even deeper reverence another dome of almost equal size which Anthemius erected a thousand years before over the aisles and altars of Sancta Sophia in Byzantium—a dome for whose stability Justinian's architect had relied, not on the hidden devices of the great Florentines but on his own skill and on the virtues of the holy relics, buried in each twelfth layer of the stones to the prayers, hymns, and chants of priests in the choir below.

We must also remember, if we are to understand, that the Renais-sance in Italy was a revolution whose leaders sought to snap the bonds that had been forged throughout a thousand years. Ever since the days of Constantine the history of church architecture had been one of continuous growth. The Flamboyant and the Rayonnant had been either an elaboration or an over-simplification of the pure Gothic; the Gothic was the achievement of a goal the Romanesque had sought in vain; the Romanesque in turn was a Carlovingian basilica, grown to full stature and turned to stone, while the Carlovingian only sought to build as closely as he could *juxta Romanorum morem.*

[2] Sturgis and Frothingham, *History of Architecture*, Vol. IV, p. 97.

Italians of the Fifteenth Century, however, sought to create a new architecture, based upon the models and canons of classic Rome. While retaining the floor plan and the structural elements of the Basilican, Romanesque, or Gothic church—types of architecture "which sought a reasonable system which should pervade the entire mass"— they so buried this structure beneath a flood of classical or Renaissance decorations that M. Brutails, Archivist of the Gironde, could say with reason, "The architecture of the Renaissance is merely the triumph of a style." In this judgement Professor Frothingham concurs: "It was only on the decorative and æsthetic side that the Renaissance could make a successful appeal." To make that appeal they resurrected the Old Orders—Doric, Ionic, or Corinthian—from the graves where they had been buried centuries before with the ghost of ancient Rome; they framed or replaced the columns with pilasters, and often substituted the lintel for the arch. They ornamented their churches with the adornments of Roman villas—wreaths, scrolls, figures suggestive of the Seasons or the nymphs; they borrowed the glyphs and the egg-and-dart motives from pagan temples. They moulded plaster or carved stone into flowing ribbons interlaced amid circles, and varied these with vines, flowers, fruits, or with classic masks amid a maze of intricate designs.

In the secular field, better adapted to this sometimes florid ornamentation, the architects of the Renaissance were often splendidly successful. The palaces that look out upon the sea from Genoa, line the banks of Venetian canals, rise above the narrow streets of Florence, or climb the hills of Rome, eclipse the castles of the Middle Ages. Philippe de Commines, French ambassador to Venice in 1495, thought the Grand Canal to be "the goodliest street in the world, and the best built." In a similar strain Bishop Briconet, who went with Charles to Naples, wrote to Queen Anne: "Madam, I would that you might have seen this city and the fair things that are therein, for it is an earthly paradise."

It is possible, of course, that as Palestine appeared a land of milk and honey to men who had long sojourned in the desert, so these

THE CHURCH OF SS. PAUL AND LOUIS, PARIS

Its Romanesque structure is concealed beneath a sheath of Italian decorations. The English Evelyn called this church, "that noble fabriq, which I esteeme to be one of the most perfect pieces of architecture in Europe." Such churches illustrate the temporary triumph of a style.

"sun-bathed piazzas and colonnades, paved streets lined with palaces that glowed with marbles and frescoes, airy villas among terraced gardens set with fountains, statues, orange trees, and vine-covered pergolas" may have possessed an unearthly beauty to those who came from the narrow and muddy alleys of French cities, the grim blank walls of uncomfortable feudal castles, or the grey stone and smoke-darkened timbers of the North, as Mr. W. H. Ward suggests. Nevertheless we today, who come from green mountains, from grain-carpeted valleys, and well-built cities, respond to the appeal of Renaissance Italy even as did the ambassador of France, who thought the Certosa di Pavia "in very deed the fairest I ever saw," and the Bishop of Meaux, who deemed Naples "an earthly paradise."

In the field of ecclesiastical architecture, however, such admiration we may feel is often shadowed by regret and embittered with indignation, for these revolutionists of the Renaissance, holding in disesteem that against which they had rebelled, did not scruple to destroy, and by destroying to impose a tragic cost upon all later generations—a cost to which S. Peter's Church bears eloquent witness. To provide a building site for the new edifice of Pope Julius II, the venerable basilica which Constantine had begun in 319 and Pope Symmachus I had consecrated in 326, which successive generations had enriched with precious mosaics, frescoes, sculptured marbles, with historical inscriptions and papal tombs, was torn down instead of being strengthened and repaired. The loss to art, history, and Christian antiquities is beyond our calculation. But that is not all; in 1540 Pope Paul III gave to the church all the statues that filled the Forum or lined the Sacred Way to be burned for lime and turned to mortar. This passion for destruction flames all through the Renaissance.

Alexander VI levelled a temple, a forum, and parts of the Baths of Diocletian; Julius II was not too busy with his wars to tear down three other churches besides old S. Peter's. Borromini destroyed the "Mother of Churches," S. John Lateran, to make way for the colossal tastelessness of his newer structure. Fontana stripped the Septizonium, one of the most extensive and best preserved of old Roman edifices, to secure building stones for his palaces and churches. In brief, all the structures of the Golden and Silver Ages of the Renaissance, reared by popes, cardinals, patricians, and rich bankers or merchants, entailed the sacrifice of ancient buildings that were hallowed by age, by history, and by long tradition. The barbarians wrought no such havoc within the walls of Rome as did the men of the Sixteenth Century who praised with their lips what their hands destroyed with incredible brutality and stupidity.

The art of the ancient world suffered equally with the architecture. The suggestion of an architect, Piero Ligorio, that fine plaster might be secured from the Parian marble in Greek statues which Imperial victories had brought to Rome, seems to have borne bitter fruit. A lime kiln in the ruins of Tiberius' palace on the Palatine Hill was found filled to the brim with marble works of art, all ready for the burners. Many of these statues, those least injured, are now the prized possessions of Roman museums.

In 1883, when archæologists were excavating the Atrium of Vesta, the statues of the Vestales Maximae were found, not beside their pedestals but all heaped together like a cord of wood in a pile that was fourteen feet long, nine feet wide, and seven feet high—obviously waiting for carters from the lime kilns. Chrysoloras wrote: "The statues lie broken all around, ready for the kilns or to be used as building material. I have seen many used as mounting steps, as curb stones, or as mangers in the stables."

Nor was this vandalism limited to Rome; wherever the Renaissance went destruction followed as its shadow. In Spain the Emperor, Charles V, permitted a gaping hole to be torn in the heart of the marvellous mosque which the great Abd-er-Rahman had built at Cordova in 784, to make way for a huge Flamboyant church. Although Charles later repented, saying to the builders, "What you have done has been done by others and may be seen in many places; what you have destroyed had no equal in the world," yet in Belgium he himself tore down S. Bevan, one of the most beautiful monasteries and abbeys in all Europe, to erect a fortress wherewith to overawe rebellious Brussels.

The tombs of the great, however fine their artistry, were heavy suf-
ferers; let two sound the lament of hundreds. In Germany the tomb
of Bishop Brunyng, a holy man who had founded the Church of
Hildesheim, was dismantled; only his graven image, with its crozier
and mitre, was spared—to be transferred to another tomb and shown
to the people as the likeness of S. Godard. In England even the
Crown could not assure rest for the dead; in 1502 Katherine, wife of
Henry V—victor at Agincourt—was cast out of the Lady Chapel in
Westminster Abbey, and her coffin went unburied for well-nigh three
centuries.

On the same side of the Channel, the monks of S. Albans covered
with whitewash their old, priceless frescoes, while in Western England merchants—*nouveaux riches* through the wool trade—destroyed
many Norman or early English churches to erect Perpendicular edifices.

At Cambridge, in the Sixteenth Century, statues and stained glass
were ordered and paid for by the foot; at the same time, in Paris, the
Chapter of Notre-Dame threw out many jewelled windows of the
Twelfth and Thirteenth Centuries, replacing their rich and rare
colours with white glass; and as Paris suffered, so also did Chartres,
Rheims, Amiens, and many other churches.

The art and the architecture of the Renaissance in Italy were as
strange in their contrasts as were the lives of her cruel but cultured
despots. Italian architects could raise sublime domes to inspiring
heights, and then place a false façade on the Cathedral of Cremona;
they could build the great apse of S. Peter's, and paint an imitation
apse for S. Satiro in Milan; they carved stone magnificently on the
façade of S. Maria dei Miracoli in Venice, and then moulded terra-
cotta for the cloisters of the Certosa di Pavia; with the labours of three
generations they inlaid beautifully coloured marbles around an altar
of the Certosa, and then disfigured the façade with Rococo decorations;
Palladio built with a fine and delicate sense of proportions but he
also formulated rules for those proportions which clipped the wings
of genius and shackled liberty.

The architects of the Renaissance built marvellously—and marvellously destroyed.

W. H. WARD, *French Renaissance Architecture.*
G. G. COULTON, *Art and the Reformation.*
STURGIS and FROTHINGHAM, *History of Architecture,* Vol. IV.
J. A. SYMONDS, *Age of the Despots.*

Chapter Twenty=eight

THE RENAISSANCE IN FRANCE

THE Renaissance crept almost unnoticed from Italy into France, filtering into the country as clerics, traders, embassies, or travellers brought works of art across the Alps which made the new forms increasingly familiar to dwellers in Northern lands. This slow leakage, however, became a flood in the Sixteenth Century when the art and the artists of Italy poured over the frontiers with the returning armies of Charles VIII, of Louis XII, and of Francis I. Symonds, quoting Michelet, says:

> "Like a gale sweeping over a forest in bloom and bearing their fertilizing pollen, after it has broken and deflowered their branches, to far-distant trees which have hitherto bloomed in barrenness, the storm of Charles' army carried thought-dust, imperceptible, but potent to enrich the nations." [1]

France, however, except for the King and the Court, had no warmer welcome for this Italian invasion than Italy had for the armies of Charles VIII. French architects felt that those of Italy were ignorant in the field of mathematics, and incompetent in that of scientific construction. They resented the presumption of artists attempting to be architects, and although they recognized, as we do today, the skill with which the Italians rested their huge domes on a combination of the Byzantine pendentive and the Roman drum, yet they knew that the Southern builders were primarily concerned with the appearance of a church, with its ornamentation, and had only a mild and minor interest in its structure. This attitude was diametrically opposed to that of builders in the North. Throughout all the architectural history of France the form assumed by any church was based upon, and con-

---

[1] J. A. Symonds, *Age of the Despots*, p. 585; W. H. Ward, *Architecture of the Renaissance in France*, Vol. I, p. xx ff.

ditioned by, its inner and essential structure. The light wooden ceiling had determined the character of the Basilican church; the ponderous barrel vault had produced the dark and heavy forms of Romanesque churches, while an inner skeleton of stone had made possible the soaring qualities of the Gothic cathedral. Throughout a thousand years French ecclesiastical architecture had been primarily structural, and some organic principle had determined the form and nature of the church. The Italians, however, would change all this. Artists first and architects second, they were primarily concerned with the ornamentations and proportions of a church, with the relations between its voids and its solids.

The architects of France, on the other hand, viewing seriously the slow processes whereby their national architecture had evolved through many centuries, could not easily accept an architecture which, arising in opposition rather than in evolution, sought to jettison all the achievements of the Middle Ages. It was not easy to persuade builders, brought up in the older faith, to accept the new architectural heresies, heresies which made no stronger appeal to the masons, the artisans, and the guilds—elements more powerful in Northern than in Southern Europe—than they did to the architects. Finally, Gothic architecture in France, born of that complex intermixture of blood and institutions which had been superimposed upon the old Gallo-Roman stock by successive waves of Visigothic, Burgundian, Teutonic, and Norse invasions, was armed and armoured with the pride of nationality. Though it had been impoverished by the disorders of the Hundred Years' War and had lost its fervour, it continued to present a logical system of construction, and to receive powerful support from old memories and associations.

Therefore the Transalpine spirit, except among the aristocracy, was as resistant to the new Italian invasion as it had been to the old in the days of Ariovistus and Vercingetorix, and the Gothic gave way to the Renaissance far more slowly than the Romanesque had yielded to the Gothic. Consequently the new architecture had to be imposed on France from above; it did not spring from the people themselves, herein differing saliently from that of all preceding centuries.

The Basilican church came into being in a day when "not many great, not many noble," were called. Its erection was of the people, by the people, and for the people. Emperors, kings, might raise or enrich basilicas, but only in a style that had already, and more humbly, been determined. Equally democratic in its origin was the church of the Eleventh Century; monks, usually of lowly birth, planned and organized the work while countless pilgrims, long since forgotten, poured their gifts into monastic coffers to make possible the splendours of vast Romanesque abbeys. So also Gothic churches and cathedrals, striking their roots deep into the devotions of the masses, drew their strength from the common soil. Bishops, cathedral chapters, guilds, and citizens bore equally the burden and shared a common task. Kings and princes might be welcomed here; sovereigns might be crowned before their altars and buried in their aisles, but until the Sixteenth Century the church, whether it was Basilican, Carlovingian, Romanesque, or Gothic, was democratic in its origin.

The church of the Renaissance, on the other hand, was essentially aristocratic; her sponsors and patrons in France were the kings and the nobility; the dominant factor was wealth, and wealth is written in every line of her architecture. Yet it is this architecture, born in the palace and cradled in luxury, that was destined to be associated with the Revolution, for it was not from towers that democracies had raised, but from those reared under royalty, that rough hands rang out the passing bells for the *ancien régime*. There is not one Romanesque or Gothic building on the Place de la Concorde; only the classic structures of Gabriel stood around the scaffold, with the *sans-culottes*, the *bonnets rouges*, and the *tricoteuses*, when the last of the House of Capet knelt before the knife.

The architecture of the Renaissance in France, unlike that in Italy, is more easily traced through the palaces, châteaux, and civil edifices of the period than through the churches, for the land had been so well supplied with these through the activities of preceding generations that there was, fortunately, less need for new construction in an age when, because of diminished spiritual fervour, men felt no great inspiration to build for the glory of God. Such churches as were built, however, reveal no new constructive principle. French architects, borrowing from their fathers, retained for many years the structural framework of the Gothic; thence retreating, step by step, to the heavy barrel vault and solid walls of the Romanesque centuries, to the still earlier Basilican type or to the churches of radiate form like S. Vitale in Ravenna. This backward road ended at last in the cold aisles of S. Geneviève in Paris, where Soufflot combined the vaults of Constantine's basilica with the dome and peristyle of Agrippa's ancient Pantheon, or in the pagan temple on the rue Royale—Napoleon's "Temple of Glory"—now the Madeleine. Nevertheless, while the framework of the church remained as the fathers had left it—being merely covered over with a veil of classic ornamentation—forces were coming from the intellectual and political worlds that altered the church in more important ways than those of decoration, or even of structure.

It seems curious that when explorers and discoverers, of whom Columbus and Magellan were only types, were thrusting back the horizons of the seas, when Copernicus was revealing shining pathways among the stars where the imagination might travel but find no resting place, when the entire universe was being interpreted in ever-expanding terms, the walls of the church should have contracted and her aisles grown narrower. This contraction, however, was logical, for it was due to a conflict between the Schools and the Councils. Even the clergy were asking whether religion might not be a problem for the reason instead of a postulate of belief; whether it would not be possible to present the doctrines of the Church, formulated by her historic Councils, in terms acceptable to the Schools—in syllogisms that the minds of men could grasp and thus reinforce theology with intellectual conviction.

But the old cathedral could not live in such an atmosphere. Chartres and all her kin were the supreme expression of an age of faith; they belonged to a time when the worshipper was not asked to understand but only to believe; when the exercise of reason was unnecessary and even dangerous. The Church neither demanded nor expected more of the believer than that he obey, confess his sins, attend her services—

especially the Mass—and refuse the lure of heresies. Built for multitudes of pilgrims, the aisles of the cathedral were far too vast for the human voice to fill, wherefore liturgies and rituals were adapted for the eye rather than for the ear. Throughout these centuries the Church brought her messages to men through the silent movements of her servants, and every gesture of the priest, every change in his position, the actions of the acolytes, all had significances and subtle meanings which the worshipper had been taught from childhood to understand.[2]

But when the Age of Reason dawned vast cathedrals, become illogical, were doomed. Clerical preachers of philosophy—men like Bossuet and Fénelon—appealing to the intellects of men by cold reasonings, needed lecture-halls of moderate proportions where a cultured audience might gather on appointed days to listen to sermons on morality which confirmed their faith by making it seem reasonable.[3] So it came about that man's churches were becoming smaller at the very time when his world was growing larger.

The yard-stick tells the tale, for the average length of eleven Romanesque-Gothic churches of England is four hundred and sixty-eight feet, that of six French Gothic cathedrals is four hundred and sixteen feet, and that of fifty Romanesque or Gothic churches in Spain, France, Italy, Germany, and England is three hundred and sixty-eight feet; while the average length of five well-known Parisian churches of the Sixteenth, Seventeenth, and Eighteenth Centuries is only two hundred and forty-eight feet.

The church of Saltpetrière, built in the late Seventeenth Century, could hold four thousand worshippers while Chartres could accommodate eighteen thousand, and Notre-Dame in Paris twenty thousand, pilgrims.

To this S. Peter's in Rome, six hundred and thirteen feet in length, appears an exception. But the seat of the Pope at the centre of the political and financial Roman Catholic world was the goal of the politically minded prelate as well as of the devout who would visit the

---

[2] See the English translation of Guillaume Durandus, *Rationale Divinorum Officiorum.*
[3] W. H. Ward, *Architecture of the Renaissance in France*, p. 253; Hourticq, *Art in France*, p. 187.

tomb of S. Peter and the shrines where lay the veil of S. Veronica or the lance of Longinus. It was, therefore, and still is, the outstanding pilgrimage church of Catholicism. There were, however, many churches of the pre-Renaissance pilgrimage years that rivalled S. Peter's in size—old S. Paul's in London, Glastonbury, or Cluny, to quote but three instances, which were nearly, or over, six hundred feet in length. The one great pilgrimage church of the Renaissance must be great in size for the same reason that a score of other churches, built in the earlier pilgrimage years, must be great—to accommodate the hordes of pilgrims. But where pilgrimages ceased, walls and aisles contracted and grew small. The change, then, from the great cathedrals of the Age of Faith to the smaller churches of the Age of Reason was as rational as that Age, and due to that very rationality.

Other changes in the architecture flowed from the political upheaval which, begun under Richelieu, concentrated all power in the throne, and from the days of Louis XIV each succeeding reign of the House of Bourbon left its imprint on the church.

Under the autocratic *Roi Soleil*—who was not only the "First Gentleman in Europe" but also, so said the Bishop of Vente, "the visible and authentic image of Deity"—God became the First Gentleman in the universe whose church was an audience chamber where He held His matutinal levees. This explains the chapel of Versailles, with its soft colours, its purple breccia railings, gilt balustrades, flecks of gold in delicate carvings and its bright but semi-pagan vault. With the advent of Louis XV, when Society—sceptical and frivolous—regarded "morals as optional but wit and good manners as essential," when gaucherie was sin and courtliness was righteousness, social intercourse centred in the drawing-room, not in the vast halls of cold Versailles. The new age demanded freedom for caprice, for wit, for the quick flash of keen repartee; it created an atmosphere wherein the solemnities of the Romanesque and of the Gothic had no place, and the architecture of the churches corresponded to the mood wherein both priests and people shared.

When Louis XVI, earnest if vacillating, came to the throne there was a marked reaction to the Rococo and Baroque, to the *Chinoiseries* and the *Rocaille* which had invaded the church in the flippant days of Louis XV and of the Regency, and serious efforts were made to banish all ornamentation that served no structural purpose, to return to purer classical lines and to a greater simplicity in form.

But the throne was doomed; continued misgovernment, costly wars and wastes, increased burdens of taxation, the orations of poor scholars who inflamed a hungry proletariat with visions of the *panis et circenses* —the free bread and games offered by the Cæsars to the Roman people—all combined to sow a seed in whose harvest king and courtier perished.

Little parlour revolutionists, toying with ideas that were to destroy their order, copied the Roman dress, the Pompeian decorations; they put flowers in Etruscan vases, breakfasted at tripod tables, and sat in curule chairs to applaud the preachings of Rousseau.

When at last the *Dies Irae* came, architecture felt the impact, for the art which had flourished under royalty now seemed tainted, while that which came from pagan Greece or Rome was welcomed as a proper expression of that Liberty, Equality, and Fraternity with which the new order challenged the despotisms of the old. When the *Tiers Etat* leaped into the saddle it sought to suppress all the activities of the Middle Ages, and to introduce the arts of the ancient pagan world; so far as it was able to gratify these preferences it did so.

As the Madeleine closes the vista from the rue Royale, so it closes the vista of the centuries. Begun in the year 1764, its foundations had hardly cleared the ground before France began her terrible *Jeu de Paume,* playing the game with the heads of her most illustrious. The last church that the old Capetian House was destined to begin seemed to shrink back into the earth as, day after day, the tumbrels rumbled by, and the beat of drums drowned alike the prayers of the dying and the clicking needles of the *tricoteuses* on the Place de la Concorde.

Then, in 1806, Napoleon wrote from his camp on the frontiers of Russia to command the completion of the church in the form of a Grecian temple to enshrine the trophies of his victorious armies.

Purely pagan, Roman-Corinthian in form, when viewed from the rue Royale, the Madeleine, seen from its portals, is such a hall as might have belonged to a Roman Bath, but with the altars of a Christian church. So today it stands, looking back across the ages to another Roman building—the basilica—which died centuries ago in parturition, giving birth to the Christian church.

Three Parisian churches sum up the six hundred years that have passed since Suger laid the foundations of S. Denis. Notre-Dame, with frowning devils on her towers, with Christ enthroned and Mary crowned above her portals, speaks for an age when men believed that within such walls alone they might find refuge for today and for eternity. The chapel at Versailles recalls the courtly graces of a generation which once gathered here to present its compliments and adulations to its sovereign's God; while from the Madeleine we hear the deep-throated "Mountain" offering the Almighty, now restored to the throne from which it had recently, by vote, deposed Him, an altar within the walls of a pagan peripteral temple.

From Notre-Dame it is God who speaks; from Versailles, the King; from the Madeleine, Marat.

W. H. WARD, *French Renaissance Architecture.*

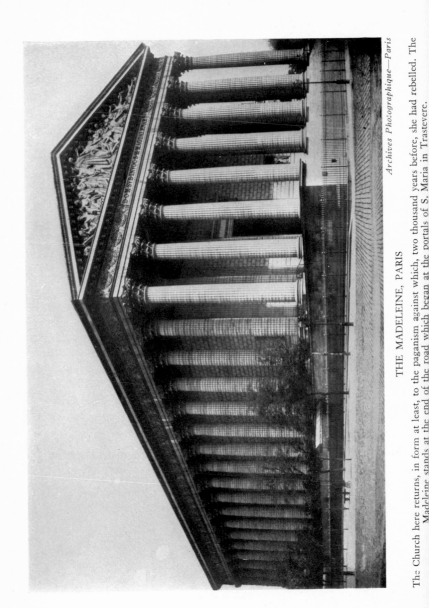

THE MADELEINE, PARIS

The Church here returns, in form at least, to the paganism against which, two thousand years before, she had rebelled. The Madeleine stands at the end of the road which began at the portals of S. Maria in Trastevere.

Archives Photographique—Paris

Chapter Twenty-nine

THE END OF THE ROAD

ACROSS Paris, on the fringe of the Latin Quarter, lie the ruins of the old Roman Arena of Lutetia, built when Gaul was a Roman Province and when Christianity was hiding in the candle-lit obscurity of the catacombs. Today nurses gossip and children play on the grass-grown soil where once men played at sterner games.

At the head of the rue Royale, looking towards the Place de la Concorde, stands Napoleon's "Temple of Glory," now the Church of the Madeleine.

These two monuments form the *terminus a quo* and the *terminus ad quem* of all church architecture. Between the time when the masons of Lutetia laid the stones of the old Arena and the day when Napoleon's builders raised the walls of the Madeleine the whole history of ecclesiastical architecture ran its course.

We have watched its upward struggles, its experiments, its failures and triumphs, and its supreme achievements in the great cathedral age in France. We have seen its decline, at first slow and imperceptible, then with increasing speed and impetus, moving ever backward towards the pagan, until at last the old gods seem to triumph on the Place de la Madeleine.

If we could step from the Arena of Lutetia to the rue Royale and stand before that peripteral Corinthian Temple which bears the name of a wanton who became a saint; if we could thus far cross Paris without passing the churches of S. Julien le Pauvre, of S. Séverin, or of S. Sulpice, and without seeing in the distance the spire of S. Chapelle or the towers of Notre-Dame, we might easily dream that Augustus was still Emperor of the World; that the days of Constantine, Justinian, Clovis, Charlemagne, and Suger were yet to come.

But one step inside the portals would shatter the dream, for though "the hands be the hands of Esau, yet the voice is the voice of Jacob." The candles burning before the marble statues, the crucifix in the chancel, the pyx on the altar, the labarum on the pulpit, alike proclaim that the old gods are dead and may not live again.

Such temples as men once raised to Jupiter or to Zeus, to Mars or to Ares, to Venus or to Aphrodite, to Diana or to Artemis, they now raise to Him whom the old world crucified, whose followers the old gods slew; to His mother, Notre-Dame—Our Lady; or to that other woman whom man made a sinner, but whom Christ made a saint.

"Christus Regnat et Regnabit"

Part Two

THE ARCHÆOLOGY

THE TEMPLE OF POSEIDON AT PÆSTUM

This Doric temple preserves the memorials of a time when men built in wood. The baseless columns, the entablature with its glyphs, triglyphs, metopes, and guttæ carry us back to the forest dwellers of very early days. If these columns bulge slightly it is because a straight column would deceive the eye and appear concave.

Chapter Thirty

WHAT PRIMITIVE MAN CONTRIBUTED TO CATHEDRAL ARCHITECTURE

THE Book of Genesis—in the Hebrew tongue *Breshith*, "The Book of Beginnings"—may be quickly read; not so the *Breshith* of the Church. Here is no proper study for one who loves overwell his hearth for he must run who reads; he must gird his loins, don his sandals, take his staff, and prepare to travel up the ages.

The first Christian church has already pointed us to the Roman law-court, thence to a market that Marcus Porcius Cato built in the Second Century before Christ, and to a Grecian Council Hall erected at Olympia in the Sixth Century B.C. The Baptistry sent us on to the Age of Bronze, to the shepherds of Alba Longa. The gateway to the cloister will presently place our feet on a long trail leading to distant gardens where the gods walked in the cool of the evening and spoke face to face with men.

Then when, like crystal gazers, we peer into the still waters of the Basin of Holy Water, we shall see the childhood of our race unfold; we shall see men who have not yet learned fully to distinguish between persons and things, for whom there were literally tongues in stones and sermons in running brooks, who dealt softly with all living waters, lest they anger the spirits in springs or streams. But even here we may not find a resting place; driven back, step by step, from the Age of Iron to that of Bronze, and from Bronze to Copper, we come at last to the Age of Stone where men move vaguely in the mists of an early dawn, mere silhouettes against an unfamiliar background.

Into these shadows and silences we must enter if we would find the beginnings of our architecture, discovering, before we have travelled far, that the architect's axioms today were once a builder's problems, and that familiar, commonplace features in our churches have strange and illuminating origins.

Why should the cathedral have a rounded apse? Why should the builders bend one wall of their churches into a curve, yet cling tenaciously to the straight line in their secular architecture?

Why is a base placed beneath the column when it needs no firmer support than the stone pavement on which it stands? The great columns of Pæstum have none, and those of Girgenti did not need them.

Why do we crown our columns with capitals? Byzantine architects interposed stone blocks to protect them; the Fourteenth Century minimized, and the Fifteenth Century abandoned them. Although the Renaissance once more adopted them, the classical architecture of the Eighteenth Century could, sometimes did, dispense with them.

Why are the splendid carvings of the frieze on pagan temples and Renaissance churches placed so far above the level of the eye? Why are its bas-reliefs often interrupted by projecting beam-ends of stone? What is the meaning of the channels grooved on the ends of these beams, and of the bead-like decorations placed beneath them?

Today asks, and yesterday replies—a yesterday when the Baltic Sea was only a lake; when the ice-cap over Europe was receding before warm winds from the South; when continuous rains were driving out the beasts who had long fed, fought, and begot where our cities now stand—the white bear and the reindeer to the North, the lion and the hyena to the South—and when the hut-building Azilian entered the land, driving before him the cave-dwelling Magdalenian.

Inevitably we must travel dim trails as we retrace the years; we must pick our way through mist and fog, looking here and there for footprints, and finding few; the centuries have passed over them, and they are gone. Here is no Tell el-Amarna, with its treasury of buried letters from dead kings, to throw light upon our path. But there are tombs, as in Lycia and in Persia, whose builders have repeated in stone the lines of earlier timber work construction; and the entablature, whether of stone, as in Grecian temples, or of wood, as in Persepolitan palaces, interprets to us the cruder architecture of Neolithic days from which it is derived. These will help us to see below the horizons of the years. Furthermore, life as it is being lived today by the more primitive peoples of the world enables us to picture the ways of Neolithic and of Palæolithic man, for the clay roofs and walls of Transjordania, the circular huts of branches in the depths of Africa, and the skin-covered, cone-shaped tepees of our own American Indians carry us back to the thresholds of Magdalenian caves.

If Cuvier, being given a single bone, could reproduce from that fragment the character and appearance of an unknown prehistoric animal, the archæologist may as confidently re-create the life of Azilian days from the habits of backward peoples which repeat those of ages past, and reproduce a perished architecture from the stone constructions of a later day which perpetuate more primitive habitations wrought in wood.[1]

Of all the elements of our church architecture the apse is the first-born, for it was cradled among Azilians who, invading Europe, drove the Magdalenians from their caves and country, conquering probably because they were not only more numerous but were also better armed.

Although the Azilians seem to have been the first builders of houses, yet they inherited something of their skill from earlier Palæolithic ancestors who needed some protection from biting winds when their periodic expeditions of fishing, hunting, scouting, or fighting called them forth from their caves and forced them into the open. Inclement weather made man an architect. His first venture in this field was the erection of a wind-break—sometimes a straight wall of stones or boughs on the leeward side of which he slept; beside this he presently raised a parallel wall that he might sleep with protection on both sides. Then, perhaps because some prowling animal disturbed his rest, he closed up the ends with stone or boughs and covered his walls with

---

[1] Since we shall have occasion, in this chapter, to refer to the various stages of pre-history it may be helpful if we arrange them in order here. Although the attempt to assign dates is admittedly presumptuous, Miss Boyle, in *In Search of Our Ancestors,* has cautiously ventured the following scheme:

Mousterian Period ....50,000 to 25,000 B.C.
Aurignacian Period........................25,000 to 18,000 or longer
Magdalenian and Solutrean Period............18,000 to 10,000
Azilian Period..............................10,000 to 8,000

branches and with skins, thus building the first rectangular house to exclude discomforts from the skies and dangers from the forests.

Often, however, these men of long past years leaned branches against the trunk of some stout tree and slept within the circle, but the rain trickling down the tree and forming unpleasant puddles in his bed may have caused Mesolithic man to forsake his tree; at any rate he soon made himself a shelter by thrusting a ring of branches into the ground, bending their tops over and fastening them with vines to form a roof which he covered with skins, thus building the first round hut.

These two forms, the rectangular house and the round hut, descended the ages side by side until they were merged into one pattern—a form that is still preserved in the Christian church with its three straight sides and one curving end.

With the coming of the Azilians the Odyssey of the apse begins— the story of an evolution whose almost continuous development may be traced through the ruins of houses built by man centuries before even the legendary history of Europe was begun by the Epic of the Trojan War.

The huts themselves have long since perished; their walls of mud-cemented reeds or straw have been scattered to the winds; the trees that lent their branches have moulded and decayed; clay bricks have crumbled into dust. But here or there the floors of these vanished dwellings, sometimes of hard-packed earth and sometimes paved with stone, have been uncovered to give us some knowledge of their plan and outline.

A box from Melos represents the seven round houses of a *genos* (a family-clan, or blood-group) gathered around a walled court with a covered entrance.

Then these small, round houses vanished and an elliptical "long house," with curving sides and rounded ends, was built in order to collect all the members of the blood-group under one roof. At Orchomenos, in Greece, archæologists have laid bare the foundations of a city of these elliptical dwellings which was built in the middle of the Third Millennium on the ruins of an earlier settlement of round houses.

During the same years rectangular houses also continued to be built but in the first years of the Second Millennium the two plans, the round and the rectilinear, were merged and dwellings began to appear, first in Thessaly and later throughout all Greece, with one curving and three straight sides. The rooms within these houses were grouped around a large central hall, or *megaron,* which was divided into aisles by the columns that supported the roof, and often had a rectangular, or semi-circular, recess at the further end.[2]

So from the wind-breaks of Palæolithic days we pass to the rude huts of Mesolithic times, thence to the round houses of Neolithic centuries, to the elliptical dwellings of Orchomenos of the Third Millennium, to the Fifteenth Century Throne Room of Cretan Knossos with its rectangular apse, to the Sixth Century Bouleterion at Olympia with its curving apse, to the Greek basilica which Marcus Portius Cato translated into the Roman law-court and market, until we reach the early Christian church whose three straight sides and curving end carry us back through ten thousand years to Azilian days.

When, then, we stand in the nave of any church, whose rectangular walls repeat the wind-breaks of Palæolithic years, and look towards the chancel where the priest stands in his embroidered vestments, holding the chalice in his hands, we may see—in the curving walls around him—a survival of the little round hut of branches wherein our Azilian ancestor stands, with long hair and shaggy beard, clad in skins instead of in silks, and gripping a club instead of a chalice in his gnarled and hairy hands.

The quest for the origin of the base and the capital of the column will not carry us into quite so remote a past, for Azilian huts, which never seem to have exceeded eight feet in diameter, were so small that no medial support was needed for their light roofs. Even when the hut gave place to the house, when the light roof of skin-covered branches was succeeded by a heavier roof of timbers and wattled branches plastered with five or six inches of clay, the walls were still able to bear the weight. But when the tribe grew stronger and the family larger, when the householder thrust out his walls to increase

2 Gustave Glotz, *Ægean Civilization,* Chap. IV.

the area of his home and accommodate his growing family, then the roof threatened to collapse.

To prevent disaster the owner hurried into the forest, cut down a tree and brought a section of the trunk into his house to support his sagging roof. This, the first column, did not long meet the need, however, for it was driven, inch by inch, deeper into the ground by the pressure of the roof, giving—as it sank—less and less support until finally it failed to function and the roof again began to crack and threaten. Therefore the stone-age inventor sought a flat stone which he brought in and placed beneath his column, thereby giving it a base that was too broad to be driven into the ground. From this flat stone came the bases upon which the builders of ancient Greece, of mediæval France, and of modern America alike have rested their piers, even though they stand on pavements of solid stone instead of on softer Mesolithic earth.

The problem was not yet solved, however, for when the tree trunk could no longer burrow into the ground under the weight of the roof it began to pierce the wattled clay above and, when it had broken through, the ceiling once more began to sag. So the builder went again into the forest with his hatchet of obsidian, returning presently with a short log which he placed across the top of his column to blunt its point and prevent it from penetrating, like a spear, the roof it had failed to support. Thus was born the capital with which we continue to crown our columns, even though they have become merely decorative at the best, and a source of weakness at the worst.[3]

It is a long journey, in years but not in thought, from Mesolithic to Modern Europe, from the forests where once the Azilian built his hut to the cathedral, doubtless standing on the self-same ground; but hav-

[3] It has been assumed that primitive man possessed tools for the felling of trees long before he began to build huts. This assumption is supported by Jacques de Morgan, who writes of "flint knives with backs," and of "tools intended for work in tough material, such as hard wood," in Aurignacian days. He also speaks of flint saws in the Solutrian Period that were "analogous to those of Mousterian and Aurignacian industries." (*Prehistoric Man*, Chap. II.) G. Renard carries cutting implements even farther back than the Stone Age: "First of all man used shell. Shell, before stone was used, played a great part in human development; it gave to man knives, even tomahawks, and was used to dig the ground and to fell trees." (*Life and Work in Prehistoric Times*, Chap. III.)

ing made it, we can look down the aisles to the apse with clearer eyes and a better understanding of our inheritance. It does not need any wealth of imagination to enable us to see a forest of rough tree trunks coming from the ground to replace the clustered columns; rows of flat stones, with the mosses and wood-ferns still clinging to them, appearing to supplant the bases with their rolls, griffes, or spurs; and round logs, bark-covered, superseding the Ionic, Corinthian, Composite, or Storied capitals—the fathers visiting the sons.

The hand of Neolithic man has also left its imprint on the frieze—that band of stone, often covered with bas-reliefs, which runs along the top of the wall, just beneath the eaves. We have seen it around the domes that Brunelleschi raised in Florence, Michelangelo in Rome, Soufflot in Paris, and Christopher Wren in London; we have seen it so often in Romanesque and Renaissance churches that the details are familiar. Stone beams—whose projecting ends are grooved from top to bottom, where a row of little decorative beads depends—divide a band of stone, often sculptured in relief, into a succession of compartments. To give them their rightful names, the plaques in the compartments are called the *metopes,* the beams are the *triglyphs*, the grooves are the *glyphs,* the little beads are the *guttæ,* and we shall hereafter so address them.

Since artistic genius of the highest order has often been spent upon the sculpturing of the metopes (on those of the Parthenon, for instance) one wonders why they have been placed so far overhead where they may not be rightly seen, instead of on a level with the eye. Why are the glyphs chiselled down the ends of the beams, and what, if any, is the meaning of the guttæ?

Neither the stone-cutter nor the building contractor can tell us—all they know is that the blueprints call for them. The architect may be able to answer us, but not with the authority of Neolithic man; if we cannot understand the speech of the men who lived in the late Stone Age, we can understand their handiwork and learn, as we watch them build, the meaning of our own architecture.

When men began to raise more solid and pretentious houses than the crude huts of earlier days they first raised the four walls, and then placed upon them the trunks of light trees which, running from side to side, formed a framework for the ceiling and also a foundation for the roof. These rough and untrimmed logs, when they were laid in place, left openings on either side, openings that were framed between the walls below, the roof above, and the beams on either hand. These empty spaces permitted ventilation, to which the builder was probably quite indifferent, and also served to let light in and smoke out, for the fire blazing on the hard earth floor of his dwelling had no other chimney. In these openings beneath the eaves man placed his weapons and the skulls of slain enemies and beasts—the trophies of his two absorbing pursuits, war and the chase. Down the ends of his projecting beams he cut grooves, possibly to hold the tough vines with which he secured his roof of wattled branches against the force of heavy winds; however, the original purpose of these glyphs is a subject of high controversy. It seems more probable that they were first decorative bands of colour painted down the ends of the beams; later, still for ornamentation, these lines were carved into the wood. The guttæ, which he drove into the bottom of these beams, were originally tree nails, used structurally in other parts of his building, but driven in here for their decorative values.

These men of Neolithic days lived out their lives and died; their huts and houses have crumbled into dust, but their memorials survive. True, there are no longer fires burning on hard earth floors; no heads of enemies are being dried and cured in smoke that billows among the rafters; no roof of wattled branches must be lashed down with vines lest storm winds carry it away; stone beams need neither glyphs nor tree nails. Nevertheless, short blocks of stone continue to project above our walls where once the tree trunks lay; glyphs groove and guttæ decorate their ends. The spaces between these blocks, no longer needed to hold the ghastly trophies of head-hunting warriors, are closed with marble metopes whereon the Greeks carved the triumphs of their cities, or the praises of their gods; where the mediæval monk carved his grotesque heads and faces, as at Sugères, Poitiers, and many a church besides, and where we place the symbols of our industry or commerce. Thus to Palæolithic and to Neolithic man we owe the curving apse of our cathedrals, the column, with its base and capital, and the frieze with its triglyphs, glyphs, metopes, and guttæ.

Many millennia have passed since those far days when man and the mammoth dwelt in the depths of vanished European forests; countless generations have buried their dead, with all the tools and weapons that their spirits might need in the World to which their souls had gone. Where the hands of the dying laid the dead, there mourners and mourned alike have rested until we, eagerly questioning, disturbed their graves and disinterred their bones. Now they lie in innumerable museums surrounded by their stone hammers, their flint or obsidian axes, their spears, arrow heads, bone knives, harpoons, and needles. They were doubtless rude, barbarous, uncouth, and ignorant but— there is the apse of Chartres; there are the soaring columns of the church of the Jacobins at Toulouse, the moulded bases of Rheims, the storied capitals of S. Nectaire; there are the friezes of the Parthenon, of S. Peter's, of S. Geneviève, and of S. Paul.

What was in the beginning is now, and apparently shall always be.

MARY E. BOYLE, *In Search of Our Ancestors.*
JACQUES DE MORGAN, *Prehistoric Man.*
MARCEL DIEULAFOIX, *L'Art Antique de le Perse.*
GUSTAVE GLOTZ, *The Ægean Civilization*
G. RENARD, *Life and Work in Prehistoric Times.*

Chapter Thirty-one

THE ORIGIN OF THE CLOISTER

THE Fourth Chapter of Exodus, in a few verses that belong to the oldest stratum of the Pentateuch, relates a curious and surprising story. According to this account Moses, journeying from Horeb, "the Mountain of God," to Egypt, in obedience to the command given by Jehovah from the Burning Bush, was met near the day's camping place by the Lord who sought to slay him; not until Zipporah, his wife, seizing a sharp desert flint, circumcised their son did the Lord let Moses go. No reason is given for this attack by Jehovah upon His own obedient messenger, but the explanation is written in the ways and thoughts of that distant generation.

The territories of Jehovah lay around Mt. Sinai, or Horeb as it was also called. In traversing the desert Moses had unwittingly trespassed upon the territory of some local god and this deity, irritated by the attempted passage of a stranger who offered neither reverence nor sacrifice, laid violent hands upon the trespasser. When, however, the blood of the circumcision fell upon the ground the god accepted this as a sacrifice and suffered Moses to resume his journey.

Some later writer or story-teller, repeating the tale because it explained the origin of circumcision but thinking it unbecoming that any lesser god should have had power over the great prophet of his people, or that Moses should ever have offered sacrifice to a stranger god, substituted the name of Jehovah for that of the deity in the original tale, otherwise leaving the story unchanged.

This incident illustrates one of the terrors that must have burdened the mind of early man—the dread of unwitting trespass upon ground that was taboo, trespass that could not fail to kindle the wrath of some one of the multitudinous known or unknown gods.

The necessity of finding explanations for the varying phenomena of nature imposed the belief in many gods upon the mind of primitive man. The wind that blew down his hut, the lightning that killed among his flocks and herds, the sun, rain, or dew that turned his seed into harvest, seemed each actuated by an indwelling spirit not unlike his own, sometimes vengeful and jealous, sometimes kindly and protective.

The territory of each tribe was also the territory of its god, and somewhere within that territory lay his holy place; it might be a cave, a spring, a boulder of unusual shape, a fountain of healing water, a tree with wide spreading branches, land that had been struck by lightning, or the site of an unusual echo, but from each holy place, whatever it might be, there radiated out to an undetermined distance an area of dangerous ground which shared, in diminishing measure, the power of a mysterious and terrifying taboo. One incautious step upon that ground might turn a quiescent god into a menace of destruction, for not every god would be merciful enough to warn a trespasser to "put off thy shoes from off thy feet, for the place whereon thou standest is holy ground," nor would every god be sufficiently mindful of human life to caution his people, as Jehovah cautioned Israel, to set bonds around his mountain and not to touch it "lest they die." Many gods would have struck without notice. The assault upon Moses in the desert, the fate of the two men who set well-intentioned hands upon the Ark of the Covenant, the leprosy that smote King Uzziah in the Temple and, in Greek mythology, the doom of Actæon who had accidentally entered the presence of Diana, are well-known instances of the perils that lurked in places or objects that were taboo.

Property as well as life might be the forfeit of trespass, for many gods claimed the right to possess whatever crossed their boundaries. The axe that the woodman carried a step too far, the flock of sheep browsing too near the sanctuary, might not be reclaimed. At Mecca even the clothing the worshipper wore as he ran around the Caaba ceased to be his own property. The present custom of leaving the shoes at the door of the mosque is merely the survival into modern times of this ancient law.

It was, therefore, of primary importance to the peace of mind of these remote ancestors of ours that Holy Ground, land that was taboo, should be clearly marked off by unmistakable boundaries in order to protect men against penalties of accidental trespass.

The consequent practice of enclosing the land around a shrine by danger-lines was common throughout the ancient Semitic world, in Roman territory, and also in the Grecian world where such enclosures were called *temenoi*, and the word *temenos*, with its plural *temenoi*, will hereafter be used for the sake of brevity. Their meaning is quite clear; a temenos was "a piece of land marked off from common use, and dedicated to a god." Such courts encircled the Temple of Jerusalem and lay behind the pylons of Egyptian temples.

Little by little, as the years passed, these earth-bound gods became detached from their local shrines, to become the deities of a people rather than the gods of a land. The steps by which the transfer might be made are clearly indicated in the history of Israel.

Jehovah, at first a local god dwelling on Mt. Sinai, went forth with the fugitives from Egypt to give them victory over their enemies and possession of their promised land. Nevertheless the local baalim remained—they were still the gods of the fields to whom sacrifice must be made whenever seed was sown or harvests reaped. Thus Jehovah, detached from his mountain, became the supreme God of a new land by the right of conquest, without entirely displacing the gods of the conquered.

When, centuries later, the armies of Babylon captured Jerusalem, destroyed the Temple and carried the people into captivity, Israel despaired. If victory proved the presence and favour of their God, such an overwhelming disaster equally revealed His anger and abandonment. Godless and alone, they could but hang their harps upon the willows of Babylon and weep beside her waters, for "how could they sing the Lord's songs in a strange land," or how could He hear, Whom they had left so far behind?

But in the fifth day of the fourth month of the thirtieth year the heavens were opened; a captive by the waters of Chebar saw visions of God and the word of the Lord came to Ezekiel, a priest. With the return of the prophets saying, "Thus saith the Lord," Israel rose to new heights of understanding, for a God who could thunder from Sinai and command in distant Babylon must be none other than the God of the whole earth beside Whom there were no other gods. Heaven and earth could not contain Him; darkness could not hide from Him, nor could the wings of the morning find, even in the uttermost parts of the earth, a place where His hand did not hold, or His right hand lead. Since, then, Jehovah alone ruled, the gods of the heathen could be no more than wood or stone.

A similar, if less ennobling, transition of the idea of deity took place in other nations; in nations which, if hampered by their polytheism, were also aided by their commerce which often called their ships to strange waters and to almost unknown lands. Those Greeks who, from the Eleventh Century before Christ onward, sailed from the Black Sea to the extreme limits of the Western Mediterranean, could not feel that their gods were left behind on Mt. Olympus. The sailors of Tyre, whose sails caught the winds and suns of the Western Mediterranean in the Twelfth Century before Christ, who established colonies, not only in Northern Africa and in Spain but even beyond the Pillars of Hercules where the waters of the Atlantic wash the African shores, knew well that it was Melkarth of Tyre who made their pathway in the great deep. The citizens of Carthage, who began their phenomenal rise to power in the Eleventh Century before our era, sending their ships northward past Gibraltar to Britain and southward nearly to the Equator, could not doubt but that their gods sailed with their ships. Inevitably the very success of this extensive trade, the deliverances of their ships from the perils of the sea, the wealth poured out upon their quays, proved the all-seeing eyes and the powers of the outstretched hands of the gods they worshipped. No temenos could limit or contain the might of such as these, and Phœnician, Greek, Roman, and Carthaginian alike lost faith in the primitive taboos. In Italy the great gifts of the gods, which undermined the temenos, even tended to destroy the gods themselves, for Rome's rise to world supremacy, and the enormous wealth poured upon her shores from her subject races, fostered a spirit of materialism, as the possession of power and prosperity often does, which impaired and sapped an already diminishing feeling of religious awe.

Meanwhile agnostics like Protagoras and Prodicus, doubting even the existence of gods, were hardly more destructive to the temenos than was the vague faith of the philosophers; the Psalmist poured out no more bitter scorn upon idols than did Xenophanes the Greek when he mocked men for making gods in their own image, flat-nosed and black among the Ethiopians, blue-eyed and fair-haired among the Thracians. Surely, he said, if a cow could draw she would make an image of a bull and worship it. Isaiah never denounced more scathingly the whole system of sacrifice than did Heraclitus when he asked if a man who, having stepped into the mud, attempted to cleanse himself with more mud was less ridiculous than he who, stained with blood-guilt, thought to purify himself by shedding still more blood before an altar.

In all these ways, in the contact of tribe with tribe, of city with city whether by war or by trade; in the impacts of philosophy and of science on the minds of men, the processes were quickened by means of which the gods were set free from the land and clothed with more universal attributes.

Thus the terror in which definite spots of ground were held began to wane and died down to a passive superstition, while the fear of the gods, decreasing as the gods receded, lost its early force. Even this superstition dwindled, for it is evident that its power was ebbing when, as early as 293 B.C., a Roman *pullarius*—a keeper of the sacred chickens —could falsely report good omens when his charges clearly foretold disaster by the way in which they pecked the corn from the ground; when Claudius Pulcher could throw the birds into the sea and sail on to battle, even though their omens had been unfavourable, and when, in the Second Punic War, Marcellus—an *augur optimus*—rode in his litter with drawn blinds to avoid seeing any warning sign.

At the very moment when men's faith in the taboos, which had created the temenoi around the older temples, was dwindling, the pres-

sure of growing populations, surging against the temple courts, made
it increasingly difficult to preserve these areas. The economic conditions
of early Christian centuries led to peasant emigrations from the country
to the city which, depleting the rural districts, overcrowded the cities;
and this shifting of the population, increasing throughout the times of
the Antonines (138-180 A.D.), was not checked until after the reign of
Aurelian (died 275 A.D.). Lepsius estimated the population of Rome at
four million while Gibbon put the number at one million two hundred
thousand. There were eight hundred thousand in the city of Alexandria; Jerusalem is said, at least, to have contained over half a million
Jews, although the figure is probably too high, and houses eight stories
in height were built to accommodate the growing populations of the
cities of Apamea, Cæsarea, Cyzicus, Tyre, and Sidon.[1] In Gaul, Lyons,
Arles, Narbonne, Trier illustrated the general concentration of population caused by the tide of emigration from the country to the city.

This congestion of the cities, where opportunities for expansion were
limited by the constriction of the city walls, forced the populations to
move against all unoccupied areas of land within the city's gates in
order to satisfy the need for building space. Although the ancient, all-
encircling temenos might linger in the country, where land was
plentiful, within the city the pressure of the populace would naturally
lead to the surrender of the less important ground behind the temple,
and then to that on either side. Thus, bit by bit, the old temenos would
be absorbed until only that part remained which lay before its portals.
The only surviving temple in Rome, completely surrounded by a
temenos, is that of Venus and Rome, built by Hadrian on an open area
of ground that measured five hundred and forty-one feet by three hundred and twenty-seven. There were other temples also encircled by
land that was reminiscent of the temenos, such as the temple of Jupiter
and Juno in the Portico of Octavia; of Venus in the Forum of Julius
Cæsar; of Neptune in the Portico of the Argonauts, and finally the
temple dedicated by Hadrian to Trajan. But in these instances the
land on either side of the temples had shrunk to a mere passageway,

[1] Paul-Louis, *Ancient Rome at Work*, p. 227.

and even this was sometimes lacking in the rear, to which aspect of the temple the Romans attached but slight importance.[2]

When Christianity entered the Roman world and Christians took the old law-court as the model for their churches, they not only found themselves surrounded by pagan temples with atria before their portals, but also felt the pressure of demands which, while they could not be met within the sacred precincts of their basilicas, could be admirably served in the arcades of an atrium. There were pagans who wished to know the meanings of this new religion from the East, there were converts who must be instructed before coming to the altar, and penitents who must be purged before again entering the sacred aisles. For all these purposes and uses some place must be found, other than the church itself which, being holy ground, was reserved for those who lived their lives in the keeping of the faith.

Therefore the Church adopted the atrium—last survivor of the old temenos—gave it a fountain for ceremonial ablutions, and placed it before their basilicas; in its colonnades Christian priests and teachers ministered to the curiosity of pagans, the aspirations of converts, and the penitence of sinners.

Quite possibly the same shrewd judgement which prompted the Church to adopt the festivals of the pagan calendar that new converts might find something familiar in her succession of holy days, also played some part in the adoption of the atrium from the pagan temples. Certainly converts who, from childhood, had passed through an atrium into their temple would find the way that led through such a colonnaded court into the basilica less strange.

So for many years the builders continued to erect atria before their churches until their knell was sounded by the fall of Rome.

When barbarians flooded the fallen Empire; when civilization

[2] It should be remembered that the temples that remain to us in the city of Rome were built after the beginning of the Christian era, when the processes which freed the gods from particular sites of ground had been long completed. The feelings of awe and of reverence now centred in the contents of the shrine rather than in the land whereon it stood. There was, therefore, no reason for surrounding these later temples by encircling areas of ground, and the influence of the temenos would remain only in the preservation of an open court, or atrium, before the temple.

Archives Photographique—Paris

THE CLOISTER OF MOISSAC

The cloister at the side of the church is the offspring of the atrium which lay before the portals; in turn the atrium is descendant from the *temenos*, the land which surrounded the shrine of a pagan god. Notice the alternations of double with single columns, and the capitals, each of which is individual in its carvings.

throughout the West went into eclipse; when force became rampant and reason silent, there was no longer time for the slow discipline and education of the atrium. Converts must be brought swiftly under the influence and authority of the Church; baptism must precede instruction, and not follow it as hitherto. So the doors of the basilica were flung wide for the multitude and the atrium—useless now for the laity —was eventually moved around to the side of the church and turned into a cloister for the use of monks or priests.

Thus this colonnaded court, shut off from the world and opened only to the sky, with its gravelled walks, its scent of flowers and its song of birds, with the occasional flash of feathered wings splashing the waters of the fountain, carries our thoughts far back into the past; it takes us beyond the atria of Christian basilicas or pagan temples; beyond the wall of the Court of the Gentiles in Jerusalem, with its oft-repeated warning, "He who crosses this line must surely die;" it leads us on until we come to those old boundary lines that men once drew around their holy places to warn the ignorant or unwary that they must now begin to step slowly, advancing with fear and reverence, with a sacrifice in their hands, lest a god should "meet them on their way and seek to slay them," as a god of the wilderness had once met Moses in the desert of Mt. Sinai.

Chapter Thirty-two

STRANGE VOICES FROM THE STOUP

AN OLD man, with a black skull-cap on his head and a long-handled brush in his hands, sits at the entrance to the cathedral beside the Basin of Holy Water. As the worshippers enter, singly or in groups, he dips his brush into the basin and holds it out to the faithful who run their fingers through the wet bristles and then cross themselves as they pass on.

By this act the old man and the worshippers alike believe that those thus blessed by the drops of Holy Water are set free from certain temporal penalties for sin, and released from some of the long years in Purgatory.

The basin beside which the old man sits is worn with years and by the touch of countless fingers. It was just as worn when he first began his service with the brush; it was old in his father's time; old when his father's father dipped his fingers here and crossed himself. Beyond that his memory does not carry him; the centuries that lie behind the days of his grandfather are hidden from him as by an impenetrable veil; here his knowledge, and probably his interest, halt.

He does not know that the Basin of Holy Water is the far descendant of the old *catharus*, or *phiala*—the fountain of ablutions—that once stood in the atrium of the early Christian church; he does not know that its still more distant ancestors may be found in the Brazen Sea of Solomon's Temple, and in those yet more remote stone basins which may still be seen in the *hanifeyeh* chambers of the Sinaitic temple of Serabít el-Khádem, begun five thousand years ago, where seekers for Hathor's favour purified themselves before entering her sacred cave. He does not dream that the formula by which the water he dispenses has been blessed echoes the primitive belief that there is power in a

252

Holy Name, to know that Name is to possess the power, and to pronounce it over a person or a thing is to transfer the power. He cannot know that the water he offers on his brush is the heir of an ancient faith that running water had a will and an intelligence of its own; that within it dwelt a spirit which could hurt or help, which might be conciliated or offended, rewarded with gifts or punished with lashes.

To pass behind the curtain that limits the old man's sight, to seek the ancestry of the Holy Water Basin, means a long journey to many peoples and through many lands; it means following twisting trails through a confusing labyrinth. One path leads us past the habitations of countless generations who have believed that water cleanses from ceremonial uncleanness, frees men from guilt, and protects them from the anger of the gods. Along another interlacing road they dwell who believe that there is inherent power in a sacred Name, a power that may be transmitted to the waters, mysteriously increasing their potency to deliver men from all evils of body or of soul.

Then, travelling a third pathway, also interlacing, we follow the myriad footsteps of those who, even before History began her written record, sought the aid of living spirits who dwelt in bubbling springs or where swift waters flow.

The Babylonian incantation of Maklu bears its own clear witness to the virtue of running water, even over menaces that come from beyond the veil of sense:

"I have washed my hands, I have cleansed my body with the pure spring water that flows forth in the city of Eridu.

"All that is evil, all that is not good, which is in my body, my flesh, my sinews, the evil dreams at night, the evil signs, and omens that are not good." [1]

Such waters healed the sick in days when illness was commonly ascribed to the baneful activities of an indwelling evil spirit. In the Third Millennium before Christ the following prescription was given by a Babylonian god for the exorcism of a demon;

[1] Morris Jastrow, *Religious Belief in Babylonia and Assyria*, p. 306.

"Fill the jar with water;
Put tamarisk and nard in it.
Cast the incantation of Eridu upon the water.
Wash this man.
The curse which is in his body
Will flow away like water." [2]

Water also made it possible to welcome the returning traveller who had crossed the priestly protected boundaries which divided the lands of his own people, and of his gods, from those of other peoples and of other gods—the clean land from the unclean. Since uncleanness was contagious the stranger and the traveller alike must be thoroughly disinfected by washings in water before hospitality might be shown them. [3]

Dangerous as the returning voyager might be the warrior was doubly so, for not only had his campaigns taken him into those unclean lands where strange gods were worshipped by unfamiliar rites, but he had also killed, thereby setting free a vengeful spirit who would injure, if he could, both the slayer and his tribe. Therefore the warrior must be cleansed with especial care before resuming the intercourses of ordinary life.

The law given in Numbers (31:19-24) ordained purifying ceremonies that included both fire and water:

"Fire for everything that may abide the fire; all that abideth not the fire ye shall make to go through the water. And ye shall wash your clothes on the seventh day, and ye shall be clean, and afterwards ye shall come into the camp."

Especial precautions must be observed by the worshipper when he approached the altar of his god, for he must draw near with clean hands as well as with a pure heart. Therefore basins of ablutions were placed in temples, as at Serabít el-Khádem, in the Tabernacle ("that

---

[2] *Journal of the Royal Asiatic Society*, January, 1934.
[3] J. G. Frazer, *Golden Bough*, pp. 196-198. See also W. Warde Fowler, *Religious Experiences of the Roman People*.

Aaron and his sons may wash their hands and their feet when they come near the altar that they die not") and in the Temple of Jerusalem. But the sacrificer must also purify himself after presenting his offering at the shrine, for the holiness that was transmitted by contact with a sacred object must be removed before a man was free to mingle with his fellows. The Greeks, after offering sacrifices, washed themselves and their garments in some spring or river before entering their city or their homes; the Jewish High Priest bathed before leaving the Tabernacle after the presentation of the sin-offering, and strict Jews today wash their hands after touching their holy scriptures.

Thus the Basin, carrying an old and a rich inheritance, passed from the East to Greece; from Greece it came to Rome in whose religious rites it played its part until the Christian Church, inheriting it, placed the fountain of ablutions in her atriums. This fountain vanished with the atrium, but the memory of it still survives in its offspring—the Basin of Holy Water—which preserves the lingering recollection of the primitive belief that the cleansing power of water must be sought before drawing near to a holy place.

Effective as might be the cleansing virtue of pure water, its efficiency would be measurelessly increased if it could be endued with the power of a sacred Name.

Serapion of Thmuis, a bishop of the Fourth Century, gave the formula by which oil or water should be blessed, and in this formula the mighty Name of Jesus is many times repeated:

"We bless these creatures in the Name of Jesus Christ. We invoke upon this water and this oil the Name of Him who suffered, Who was crucified, Who rose from the dead, and Who sitteth at the right hand of the Uncreated. Grant unto these creatures the power to heal; may all fevers, every evil spirit, and all maladies be put to flight by him who either drinks these beverages or is anointed by them, and may they be a remedy in the Name of Jesus Christ." [4]

[4] *Catholic Encyclopedia*, Vol. VII, "Holy Water."

S. Ephanius records the healing of a madman by one Joseph, who made the sign of the cross over water which he then poured upon the possessed, saying:

"In the Name of Jesus Christ of Nazareth, depart from this unhappy one, thou infernal spirit, and let him be healed." [5]

It is quite evident that we are here in the presence of a primitive belief that there is power in a Holy Name, and that that power may be imparted by the pronouncement of the Name.

In all corners of the earth the belief that a Name possessed personality was shared by men who dwelt in the dim half-lights of early years. Therefore, believing that name and body are inextricably bound together, the savage guards both with equal care lest the malicious, by magic arts, inflict suffering on the one through the misuse of the other.[6] In ancient Egypt, as still among the Brahmins, two names were given to a child, one of which was carefully concealed.[7]

But if the names of human beings possessed such attributes of personality that they must be spoken with extreme caution, or even never pronounced at all, those of the deities, quite apart from the gods themselves, were dangerously surcharged with power. "In all the religions of ancient Asia the mysterious Name was conceived as a real and divine being, who had personal existence and power over both nature and the world of spirits." [8]

An Egyptian formula, placed in the mouth of a god, reads: "I am the elect of a million years. Were my Name uttered on the banks of a river it would be consumed; were it spoken on earth, fire would burst from the ground." [9]

---

[5] *Catholic Encyclopedia,* Vol. VII, "Holy Water."

[6] J. G. Frazer, *Golden Bough,* p. 244.

[7] E. Bendann, *Death Customs,* p. 145. When the savage assumes, or is given, the name of an animal something of the character of the bird or beast is believed to be imparted—the swiftness and keen vision of the eagle, the strength of the bear, the cunning of the fox. So the name of a Saint, given to a child in baptism, not merely places the infant under a mystical protection, but also preserves the recollection of the confident belief that the Name will endue the child with something of the character of the Saint.

[8] Lenormant, *Chaldean Magic,* p. 104.

[9] *Ibid.,* p. 103.

When the Hebrews dropped the vowels from the Name of their God, so that the real pronunciation of *Yawe* has been lost, they followed a practice which has obtained the world around.

The Romans believed that, by addressing the gods of their enemies by their secret names, they could force them to abandon their own peoples and to serve the purposes of Rome. For such a reason the names of her own guardian deities were never uttered lest the enemies of Rome, overhearing, should be able to take, or to lure, their gods away.[10]

It was a wide-spread belief that he who knew the Name could command its owner, be he god or man, as a master directs his slave; thus Isis gained control of Ra, when she tricked him into the disclosure of his secret Name.[11]

This belief echoes through the pages of the Bible. When Jacob, wrestling with the spirit in the waters of the Jabbok, cried: "Tell me, I pray thee, thy Name," the spirit answered, "Wherefore doest thou seek my name?" But the question was not necessary, for both Jacob and the angel knew that the possession of the Name meant power.

When the angel appeared to Manoah at Zorah to foretell the birth of Samson:

"Manoah said unto the angel, 'What is thy Name, that when thy sayings come to pass we may do thee honour?' And the angel of the Lord said unto him, 'Why askest thou after my Name, seeing it is a secret?' "

In the Book of Revelation it is written:

"His eyes were as a flame of fire, and on His head were many crowns, and He had a Name written that no man knew but He Himself."

John's words are rich with a significance that few readers of the Apocalypse understand when he declares that the time is coming

[10] J. G. Frazer, *Golden Bough*, p. 261.
[11] G. F. Moore, *History of Religions*, p. 190; J. G. Frazer, *Golden Bough*, pp. 260-261.

when the secret Name shall be revealed, and when the glory and the power of it shall become the possession of the Redeemed, for

"I will write upon him that overcometh the Name of My God, and the Name of the City of My God, and I will write upon him My New Name. And His servants shall see His face, and His Name shall be on their foreheads."

So at last, reads the promise, men shall lay down their little names, with their futility and their weakness; instead they shall receive the secret Name of the Lord their God, and be clothed with its majesty and splendour.

But the power of the Holy Name was also available for men on earth, as the verses that were later added to the Gospel of S. Mark (16:17-18) clearly taught:

"In My Name they shall cast out devils; they shall speak with new tongues; they shall take up serpents, and if they drink any evil thing it shall not harm them; they shall lay their hands upon the sick and they shall recover."

In this belief Arnobius wrote, when the Third Century was drawing to its close:

"His Name, when heard, puts to flight evil spirits, imposes silence upon soothsayers, prevents men from consulting the augurs, and frustrates the efforts of magicians." [12]

So when Serapion of Thmuis pronounced the Name of Jesus, or its equivalent, nine times over the water and the oil he was transferring to "these creatures" the mighty power of that Name by which "all fevers, every evil spirit, and all maladies may be put to flight."

Apart from the magic grace that might be conferred by the use of a sacred Name, "living waters" had inherent powers of their own, wherefore they were held in peculiar reverence among all primitive peoples. This was particularly true in such sterile countries as Mesopotamia and Syria, where so much depended upon irrigation, on seasonal rains, and on wells, springs, and streams.

[12] D. G. Brinton, *Religion of Primitive Peoples*, p. 100 ff.

The gods were in all nature, and not least in the depths of life-giving waters. Here dwelt those whose favour must be sought, for if the spirit of the water were favourably disposed the spring would flow for the needs of men; if it were offended, the water would be refused and the spring or stream would dry up at its source.

Like every other spirit, the Intelligence within the water could be moved by sacrifices, offerings, or by music and dancing. Rites and rituals might win its favour or avert its wrath. The Song of the Well, recorded in Numbers (21:17), is obviously an incantation, intended to persuade the well to flow.

Professor G. L. Robinson tells of a recent visit to the "Bath of Pharaoh," a healing hot spring near Tafileh, in Moab.[13]

> "Some of the men brought a kid to the edge of the basin and cut its throat over the water, so that the blood flowed into the stream. Others then bathed with much shouting and hilarity. . . . I asked them why they did so; they replied: 'So that the Lord Solomon may be pleased and cause the spring to boil and bubble.' Here was propitiatory sacrifice."

Obviously "The Lord Solomon" has displaced the original, and local, spirit of the spring.

When the waters of Ilabistan failed a feast was held at the source, with music and dancing, to induce the waters to flow again.[14]

As late as the Seventeenth Century of our era the peasants of Esthonia were stirred to revolt by a succession of bad harvests, which they traced to the resentment of a stream whose current had been impeded by the erection of a water mill.

Naaman's reluctance to bathe in the Jordan at Elisha's command sprang from his belief that such an act would be apostasy from the river-gods who moved so tumultuously in Abanah and Pharpah waters of Damascus.

In parts of Europe the belief persists that he who has saved another from drowning will, some day, be injured by him whom he has

---

[13] *Sarcophagus of an Ancient Civilization*, p. 59.
[14] W. Robertson Smith, *Religion of the Semites*, p. 183.

saved. This superstition is rooted in the primitive belief that a drowning man has been "called," or seized by the water-spirit as a sacrifice; to interpose between that spirit and its victim invites disaster for the god within the waters will surely seek revenge, and will use his intended victim as the instrument of his justice.[15]

But water deities who seize human beings as sacrifices should be propitiated by voluntary offerings and these, from early times, have been cast into streams or rivers. The treatment an offering received revealed the favour, or the disfavour, of the gods; those that sank were accepted; those that floated, or were cast upon the shore, were rejected together with the petitioner and his prayer.

It was no long step for men to take, nor an illogical conclusion for them to draw, when they inferred that waters which could thus discriminate among offerings could also distinguish among men, to separate the innocent from the guilty; hence arose the judgement of the gods through the Ordeal of Water. In this Ordeal, however, they reversed the interpretation of the omen as applied to offerings, and wisely, since it would be small comfort to the accused if he must sink and drown in order to establish his innocence.

The earliest application of this Ordeal that I can quote is given in the Babylonian Code of Khammurabi, and dates from about the year 2300 B.C. One provision of that Code reads:

"If a man charge a man with sorcery and cannot prove it, he who is charged shall go to the river; into the river he shall throw himself, and if the river overcome him his accuser shall take to himself his house [estate]. If the river show that the man is innocent, and he come forth unharmed, he who charged him shall be put to death."

The early Celts threw infants suspected of bastardy into the Rhine; those of illegitimate birth sank and were drowned; those whom the river spared were thereby freed of every taint.

The mediæval practice, on the other hand, held the accused innocent if he sank and guilty if he floated, for

15 J. G. Frazer, *Folk-lore in the Old Testament*, Vol. II, p. 416.

"The pure nature of the water recognizes as impure, and rejects as incompatible, human nature that has been infected with untruth." [16]

This is the explanation given by Hincmar of Rheims in the Ninth Century, but in 1583 Scribonius had another interpretation:

"Sorcerers, from their intercourse with Satan, partake of his nature; he resides within them, and their human attributes become altered to his; he is an imponderable spirit of air and therefore they likewise become lighter than water." [17]

When the sacred vessels were stolen from the Cathedral of Laon those who had easy access to the church were subjected to this test. Among the three whom the Ordeal declared guilty was one Anselm, a most learned doctor of the diocese, who had himself first proposed the "trial by water." Despite his protestations of innocence, he was punished, together with two others whom the Ordeal had revealed as his accomplices.[18]

In 1083 Henry IV of Germany and Pope Gregory VII were alike subjected by proxy to this test; as the water refused to accept the representative of the Pope while welcoming that of the Emperor the matter was hushed up.[19]

But waters that were cruel, unreasonable, or unjust might be punished. According to Herodotus, when Xerxes saw the bridge with which he had spanned the Hellespont swept away by a storm he sentenced the Strait to receive three hundred lashes and be put in chains. The chains were duly sunk into the waters, and as the royal executioners plied their whips they explained to the waves the offences for which they were being chained and scourged:

"O bitter waters, thy master inflicts this punishment on thee because thou hast wronged him who wrought no harm to thee.

[16] H. C. Lea, *Superstition and Force*, p. 280.
[17] *Ibid.*, p. 288.
[18] *Ibid.*, pp. 285-286.
[19] *Ibid.*, p. 285.

Thou canst not halt thy Lord, our King, but because thou art a treacherous river, hereafter shall no man sacrifice to thee." [20]

But in the mediæval ecclesiastical judicial processes the water, even if wishful to do otherwise, could be compelled to reveal the truth, for the priest, by speaking over it the Name of Him who is Infinitely Just, constrained it to right decisions.

In preparation for the Ordeal of boiling water the priest, having exorcised the water, bound it to justice by the mighty power of the name of God:

"O creature of water, I adjure thee by the Living God who separated thee from the dry land; Who led thee from the fountain of Paradise and in four rivers commanded thee to compass the earth; I adjure thee by Him who at Cana of Galilee changed thee from water into wine, Who trod on thee by His holy feet; I adjure thee by the God who in thee cleansed Naaman of his leprosy, that thou show thyself pure, nor retain any false image, but that thou shalt make manifest all truth and reveal all falsehood." [21]

The same element that could exercise judicial functions might also fall as a benediction on the farms and homes of men, and by it their firesides, fields, barns, herds, and harvests might be blessed.

The first appearance of the weekly blessing and sprinkling of Holy Water in the West was in the Ninth Century when Pope Leo IV ordained that all priests:

"On every Sunday before Mass make Holy Water by which the people and the homes of the Faithful may be blessed."

Hincmar of Rheims, in 845, issued the following instructions:

[20] The invention of gunpowder has now made it possible to deal even more severely with mischievous water-spirits than it was in Xerxes' day: "When a party of Arafoos [mountaineers of Dutch New Guinea] were disporting themselves in the surf, three of them were swept out to sea by a refluent wave and drowned. To avenge their deaths their friends fired on the in-rolling billows for hours with guns and with bows and arrows." J. G. Frazer, *Folk-lore in the Old Testament*, Vol. II, p. 423.

[21] H. C. Lea, *op. cit.*, p. 246.

"Every Sunday, before Mass, the priest shall bless water in his church. The people, when entering the church, shall be sprinkled with this water, and those who desire to do so may carry some away in clean vessels, so as to sprinkle their houses, fields, vineyards, and cattle; the provender with which the cattle are fed, and also to throw some over their own food."

Perhaps the great Bishop of Rheims recalled the fate of a woman, reported in Gregory's *Dialogues*, who, failing to make the sign of the cross over a head of lettuce, swallowed a little devil who had been hiding among its unexorcised leaves, and thus became possessed. From all such dangers he would guard his people by the grace of Holy Water, sprinkled upon their food.

That such beliefs persist today is evidenced not only by the blessing of horses in Normandy, of cattle in Brittany, and by countless similar ceremonies with which every traveller is familiar, but also by the experience of a German archæologist. This savant, unluckily dressed in black and riding a black horse, was slowly climbing the steep road that led to an Italian hill-town to inspect certain old inscriptions. When the villagers, working in their fields, saw an indubitable black devil steadily drawing nearer they dropped their tools and fled for the protection of the church. The priest, however, being summoned by his flock, went forth to meet the ominous stranger at the entrance to the village where, holding up the crucifix, he forbade his further progress in the Name of Christ, of the Virgin, and of the Saints. Only when the archæologist had been thoroughly tested by Holy Water, which no devil may endure, was he permitted to continue on his way.

Such experiences are by no means unparalleled or even unusual. A servant in my own employ encountered the devil in our attic who shot a beam of fire at her which scorched her garments and burned her flesh. (The devil in this case was an arc light in the street whose rays passed through an oriel window.) Not until her room and her person had been liberally sprinkled with Holy Water was she delivered from the terror that possessed her.

So the Holy Water comes down to the Twentieth Century, a direct descendant of the rich rivers of Eridu and of the poor springs of Sinai, through the fountain of ablutions which once stood in the atrium of the early Christian church, to the Basin of Holy Water at the entrance of the cathedral where an old man sits, a black skull-cap on his head and a long-handled brush in his hands.

Chapter Thirty-three

THE ORIGIN OF THE ALTAR RAIL

THE altar rail that today divides the chancel from the choir, where communicants kneel to receive the consecrated wafer from the hands of the priest, is the last survivor of a high barrier which once ran in front of the chancel to separate the altar from the aisles, the clergy from the laity. This barrier appears clearly in early Anglo-Saxon churches, fades in the Eleventh and Twelfth Centuries and vanishes in the Thirteenth, leaving the altar rail as its sole memorial. Because of the relation between this rail and that primitive barrier which guarded the altar in these early churches, some of which date from— or even predate—the landing of S. Augustine in 597, the American visitor errs in his haste when he hurries past the ruined church of S. Pancras at Canterbury, or the churches of S. Peter-on-the-Wall at Bradwell-by-Sea, of S. Mary at Lyminge, or—in the North—of Escomb and Monkwearmouth to visit the cathedrals of Winchester, Canterbury, Ely, Lincoln, York, or Durham.

"To the stranger who visits England nothing, perhaps, makes such an impression of stability as the vast abbey and cathedral churches which have come down to us from far-off dynasties of Norman and Plantagenet kings. . . . Nevertheless, hoary though their aspect is with age, . . . they rose . . . only midway in the long record-roll of the English nation.

"Take up a plank in the Twelfth Century transept of South-well minster and beneath is seen *in situ* a mosaic pavement of the Roman occupation. That transept has now eight centuries of age upon it; another nine centuries had elapsed before Norman work overlaid Roman work at Southwell. To these nine centuries not one of our great abbeys or cathedrals belongs; not one has a stone above ground earlier than the Eleventh Century. But from the Third Century of our era there were parish churches in the land, many built by British, some possibly by Roman, converts. . . .

"The Anglo-Saxon chronicles are full of the glories of great churches, but of these practically nothing remains above ground. . . . The greater pre-Conquest churches have disappeared. In their place the mighty builders of Normandy, with all a nation's ransom to build with, erected in about seventy years some of the most gigantic churches of Christendom. . . . To rear them, the ancient Anglo-Saxon minsters were everywhere destroyed; not one is left for our edification. Many must have wept like S. Wulfstan at Worcester when they saw the churches of their fathers, hallowed by the associations of centuries, go down before the Norman hammers. 'We wretches,' he said, 'destroy what the saints have wrought.' . . . It is not so with the parish churches. . . . Probably few realize what a wealth of primitive Romanesque architecture survives in England or how far more venerable than 'the proudest church of bishop, prior or abbot' is the English parish church.

"From the Greater churches the record of one long period of English Christianity has been almost wholly obliterated; it lingers in the structure of many a humble parish church, bearing witness in its stones to the long ages that bind the religion and the art of the Norman to that of the Briton and the Roman.

"We never accost the humblest parish church without a chance of learning something of the five centuries of Anglo-Saxon or Danish rule which had elapsed before the Norman reached our shores." [1]

Let us not, then, leave Canterbury until we have visited the ruins of old S. Pancras, one of seven churches built in England in the Seventh Century by S. Augustine, or under his influence. Four of these churches, and probably all seven, possessed a triple arcade, resting on two columns, which divided the chancel from the nave.

It may be well to recall now that in the early churches of the West there was no choir between the nave and the chancel; the musical

---

[1] Bond, *Introduction to English Church Architecture*, p. 177.

Alinari

THE CHANCEL SCREEN AT TORCELLO

The low wall between the chancel and the nave is the "cancelli," from whence the word "chancel" is derived. On the cross-bar are the pictures of the Virgin and Child, flanked by those of the Twelve Apostles. From the rocks beneath the cross the skull of Adam peers with sightless eyes. In the background portions of the service were rendered by priests who sat on the curving stone benches which flanked the bishop's throne and followed the curving wall of the apse, as at Torcello. With the expansion of the liturgy a portion of the nave was isolated by low walls to form the Schola Cantorum for the use of the minor clergy who composed the choir. With the addition of transepts in the larger metropolitan churches, and the importation of antiphonal singing from the East, the wings of the transepts were probably used for an enlarged antiphonal choir, and the altar was placed in the Crossing where the Great Altar, used by the Pope alone, still remains in S. Peter's basilica. In the less important churches, where transepts were lacking, the altar was placed beneath the chancel arch whence it was later removed to the rear of the apse.

When the altar stood in the Crossing it was surrounded, as in the cruciform church at Tyre of which Eusebius speaks, by a *transenna*— a decorated latticed screen of stone or wood. Only where the altar was in the chancel could the colonnade arcade, from which the altar rail is descended, be employed. In later examples, and probably in the earliest, the columns of this colonnade rested on, or were joined together by, the *cancelli* from which our word chancel derives its name. This was a low wall, three feet or less in height, which was broken only by the archway, or archways, that led into the holy place where stood the *adyta*—the "unapproachable" altar. In the West only the clergy might pass these archways; in the East the third Council of Constantinople, meeting in the Trullan Palace in 681, made a single exception to this otherwise inflexible rule when it permitted the Emperor to sit with the clergy.

The triple arcade of the Anglo-Saxon churches of Kent occurs but rarely on the continent—as in the Fourth Century Pyrenean Church of S. Bertrand de Comminges, which was destroyed by the Visigoths in the Sixth Century. It was common, however, in North Africa and in the Byzantine East, where it appears for instance in the Cathedral of Parenzo, on the eastern shores of the Adriatic. Thus it reveals, together with the narthex, influences from Byzantium transmitted through Sicily or through North Africa by way of Spain. Perhaps the fact that Theodore of Tarsus, Greek by birth and early training, was archbishop of Canterbury from 668 to 690 helps to explain these Oriental influences in Anglo-Saxon architecture, while letters of Origen, a Greek theologian of the Third Century, show knowledge of, and interest in, "that land so far divided from our own." But that Byzantine influences did penetrate England in these early days is evidenced by the narthex (the porch extending the entire width of the church) as well as by this triple arcade.

Mr. Thompson, in his *Historical Growth of the English Parish Church,* suggests that this barrier may have been derived from the screen of embroidered needlework, of cloth-of-gold or of tapestry, which at an early date was placed behind the altar (whence came the reredos) and was often carried along the sides. At times during the celebration of the Mass the entire altar was thus enclosed. Possibly in distant and barbarous countries, like Anglo-Saxon England, where it was difficult to secure tissues worthy of the altar, it would be easier to screen the chancel by a solid wall with a narrow chancel arch— as in the North of England, or, as in the South, by a triple arcade from which curtains might be hung.

However, although this triple arcade was rare in Europe, some form of barrier between the altar and the aisles was well-nigh universal. In the Eighth Century Church of S. Riquier, in Picardy, six bronze columns crossed the nave in front of the chancel, bearing thirteen shrines that held relics of the saints. In the Seventh Century Church of Torcello, in the Venetian lagoon, six columns connected by a low wall (the cancelli) carried a cross-bar whereon were painted representations of the twelve apostles, the Virgin, and the Infant Jesus. Above this bar a pile of rocks enclosed a skull and supported a crucifix, recalling the tradition that Christ had been crucified above the grave of Adam that His blood, seeping into the ground, might touch the bones of our first father with its redeeming grace.

In old S. Peter's, built by Constantine in Rome early in the Fourth Century, a chancel screen of six columns carried statues of Christ and the apostles on its entablature. In the Church of the Anastasis (the Resurrection) in Jerusalem, also built by Constantine, a row of twelve columns dedicated to the apostles and bearing their images surrounded the rotunda where lay the tomb of Christ and its altar.

These images, however, were not intended merely for the adoration of the faithful; their presence placed the altar screen under the protection of apostles, saints, and martyrs; he who passed that barrier and violated the altar, if only by his intrusion into the holy place, did so to the peril of his soul hereafter and at the risk of temporal penalties today at the hands of roused and indignant saints.

Therefore the fact that, from the early Fourth Century onward, the columns, arcades, cancelli, and lintels that barred the altar from the aisles bore the shrines of the saints, or paintings of our Lord, the Virgin, the apostles, or the martyrs and saints, makes it altogether probable that such images also decorated the screen wall in other churches, such as those of Anglo-Saxon England, where no evidence of their presence has survived the havoc of the years. Indeed the use of such images would seem more logical in remote and barbarous countries than in civilized Byzantium and Rome, for they gave the altar protection from the barbarian that would be less needed from the cultured Greek or Latin. However this is clear, that in both Northern and Southern Europe the altar was placed, for many centuries, under the guardianship of the apostles and the saints. In later years the growing power and authority of Rome, diminishing barbarism and increasing culture, made this high barrier with its holy images decreasingly necessary; the altar was safe without its protection, and it gradually disappeared. The narrow chancel arch persisted in the North of England throughout the Eleventh and into the Twelfth Century, but in the Thirteenth it vanished and from Rome to Durham only the altar rail remained.

This sacred barrier with its single or triple arched entrance, or with its barrier-colonnade, under holy protection that kept the unconsecrated from the sanctuary, although not descended from, yet belongs to, the same family of ideas as did the barrier of another arch, erected with mystic rites and magic spells by Roman priests in the early days of the Republic, through which no unclean thing might pass.

To these two, the barrier-arcade of the early Christian church, and the barrier of the Roman magic arch, the one protected by the holy images and the other by priestly spells, we owe two familiar features of our modern life—the altar rail of our churches, and the monumental triumphal arches of our cities.

We turn, then, from the present to the past; from the chancel arch and rail of our churches to the *porta triumphalis* of pagan Rome, and to the forgotten world of ideas which called it into being.

To the Romans of the Republic, as to all primitive peoples, frontier lines did not merely divide the territories of tribes; they also demarked the lands of the gods; on one side lay the Clean, on the other side the Unclean. The very language is significant, for the primitive idea beneath the Latin word *hostis* is not "enemy" but "stranger." The stranger was an enemy, not necessarily because of hostile feelings or intentions, but because he came from that outer world which lay beyond the sacred boundary where strange gods were worshipped with unfamiliar rites and sacrifices. Therefore he brought with him magical influences and baneful powers which must be destroyed lest he infect others. Only when the stranger had been thoroughly disinfected by the priests might hospitality be shown him.

For this reason the member of the tribe, before crossing the boundaries of his own gods and people, sought those priestly rites that would make him immune to the "powers" that ruled the Unclean lands towards which he journeyed. When he returned from his wanderings he must, like the stranger, be ceremonially purified and cleansed before entering his city or his home, lest he carry infection with him.

Dangerous as the returning traveller might be, the warrior was doubly so, for if he had killed, albeit "for the temples of his fathers and the altars of his gods," he had set free a vengeful spirit who would injure, if he could, not only the slayer but also any of his tribe. Therefore the killer must appease the *manes* of his victim, or else render it powerless, before he could be readmitted to the fellowship of his family or his clan.

The belief that blood, when shed and left uncovered, cried aloud for vengeance is illustrated not only in the story of Cain and Abel—

"the voice of thy brother's blood crieth unto me from the ground"—but also in the Seventeenth Chapter of Leviticus where the hunter is commanded to cover blood with dust lest the cry of the slain animal might make itself heard by the powers that are always just.

Such blood, poured out upon the ground, was doubly dangerous, for it might have been accepted as a sacrifice by some non-tribal deity or demon who would thereby gain the right to make demands upon the careless hunter.

The warrior, when setting out on any military expedition, knows that he will be both a traveller and a prospective killer; he will encounter not only the armed forces of the enemy but also the antagonisms of their gods and the incantations of their priests. He will, therefore, be careful to receive from his own priests the charms and spells which will protect him from the unseen powers who fight with his foe, from the indubitably potent curses of strange priests, and which will enable him to penetrate, with his spear or arrow, both the magical and the material armour of the enemy.

When he returns from the campaign he will make the proper sacrifices to the spirits of those whom he has slain and will undergo the necessary purifying rites before attempting to enter the gates of his city or the door-way of his home.

The Roman army of early days was composed of men who were going forth on a journey to the unclean lands of strange gods for the purpose of killing Rome's enemies, extending her authority, and enriching her city with the spoils of battle. The same precautions, therefore, must be taken for this host that were taken for travellers and for the killers of men.

In the month of March the army was gathered in the Campus Martius, outside the city's walls, where the priest in procession thrice drew the magic circle around the fighting men, offering a sacrifice at the conclusion of each round. Thus equipped, the army went forth to battle, strong in the conviction of immunity from the hostile powers of the gods or the priests of their enemies.

In October, when the campaign was over, the army was again gathered in the Campus Martius where the sacred circle was once more thrice drawn around the host; but as a final precaution against contamination the priests erected a magic arch with priestly spells through which no uncleanliness might pass; the arch was a barrier which excluded all infection contracted in the lands of strange peoples and strange gods. When the soldiers of Rome marched through that arch, erected before the city's gate, they shed the last contagions brought with them from the war.

This also explains the "yoke"—the two spears thrust into the ground with a third spear bound across the top—under which the Samnites made the defeated Romans pass after the battle of the Caudine Forks. This "yoke" was not a symbol either of victory or of disgrace; it was a magic arch, hastily constructed to strip the Romans of the protection of the spells and charms by which they had been armed by their own priests. Thus the helplessness of the defeated was made complete; already deprived of their weapons, they were now stripped of the protection of their gods.

When Rome became mistress of the world as well as of the peninsula her legions carried the Imperial Eagles into Egypt, Syria, Asia Minor, Pannonia; they went to Spain, Gaul, the Rhine, and Britain. Thereafter Rome fought her wars far from the capital city and the arch was no longer erected in the Campus Martius. Its purpose was consequently forgotten and men, merely remembering that Rome's victorious armies had marched through an arch after a successful campaign, erected triumphal arches within the city's walls through which the triumphant legions, their commanders, spoils, and prisoners passed along the Sacred Way to the Temple of Jupiter Capitolinus.

But if the magic arch had lost its early meaning, so also had the gods. *"Primus in orbe,"* said Statius, *"deus facit timor"*—"first in the world the gods made fear." Although this is only partially true, nevertheless in the primitive world men, casting the veil of their own fear around their gods and drawing danger lines around their holy places, approached the altars of their gods with care and caution lest they suffer from their deities for accidental trespass.

With the increasing wealth of Rome, and with the materialistic spirit that came with wealth, the sense of religious awe so dimmed that any man might enter the temples, lay his wreath before the statues of his deities and place his offering upon their altar. Thus the gods, once almost unapproachable, became the objects of a formal courtesy.

But a new God appeared on the Syrian hills; a God who had been born in humble surroundings—in a stable; who had grown as a child grows, played with other children and then, in boyhood, worked at His father's side in a carpenter's shop of Nazareth. Throughout His short manhood He had walked the Syrian roads with men, sharing their daily life, until that last night when, in Jerusalem, seated at table with His followers He had broken bread, blessed it and given it to the few who sat with Him. Before cockcrow He had been arrested by the temple guard. God though He were, yet He had been tried by men like an ordinary criminal; He had been mocked, scourged, and at last crucified by men on Calvary.

But year after year, as the pagan deities lost the awe, even the respect of men, until Theodosius dragged their statues through the dust of Roman streets, this new God from Syria rose higher and higher in the reverence of men until He passed beyond the reach of ordinary mortals. The simple table where, in simple manner, He had taken wine and blessed it, taken bread and broken it, became an altar kept aloof alike by saints and priests whereon, by divine miracle, the common bread and wine were turned into the very flesh and blood of the body of the Christ. None but those dedicated to its service, not even an emperor (until the rule was modified by the Council of Trullo in 691) might draw near that altar, wherefore barriers, defended by the image of Christ Himself, by that of the Mother of God, or by those of the apostles and the saints, were erected between the altar and the nave, between the clergy and the people.

So the magic arch of pagan Rome sank into oblivion; the old gods lost the fear, even the esteem, of men, and their once dangerous shrines fell from the heights of terrifying awe until they came within the easy reach of man.

The new God from Syria, on the other hand, appearing first in the common ways where all men walked, was more and more clothed upon with reverence until He was exalted to the glory of infinite Deity whose ways are not our ways and whose thoughts are not our thoughts. The table where He once sat, talked and ate with men, shared His exaltation and became the adyta—the "unapproachable" altar—guarded from the common touch by the hosts of heaven and the army of the saints and martyrs.

Thus the barrier of the early Christian church—the cancelli, columns, and lintels—which separated the chancel from the nave, the altar rail of the mediæval and modern church—the last survivor of that barrier; the primitive magic arch of Republican Rome, the "yoke" of the defeated, the Victory arches of Titus or of Constantine, and today's civic triumphal arches are all bound together, either by kinship or by a similarity of purpose and of function.

A. W. CLAPHAM, *English Romanesque Churches Before the Conquest.*
W. WARDE FOWLER, *Religious Experiences of the Roman People,* pp. 216-217.
J. G. FRAZER, *Golden Bough,* pp. 194, 197, 210.
A. H. THOMPSON, *The Ground Plan of the English Parish Church; The Historical Growth of the English Parish Church.*

Chapter Thirty-four

THE BELLS AND THE DEVIL

LONG before the appearance of bells the congregations of early Christian churches were called together, for religious and secular purposes alike, by gongs of brass or of bronze, or by the strokes of a hammer on boards—a method that is still in use in the Greek monasteries of the Levant and in Abyssinia.

But church bells were certainly in use in the West before the Ninth Century since the chronicles of Fontenelle, as we have seen, record the placing of a bell in the tower of that church by the Provost Tentsindus in 734, "as is customary in churches," and the Liber Pontificalis speaks of the installation of a bell in the tower of the Vatican basilica by Pope Stephen II, about the year 752.

Small, portable bells were used in England about the middle of the Fifth Century, but there is no very satisfactory evidence for the use of large bells in churches before the days of the Provost Tentsindus.

Church bells, however, had an even more serious duty to perform than that of calling worshippers together, for they were charged with the high commissions of routing the spirits of Evil that rode upon the storms, of protecting the harvests, and of guarding the souls of the dying. Here, again, we touch the primitive beliefs of men in all parts of the world.

At Ningpo, in China, there is a modern electric light plant operated by Chinese engineers:

"For some reason it balked lately, the wheels would not turn. Try as they would, using purely American tests, the natives could not locate the trouble. Thereupon they called in the necromancers. Around and around this modern electric plant the medicine men marched, beating their drums to scare away the demons that had

275

bewitched the machinery. Ridiculous as it may sound, the machinery soon began to run. Whatever the trouble, it had corrected itself, and now any devil-doctor in Ningpo can take his drum and get a job at the light plant." [1]

The incident is significant and interpretative, for among primitive peoples in all times and lands the beat of drums and the sound of bells have been held to possess great power for the exorcism of evil spirits. In the Congo country a chief will commonly ring a bell at each draught of beer that he swallows, to keep at bay the spirits that might try to sneak into his body by the same road as the beer. [2]

"On the Slave Coast when a woman sees her child gradually wasting away, she concludes that a demon has entered into the child and takes her measures accordingly. To lure the demon out of the body of her offspring, she offers a sacrifice of food; and while the devil is bolting this she attaches iron rings and small bells to the child's ankles, and hangs iron chains from his neck. The jingling of the iron, and the tinkling of the bells, are supposed to prevent the demon, when he has finished his repast, from entering again into the body of the little sufferer. Hence many children may be seen in this part of Africa weighed down by iron ornaments." [3]

The golden bells worn by the mules in the funeral rites of Alexander; the jingling brass, hung by Arabs around the necks of their caravan camels; the clash of spears upon shields which attended the birth of the infant Zeus; and the "bells" on the horses mentioned in Zechariah (14:20) all spring from the same belief, that demons and evil spirits may not abide the sound of drums, bells, or cymbals.

The Law given in Exodus (28:33-35) ordained that golden bells should be sewn to the hem of the High Priest's robe that "the sound should be heard when he goeth in unto the holy place; and when he cometh out, that he die not." Apparently the threshold, which the High Priest must pass as he went in and as he came out, was recognized

1 Frederick Simpich, *Saturday Evening Post*, Sept. 8, 1923.
2 J. G. Frazer, *Folk-lore in the Old Testament*, Vol. III, p. 478.
3 J. G. Frazer, *Golden Bough*, p. 226.

as being a spot of danger; this is again evidenced by Jeremiah (35:4)
and elsewhere in the Old Testament, where we read of men appointed
to be the "Keepers of the Threshold." The many provisions among
many peoples which forbid stepping on, or even touching, the threshold, the sacrifices offered upon it, the still persistent custom of carrying a bride across it, and the wooden bar that is placed today on the
threshold of Moslem mosques to compel entrants to step over, but
not upon, the door-sill, all bear witness to an ancient belief that he
who passed the threshold was, in the moment of crossing, especially
exposed to the attack of demons.[4] The bells on the hem of the High
Priest's robe were worn for his protection lest the devils of the threshold assail him and he die.

A bronze bell has recently been recovered from Assyria which bears
the figures of seven devils in repoussé upon its surface; the further
fact that this bell was called "the copper instrument of power" clearly
indicates that its function was the protection of men from demons.

A ritual of 2400 B.C. tells of an attack made by devils upon a man
who "was torn asunder from his soul":

> "Like water in full flood he trembled.
> Food he ate not; water he drank not."

Then the god Marduk, pitying the man, went to his father, the
water-god Ea, for advice, and Ea told him in part:

> "The bell, champion of the heaven-god,
> whose awful peal terrifies,
> which expels all evil, take thou;
> where its peals fall upon him,
> verily it is thy helper." [5]

Throughout the Middle Ages, and down to modern times, the
night-watchman was armed with a little bell whose sound, ringing
through the streets of the sleeping city, guarded the homes of those
who, being asleep, were the more helpless to defend themselves from

[4] J. G. Frazer, *Folk-lore in the Old Testament,* Vol. III, Chap. XII.
[5] *Journal of the Royal Asiatic Society,* January, 1934.

the demons who were ever seeking to take possession of their bodies.

Bells were particularly useful on the Eve of S. Agatha, on Twelfth Night, on Walpurgis Night, and on Midsummer Eve; when, as everyone knew, witches were especially active. But far more potent than the little handbells in repelling evil were the consecrated bells of the churches wherefore, on the four nights of the year when witches were mobilized in force, these bells were rung from dusk till dawn.

That the bells might be equipped for their great mission they were consecrated by the priests in full regalia, and with a ritual which probably dates from early Carlovingian times. They were bathed, both in water and by the smoke of the censers, and dried with towels; the prayer of the Bishop implored divine power to enable them to overcome the evil influences of the air—phantoms, storms, and lightning. Finally the bells were consecrated and hallowed "in the Name of the Father, and of the Son, and of the Holy Ghost." [6]

Although Charlemagne found it advisable to include in his Capitularies a decree that "bells shall not be baptized," and despite the rubrics in at least one or two extant pontificals which provide that the bell may be given "a name with the triple infusion of Holy Water," Father Delrio, a Jesuit of the early Seventeenth Century, indignantly denies, as do modern Catholic authorities, that church bells ever were baptized:

"that the ringing of church bells laid a wholesome restraint on evil spirits, and either averted or allayed the tempests wrought by these enemies of mankind was, in the opinion of the Jesuit, a fact of daily experience too patent to be denied, but he traced these happy results to the consecration or benediction of the bells." [7]

With this judgement the Middle Ages confidently agreed; all the world knew that thunder-storms, hail, and lightning were caused by maleficent demons and no man doubted the efficiency of the consecrated bells to defeat the evil spirits of the air; therefore they were called into action whenever the clouds began to gather.

[6] *Catholic Encyclopedia*, Vol. VII, "Bells."
[7] J. G. Frazer, *Folk-lore in the Old Testament*, Vol. III, p. 460.

In old S. Paul's, in London, the church bells were given a special endowment to pay the costs for ringing them when the first mutterings of thunder were heard. In Germany the peasants paid in corn to have the church bells rung when storms threatened the crops, and these payments were, in various places, continued until well into the Nineteenth Century. Five sheaves of corn, called "thunder sheaves," were paid to drive the clouds away and save the harvests.[8]

Longfellow, in the *Golden Legend,* portrays Lucifer and his demons hovering in the air about the spire of Strassburg Cathedral, trying to tear down the Cross, and to silence the holy bells by the might of the hurricane upon which his cohorts ride, and by the bolts of lightning which they hurl earthward. But the bells persist, their solemn tones ring steadily out above the turmoil until at last the thwarted Powers of Evil slink away in the darkness, pursued by the notes of the blessed bells, by the pealing of the organ, and by the praying voices of the choir.

But bells, like men, might sin, and when they sinned they must be punished.

In 1685, after the Revocation of the Edict of Nantes, the Protestant chapel at La Rochelle was condemned to be destroyed, but the bell, perhaps because of its value, was spared. However:

> "To expiate the crime of having rung heretics to prayers, the bell was sentenced to be first whipped, and then buried and disinterred, by way of symbolizing its new birth on passing into Catholic hands. Thereafter it was catechized, and obliged to recant, and promise that never again would it relapse into sin.
>
> "Having made this ample and honourable amends the bell was reconciled, baptized, and sold to the parish of S. Bartholomew. But when the governor sent in the bill for the bell to the parish authorities, they declined to settle it, alleging that the bell, as a recent convert to Catholicism, desired to take advantage of a law lately passed by the king which allowed all new converts a delay of three years in paying their debts."[9]

[8] J. G. Frazer, *op. cit.,* Vol. III, p. 457.
[9] J. G. Frazer, *op. cit.,* Vol. III, p. 443.

But sometimes old memories quicken when the church bells ring, solemnly tolling for the passing soul.

There are nonagenarians still living who can remember New England church bells tolling from their spires when the "black horses" swept over the village green; they remember too how—up and down the valley—the people woke to count the strokes, for the bells always told both farm and village whether the dying were man or woman; if the first strokes were even, the soul of a man was slipping away on the night tide; if they were uneven, then let the women close a woman's eyes. Then the bells began again, now flinging to the night winds the tally of the years: one, two, three, five, ten, thirty, sixty, eighty, eighty-one, eighty-two, eighty-three—no more; but the long silence told the countryside that old Peter Robinson had passed to his account.

Further back towards the dawn of life men beat their brazen gongs to drive away the demons, and this belief has descended to the bells, for countless mediæval legends assure us that the foul fiends cannot abide the ringing of the blessed bells which, tolling for the dying, thereby scatter all devils far beyond their faintest sound, and thus secure for the poor soul, speeding on its frightened way to Heaven, freedom from all demoniacal pursuit.

"The English antiquary, Captain Francis Gosse, writes as follows: 'The Passing-Bell was anciently rung for two purposes; one, to bespeak the prayers of all good Christians for a soul just departing; the other to drive away the evil spirits that stood at the bed's foot, and about the house, ready to seize their prey, or at least to molest and terrify the soul in its passage; but by the ringing of that bell . . . they were kept aloof; and the soul, like a hunted hare, gained the start. . . . Hence, perhaps, exclusive of the additional labour, was occasioned the high price demanded for tolling the greatest bell of the church; for that being louder, the evil spirits must go the further off, to be clear of its sound, by which the poor soul got so much more the start of them.' In some parts of the Eifel mountains, a district of Rhenish Prussia, when a sick person was at the point of death, the friends used to ring a small hand-bell, . . . 'in order to keep the evil spirits away from the dying man.'"

"Again, at Neusoil, in Northern Hungary, it is said to have been usual to ring a small hand bell softly when a dying man was near his end, 'in order that the parting soul, lured away by death, may still linger for a few moments on earth near its stiffening body.' When death has taken place, the bell was rung a little further off, then farther from the body, then out at the door, and once around the house, 'in order to accompany the soul on its parting way.' After that, word was sent to the sexton that the bell of the village church might begin to toll. A similar custom is said to have prevailed in the Bomerwald mountains, which divide Bohemia from Bavaria. The motive assigned to it—the wish to detain the parting soul for a few moments by the sweet sound of the bells, is too sentimental to be primitive; the true original motive was doubtless, . . . to banish the demons that might carry off the poor soul at the critical moment. Only when the little bell has performed this kindly office, tinkling for the soul at its setting out, does the big bell in the steeple begin to toll, that its sonorous tones may follow, like guardian angels, the fugitive on its long journey to the spirit land." [10]

Such beliefs still live, and men continue to follow the old ways. When Uncle Yanez died in the little Yugoslavian village of Brankovo, the windows of his room were opened to let his soul pass out —and quickly closed lest it should return; then the church bell across the river began to ring, calling into action the bells of other churches up and down the valley, some of them quite out of sight. So, "far, far away the bells at evening pealing" spoke comfort to poor, frightened Uncle Yanez, saying, "Fear not thou, for we are with thee," and when their last echoes died away all the valley knew that Uncle Yanez was beyond the reach of any evil thing.[11]

[10] J. G. Frazer, *op. cit.,* Vol. III, Chap. VII.
[11] L. Adamic, *The Native's Return,* pp. 68-70.

Chapter Thirty-five

THE TOWERS OF GUDEA

OVER four thousand years ago Gudea, *patesi* or governor of the
Babylonian city of Lagash, built a strong acropolis to defend his city.
Proud of his achievement, he had a plan of the fortress cut deep into
a tablet of diorite, and the visitor to the Louvre today may see him
with his beatific expression, round hat, hands clasped across his breast,
and the tablet resting on his knees for all the world to see.[1]

Few of the hundreds who pass his diorite image will associate the
old Sumerian with the builders of mediæval churches, but Gudea,
dead yet speaking, tells us that he raised flanking towers beside each
of the six gates of his citadel at Lagash more than three millennia
before William the Conqueror erected towers to flank the portals of
his Abbaye-aux-Hommes at Caen.

It is now our purpose to trace the links of the chain that binds the
Sumerian to the Norman, and to follow the fortified gateway from
Babylonian Lagash to the Hittite stronghold of Zindjirli, thence to
Roman Temples at Baalbec, to the Syrian churches of Kalb Lauzeh
and Kasr-il-Benat, then over the sea to German Frankfort on the
Main, and so to the churches of the great Norman in the city of Caen.

Gudea of Lagash was not the first to defend his gates with towers;
Ur-Nammu erected them beside the entrances to his city whose walls
were seventy feet thick and, long before his day, A-aani-pad-da, whose
father founded the Third Dynasty after the Flood in Ur, built a

---

[1] The statue has lost its head, perhaps as an expression of pride, or venom, on the
part of some later conqueror of Lagash; there remains another statue in the Louvre,
however, whose severed head was found, identified, and restored to its place upon his
body, so we are familiar with his likeness. It is also not quite certain whether Gudea's
structure was an acropolis or a fortified palace but this, for us, is a minor matter.

GUDEA AND HIS ACROPOLIS

The statue of the "patesi" of Lagash and the plan of the fortress he built forty-five hundred years ago, little dreaming that he was preparing an inheritance for Benedictine monks who, thirty-five hundred years later, should build an abbey where Durham looks down on the River Wear.

temple in the suburbs of his city with encircling walls and, apparently, with towers beside the gates.[2]

The Third and Fourth Millennia in Mesopotamia, however, are richer in archæological possibilities than in certainties, for—unlike Egypt—stone was lacking while clay was plentiful, wherefore the builders made the walls of cities and palaces of sun-dried brick, which cannot be expected to survive the rains, floods, and wars of five thousand years. We may learn something, however, from occasional bas-reliefs and from the mosaics of the royal tombs of Ur which reveal the existence of an advanced civilization three thousand five hundred years before the birth of Christ. In that far day the armies of Ur were well organized, armed, and disciplined; her architects were familiar with all the basic principles of construction known to us today; her artists, goldsmiths, and workers in metal were skilful; their work discloses a marked delicacy of taste, while her merchants carried on an extensive trade and her wealth gave scope to luxury.[3]

It is quite conceivable, therefore, that such walls, towers, and gates as those that A-aani-pad-da probably built in 3100 B.C., and that Ur-Nammu and Gudea certainly erected some six hundred years later, were not unknown in the high civilization of the days of Mes-kalem-dug who lived, died, and was magnificently buried over five thousand years ago. Lagash and Ur were not alone in their possession of walls, towers, and fortified gates; there were many other cities equally well protected in the "Land of the Rivers"—cities of Sumer and of Akkad —Eridu, Erech, Larsa, and Agade; there were others still beyond the sweeping curve of the Euphrates—"The Great Bend of the Naharin" —cities behind whose mighty ramparts men slept well, from Ilium in the North, past the Hittite strongholds of Boghaz Keui and Zindjirli, to Kadesh on the Orontes where the great Rameses, ambushed by Metella, came so near defeat; and the gates of this Hittite capital, protected by flanking towers, appear in Egyptian bas-reliefs from Abydus to Abu Simbel. Recent excavations at Shechem, where lies "Jacob's Well," have brought to light a fortress city with an enclosed

[2] C. L. Woolley, *Ur Excavations at al-Ubaid*, p. 114.
[3] C. L. Woolley, *Ur of the Chaldees*, pp. 84-89.

area of fifteen acres which was erected in the Fourteenth Century before Christ to defend the pass between Mt. Ebal and Mt. Gerizim. Its walls of cyclopean masonry were thirty-five feet thick and sixty-five feet high, and its entrance gate was defended by four massive corner towers. Still farther to the South lay the cities of Canaan, encircled by walls upon whose crests two chariots might drive abreast.

The storm waves of History have broken against these towers and her tides have flowed through these gates. In a past where we may but dimly see through the mists of more than three millennia Abd-Khiba the Amorite stood on the gate tower of Jerusalem and watched his messengers take the long road to Egypt, bearing letters to implore Amenhotep's aid against the Khabiri who had crossed the Jordan and were ravaging the land—aid that was never given although the pitiful letters have been found beneath the sand that, long since, covered Pharaoh's palace at Amarna.

The spies sent by Moses from Paran to survey their promised land, seeing from afar the mighty ramparts and towered gates of those cities of Canaan which the great Thutmose—the Alexander of Egypt —had only conquered after five hard fought campaigns, returned with quick and fearful steps saying: "There are giants in the land, in whose sight we are as grasshoppers." From the "divine tower" that Poseidon built over the Dardanian Gate of Troy Priam and Hector watched as Agamemnon, Ajax, Achilles, and the wise Odysseus deployed their Greeks on the Plain of the Scamander, and beneath this same tower the fatal gift of the Greeks, the Trojan Horse, was drawn into the city, now abandoned of the gods. So we may journey from the Scamander to the Nile, from the days of Akkad to those of Rome, finding always and everywhere the cities of men defended by such towers as those which Gudea built. They appear not only by the gates of cities but also at the portals of the palaces of kings, for the "Great House" where dwelt the "Mighty in Valour, the Crusher of Lands" was a little city in itself, and surely the place where Majesty dwelt must be no less secure than were the abodes of his subjects.[4]

---

[4] The Palace of the King was known as the "Great House" throughout the East; it was the *per-o* in Egypt, a name which gave rise to the title "Pharaoh;" in Akkad it was the *e-gal;* in Babylonia the *ekallu;* and in Jerusalem the *hekhal.*

From the palace the flanking towers passed naturally to the temple, for this also must be protected since it was considered as truly the dwelling place of the god as the palace was the residence of the King. This belief that the gods actually dwelt in their shrines is very old and is implicit in the names that men bestowed upon them.

Jacob, sleeping at Bethel with a stone for a pillow, dreamed of angels and heard the voice of God. When morning broke he awoke with the cry upon his lips, "How dreadful is this place; this is none other than the House of God;" wherefore he made a pillar of the stone on which his head had rested, anointed it with oil, and said: "This stone shall be *bayith-Elohim*"—the "House of God." [5]

Since the temple was the earthly residence of deity men fashioned it after the most splendid dwelling they could conceive and repeated, so far as was practicable, the dispositions of the palace. If this had gardens, colonnades, an audience hall, and chambers for the royal concubines, the temple also had gardens, colonnades, an audience hall, and apartments for the *quedeshim,* or temple prostitutes. If the King's house had an enclosing wall, with gates and towers, the house of the god must be as well guarded and secure, for gods might be taken prisoners as well as kings and peoples. Egyptian conquerors brought the statues of Syrian gods, captured with their cities, back to Egypt, placed them in their temples, carving upon the stone the dates of their capture and, later, the dates of their release. When the ark of God was brought into the camp of Israel on the eve of battle the Philistines, hearing the welcoming shouts of their enemies, were terrified and said to one another, "Their god is come into the camp." But before another sun had set the ark was a spoil of the men of Gath who took it to their temple that Jehovah might serve their fish-god, Dagon. Captured idols of Amorite Jerusalem were dragged to Gezer; while others of Atoroth and of Nebo, seized in the sack of those cities, were carried

[5] Back of this story lies the primitive belief, unrecognized but still surviving in the procedures of our courts, that the holiness within an object is communicated to him who touches it. When Jacob used the stone for a pillow he established contact with the spirit that dwelt within and that spirit, entering his sleeping brain, spoke to him in the watches of the night. So when the witness in our courts "kisses the Book," the holiness within its covers enters and seals his lips to all except the truth.

away by Mesha to his city of Kir and set up before Chemosh, his god.[6] Therefore, since gods might be captured, walls, towers, and fortified gateways must defend their temples.

Such fortifications however, especially of cities, became intolerable to the sovereigns of Assyria and of Babylon when, increased in power, they began to challenge the supremacy of Egypt. They dared not send their armies across Syria and Palestine—"the Bridge of the World"—without protecting their communications by the reduction of hostile cities lying along their path, yet the capture of these cities was no light undertaking. Shalmaneser spent five fruitless years before the walls of Tyre; Sennacherib was forced to withdraw from the strong defences of Jerusalem, and Samaria successfully defied the armies of Assyria for three years until famine, not force, unbarred her gates. Such difficulties, delays, or defeats made the Mesopotamian kings reluctant to allow the existence of walled towns along the roads by which their armies marched; therefore the defences of captured cities were cast down, and the rebuilding of fortifications once levelled was accepted as a sign of premeditated rebellion and a *casus belli*. Nehemiah might not repair the walls of Jerusalem, breached and burned by Nebuchadrezzar, until he had received permission from Cyrus, and his work had hardly been begun before hostile lips were whispering in Persian ears that Nehemiah was fortifying his city as a prelude to revolt. Only the unprecedented speed with which the Jews worked, completing the rebuilding of their walls in fifty-two days, enabled them to outstrip the royal couriers, speeding swiftly from Babylon with orders that the work should halt.

Thus with the rise of world empires, whose sovereigns were jealous of rivals and impatient of lesser kings, the towers which flanked the gates of cities, palaces, or temples began to lose their defensive character and to assume a decorative, rather than a military, rôle. In the ruins of the Hittite cities of Bogaz-Keui, and especially of Zindjirli, we may trace this evolution for centuries until, with the overthrow of the Hittite Empire, the fortress was turned into a château whose towers were intended to embellish rather than to serve their ancient purpose

---

[6] Stewart Macalister, *Bible Side-Lights from the Mound of Gezer*, pp. 57-61.

of defence, and after Esarhaddon (660-668 B.C.) captured Zindjirli "the fortress towers gave place to purely decorative motives, that of the towered façade, which was destined to have a long and honourable place in Christian architecture." [7]

So, by the long road which descends the centuries from the cities of Gudea and of Ur-Nammu, and very probably from those of A-aani-pad-da and of Mes-kalem-dug, we travel down the ages from Akkad to Ilium, to the cities of the Hittites, the Amorites, and the Canaanites; from the days of Sumer to those of Rome; seeing the fortress changing to the residence and the towers becoming decorative features, even as the stern feudal strongholds of France developed into the moated châteaux of the Renaissance along the Loire and are reflected in the turreted dwellings which scowled upon the Victorian world with a timbered frown.

The survival of the age-old flanking towers as an important decorative device in Roman Syria is evidenced by early Third Century coins of Caracalla, of Philip the Arabian, and of Oticilia, his wife, which show that the temples of Baalbec were supplied with enclosing walls and with gates that were flanked by towers even as were those of Gudea's acropolis at Lagash. With the rise of Christianity the ancient gods of Baalbec were dispossessed, their temples became churches, their shrines were turned into Christian altars, and their towers began to look down upon long processions of priests and people passing through the entrances which they had so long guarded for vanished gods.

From Baalbec these flanking towers passed on to the great Fourth and Fifth Century basilicas which sprang up in Central Syria long before the Moslems came to separate Syria from the Christian world. The connection between the towers of pagan Baalbec and those of Christian Kasr-il-Benat is attested by the fact that it was only in Asia that the temple areas possessed these towers, and that it was only in Asia that Christian churches had them before the dawn of the Eighth Century.

With the Moslem conquest of Syria the flanking towers might conceivably have vanished completely had not the disappearance of the

[7] Gertrude Bell, *The Palace and Mosque of Ukhaidir*, p. 60.

atrium in the West, exposing the angular façade of the basilica, created a sudden need for compensation wherefore, after a lapse of two hundred years or more, the towers which had last appeared in the land of the Syrian Orontes began to reappear along the banks of the German Rhine.

We are impelled to believe that these Carlovingian towers were the offsprings of the Syrian. Of course it is possible that they had an independent origin in Eighth Century Germany, for the Moslem conquest had severed the Christian West from the now Moslem East and the Syrian churches were involved in the debacle. But when Kasr-il-Benat was built, that conquest was still two hundred years in the future; throughout those two centuries, when Spanish bishops were attending Eastern councils, when Syrian ecclesiastics were visiting Spain, and Syrian laymen were colonizing Western cities (they were settled in Narbonne before the year 600) some knowledge of these great churches must have reached the West; and this knowledge must have been still more widely diffused when multitudes of Syrian refugees, fleeing from the advance of Moslem armies, sought refuge in the Christian cities of the Mediterranean basin. Even after the conquest, when the Omayyad and the Abbasside caliphs were established in Damascus, it was made evident that frontiers, however hostile, cannot interdict the passage of ideas; there were embassies, armies, traders, and pilgrims passing to and fro, and ideas travel with the impedimenta of armies, the packs of traders, and the wallets of pilgrims. With so many points of contact, by any one of which a knowledge of these Syrian towers might have reached the West, it seems safe to agree with those many eminent scholars who have seen a direct connection between early Syrian architecture, and that of the Carlovingian period in Western Europe.[8]

So the towers of our churches come down to us with an illustrious lineage; we may not be able to follow a distinguished archæologist and student of Babylonian culture when he suggests the Zikkurat, with its gilded peak and superimposed terraces green with trees, as the progenitor of the towers of mediæval churches; nevertheless we

[8] A. K. Porter, *Mediæval Architecture*, Vol. I, p. 82.

believe that we may trace them back to those earlier towers which, throughout the ages, have guarded the portals of the House of God, by whatsoever terms men may have called upon His Name, and that these, surviving the passing of five millennia, reappear on our cathedrals to repeat the essential lines of the façades of the Temple of Ur, and of the acropolis that Gudea built in his city of Lagash.

Not all the cathedral towers of Europe can be traced back through Kasr-il-Benat, Baalbec, and Zindjirli to those of Sumerian cities. The square campaniles, or bell towers, that rise above the roofs of Italian towns or cities doubtless have a common origin with the flanking towers of Northern Europe and are related to those of Gudea's acropolis, although they were directly derived from the rectangular fortress towers that guarded the walls and gates of the armed camps of Roman legions, that rose at intervals along the great Wall in Northern England, and which, later still, defended the wall which Aurelian, in fear of the barbarians, built around the city of Rome itself. But the round campaniles that appear nearer the Italian coast, as at Ravenna and at Pisa, have a quite different origin; they spring from the watch towers whose ruins, still dotting the Mediterranean shores, remind us that this ancient sea, from the days of the Dorian invasion in the Eleventh Century B.C. to those of the Tripolitan Beys whom Decatur fought, has been swept by pirate fleets. Therefore the early dwellers by the sea, living in dread, raised round watch towers that were also lighthouses, from which their sentries scanned horizons for the first glimpse of hostile sails. From such observation posts as these sprang the famous round tower of Galata, in Constantinople, whose base predates the circular campaniles of Ravenna by over two hundred years, and Thiersch is convinced that the round Italian campaniles derive their origin from the tower of Galata and thus ultimately from the earlier watch towers by the sea.[9]

So the stones of our church towers have more tales to tell us than ever Scheherazade told, for her life, to Schariar, Sultan of India. In Pisa and Ravenna, round campaniles tell us stories of pirates of all ages and of many races as, through their portals, we see the sun shining

[9] Thiersch, *Pharos*, p. 176.

on sinister sails or flashing on blue Mediterranean waters beaten into foam by corsair oars as Ishmaels of the sea raid coastal settlements for slaves and spoils. At Palermo, Verona, and Florence, square campaniles tell us martial tales, opening their door-ways that we may see Rome's legions marching the long roads towards far frontiers to build there those dams and dykes of walls and towers by which the barbarian floods were long held in check. At Canterbury, Caen, and Chartres, the flanking towers of cathedrals tell us of Hector and Achilles; of crafty Metella of Kadesh; of Abd-Khiba, vainly watching for the horsemen of Egypt and the chariots thereof; they also tell us tales of Ur of the Chaldees from whose fortified gateways Abraham went forth to lay the foundations of a faith that should one day rear the towers of Amiens and of Rheims.

Chapter Thirty-six

ICONOGRAPHY
A LITERATURE FOR THE ILLITERATE

PERHAPS the first impression the European cathedral makes upon the American visitor is one of amazement at the wealth of carvings that often covers the façade, frames the portals and the windows, peers beneath the eaves, and climbs the towers. Some of these are merely decorative, others illustrate the narratives of the Bible, the lives of the saints, or the fables of the Bestiaries. When we cross the threshold and enter the church we find identical, or similar, tales repeated by the sculptor on the capitals of the columns, and by the glazier in the medallions of the windows.

It is all very amazing, but it is also often puzzling; when we look at the windows we wonder what these quaint, archaic figures are doing in the jewelled glass. Why are these golden idols falling from their pedestals at Chartres? Why does that long-necked bird perch on a sick man's breast at Lyons? Why does the lion stand over his dead cubs in a medallion of Bourges?

Equally perplexing are the carvings; at Notre-Dame in Paris two hands without an owner cling to the sides of a casket borne in a funeral procession; at Amiens three kings go sailing while men with torches set fire to ships anchored in a harbour; at Modena, in Italy, a man with a pole in both hands dangles something before the eyes of two winged griffons harnessed to his chariot. What do these scenes mean? What was the thought of the artist who carved them in the stone or leaded them into the glass? Very few know; to most visitors the art of the cathedral has all the mystery of the hieroglyphics on Egyptian monuments.

Yet they were never meant to be obscure; on the contrary, the Church had, from early times, wished the artists to teach her children

291

so clearly the things they ought to know that none could fail to understand their meaning. Back in the Sixth Century, Gregory the Great wrote his desire that art might be so used, that "those who do not know their letters may be taught from the pictures on the walls what they cannot learn from books."

So also thought Benoît Biscop, abbot of Weremouth in the Seventh Century, and Walafrid Strabo in the Ninth; while the Council of Arras, in the Eleventh Century, called pictures (and the word includes all forms of pictorial art—bas-reliefs, mosaics, frescoes, or glass) "the literature of the illiterate."

Moreover neither the sculptor nor the glazier could have understood an art that was abstruse or profound; for them to express the dialectics of the Church would have been as difficult as it would be for one, ignorant of Hebrew, to copy intelligibly an old Hebraic cursive manuscript. Indeed, the man who carved these stories of the Bible or of the Golden Legend, who trained the graceful vines with their bursting buds around the portals of the church, was not an artist at all as we understand the term. He was just a mason with the status of a peasant who, when work at his craft was light, often worked as a peasant, farming his small holdings of land. Speaking and understanding only the common speech, the subtle dialects of the Church were far beyond his understanding, and therefore beyond the capacities of his chisel. Wherefore the subjects that he carved must have the simplicity of the folk-lore of his day. They must lie within the scope of his comprehension and within that of the plain people, of whom he was one. This will be more clear, perhaps, if we follow the training of this man who, peasant though he was, yet gave to the Twelfth and Thirteenth Centuries an art unexcelled in Europe since the days of Praxiteles.

He began as a labourer in the quarries, a hewer of stone. But because of the high cost of cartage (in 1415 it cost twenty-one English pounds to draw stone from Huddleston to York cathedral; to quarry the same stone at Huddleston cost only fourteen pounds) it was expedient to send masons to the quarries to dress the stone on the spot, and sometimes to carve the capitals and the mouldings. Thus the quarryman could learn much by watching the skilled masons at their work, and perhaps get some practice. When he showed adaptability he would leave the quarries to become a mason's helper—a carrier of dressed stone and of mortar; next he would be given a trowel and, as a "rowmason" or *positorus petrarum,* would set the stones with mortar in their courses. Then, as a *cissorus* or a *batrarius,* he would begin to dress the stone and shape it with axe, hammer, or chisel. But let him now be careful, for the guild to which he aspired was jealous of its reputation and quick to exclude from membership the incompetent and careless. There were penalties attached to slipshod work that would be as impossible to impose as they might be valuable in our day. Janner reports a lodge custom which seems to have had considerable antiquity. If the aspirant should chance to spoil a stone all work stopped; the victim of his malpractice would be placed on a bier and carried in procession to the last resting place of ruined stones—nicknamed the "charnel-house." He himself must march directly behind the bearers, followed by the other workmen, and look forward to a beating when he returned, which might be rather severe if the work were important enough to call for many workmen, since each of his fellows was permitted three or four blows.

If, however, his record was good, if he had escaped the office of chief mourner in the dead march to the petrine cemetery, he might be entrusted with some minor details in the carving, and so at last the exceptionally gifted mason would join the ranks of the *imagours* who carved the mouldings, the capitals, bas-reliefs, and statues. As a member of the mason's guild he would be taught the password and the grip, for these were his certificates of competency when, of necessity a wanderer in search of work, he came among strangers.[1]

This is the man, and such his training, who carved the story of Noah at Ely Cathedral; of Abraham and the fall of Sodom at Salisbury, and of Jonah at Ripon. Such also must have been the training

---

[1] Thus the secret clasp of hands, the whispered password, of today's Masonic Lodges, as well as of those guarded chambers to which hooded figures with masked faces led us in our college days, came into being as the credentials of the mediæval mason. See G. G. Coulton, *Art and the Reformation,* p. 171; D. Knoop and G. P. Jones, *The Mediæval Mason.*

of his brother artist across the Channel whose chisel told the story of the Creation at Amiens; of Gideon and his fleece at Laon; of David and Goliath at Rheims, of the sacrifice of Abraham at Chartres, the Kiss of Judas at Arles, until the entire record, from the Creation through the stories of both Testaments and the Lives of the Saints to the End of the World, the Resurrection of the Dead, and the Day of Judgement, was written on the stones.

Obviously such a story must fail of its purpose if it were not easily understood; commissioned by the Church to teach men clearly, the artist meant to speak, through his chisel, in a common tongue so that men of every age would understand his thought. And for the Christian of his day he rarely failed, for he spoke to a generation that had been brought up in the stories of the Bible and the Golden Legend. When he carved at Amiens ships on fire and three kings sailing, he expected men to remember that Herod had burned the ships at Tyre in a vain attempt to seize the Magi who had brought gifts to Bethlehem.

When he drew with his leads, in an upper window of Chartres, the figure of a woman holding three loaves of bread in her hands, he felt that all would know the story of Mary of Egypt—first a sinner and then a saint—who had been miraculously sustained for forty days in the wilderness on such scanty fare, and who slept at last in a desert grave, dug for her body by a lion sent of God. When, also at Chartres, the sculptor carved an emaciated saint with a dove on his shoulder, beneath whose feet the head of a man peered upward through the parted folds of a curtain, he knew that men would recall the tale of S. Gregory, caught by his secretary in the act of writing to the dictation of a heaven-sent dove.

Neither did the artist often fail for the men of the Fourteenth and Fifteenth Centuries; the old tradition might be dying but it was far from dead, and men could understand his purpose, even though they might be untouched by scenes that had deeply moved their fathers, and be unresponsive to traditional appeals. Even in the Sixteenth Century, most Christians could still interpret the medallions in the windows and the carvings on the stones, for the denunciations of "idol worship" by the Protestants, the proceedings of the Council of Trent, and the writings of Molenus of Leyden University clearly show familiarity with the legends. These men knew the story of the miracles whereby S. Thomas had converted Gondoforus, King of India; of S. Nicholas who restored life to three little children, killed, dressed, and salted away for the winter's meat by an evil inn-keeper; of the giant S. Christopher who had sought the devil and found Christ; and of the battle of S. James with the magician Hermogenes which was carved at Amiens in the Sixteenth Century.

From this time on, however, the visions dimmed, partly because of the mockery of the Protestants, partly because of diminished spirituality, of increased secularity, and the deepening of the scientific spirit. By the Eighteenth Century they had quite faded out, and Parisian scholars had so far lost contact with the Middle Ages that they thought they saw in the carvings of Notre-Dame the secret formula whereby base metals might be turned to gold; Lenoir saw Bacchus in the figure of S. Denis, patron saint of France, carrying his head in his hands as he walked from Paris, where he had been beheaded, to the Abbey without the walls where he should be enshrined; and Revolutionists smashed the statues of the royal Judean ancestors of Christ on the gallery of the kings at Notre-Dame, mistaking them for images of the kings of France whom all good patriots must detest.

Yet, trained in understanding as the men of the Middle Ages may have been, familiar as they doubtless were with the stories their churches silently told, there were values and meanings, important and significant, that were hidden from their eyes. It is only in our day that scholars and archæologists like Emile Mâle and Louis Bréhier, studying the gifts the living buried with their dead in Scythian or Sarmatian tombs of Central Asia, sculptures of Babylon and Assyria, tapestries from Persia, and illuminated manuscripts from Mesopotamia, Byzantium, Greece, Syria, Egypt, and on to Spain, which monks of the Romanesque century copied for the decorations of their abbeys, have opened doors to us that were closed to the mediæval mind. It is their researches into the sermons and philosophies of the Gothic centuries, when men saw the universe as a cryptogram of

God eloquent with His messages, that pathways have been revealed to us that men, before our day, had never seen.

In a chapel of Amiens, and in many churches until the clerics of the Renaissance destroyed them, a bearded figure in a long robe is nailed upon a cross. The Twelfth Century, not understanding this man in a woman's dress, invented an explanatory legend. It was Wilgeforte, they said, a Christian princess of Portugal, betrothed by her pagan father to a prince who knew not Christ. Shrinking from the unhallowed union, Wilgeforte, when all other efforts failed, besought God for an ugliness so great that no man could desire her and He, hearing the prayer, caused a beard to cover her face from eyes to throat. Thereupon the suitor hurriedly sailed away as the angry father crucified his daughter. Thus they explained the cross, the man's beard, and the woman's dress.

We, however—finding the same figure in a Tenth Century Catalonian Bible, a copy of which, the Bible of Farfa, is in the Vatican Library; in a Seventh Century fresco on the walls of S. Maria Antiqua in Rome; in the Sixth Century Gospel of Rabula in Florence, on an ampoule of the Fifth Century in Monza, and in a famous crucifix at Lucca which the legend says was carved by Nicodemus—know that this bearded figure in a woman's dress reveals the early Syrian conception of the Christ. To the Syrian Christian Jesus was mature, sacerdotal, bearded as became a man, and clad in a long robe even on the cross (where the Greek would have him nude) since nakedness had been the reproach of Noah, and the evidence of Adam's sin.

In a church near Rouen a man strangles a lion in both hands; whatever interpretation the Twelfth Century may have given to this hero no man then could have known, as we do now who find the same scene in an Assyrian carving at the Louvre, that this is Gilgamash, once a Sumerian king of the First Dynasty of Erech, later transmuted into a Babylonian demi-god and, millennia after the fall of Babylon, transported to the West in the weavings of such a tapestry as may today be seen at Sens, to delight some unknown artist and be copied on a capital of S. Georges-Boscherville.

The more we visit the churches where these artists wrought, the longer we listen to the stories told—in mosaics, frescoes, glass, or stone —the deeper grows our conviction that we have heard these tales before, that we heard them when we were listening to the voices of the cathedral, to the whisperings of the stones. Sooner or later, as we pass from cathedral to church and from church to abbey, a moment comes when we suddenly realize that the artists are telling in poetry what the masons told in prose; that iconography illustrates the history which architecture records.

This new understanding may come to us in such a church as S. Trophîme at Arles, where the iconography of a thousand years passes us in review. Here is the symbolism that was frescoed on the walls of the catacombs; here is the narrative and creedal art of the Fifth and Sixth Centuries that may still be seen in the churches of Ravenna, and here, too—forming the background—is the purely decorative art which, born in Asia, entered Europe with those invading tribes that overthrew the ancient civilization. The earlier Christian art, obliterated for five hundred years by that of the barbarians, might conceivably have been wholly lost to the mediæval church had it not been preserved by monks who, often in remote monasteries, preserved it in their innumerable manuscripts, whose miniatures were copied in stone and repeated in bas-reliefs by other monks in Romanesque centuries.

So also the story of the past is repeated in the architecture—in cloister and in crypt; in curving apse and ambulatory; in transepts, nave arcades, and triforium galleries.

When we enter the crypt it tells us tales of the cubiculum from which it is descended; of Christians once gathered in underground chapels whose altars were martyrs' graves, whose frescoed walls were eloquent with Christ's promise of resurrection for those who kept the faith, even at the cost of life. The same story is repeated in the glass of Chartres, the carvings of Moissac, the mosaics of Monreale, and the Cosmato work of Salerno. In the cathedral and cubiculum alike, Lazarus rises from the dead; the lions fawn at Daniel's feet; Shadrach and his comrades stand unharmed amid the flames; Jonah is delivered from the whale, and the Ark rides safely over a submerged world.

Thus art and architecture, the cathedral and the cubiculum, echo the same tale, and when we stand before the jewelled window of Chartres where Jesus bids Lazarus "Come forth," or in the cloister of Moissac where the Son of Man stands with Meshach and Abed-nego in Nebuchadrezzar's flaming furnace, we hear the murmurs of Christians praying underground; we hear Rome's proletariat shuffling through narrow streets towards the Circus Maximus, and then—the soft patter of padded feet moving swiftly over the sands of the arena.

When we were passing down the aisles the arches in the nave's arcade told of the crowds who had followed Constantine into the church, whose very numbers had forced the builders to open wider vistas from the side aisles towards the altar by placing arches instead of lintels on the columns.

The iconography adds something to the tale the arches have already told, for the narrative form it now assumes, the detail in which the stories of the Old Testament and of the New are portrayed, as at S. Apollinare Nuovo in Ravenna, clearly indicate that the Church was ministering to a new order of Christians, to men who were far less familiar with the Bible than they had been who had worshipped in the catacombs before Constantine had made confession safe.

This tale of Christian security through Imperial favour is again emphasized by the size and splendour of the churches that were built in and after the Fourth Century, and here again art adds a chapter to those already related in the architecture. Throughout the years of persecution, when the Church had been unable to call her Councils and to define her faith, confusion had spread across the Christian world—especially as to the nature of Christ and of the union, in His person, of the human and the divine. When the conversion of the Emperor gave the Church her opportunity she called the Council which met in Nicæa in 325; thereafter Council followed Council, among the most important being those that met in Ephesus in 431, and at Chalcedon twenty years later, whose decrees still echo in the iconography of the Middle Ages.

When, at Paris or at Chartres, we see Our Lady crowned and

CAPITAL FROM AUTUN

Woman, accomplice of Satan, surrenders the man she
has seduced to her master.

BAS RELIEFS FROM THE PORCH OF AMIENS CATHEDRAL

Above, right to left: Balaam prophesies a star; Micah promises a ruler; Herod consults
the wise men; massacre of the innocents. Below (extreme right): An angel warns the
sleeping kings. (From left to right) Herod orders the ships to be burned; they are set
afire; the kings have already escaped.

seated at the right hand of Christ in glory; when we see her at Char-
lieu flanked by the apostles and enthroned among the stars, we hear
—as the Twelfth Century could not—the voice of the Council of
Ephesus affirming that Mary was not only the mother of Jesus, she
is also "Theotokos"—"The Mother of God." When mediæval artists
placed the sun and the moon on either side of the cross, as on Calvaries of Brittany, they were unwittingly repeating the utterances of
the Council of Chalcedon which, in 451, declared that Jesus was both
Son of God and Son of Man, that in His person the two natures were
"inconfusedly combined."

Thus the brief centuries of the Church's triumph are recorded for
us in the architecture, and also in the narrative or creedal art of the
great churches of Ravenna, and again repeated in the carvings, frescoes, mosaics, and glass of the Middle Ages.

When we were sitting in the transepts we heard the stones chanting
a requiem for dying Rome, while the north winds brought us distant
echoes of the conquering barbarians' guttural *vae victis*. From the
narrow windows of the ambulatory we saw wave after wave of Asiatic
hordes sweeping over the old frontiers, and listened to the *Ora pro
nobis* tremulously chanted by priests, now living among "wild beasts,"
protected, not by the ancient majesty of Rome, but by the barbarians'
fear of the Holy Relics. The tale that the transepts told, that the
ambulatories and the double apses of Albi and of Garde Adhémar
repeated, is carried on by the artists. The old symbolic, narrative, and
creedal art of Rome vanishes, not to reappear for five hundred years
and is replaced by barbaric forms that are purely decorative, by geometric patterns, swirling, interlacing lines, and by misformed or em-
battled animals. The relics, feared by Goths and Huns alike, were
enclosed in such reliquaries as that which Pépin gave to the abbey at
Conques whose sides are decorated with barbaric forms—with cabochons (large, uncut jewels) set in cloisonné. Similar reliquaries are
preserved at S. Maurice d'Agaune and at Benoît-sur-Loire. The same
barbaric art decorates "The Gospel of Theodolinda" at Monza and
appears in the votive crowns, offered by Receswinth and other Visi-

gothic kings, some of which are preserved in Madrid while others are in the Cluny Museum in Paris.

Such decorative forms are also found in the architecture—at Notre-Dame-le-Grand at Poitiers, for instance, and on the arcades of a vanished abbey whose ruins lie beneath the corridors of the Prefecture at Angers.

But these same swirling, interlacing, decorative lines, these cabochons set in cloisonné, have been found in Scythian and Sarmatian tombs of Central Asia, some of which date from the Sixth Century before Christ.

If, now, we have the eyes to see we will find details in these confusing patterns on our churches which tell us stories of the migrations of these barbaric peoples. Here or there, among the scrolls or interlacing lines, classical motives appear—the acanthus leaf or the *rinceau*, a graceful scroll of delicately carved foliage—which tell us that the Sarmatians, teachers of the Goths—who carried this art across the Rhine—on the Steppes of Russia, halted on their westward trek beside the shores of the Black Sea where, through contact with Greek trading settlements, they enriched their art with designs that were familiar to the entire Hellenic world.

Still other forms—twisted serpents, queer animal figures, lions on either side of the Tree of Life—indicate that this Asiatic people had camped for years on the borders of Persia, heir to the art of the oldest civilizations of the world, and had there learned those lessons which Iran had herself received from Assyria, Babylon, and Sumer.

Five centuries later the stones of huge foundations and of great abbey churches, raised—like S. Guilhem-le-Désert—in desolate places, and far too vast for the needs of any local congregation, speak to us of a monastic age; they echo the chants of pilgrims, come from far, over weary roads, to seek the help of potent saints enshrined among the abbey's dead.

The art also tells us tales of those monks whose influence permeated the Eleventh Century, for the monastic fear of woman and scorn of wealth are dramatically told in the naked woman devoured by snakes and toads in the porch of Moissac while, near by, Lazarus the beggar rests in Abraham's bosom as exultant devils drag rich Dives down to Hell, his heavy but useless purse dangling from his neck.

Then Cluny dies and Cîteaux is born; the disappearance of all richly coloured windows, the substitution of soft browns, or cool green, or grey in the glass that merely please by their delicate colours and graceful patterns, tell us that a twilight has fallen upon the monastic world; that a new Order, austere and hostile to all forms of art, has surrendered the iconographic field to the cathedral chapters; that the Gothic sun is rising to shine brightly for four hundred years, and then to set "behind the mighty printing presses of Mayence."

The artist also records the change for whereas the monk, secluded in his cell, letting the world he had foresworn come to him, had copied in his bas-reliefs the miniatures of manuscripts which princes gave, or which pilgrims brought from the far corners of the world—from Mesopotamia, Byzantium, Greece, Syria, Egypt, and on to Spain—the priest of the new order went forth into the world, seeing God's cryptogram in His creation, and in every created thing a secret message from God to man.

Three leaves had been given to the clover that it might bear witness to the Triune God; the twisted beak of the crossbill and the red breast of the robin carried a divine reproach for they revealed that there were sufferings which even the birds aspired to share. The crossbill had broken his beak in desperate efforts to wrench the nails from the feet of Christ, while the robin's breast had been stained red from wounds received as he pulled the thorns from the brow of Jesus.

Thus all nature, animate or inanimate, brought God's messages to men. So also did history in countless ways that we can only briefly illustrate. If Gideon chose three hundred men, no more, to repel the threat of Midian it was because the Greek letter *Tau* (T) not only stood for the number three hundred, but was also the emblem of the Cross. Therefore Gideon limited the number who marched with him that he might foretell the victory of Christ on Calvary. So in all forms possible to his art the Gothic artist interpreted the cryptogram of God.

Of course the artists were not always concerned with the souls of men; even the monk could jest. On a capital, now in the Museum of Poitiers, two bald men tear at each other's beards above a Latin inscription which may be freely translated: "It is permitted to pull your adversary's beard if he has no hair to grasp."

Another capital in the nave of S. Pierre at Caen jests at the plight of Virgil, left suspended in a basket half-way up to the tower chamber of a lady whose arm was as stout as her virtue was frail, for the mockery of the people when day should dawn. Here also the vengeful Campaspe rides Aristotle with bit and bridle to the amazement, and amusement, of Alexander—rebuked yesterday by the great philosopher for too often yielding to the wiles of the famous courtesan. At Bristol, England, a wife drives her husband from the kitchen with a barrage of flying dishes, while on misericords of Beverley and Lincoln husbands trundle their scolding wives in wheelbarrows to the Ducking Pond. It is all very human, even when the laughter of the stones is raucous, and the capitals guffaw.

Then a different note is struck as the medallions or the carvings tell us of strange beasts and stranger peoples who dwell beyond the frontiers of the known world—tales that Ctesias, Court Physician to Artaxerxes of Persia, related four hundred years before Christ.

The tympanum of Vézelay tells us of the Cynocephali, a dog-headed race, keepers of flocks and herds, weavers of wool, who were also sons of Adam and victims of his fall; it tells us, too, of the Panotii, a strange people whose huge ears encase their skulls like the shells of the oyster. Sens shows us the Sciapod, a man with a single leg who can run marvellously but is here outstretched on the sands using his foot as a parasol against the heat of a blazing sun.

A column of Souvigny gives us the Ethiopian, with his four eyes; a capital in the Museum of Nevers adds the Mantichore to the list— a curious beast who hisses like a serpent through the face of a man. Amiens gives us the Aspic, a kind of dragon who fears the sound of music and, at the first note, buries one ear in the ground and seals the other with his tail—he is therefore the symbol of the sinner who refuses the music of the Gospel. The Owl at Le Mans is the natural symbol of the Jew, because he flies by night and hides from the sun. All these, and many others that we have not time to question here, are given us either in the stone or in the glass.

From the beasts the artists turn to tell the Golden Legend—the lives of the saints who, living or dying, blazed for us the way of life. The glass of Bourges, of Chartres, and of Tours tell the fate of Simon, a great magician at the court of Nero who could make stone dogs bark, brass statues laugh, and bronze serpents crawl. Defeated in a contest of powers by S. Peter, Simon angrily launched into the air and flew away, but at the prayer of S. Peter the devils who sustained him in his flight were forced to flee, whereupon Simon fell and broke his neck. Chartres tells, in stone, one of many stories of S. Nicholas, protector of little children. A certain nobleman, unable to endow his daughters because of poverty, feared lest starvation might ultimately force the sacrifice of their virtue. This fear was partially relieved when a heavy bag of gold fell through an open window to provide a dowry for one daughter. Soon after a second purse, also dropped by an unseen hand, enabled a second daughter to be likewise married. Thereafter the father kept watch until he caught the good S. Nicholas in the act of providing for the third and last daughter. But when he would spread his fame abroad the saint, like his Master, "straitly charged him that he should tell no man."

The artists also followed the pilgrim roads, and their art reveals the songs sung by troubadours, tales told by the story-tellers, the dances and acrobatic feats whereby the pilgrims were entertained when, their devotions finished, they came from the church to stand before the booths which strolling minstrels had erected in the little piazza before the cathedral's portals.

The walls of Fidenza repeat in stone a song of Alberic of Besançon who told of Alexander, ambitious to explore the heavens, who first starved and then harnessed two winged griffons to his chariot. By holding tempting joints of meat before the eyes of his winged steeds Alexander kept them for seven days mounting higher and higher into the blue until an angel rebuked him and ordered his return to earth.

Over a portal of Modena King Arthur and his knights of the

Round Table ride to rescue a damosel from the false knight Sir Caradoc and his yet more evil mother. Within the church, over the entrance
to the crypt, a tale of Æsop comes to life—the story of the crafty fox
who pretended to be dead that he might tempt the barnyard fowl
within his reach.

These scenes show the influence of Northern legends upon the
churches of Italy. In return Salome, dancing on her hands before
Herod and Herodias for the head of John the Baptist, shown on the
façade of Rouen Cathedral, evidences the pleasure such acrobatic dancing had given the pilgrims along the roads that led to Lucca, to Bari,
or to Rome. The statue of S. Michael, high above his famous abbey
in Normandy, of S. George and the dragon at Bordeaux, and of Constantine at Civray, bear witness to the influence of the pilgrim roads
upon the churches of France.

Then the pilgrims vanish and armies come; the rumble of artillery,
infantry, and cavalry drowned out the last echoes of the Pilgrims'
chorus as the regiments of Charles VIII, Louis XII, and Francis I
fill the once hallowed roads. A twilight is falling over Italy; and the
Church, her spiritual influence and her authority lost in the disasters
of the Fourteenth Century, her clergy decadent and her prelates often
agnostic, welcomes an art risen from the classic pagan world because
she herself is semi-pagan.

Nevertheless, although a secular spirit pervaded the art of the Renaissance and many artists used the gospels and the Golden Legend merely
as sources from which to draw backgrounds for their canvases—a martyrdom of S. Sebastian to honour the Archers' Guild; Christ dining
with Simon to show a Venetian palace with soldiers drinking, and the
Pharisee's Jester toying with a parroquet on his wrist—yet the individualism of the period gave room for Christian artists, even though
the age was antithetic to Christian art. Such men as Giotto, Benozzo
Gozzoli, and Perugino might be sceptics while others, like Lippo
Lippi, might also be profligates, yet Rubens could belong to the Renaissance and still paint his "Descent from the Cross," Rembrandt could
give us "Christ Healing the Sick" and "The Road to Emmaus," and
Raphael could portray with feeling the "Crucifixion" and the "Resur-

rection." The list of Christian artists and of Christian works of art is long. And yet side by side with those whose work would have been welcomed in the Thirteenth Century there were other artists whom that age would have cast out as leprously unclean.

The contrast between "The Labours of the Months" as conceived by the Gothic and by the Renaissance artist is more significant than may at first sight appear.

On many Thirteenth Century churches the sculptors have carved delightful little scenes which show the peasant at his work—sowing his seed, planting or trimming his vines, gathering the harvest, or treading the grapes—month by month he is seen performing all the labours of the year. In showing these scenes the sculptor was acting more as a preacher than as an artist, for he was warning men that, if they were to hope for grace from God, they must work together with His sun and rain to redeem the land from the primal curse.

In the Renaissance all this is changed; each month now represents six years of man's life; as the year advances we see him gathering lands, wealth, and honours until in his December he dies, rich and increased in goods, master of many servants, wanting nothing. This is the type of man the Renaissance held in honour. The generation that carved the porch of Moissac, however, would have called him "Dives," tied his fat purse around his neck, and delivered him to devils.

It would not have been possible in the Thirteenth Century for courtesans of Florence to pose as models for the holy saints; to represent the Virgin as a Flemish bourgeois mother, beer stein at her side, warming her hands at an open fire before changing the linen of the baby on her lap. Nor could that century have taken from the tiny hands of the Infant Jesus the globe of the world He came to save in order to place Him astride a hobby horse and send Him prancing across His nursery floor.

Thus two currents, one Christian and one pagan, flowed frettingly side by side throughout the Renaissance. Titian shows us Christ, no longer a man of sorrows and acquainted with griefs, but as a conqueror of old Rome, riding in His triumph, preceded and followed by the patriarchs, heroes, and prophets of the Old Testament and by the martial forces of the Christian Church instead of the Imperial Legions. The Saviour of the world whom Michelangelo painted in the "Last Judgment" of the Sistine Chapel is not He Who said "Father forgive them, they know not what they do," but a wrathful Jove hurling His thunderbolts upon His enemies. The little woolly sheep, symbols of the sacrificial Lamb of God, that warm the marble feet of Agnes of Sorel at Loches, become a lap-dog for milady and a hunting dog for her lord, or two little crouching donkeys for André Lasne and his wife in a window of the Abbey des Vaux-de-Cernay. The figures of the apostles that the men of the Thirteenth Century carved upon their tombs, to show the faith of the dead in his Redeemer, become the *Pleurants* of Claus Sluter on the tomb of Philip the Bold—little hooded figures, clad and cowled in black, emblematic of grief, and of grief alone. The tombal figure of the Thirteenth Century dead, eyes open to the first vision of Paradise and hands clasped in thankful prayer, yields to *Il Penseroso*—"The Thinker"—whereon the chisel of Michelangelo has carved not one line of Christian faith or hope.

Steadily the path descends until we seem to have reached a limit beyond which even paganism cannot pass, when an artist, probably a pupil of Van Eyck or of Memling, painted Mary "Theotokos," whom the Council of Ephesus had enthroned upon the clouds and diademed with stars, stripped of her halo and her garments, in a nudity that was but thinly veiled by the strands of her dishevelled hair.

But the twisted panels that frame Ottaviano Nelli's picture of the Virgin and Child at Gubbio show that there were still deeper depths to which the art of the Renaissance could fall, for they form a halo of obscenity where little scenes are wrought which, passing the last frontiers of decency, rival the frescoes on the walls of the brothels of Pompeii.

Thus art and architecture, both born in paganism, follow the same pathway. Together they climb the years; side by side they stand on the summit of the Gothic Age, and side by side they follow the downward road until they return to the paganism from which they came. The cloud "like a man's hand" that rose above the horizon of

Avignon in the Fourteenth Century has overspread the heavens in the Sixteenth; sun, moon, and stars are gone and darkness covers the earth.

With this brief glimpse into the atelier of the artist we must close the door and come away. He has much to tell us, but we cannot wait to hear. Some day we shall return and listen as he shows us how Christian iconography, rejected by the Fathers, nurtured partly by Christians and partly by pagans, was finally laid as a foundling upon the doorsteps of the Church and by her reluctantly adopted to prevent desecration of her aisles and altars. Then we shall see how the faith of an emperor opened the door, barred by a school-boy's scorn, and admitted the Cross to the field of Christian art; how a dangerous heresy forced the Church, although unwillingly, to call upon her artists to represent the Crucifixion in all its humiliating details. We shall study the famous ampoules of Monza and listen as they tell us many tales—for one, how the head-dress worn by the Magi in mosaics or frescoes of the Church in Bethlehem saved that basilica from destruction when Chosroes was ravaging the land. There is much of history that we may learn, many stories of saints and devils, of men living and of men dead, of ghosts and goblins. In carvings, mosaics, frescoes, or in glass we can discover something of the way our ancestors lived, dressed, behaved, and believed; but for the present at least the door is closed and we must take our way.

EMILE MÂLE, *L'Art Religieux du XII Siècle en France. L'Art Religieux du XIII Siècle en France.*

LOUIS BRÉHIER, *L'Art Chrétien.*

G. G. COULTON, *Art and the Reformation.*

D. KNOOP and G. P. JONES, *The Mediæval Mason.*

L'Envoi

"Farewell! A word that must be, and hath been—
A sound which makes us linger—yet, farewell!
Ye, who have traced the Pilgrim to the Scene
Which is his last, if in your memories dwell
A thought which once was his, if on ye swell
A single recollection, not in vain
He wore his sandal-shoon and scallop-shell."

Byron—Childe Harold's Pilgrimage.

THE day is ending and the evening calls us home.

We turn reluctantly from the darkened windows of the chevet and descend the wide nave to the Western portals. Long shadows are gathering in the vault, beneath the arches, and around the columns; level rays from the setting sun are pouring through the Western Rose Window while, here or there, a candle shines on a saint's altar with a brilliance that is borrowed from the growing dusk.

We have the cathedral to ourselves; and yet we are not, and never again shall be, quite alone within these aisles, for whisperings come to us from right and left; they rise behind us and follow us; they descend from above—from vault, clerestory, triforium, arch, capital, and column; they rumble up from the crypt, and come to meet us from the portals. They fill the church like the music of a great chord; *langue d'oc* and *langue d'oui;* Teuton, Celt, and Lombard; Latin and Greek; Syrian and Arab; Scythian and Sarmatian; Persian and Babylonian; while, beneath them all, like the inarticulate murmurings of a great multitude, come distant voices from the world's childhood, and even from its infancy.

But something of the gift of Pentecost has fallen upon us here, for we too have received a "gift of tongues" and although there be confusion in the tones, the overtones and undertones that rise about us, yet we understand their meaning. All this, they tell us, from crypt to keystone is their work. They have laboured and we have entered into their rest. We reap where they have sown, gather fruits from vineyards that they have planted, and drink from wells their hands have dug.

Nor is it strange that we should understand for these are the voices of our fathers of half a thousand generations, of men whose blood, borne on the tide of well-nigh a score of millennia, pulses in our veins.

"Si monumenta eorum requiris, circumspice"

Index

Index

A-aani-pad-da, 282, 283
Aachen (Aix la chapelle), 81
Abbeys, see Monasteries
Abd-er-Raman, 88, 220
Abd Khiba, 22, 284, 290
Abed-nego, legend of, 298
Abélard, 113, 123
Abraham, 290; carved story of, 294; with the souls of the saved, 64
Absolutions, sale of, 192 n.
Abu Simbel, 283
Abydus, 283
Acanthus, 300
Achilles, 284, 290
Actæon, legend of, 245
Acy-en-Multien, 157, 158
Adam of Bremen, 136
Adam of St. Victor, 122
Adamic, L., *The Native's Return,* 281
Adams, Brookes, *Law of Civilization and Decay,* 139 n., 143 n.
Adult baptism, 73
Adyta, 267, 274
Ægean architecture, 28
Æneas, 15
Æsculapius, 23
Africa, huts in, 237
Africa, Roman, see North Africa
Agade, 283
Agag, the Amalekite, 22
Agde, fortified church, 111, 196
"Age of Faith," 123-130; collapse of, 205, 304, 305
Agnes of Meran, 126
Agnes Sorel, tomb of, 306
Agrarian Policy, see Land Holding System
Agriculture, monasticism advances, 96, 97
Ahab, King, 23
Airaines, Notre-Dame, 157, 181
Aisles, see Side aisles
Aix-la-Chapelle, see Aachen
Akkad, Land of, 283, 284, 287
Alaric, the Goth, 16; captures Rome, 17
Alba Longa, 235
Alberic of Besançon, 303
Alberic de Humbert, 142
Albertus Magnus, 124
Albi, cathedral, 70, 111, 196, 299

Albigenses, 124
Albigensian Crusade, 126
Alboin, 5, 56, 64, 65
Aldus Manutius, 212
Alexamenos, 30, 31 (fig.), 32
Alexander, legends of, 302, 303
Alexander of Hales, 124
Alexander III, Pope, 129
Alexander VI, Pope, 83, 219
Alexandria, 11, 140; population of, 249
Alexius Commenus, 134
Altar, altars, 5, 11; five crosses on, 167; magic powers of, 70, 71; origins of, 11, 17; protected by the saints, 269
Altar rail, 265, 274; origin of, 265-274
Altar screen, 267
Aluric, the mason, 103 n.
Amarna, palace at, 284
Ambos, 27 (fig.)
Ambrose of Milan, S., 44, 53, 166, 167
Ambulatory, 68, 69 (fig.), 79, f. p. 106, 150, 299; vaults, 237
American Indians, tepees of, 237
Amiens Cathedral, xv, 50, f. p. 59, 118, 142, 159, 181, 203, 207, 208, 221, 290; carvings on, 291, 296, f. p. 299, 302; choir stalls, 208; creation, carving of, 294; Herod story, carvings of, 294; portals of, 59
Amorites, 22, 287
Ampoules of Monza, 296, 307
Amulets, 67, 68
Anagni, 127, 128, 186; Church of S. Maria, 128
Ancient World, End of, Chapter Seven, *passim,* 52-55
André Lasne, on window at Vaux-de-Cernay, 306
Angels, carrying souls in a napkin, 64
Anglo-Saxon churches, 265-268
Anglo-Saxons, 75
Anselm, 261
Anselm, Bishop of Canterbury, 122
Anthemius, f. p. 167, 217
Antioch, 157
Antiphonals and antiphonal singing, 44, 45, 267
Antonines, the, 34, 35

313

Antoninianus, 37
Antoninus Pius, Emperor of Rome, 35
Antwerp, 193, 194 n., 213
Apamea, 249
Apocalypse, Book of the, quoted, 257, 258
Apse, 5, 26-28, 69; double, 69, 70; origin of, 237-239; triple, 69, 70
Arcades, origin of, 60, 61
Arch, arches, 46-51; allow wider column spacing, 47-50, f. p. 55; magic power of, 269, 270, 272; make vaults possible, 50, 51; moulded, f. p. 62
Arch, stepped, see Stepped arch
Arch, substitution of, for architrave, 47-49
Archæology (of Churches), Part Two, *passim,* 235-309
Arches of Constantine, Chapter Six, *passim,* 46-51
Architects, mediæval, 103 n.
Architecture, economic conditions influence, in mediæval Europe, 93; expresses men's beliefs, 72-79; triple point of view on, xviii, xix
Architrave, replaced by arch, 47-49; f. p. 27
Archon basileus, 25
Arian, Arians, 86
Arian heresy, 74, 75; its architectural effects, 74, 75
Aristocratic nature of the Renaissance, 225
Aristotle, on capital at Caen, 302
Arius, 53, 74
Ark of the Covenant, 245, 285
Arles, S. Trophîme, 104; iconography of, 297; kiss of Judas carving, 294; population, 249
Arnobius, quoted, 258
Arras, Council of, see Council of Arras
Art, as a "literature for the illiterate," 291-307
Arthurian legend, at Modena, 304
Asinarii, 30
Aspic, 302
Assisi, Church of S. Francis, 80, 81
Assyria, 300; sculptures from, 295; influence on mediæval art, 296
Athanasius, 53, 74
Athens, Parthenon, 241
Atrium, atria, 27, f. p. 71, 72, 73, 250, 251; and church façades, 75
Atticus, epitaph of, 16
Attila, leader of the Huns, 40 n.
Attis, 15
Augurs, 248
Augustine, S., 53, 265
Augustus, Emperor of Rome, 24, 35
Aurelian, Emperor of Rome, 249, 289
Aurignacian Period, 237 n., 240 n.

Autun, 34, 104; capital from, f. p. 299; Christ as Judge on, 182
Aversa, church, 156
Avignon, 129, 186, 307; plague in, 188, 189, 190
Azilians, xvii, 236, 237, 237 n., 239

Baal, baalim, 19, 21, 246
Baalbec, Syria, Roman temples, 282, 287, 289
Babylon, 300
Babylonian Captivity (of the Jews), 246
Babylonian Captivity (of the Popes), 129, 186
Babylonians, 308; ideas of immortality, 14; sculptures of, 295
Bacchus, confused with S. Denis, 295
Background of Gothic Architecture, Chapter Fifteen, *passim,* 113-121; Chapter Sixteen, *passim,* 122-130
Background of Rayonnant and of Flamboyant Architecture, Chapter Twenty-four, *passim,* 185-199
Background of Romanesque Architecture, Chapters Eleven and Twelve, *passim,* 80-90
Balaam and his ass, 120
Baltic Sea, 133, 135, 136
Baptism, of adults, 73; changing beliefs about, 72, 73; of infants, 74; by laymen, 78; mass, of barbarians, 75
Baptismal Font, see Font, baptismal
Baptistry, 72, 73; at Pisa, illus. f. p. 46; decline of the, 78; symbolism, 165, 166
Barbara of Heliopolis, S., 168 n.
Barbaric decorative forms, 299, 300
Barbarian invasions, 56, 57, 58
Bari, 92, 138, 157; pilgrimages to, 92, 182, 304
Baroque, 228
Barrel vault, f. p. 94, 102 (fig.), 154
Barter, in the late Roman Empire, 37
Base (of columns), 239, 240
Basilicas (Christian), 18, Chapter Three, *passim,* 19-29, 235; interior of, f. p. 27, f. p. 55; origin of, 25-27; T-shaped, f. p. 42; typical plan of, 27 (fig.)
Basilicas, pagan, 25, 26, 235; as origin of Church plan, 25, 26; wide distribution of, 25
Basin for Holy Water, see Holy Water Stoup
"Bath of Pharaoh," 259
Batrarius (stone cutter), 293
Baudoin de Conde, 198
Beaulieu, Abbey of, f. p. 103, 182
Beauvais Cathedral, f. p. 135, 159

Bede, quoted, 8

Bel, see Baal

Bell, Gertrude, *The Palace and Mosque at Ukhaidir*, 287 n.

Bell, bells, 76, 168 n.; as amulets, in Africa, 276; announce death, 280; antiquity of, 275; baptism of, 278, 279; censing of, 278; consecration of, 278; golden, on High Priest's robe, 276; magic power of, 275-278; magic power of, in Africa, 276; magic power of, in Assyria, 277; magic power of, in mediæval Europe, 278; as protectors against devils, 77, 275-281; as protectors against thunder storms, 279; punishment of, 279

Bell-rituals, 277

Bellefontaine, 157

Bells and the Devil, Chapter Thirty-four, *passim*, 275-281

Bendann, E., *Death Customs*, 18, 256 n.

Benedict, S., 83

Benedictines, 96

Benoît Biscop, Abbot of Weremouth, 292

Benoît-sur-Loire, reliquary, 299

Benozzo Gozzoli, 304

Bernard of Clairvaux, Saint, 113

Besançon Cathedral, 70

Bethany, 141

Bethel, 285

Bethlehem, 141; Constantine's church in, 307

Beverley, minster, misericord, 302

Bible of Farfa, 296

Bishop's Throne, 5, 26, 27 (fig.), f. p. 267

"Black Death," 5, 185, 188-191, 199, 210

"Black Prince," buried in Canterbury, 4

Blood, magic power of, 271

Blood covenant, 20, 21, 22

Blood-guilt, 248

Boccaccio, 185, 198, 215; on the "Black Death," 188, 189

Boghaz Keui, 283, 286

Boissonade, P., *Life and Work in Medieval Europe*, 94, 95 n., 143 n.

Bologna, plague in, 188; S. Stefano Rotondo, 155

Bond, F., *Introduction to English Church Architecture*, 154 n., 266 n.

Boniface VIII, Pope, 127-129, 186, 187

Boniface, S., 75

Book of Revelation, see Apocalypse

Bordeaux, 194; sack of, 89; St. George and the Dragon at, 304

Borromini, 219

Boscherville, Church of S. Georges, 296

Boston, England, 120 n.

Bouleterion, 28

Bourges Cathedral, 51; carvings on, 291; devils carved on, 64; Tympanum, frontis.; windows, 170, 303

Boyle, Miss Mary E., *In Search of Our Ancestors*, 237 n., 243 n.

Bradwell-by-Sea; S. Peter-on-the-Wall, 265

"Brazen Sea" (in Solomon's Temple), 252

Brehier, L., *L'Art Chrétien*, 307 n.

Brézé, Duke de, tomb of, 199

Briconnet, Bishop of Meaux, 218, 219

Brinton, D. G.; *Religion of Primitive Peoples*, 258 n.

Bristol, 120 n., 196; carving at, 302

Britain, overrun by the Jutes, 56; revolt of, 35

Brive, 98

Bruges, 114, 193, 194 n., 213

Brunelleschi, F., 202, 217, 241

Brunyng, Bishop, tomb of, 221

Brussels, Abbey of S. Bevan, 220

Brutails, M., 218

Building, ignorance of, after fall of Rome, 56-63

Burgundians, 56, 57, 74

Bubonic Plague, see "Black Death"

Buttress, 146, 147, 149, 149 (fig.), 150

Byzantium, see Constantinople

Caaba at Mecca, 245

Caen, Abbaye-aux-Dames, 161, 162; Abbaye-aux-Hommes, 160, 161, 282; abbeys, 111; S. Pierre, capitals in, 301; towers, 77, 160, 290

"Calvaries" of Brittany, 299

Calvin, 124

Cambridge, 221

Campanile, at Pisa, f. p. 46; origin of, 289

Campaspe, on capital at Caen, 302

Canaan, fortified cities of, 284

Cancelli, f. p. 267, 267, 268, 269, 274

Canopies, in Flamboyant Gothic, 206

Canossa, 81, 125

Canterbury Cathedral, 4, 265, 290; tomb of the Black Prince in, 4, 152; S. Pancras, 265, 266

Capitals (of columns), 49, f. p. 299; origin of, 240

Carlovingian Church, period of, 69

Carlovingian Era, 57, 58, 78

Caradoc, Sir, carving at Modena, 304

Cargoes, Caravans, and Cathedrals, Chapter Seventeen, 131-143

Cartage, high cost of, 292

Carthage, 74, 247; forum of, 54

Catachumens, 72, 73

Catacombs, f. p. 10, Chapter Two, *passim*, 9-18; inscriptions in, 15, 16

Catharus, 252
Cathedra, 26
Cathedral, cathedrals, number of, 115; plan of, 5; porches of, 59
Catherine de' Medici, tomb of, 199
Catherine of Siena, S., 186
Catholic Encyclopedia, "Holy Water," 255 n.; "Bells," 278 n.
Cato, Marcus Portius, 25, 235, 239; builds first Roman basilica, 25, 78
Celts, 308; early beliefs in ordeal by water, 260; folklore of, 67
Cement, 168
Centring, 155
Chaise Dieu, La, Danse Macabre at, 5; abbey at (*Casa Dei*), 68; frescoes at, 198
Chalcedon, Council of, see Council of Chalcedon
Chalons-sur-Marne, cathedral at, 181; Notre-Dame de l'Epine at, 206
Champagne, 193
Chancel, arches, 268, 269; screen, f. p. 267, 268; symbolism, 167, 265
Chapels, origin, 50; relics, 69, 70
Charlemagne, King of France, 55, 57, 83, 278
Charles the Bold, King of France, 93
Charles the Fat, King of France, 55
Charles the Great, see Charlemagne
Charles the Hammer (Charles Martel), 89
Charles VIII, King of France, 83, 223, 304
Charles V, Emperor, 220
Charriage, 98
Chartres Cathedral, 5, 6, 50, 51, 115, 118, 146, 152, 159, 201, 203, 221, 226, 243; carving of Abraham's sacrifice, 294; carvings on, 291, 303; fire in, 105 n.; Mary of Egypt, carving on, 294; North Porch, 119; porches of, 59, 181, 182; Rose Windows, 119; S. Gregory the Great, carving of, 294; South Porch, 119; spires of, 77; towers, 290; windows, 170, 297, 298, 303
Chemins-de-ronde, 111
Chemin de S. Jacques, 82, 200
Chemosh (Moabite divinity), 20, 286
Chevet, 69, 69 (fig.)
Chichester, 98
Chimeras, 116
Chinoiseries, 228
Choir, 264, 266; origin of, 43; symbolic interpretation of, 167
Christ, see Jesus Christ
Christianity and Semitic Tribal Beliefs, 21, 22
Christopher, S., 295

Chrysoloras, 220
Chrysostom, S., 53
Church, creates markets, 98; disorganization of, Fourteenth and Fifteenth centuries, 185-187; influences on trade, 97
Church decoration, iconography, 291-307; barbarian influence on, 299, 300; Persian influence on, 300; Roman influence on, 300
Churches, early Christian, 17, 19-29; Flamboyant, 206-211; French Renaissance, 225-229; Gothic, 144-169; Rayonnant, 200-205; Romanesque, 100-112
Circumcision, 244
Cissorus (stone cutter), 293
Cistercian Order, 114, 300; and stained glass, 177
Cîteaux, order of (Cistercian order), 301
Civray, statue of Constantine at, 304
Clapham, A. W., *English Romanesque Churches Before the Conquest*, 274 n.
Classic Revival, period of, xxiii
Claus Sluter, 306
Cleanliness, monastic rules concerning, 117
Clemens, the Martyr, 9
Clement II, Pope, 125
Clement V, Pope, 129, 186
Clement VI, Pope, 189, 190, 191
Clerestory, f. p. 126, 149 (fig.); gallery, 202
Clergy, immunities of, 40, 41
Clermont Ferrand, cathedral at, 145; Notre-Dame du Port, 100, 104
Cloister, 72; origin of, 75, f. p. 235, 244-251
Clover, symbolism, 301
Clovis, King of the Franks, 56, 74; conversion of, 75
Cluny, Abbey, 50, 145, 146, 228; order of, 114, 301
Clustered columns, clustered piers, 60, 151
Cock, weather, 168
Coinage, debasement of in Rome, 37
Cologne, 137, 152
Coloni (Rome), 34
Colonna, Sciara, see Sciara Colonna
Columban, S., 96
Columbaria, 5
Columbus, Christopher, 4, 133, 212, 226
Column, see base, clustered, arches; Flamboyant, 207
Commerce, mediæval, Chapter Seventeen, *passim*, 131-143; effects on ancient religious ideas, 247; effects on church building, 132
Como, S. Abbondio, 76
Communion Feast (Semitic), 21

Compostelle, S. Jacques de, 82, 200
Confiscation of Temple Estates in Rome, 16, 40
Conques, S. Foy, 83, 181; reliquary, 68, 299
Constantine, Emperor of Rome, 10, 38, 39, 40, 46, 79, 298; conversion of, 16, 17, 46
Constantinople, 53, 74, 132, 133, 134, 136, 137, 140, 141; fall of, 212, 214, 215; Galata Tower, 289; illuminated manuscripts, 295; plague in, 188; Sancta Sophia, 54, f. p. 167, 217; Trullan Palace, 267
Copernicus, 212, 226
Cordova, Mosque of, 220
Corinthian order, and capitals, 49, 218
Correggio, 203
Coulton, G. G., Art and the Reformation, 103 n., 221 n., 293 n., 307 n.
Council of Arras, 292
Council of Chalcedon, 299
Council of Constantinople, Third, 267
Council of Dijon, 126, 127
Council of Ephesus, 299, 306
Council of Laodicea, ruling on church singing, 44
Council of Nicæa, 74, 298
Council of Trent, 295
Council of Trullo, 273, see also Council of Constantinople, Third
Counter-thrust (of a vault), 6, see also Vault
Creation, carved story of, 294
Cremation, purpose of, 13
Cremona Cathedral, 221
Cross, on church steeples, 168 n.; early stigma lifted, 31; as source of basilican church plan, 31, 32
Crossbill, symbolism, 301
Crossing, 69 (fig.)
Crucifixion, caricatures of, 30, 31 (fig.); mediæval interpretations of, 296
"Crucifixion," by Raphael, 304
Cruciform church, f. p. 46
Crusades, 81, 114, 138-140, 157; and trade routes, 138, 139
Crypt, crypts, Chapter Two, passim, 9-18, 297; and relics, 70
Cubicula, cubiculum, f. p. 10, 12, 16, 17
"Cult of Carts," 123
Curiales, 39
Currency, inflation of in Rome, 37
Curule chair, 26
Cnyocephali, xx, 302

Dagon, the fish god, 285
Damascus, 259; caliphs in, 288

Dance, dances, influence on mediæval art, 304
Daniel, 298
Danse Macabre, 5, 198, 199, 210
Dante, 82
Danube, river, 134, 136, 137, 193
Dark Ages, 75, 79; economic state of, 90-99; make Romanesque architecture possible, 101
David and Goliath, carvings of, 294
Davis, W. H., Influence of Wealth in Imperial Rome, 37 n.
Day, Lewis F., Stained and Painted Glass Windows, 180 n.
Dead, pagan ideas on, 13
Death, ancient world's beliefs about, 13-15; mediæval representations of, 197; Renaissance representations of, 199
Death dramas, 198
"Decorated" Gothic style, 209
Delrio, Father, quoted, 278
de Morgan, Jacques, Prehistoric Man, 240 n., 243 n.
Denbigh, 120 n.
"Descent from the Cross" by Rubens, 304
Despotism, in Renaissance, 214
Devil, the, 82, 83, f. p. 299
Devils, carved on churches, 64; exorcism of, 255-258
Diana and Actæon, legend of, 245
Dieulafoy, M., L'Art Antique de la Perse, 243 n.
Dijon, S. Bénigne, 145; stained glass in, 172
Diocletian, Emperor of Rome, 10, 11, 16, 38, 52; persecutions under, 16, 52
Disorganization of the Church, Fourteenth and Fifteenth centuries, 185-187
Dispensations, sale of, 192 n.
"Dives and Lazarus," 300, 301, 305
Djeradeh, 6
Domes, f. p. 167, f. p. 215, 217, 226
Dominicans, 124
Domitian, Emperor of Rome, ii, 36
Domitilla, the Martyr, 9
"Donkey-Tenders," used of Christians, 30
Doric order, 218, f. p. 235
Dormer windows, 77
Dosseret, see Stilt Block
Double door-ways, symbolism, 163
Dove, 11
Dragon, 164
Ducking pond, 302
Duns Scotus, 124
Dunstan, S., 82

Durandus, Guillaume, 166; *Rationale Divinorum Officinorum,* 168
Durham, xviii; Cathedral, f. p. 87, 265

Eagle, 163
Ecclesiastical architecture, *passim,* xviii
Ecclesiastical taxation, see Taxation, ecclesiastical
Economic factors in fall of Rome, 32-38, 58
Economic influences on church building, 91-99, 131-143
Economic state of the Dark Ages, 91-99
Ecumenical Councils, 53; see also under Council of ——
Edict of Milan, 16, 17, 40, 43, 46, 52, 53, 64
Edict of Nantes, 279
Edward the Confessor, King of England, 70
Edward III, King of England, 197
E-gal, 284 n.
Egyptians, ideas of immortality, 14, 14 n.; illuminated manuscripts of, 295
Elijah, 19, 63, 114
Elisha, 114
Elliptical houses, 238, 239
Ely Cathedral, 120 n., 265; story of Noah at, 293
End of the Ancient World, Chapter Seven, *passim,* 52-55
England, early churches in, 88; number of churches in, 131
Ephanius, S., 256
Ephesus, Council of, see Council of Ephesus
Epitaphs, 15, 16
Escomb, church, 265
Esthonia, beliefs in water-magic, 259
Etampes, Notre-Dame, 181
Ethiopians, xx, 302
Euphemius, 85
Eusebius, 10, 267
Evreux, cathedral, 181
Exodus, Book of, 244, 276
Exorcism, 254, 256-258
Exposure of unwanted children, 73
Ezekiel, 247

Façades, 75
Fairies, 67
Fairs, 193
Fan vaulting, 150, 207
Farfa, Bible of, 296
Fear, the Gifts of, Chapter Nine, *passim,* 64-71
Fénelon, 227
Ferdinand and Isabella, tomb of, 4

Feudalism, 93-95
Fidenza, carvings at, 303
Fire, destruction of churches by, 89, 104, 105
Fire-proof churches, 101
Flamboyant Architecture, Chapter Twenty-six, *passim,* 206-211
Flamboyant Gothic, f. p. 206, 206-211; background of, 185-199; character of, 206-208
Flashed glass, 175
Florence, 203; Baptistry, bronze doors, 202; campanile, 290; Duomo, 202, 217, 241; palaces, 218; plague in, 188, 189
Flying arch, 146, 147, 148 (fig.), 149, 149 (fig.), f. p. 158
Flying Buttress, f. p. 155, f. p. 158, 160-162; The Origin of, Chapter Twenty, *passim,* 160-162; see also Flying arch
Fondaci, 140
Font, baptismal, 7, 165
Fontevrault, Richard Cœur-de-Lion buried in, 4
Fortified churches, 111, f. p. 183, 196
Forum, fora, 25
Fountain of ablution, 27, 79; in ancient temples, 254, 255
Fowler, W. Warde, *Religious Experiences of the Roman People,* 254 n., 274 n.
Fox, 163
France; commerce, Thirteenth Century, 142, 143; after Hundred Years' War, 195
Francis I, King of France, 223, 304
Francis of Assisi, S., 80, 81
Franciscans, 124
Franks, 75, 86; conversion of, 86
Frazer, J. G., *Folk-lore in the Old Testament,* 18, 262 n., 276 n., 277 n., 278 n., 279 n., 280 n., 281 n.; *Golden Bough,* 254 n., 256 n., 257 n., 260 n., 274 n., 276 n.
Frederick II, King of Sicily, tomb of, 4
Free Companies (in Hundred Years' War), 195
French Revolution, 229; its destruction of mediæval art, 295
Friburg Cathedral, 98
Frieze, origin of, 241, 242
Froben, press of, 212
Frothingham, in Sturgis and Frothingham, *History of Architecture,* Volume IV, quoted, 216, 217

Gables, in spires, 77
Gabriel, Jacques Anges, 225
Gaddi, Gaddo, 203
Galata tower, 289

Galerius, Emperor of Rome, 16, 53
Galileo, 212
Galleries, 5, 26
Gallery of Kings, 116
Garde Adhémar, 70, 299
Gargoyles, 82, 116
Garonne, river, 134
Genii, of northern mythology, 67
Genoa, 133, 137, 138, 140, 143, 194 n., 213; palaces, 218; plague in, 188
Genos, 238
Genseric, the Vandal, 17, 56
Gezer, 13 n., 285
Ghent, 114, 193, 213
Ghiberti, L., 202
Ghirlandajo, 203
Giants, in stained glass, xvii
Gibbon, 36, 249
Gideon, carved story of, 294; symbolism of, 301
Gift of an Impatient Horse, Chapter Thirteen, *passim*, 91-99
Gilgamash, 14, 296
Gilles, S., 104
Giotto, 304
Glass, early history of, 170-172; Roman, 172; technique of painting, 179; see also Stained glass
Glastonbury, Abbey, 228
Glotz, Gustave, *Ægean Civilization*, 28, 29, 239 n., 243 n.
Glyphs, f. p. 235, 241
Gnomes, of northern mythology, 67
God, cryptogram of, 295
Godard, S., 221
Goddess-mothers, 67
Goethe, on Gothic art, 144
Gold, effect on Roman economics, 36, 37
"Golden Legend," 292, 303, 304
Gonsalvo de Cordova, 4
Gospel of Rabula, 296
Gothic architecture, 113; Chapters Eighteen to Twenty-one, inclusive, 144-169; background of, 113-130; definition, 146; a stone skeleton construction, 147; symbolism, 163-169
Gothic churches, f. p. 126, f. p. 135, f. p. 138, f. p. 155, f. p. 183; destruction of, 145, 146
Gothic vaults, 146-151, 154-159; development of, 150; heights of, 151; origin of, Chapter Nineteen, *passim*, 154-159
Goths, 56, 57, 64, 74, 299, 300
Gould, Baring, 202
Gozbert, abbot of Turgensee, 172
Granada, cathedral, 4
Granada, San Jeronimo, 4

Grandmont, miracles at, 83
Gratian, Emperor of Rome, 16, 40
"Great Schism," the, 186
Greek influence in Renaissance, 214
Greeks, 308; ideas of immortality, 14; illuminated manuscripts, 295
Green, *History of the English People*, 197
Gregorius, S., 145
Gregory the Great, S., 53, 190; dialogues of, 263; legend of, 294; quoted, on church decoration, 292
Gregory VII, Pope, 81, 129, 146, 261
Gregory XI, Pope, 186
Gregory of Tours, S., 53
Grisaille, 177
Groined vault, 109, 109 (fig.), 110, f. p. 123; for ambulatory, f. p. 106, 110; with unequal spans, 109
Gubbio, Virgin and Child at, 306
Gudea, f. p. 282, 282, 283, 284, 287
Guilds, 39; formation of, 114; masons', 293, 293 n.
Guizot, 57 n.
Guttæ, f. p. 235, 241
Guy de Chauliac, 189, 190

Hadrian, Emperor of Rome, 35, 249
Half Barrel Vault, f. p. 94, 102 (fig.)
Hamurabi, see Khamurabi
Hanifeyeh, 252
Hart, symbolism, 164
Harz Mountains, 91-93
Hassall, Arthur, *The French People*, 209 n.
Hathor, Temple of, at Sinai, 252
Haymo, Abbot, 115, 118
Hekkal, 284 n.
Hell, mediæval ideas of, 82
Hellespont, the scourging of, xv, 261
Henry II, King of England, 125
Henry V, King of England, 221
Henry II, King of France, tomb of, 199
Henry IV, Emperor of Germany, 81, 125, 145, 261; excommunication of, 81
Heraclitus, 248
Herculaneum, 172
Hereford, 98
Heresy, 124
Hermogenes, legend of, 295
Herod story, carvings of, 294, f. p. 299, 304
Herodius, carvings of legend of, 304
Herodotus, 261, 262
Hewer (of stone), 292
Hilary of Poitiers, S., 53
Hildebrand, see Gregory VII, Pope
Hildesheim, church, 221
Hincmar of Rheims, 261
Hittites, 286, 287

Holy Ground, as taboo, 246
Holy Water, 263, 264
Holy Water, see Water, magic
Holy Water Stoup, xv, 79, 200, 235, 252-264
Homer, 14, 15, 28
Honorius III, Pope, 141
House, 237-239
Huddleston (quarries), 292
Hugh Capet, King of France, 88, 132
Human sacrifice, 20, 21, 259, 260
Humour, in mediæval carving, 302
Hundred Years' War, f. p. 183, 185, 194-197, 224; causes of, 194; effect on architecture, 197; effects of, England, 196; effects of, France, 195
Hungary, conversion of, 137
Huns, 56, 79, 299
Huts, 237, 238

Iconography, Chapter Thirty-six, *passim*, 291-307; effect of theology on, 298, 299
Idol worship, 294, 295
Ignatius of Antioch, S., 44
Ignorance, Gifts of, Chapter Eight, *passim*, ^ 56-63
Île-de-France, 157; see S. Denis, Abbey of
Imagours (sculptors), 293, 294
Immortality, pagan conceptions of, 13-15; Christian conceptions of, 15, 16
Impost block, see Stilt block
Inclination of the apse, 164, 166 (fig.); purpose of, 164, 165; symbolism, 164, 165
Indians, American, see American Indians
Indulgences, sale of, 192 n.
Infant baptism, 74
Infanticide, in Rome, 73
Innocent III, Pope, 123, 126, 127, 129
Innocent VIII, Pope, 83
Ionic order, 218
Isaiah, 248
Isis, 15, 257
Istradi, 135 n.

Jackson, T. G., *Reason in Architecture*, 49 n., 60 n., 109 (fig.), 148 (fig.), 149 (fig.)
Jacob, 257, 285
Jacquerrie, 195
James, the apostle, S., 12, 82; mediæval legends of, 295; tomb of, 82
Jastrow, M., *Religious Beliefs in Babylonia and Assyria*, 18, 253 n.
Javeh, see Jehovah
Jean de Vinette, 196

Jehovah, Javeh, 22, 244, 245, 246, 247, 257, 285
Jephthah, 21
Jeremiah, 277
Jerome, S., 53
Jerusalem, 118, 284, 285, 286; fall of, 9, 22; pilgrimages to, 92; population of, 249; Church of the *Anastasis*, 269; place of sacrifice, 22; temple in, 20, 255; temple in, as House of God, 22, 246; temple in, Brazen Sea in, 252
Jesus Christ, on death, 16; as judge, 182, 183, 306; as Messiah, 22; Renaissance conceptions of, 305, 306; symbols of, 122; Syrian type of, 296
Jews, symbols of, 303
Joan of Arc, S., 197
Job, Book of, 182
John, the Evangelist, S., 14 n., 257, 258; vision of Heaven, 170
John II, King of France, 195
John XXII, Pope, 125, 186
Jonah, carved story of, 293
Jordan, river, 259
Journal of the Royal Asiatic Society, 254 n., 277 n.
Julian, "The Apostate," Emperor of Rome, 16
Julius Cæsar, 78
Julius II, Pope, 219
Jumièges, abbey, 77, 91, 99, 111, 145, 146; towers of, 77
Justinian, Emperor, 54

Kadesh, 283, 290
Kalb Lauzeh, 6, 282
Kasr-il-Benat, 6, 282, 287, 288, 289
Katherine, Queen of England, tomb of, 221
Kermaria, Danse Macabre at, 198
Kir, 20, 286
Knights Templars, destruction of Order, 192
Knoop, D., and Jones, G. P., *The Mediæval Mason*, 103 n., 143 n., 293 n., 307 n.
Knossos, 28, 239
Kyrie Eleison, 44

Labarum (XP), 30
Labour Systems, in late Roman Empire, 39, 40
"Labours of the Months," mediæval and Renaissance conceptions contrasted, 305
Lack of building skill, its contribution to mediæval architecture, 56-63
Lactantius, 38

Lagash, 13 n.; citadel at, f. p. 282, 282, 283
Lamb, symbolism, 306
Land Holding System (Rome), 33, 35
Laodicea, Council of, see Council of Laodicea
Laon Cathedral, 118, f. p. 126, 142, 201; carved story of Gideon, 294; theft of vessels from, 261
La Rochelle, see Rochelle, la
Last Judgment, Bourges Cathedral, frontis.
La Trinité, Vendôme, f. p. 206
Lazarus, 104, 298; parable of, 300, 301, 305
Lea, H. C., Church History, 65, 66; Superstition and Force, 261 n., 262 n.
Legarde, André, Latin Church in the Middle Ages, 192 n.
Le Mans, see Mans, le
Lenormant, F., Chaldæan Magic, 256 n.
Léon, Paul, Les Monuments Historiques, 144 n.
Leonardo da Vinci, 203
Leviticus, 271
Lierne vaulting, 207
Lighthouses, 289
Lille, 114, 193
Lime, symbolism, 168
Limoges, S. Martial, 145, 181
Lincoln Cathedral, 265; misericord, 302
Lindsey, T. M., History of the Reformation in Germany, 192 n.   [163
Lion, in mediæval art, 296, 300; symbolism,
Lippo Lippi, 304
Liturgy, 43-44
Loches, Tomb of Agnes Sorel, 306
Loire, 134, 142
Lollards, Lollardy, revolt of, 196
Lombard ribbed vaults, 155, 156
Lombards, 57, 64, 65, 86, 308; conversion of, 86
Lombardy, 154
London, 114, 194 n., 213; S. Paul's Cathedral, 168 n., 228, 241, 279; Westminster Abbey, 68, 149 (fig.), 221
"Long Houses," 238
Loria, Roger de, 4
Lot, Ferdinand, The End of the Ancient World, 38, 39 n.
Louis IX, King of France, 119
Louis XI, King of France, 134
Louis XII, King of France, 223, 304
Louis XIV, King of France, 228
Louis XV, King of France, 228, 229; style of, 228
Louis XVI, King of France, 228, 229
Louis, the Pious, King of France, 87, 172

Lucca, crucifix at, 296; pilgrimages to, 92, 304
Lutetia, derivation of, 116, 231; see also Paris
Lyminge, S. Mary, 265
Lyons, 249; cathedral carvings, 291

Macalister, Stewart, Bible Side-Lights from the Mound of Gezer, 286 n.
Madeleine, S., 83
Madeleine, the, see Paris, Madeleine
Magdelenians, 236, 237, 237 n.
Magellan, 212, 226
Magi, carvings of, 294; headdress of, 307
Magna Mater, 24
Magyars, 86, 93, 94; raids of, 86, 87, 89, 90, 103
Mainz, 136; printing at, 301
Maklu, Babylonian incantation of, 253
Mâle, Emile, 183, 295; L'Art Religieux du XIIe Siècle en France, 67, 67 n., 307 n.; L'Art Religieux du XIIIe Siècle en France, 183 n., 184 n., 307 n.
Mans, le, Cathedral, 51; carved owl at, 302
Mantes, Notre-Dame, 181
Manuscripts, illuminated, 295; Christ types in, 296; effect on church carving, 295, 296, 301
Mantichore, 302
Marcus Aurelius, Emperor of Rome, 35, 38
Marguerite d'Angoulême, 215
Mark, the Evangelist, S., 12, 258
Marquand, Allen, Greek Architecture, 29
Marseilles, 133, 136, 137, 140, 143; plague in, 188
Martin, of Tours, S., 67, 83
Martyrs, Christian, 10-12, 17, 18
Mary of Egypt, legend of, 294
Mary, Virgin, see Virgin Mary
Mas d'Azil, xvii
Masonic lodges and mediæval guilds, 293 n.
Masons, 292-294; guild system, 293, 293 n.; number of in Thirteenth Century, 131; training of, 292-294; types of, 293
Maspero, G., Egyptian Archæology, 171 n.
Mass (sacrament), 70, 71
Matilda of Flanders, 111, 160
Maximianus, Emperor of Rome, 16
Mayence, see Mainz
Mecca, 245
Mediæval point of view, 123-130
Megaron, 28, 239
Melitonis Clavis Sanctæ Scripturæ, 169
Melos, 238
Memling, 306

Mendicant Orders, 120, 195; symbols of, 120

Merchant guilds, 39, 98

Mercury, the god, 67

Meshach, legend of, 298

Mesopotamia, manuscripts, 295

Metopes, f. p. 235, 241; origin of, 242

Michael, S., 67

Michelangelo, 202, 203, 217, 241, 306

Miette, Abbé, 198

Milan, 213; Cathedral, 76, 216

Milan, Edict of, see Edict of Milan

Milan, S. Ambrogio, 12, f. p. 71, 155, 156; S. Eustorgio, 155; S. Nazaro, 155; S. Satiro, 216, 221

Milman, H. H., 65; *Latin Christianity,* 82 n., 88 n., 139 n. [91-93

Mines, exhaustion of, 36; importance of, Miniatures, 301; see Manuscripts

Miracles, 63, 70, 71

Miracles, in mediæval legend, of Gondoforus of India, 295; of S. Christopher, 295; of S. James, 295; of S. Nicholas, 295; of S. Thomas, 295

Modena Cathedral, 120 n.; Æsop's Fables at, 304; Arthurian legend at, 304; carvings on, 291

Moissac, 156; carvings at, 297, 298, 300; cloister at, f. p. 250; ribbed vault in, 157, 158

Molière, on Gothic art, 144

Monasticism, 104, 131; aids security of travel, 97; assists trade, 97; fear of women, 300; its development of agriculture, 96, 97 [37

Monetary system, mediæval, 92; Roman, Monkwearmouth, church, 265

Montefiascone, S. Flaviano, 155

Monza, ampoules of, 296, 307; "Gospel of Theodolinda," 299

Moore, G. F., *History of Religions,* 257 n.

Morienval, abbey, 76

Mosaics, 297, 298

Moses, 244, 284

Moslems, 85; raids of, 85, 86, 88, 89; see also Saracens

Mosques, 277

Moulded arches, 60

Mt. S. Michel, Normandy, statue of S. Michael, 304

Mt. Sinai, see Sinai

Mourning customs, 13

Mousterian Period, 237 n.

Nakedness, 296

Name, sacred, magic power of, 253, 254, 255-258

Naples, 11, 213

Napoleon I, Emperor, 229

Napoleonic taste, 229

Narbonne, 89, 193; capture of, by Moslems, 89; congestion in, 249; Syrians in, 288; S. Paul-Serge, Holy Water Stoup in, 200

Nature, as symbol, 163, 301

Nave, 69 (fig.), 102 (fig.), 149 (fig.)

Nebuchadrezzar, 298

Nelli, Ottaviano, Virgin at Gubbio by, 306

Neolithic man, 237, 242

Nero, Emperor of Rome, 10, 11, 36

Nevers, Cathedral, 70; Museum, carvings in, 302

New York, S. John the Divine, Cathedral of, 12

Nicæa, Council of, see Council of Nicæa

Nicholas, S., 295, 303

Nicodemus, 296

Nîmes, Aqueduct, see Pont du Gard

Ningpo, China, 275, 276

Noah, 293

North side of a church, symbolism, 163

Northmen, 64, 79, 81, 85-90, 93, 94; conversion of, 87; raids of, 85, 86, 88, 89, 90, 103, 134; in Russia, 135, 137

Norwich, 131

Notre-Dame, Chapter Twenty-three, *passim,* 181-184

Notre-Dame, Paris, see Paris, Notre-Dame

Noyon Cathedral, 159, 181

Ogee arch, f. p. 206, 206

Olmstead, F. L., 33

Olympia, Bouleterian, 28, 239

Orchomenos, 238, 239

Ordeal of Water, 260-262

Orders of architecture, 218

O'Reilly, E. B., *How France Built Her Cathedrals,* 144 n.

Origin of the Altar Rail, Chapter Thirtythree, *passim,* 265-274

Origin of the Cloister, Chapter Thirty-one, *passim,* 244-251

Orvieto Cathedral, 76

Ostrogoths, 56, 74

Ottaviano Nelli, see Nelli, Ottaviano

Otto the Great, Emperor, 91, 137

"Our Lady," 181-184, 298, 299; see also Virgin Mary

Owl, as symbol, 302, 303

Oxford, 131

Pæstum, Temple of Poseidon, f. p. 235, 236

Palace, as "Great House," 284 n.

Palæolithic man, 237, 242

Palermo, 138, 290; Frederick II buried in, 4
Panotii, xx, 302
Parenzo, church at, 267
Paris, Arena, 231; Cluny Museum, Visigothic crowns in, 300; Latin Quarter, 231
  Madeleine, 98, 226, 229, 230, f. p. 231; mediæval conditions in, 116, 117
  Notre-Dame, xv, 115, 118, 142, 146, f. p. 155, f. p. 158, 201, 203, 221, 230; carvings on, 291, 295; gallery of the kings, 295; north Rose Window, 176; south Rose Window, xv; Virgin in, 298; number of masons in 1292, 131
  Pantheon, 226, 241; Place de la Concorde, 225; plague in, 188; population in Twelfth Century, 114; Sainte Chapelle, f. p. 138; S. Julien-le-Pauvre, 160, 231; SS. Paul and Louis, f. p. 218; S. Séverin, 231; S. Sulpice, 231; University, 123
Parma, Baptistry, 120 n.
Parthenon, 241
Pascal II, Pope, 145, 158
Passing-Bell, 280
Paul, the Apostle, S., 9, 30, 73
Paul III, Pope, 219
Paul-Louis, Ancient Rome at Work, 37 n., 249 n.
Pavia, 74; Certosa, 219, 221
Pax Romana, 9, 32, 34, 35
Peage, 98
"Peasants' Revolt," 210   [192
Peckham, John, Archbishop of Canterbury, Pelagius, Cardinal, 141
Pelican, symbolism, 163
Pentateuch, 244
Pépin, of France, 299
Persecutions of Christians, 10-12
Persepolis, palaces, 236
Per-o, 284 n.
Persians, 300, 308; mediæval trade with, 133; tapestries of, 295
Perugino, 304
Peter, the Apostle, S., 10, 12; and Simon, legend of, 303
Peter the Hermit, 81, 138, 139
Peterborough Cathedral, 103 n.   [29
Peters, Dr. J. P., Religion of the Hebrews,
Petrarch, 186, 195, 215
Phiala, 252
Philip the Apostle, S., 72
Philip the Bold, Duke of Burgundy, tomb of, 199, 306
Philip Augustus, King of France, 126, 127
Philip the Fair, King of France, 127, 192
Philip III, King of France, 142

Philip VI, King of France, 195
Philip, King of Macedon, 29
Philosophy, ancient, agnosticism in, 248
Phœnicians, 247
Piers Ploughman, 196, 210
Pilgrimages, architectural results of, 50, 69, 70, 157, 303, 304; character of, Eleventh Century, 80, 81; popularity of, 81, 82
Pilgrim Way, 69, 70
Pinnacle, 149 (fig.); purpose of, 162
Pirates, 196
Pisa, 137, 138, 140, 213, 289; cathedral, baptistry and campanile, f. p. 46
Pleurants, on tomb of Philip the Bold, 199, 306
Pliny (the Elder), 36; on glass, 171
Plutarch, 34
Pointed arch, 107, 148, 149 (fig.), 151
Poitiers, 83, 242; Baptistry of S. Jean, 88; Museum, capital in, 302; Notre-Dame le Grand, 100, 146
Pont du Gard, 54, 216
Population, Germany, doubling of, 92; shrinkage of Roman, 34; urban, growth of, 114, 249
Porch, porches, 59, 60
Portals, recessed, f. p. 59; symbolism, 167; triple, 163
Porter, A. K., The Construction of Lombard and Gothic Vaults, 159 n.; Mediæval Architecture, 41 n., 102 n., 159 n., 187 n., 208 n., 288 n.
Portocarrero, Cardinal, tomb of, 3   ]236
Poseidon, Temple of, at Pæstum, f. p. 235,
Positorus petrarum, 293
Pot-metal glass, 174
Preaching, 227
Preaching friars, 120
Priests, immunities of, 40
Primitive man, contributions of, to cathedrals, Chapter Thirty, passim, 235-243
Printing, effect of, 212
Probus, Emperor of Rome, 34
Prodicus, 248
Prosper of Aquitaine, 55
Protagoras, 248
Protestants, denounce "Idol Worship," 295
Psalms, 23
Public baths, mediæval, 117
Pulverino, see Stilt block
Purification, by water, 263; by passing under arch, 271, 272

Querqueville, chapel at, 88, 91, 99

Rabelais, 215
Rabula, Gospel of, 296

Racine, on Gothic art, 144
Rainy, Robert, 10; *Ancient Catholic Church,* 41 n.
Rameses the Great, Pharaoh, 283
Rammelsberg mines, 91-93, 133
Raphael, 202, 203, 304
Ravenna, 74, 289; fall of, 64, 215; mosaics in, 297, 298; S. Apollinare Nuovo, 100, 298
Rayonnant Architecture, Chapter Twenty-five, *passim,* 200-205
Rayonnant Gothic, f. p. 62, 159, 200-205; background of, 185-189; character of, 200-202; unity of design in, 204; vertical lines, 203, 204
Reason, in French Renaissance architecture, 226, 227
Receswinth, votive crowns of, 299
Regency, in France, 229
Relics, 12, 17, 18; influence on church architecture, 68-70; power of, 83, 84, 299; safety of, require fire-proof churches, 101, 104, 105; worship of, 82
Reliquaries, 68, 299
Rembrandt, 304
Rénard, G., *Life and Work in Prehistoric Times,* 240 n., 243 n.
Renaissance, the, 55; literary character of, 215; pagan quality of, f. p. 231, 305, 306; philosophy of, 215; religious painting of, the, 304, 305, 306
Renaissance architecture, 212-230; as decorative art, 218; birth in Italy, 213; character of, 216; lack of constructive idealism, 216, 217
Renaissance in France, Chapter Twenty-eight, *passim,* 223-230, f. p. 231; aristocratic nature of, 225; character of, f. p. 218, 224, 225, 227-229; origins of, 223, 224; philosophy of, 226; reason in, 226, 227
Renaissance in Italy, The, Chapter Twenty-seven, *passim,* 212-222
Renaissance palaces, 218
Revelation, Book of, see Apocalypse
Rheims Cathedral, 142, 152, 159, 181, 221, 290; bombardment of, 105 n.; David and Goliath carvings, 294; porches of, 59
Rhine, river, 134, 136, 137, 260
Rhône, river, 134, 136, 142, 193
Rhuis, ribbed vault in, 157, 158
Ribbed vault, 146-150; in ambulatories, 150; origin of, 154-159
Richard Cœur-de-Lion, King of England, 4, 126, 140
Richelieu, Cardinal, 228

Ridge ribs, 150
Rienzi, 213
Rinceau, in mediæval art, 300
Ripon, 120 n.; story of Jonah at, 293
Ritual purification, 263
Rivers, as trade routes, 133-135
"Road to Emmaus" by Rembrandt, 304
Robe, which Jesus wore to the Cross, 81, 83
Robin red-breast, symbolism, 301
Rocaille, 228
Rochelle, La, Protestant chapel at, 279
Rococo, 228
Roman development of triumphal arch, 270-272
Roman religion, state character of, 10; tolerance of, 10
Romance and Tragedy of Stained Glass, Chapter Twenty-two, *passim,* 170-180
Romanesque Architecture, Chapter Fourteen, *passim,* 100-112; background of, 80-90; effect of pilgrimages on, 104
Romanesque churches, f. p. 87, f. p. 94, f. p. 103, f. p. 123; character of, 100, 106-110; development of, 101, 102; monasteries and, 103; period of, xxiii; vaulting of, 106-110; windows in, 108; wooden roofs and ceilings of, 100, 104, 105
Roman idea of immortality, 15
Rome, 157, 213; pilgrimages to, 92, 304; sack of, by Saracens, 87
Rome, ancient, destruction of, in Renaissance, 220; economic state of, 32-38; labour system of, 39-40; mines, exhaustion of, 36; peasant farmers, impoverishment of, 33; population of, 249; prosperity of, 32, 33; ruins of, 214; tax system of, 38-40; urban overcrowding, 33
Rome, Arch of Titus, 9, 54; Atrium of Vesta, 220; Baths of Caracalla, 214; Baths of Diocletian, 216, 219; Campus Martius, 271; Church of Tre Fontana, 9; Circus Maximus, 53, 298; Circus of Nero, 53; Forum of Julius Cæsar, 249; Golden House of Nero, 214; Museum of Prehistoric Antiquities, 13 n.; Palace of Tiberius, 219; palaces, 218; Palatine Hill, school for pages, 30; Pantheon, 216; Portico of the Argonauts, 249; Portico of Octavia, 249; Sacred Way, 272; S. Agnese, 47 n.; S. Clemente, 47 n., 100; *Schola Cantorum* in, 44; S. John Lateran, Basilica of, 12, 219; baptismal font, 200; S. Laurent (Lorenzo), 47 n.; S. Maria Antiqua, 47 n.; fresco in, 296; S. Maria in Aracœli, 47 n.; S. Maria in

Cosmedin, 47 n.; S. Maria Maggiore, 47 n.; S. Peter's, 53, f. p. 215, 217, 219, 221, 227, 228, 241; bell in, 275; chancel screen in, 268; great altar in, 267; S. Pietro al Monte, 47 n.; S. Pietro in Vinculi, Moses statue, 202; S. Prassede, 47 n.; S. Sabina, 47 n.; Senate House, Statue of Victory in, 16; Septizonium, 219; Sistine Chapel, ceiling, 202; "Last Judgment," 306; Temple of Jupiter Capitolinus, 9, 214, 272; Temple of Jupiter and Juno, 249; Temple of Neptune, 249; Temple of the Sun, 214; Temple of Trajan, 249; Temple of Venus, 249; Temple of Venus and Rome, 249; triumphal arches, 272, 274; Vatican Basilica, see S. Peter's; Vatican Library, 296
Roof tiles, symbolism, 167
Rose Windows, 115, 201
Rouen, Cathedral, 181, 207, 208, 304; S. Ouen in, f. p. 62, 145 n., 200, 201, 203, 204
Round Table, see Arthurian legend
Round towers, 289
"Rowmason," 293
Royat, fortified church, iii, 196
Rubens, 304

Sabazian Jupiter, 23
Sacerdos, 19
Sacraments, the Christian, 12, 26, 70, 72-75
Sacristy, symbolism, 167
S. Abbondio, Como, 76
S. Agnese, at Rome, 47 n.
S. Albans Abbey, 221
S. Albans, at Washington, 12
S. Ambrogio at Milan, 12, f. p. 71, 155, 156
S. Andoche, at Saulieu, 120
S. Apollinare Nuovo, at Ravenna, 100, 298
S. Beât, f. p. 94
S. Bénigne at Dijon, 145, 172
S. Benoît-sur-Loire, f. p. 106
S. Bertrand de Comminges, church, 267
S. Bevan Abbey, 220
S. Clemente, at Rome, 44, 47 n., 100
S. Denis, Abbey of, 142, 159, 201, 230; ribbed vault in, 157; window in, f. p. 174
S. Etienne, at Toulouse, 181
S. Eustorgio, at Milan, 155
S. Flaviano, at Montefiascone, 155
S. Foy, at Conques, 68, 83, 299
S. Georges-Boscherville, capital at, 296
S. Guilhem-le-Désert, 300
S. Jean Baptistry, at Poitiers, 88

S. John Lateran, Basilica of, at Rome, 12, 200, 219
S. John the Divine, New York, 12
S. Julien-le-Pauvre, in Paris, 160, 231
S. Laurent, at Rome, 47 n.
S. Lo, Notre-Dame, 181
S. Madeleine, at Vézelay, 104, f. p. 123, 302
S. Maria, in Trastevere, f. p. 27
S. Maria Antiqua, at Rome, 47 n., 296
S. Maria dei Miracoli, Venice, 221
S. Maria in Aracœli, Rome, 47 n.
S. Maria in Cosmedin, Rome, 47 n.
S. Maria Maggiore, at Rome, 47 n.
S. Maria Maggiore, at Toscanella, f. p. 42
S. Marks, at Venice, 12, 134
S. Martial Abbey, at Limoges, 145, 181
S. Martin, at Tours, 145
S. Mary, at Lyminge, 265
S. Maurice d'Agaune, reliquary, 299
S. Maximim, Church of, 83
S. Nazaro, at Milan, 155
S. Nectaire, Auvergne, xvii, 181
S. Ouen, in Rouen, f. p. 62, 145 n., 200, 201, 203, 204
S. Paul's Cathedral, see London
S. Paul-Serge, at Narbonne, 200
S. Peter, Cathedral of, Rome, 53, f. p. 215, 217, 219, 221, 227, 228, 241; altar in, 267; chancel screen in, 268; bell, 275
S. Peter-on-the-Wall, at Bradwell, 265
S. Pietro al Monte, Rome, 47 n.
S. Pietro, at Toscanella, f. p. 55
S. Pietro in Vinculi, Rome, 202
S. Prassede, at Rome, 47 n.
S. Riquier, church, 268
S. Sabina, Rome, 47 n.
S. Satiro, at Milan, 216, 221
S. Sernin, at Toulouse, 160, 161, 181
S. Séverin, in Paris, 231
S. Sulpice, in Paris, 231
S. Trophîme at Arles, 104, 294, 297
Sainte Chapelle, Paris, f. p. 138
Saintes-Maries, Les, fortified church, 111, f. p. 183, 196
Saintes, ribbed vault in, 157, 158
Saints, importance of, in mediæval art, 182-184
SS. Paul and Louis, at Paris, f. p. 218
Salisbury Cathedral, 168 n.
Salome, legend of, 304
Salpetrière, church of, 227
Sancta Sophia, Constantinople, 54, f. p. 167, 217
Sanctuary, 23
Sand, symbolism, 168

Santiago de Compostella, 12; pilgrimages to, 82, 92, 182
Saracens, 79, 85, 87, 93, 94; raids of, 85, 86, 103
Sarcophagus of an Ancient Civilization, 259 n.
Sarmatians, 308; tombs of, 295, 300
Satan, see Devil
Saul, of Tarsus, see S. Paul
Saulieu, S. Andoche, 120
Scallop shell, as symbol, 68
Schliemann, 28, 171
Schola Cantorum, 44, 267
Scholasticism, 123, 124, 185
Sciarra Colonna, 127
Sciopode, xx, 302
Sclavs, 56, 64
Scribonius, 261
Sculptors, mediæval, 293
Scythians, 56, 308; tombs of, 295, 300
Sea-borne commerce, importance of, 133-138
Sebastian, S., 304
Secular clergy, 120
Segovia, 82
Segregation of women, 26
Seine, river, 134, 142, 193
Semitic religions, 19, 20, 21, 22, 23
Semitic tribal beliefs, 19-21
Sens, carvings at, 302; oriental tapestry at, 296
Serabít el-Khádem, Temple of, 252, 254
Serapion of Thmuis, 255, 258
Seville, 4
Shadrach, legend of, 297
Shechem, fortress at, 283, 284
Sherrill, C. H., *Stained Glass Tours in France,* 180 n.
Ships on fire, carvings of, 291, 294
Side aisles, 26, 27 (fig.), 28, 102 (fig.), 149 (fig.)
Silver, effect on Roman economics, 36; exhaustion of Roman supply, 36, 37; importance of, 91-93; mediæval discovery of new supplies, 91, 133
Silver stain (for glass), 174
Simeon of Durham, 86
Simon, the magician, 303
Simpich, F., *Saturday Evening Post,* 276 n.
Sinai, Mt., xviii, 244, 246, 251; Temple of Serabít el-Khádem, 252, 254
Sistine Chapel, 202, 306
Slavery (Rome), 33, 34
Sodom, 293
Smith, H. P., *Religion of Israel,* 18
Smith, W. Robertson, *Religion of the Semites,* 29, 259 n.

Soissons Cathedral, 142
Solutrean Period, 237 n.
Soufflot, 226, 241
Southampton, 194 n.
Southwell, Minster, 265
Spain, 36, 87; early churches, 88; manuscripts, 295
Spalato, Diocletian's Palace, 49
Spear, which pierced Christ's side, 83
Spire, spires, 77, f. p. 78, 78
Splays, in windows, 62, 62 n.
Stained glass, 115, f. p. 138, 170-180, f. p. 174; antiquity of, 172; colours in, 174, 175; drawing in, 175, 176; effect of glass painting on, 177; leading in, 173, 174; manufacturing technique, 173-176; Renaissance types of, 177, 306
Stalius, 272
Stephani, the press of the, 212
Stepped arch or arches, 59, 60
Stereotomy, 102
Stilt block, 49
Stoa basilike, 25, 28
Stone Age, 7; see also Palæolithic man and Neolithic man
Stone building, 84
Stoup, the; see Holy Water Stoup
Strange Voices from the Stoup, Chapter Thirty-two, *passim,* 252-264
Strassburg Cathedral, 279
Sturgis and Frothingham, *History of Architecture,* 156 n., 216 n., 221 n.
Suger, Abbot, 142, 201
Sugères, church at, 242
Sumer, Land of, 283, 287, 300
Supernatural, 66, 67, 68
Symbolism, mediæval, 122, 123; Chapter Twenty-one, *passim,* 163-169
Symmachus I, Pope, 219
Symonds, J. A., *Age of the Despots,* 83 n., 214 n., 221 n., 223 n.
Synagogue, synagogues, 20, 25, f. p. 174; as origin of Church plan, 25
Syrians, 308; manuscripts, 295

Taboo and taboos, 244, 245
Tariffs, feudal, 98
Tau (Greek letter), as symbol of cross, 301
Taylor, H. O., *Ancient Ideals,* 18
Taxation, in Fifteenth Century France, 209; in late Roman Empire, 38-40; ecclesiastical, 192, 193
Temenos, temenoi, 246-249; effects of urban growth on, 249; reverence for undermined by commerce and philosophy, 247, 248; as tabooed ground, 246
Temple, as the House of God, 285

Temple of Jerusalem, 20, 255
Temples, Egyptian, 246; Roman, 23, 24; Semitic, 20-22
Tentsindus, Provost, 275
Tertullian, 10, 30
Teutons, 56, 308; supernatural beliefs of, 67
Theodore of Tarsus, Archbishop of Canterbury, 268
Theodosius, Emperor of Rome, 16, 52, 121, 273
Theodosius II, Emperor of Rome, 40 n.
Theology, mediæval, effect on iconography, 298, 299; of the Twelfth Century, 122
Theophilus, the Monk, 96, 182
Theotokos, Mother of God, 299; see also Virgin Mary
Thiersch, 289
Thomas, the Apostle, S., 295
Thomas Aquinas, S., 113, 123
Thompson, A. H., The Ground Plan of the English Parish Church, 274 n.; Historical Growth of the English Parish Church, 268, 274 n.
Thompson, J. W., Economic and Social History of the Middle Ages, 41 n., 95 n., 143 n.; Economic and Social History of the Later Middle Ages, 188 n., 191 n., 192 n., 194 n.
Thor, 67
Threshold, burials under, 13 n.; "Keepers of the," 277; magic power of, 276, 277
Throne, Bishop's, see Bishop's Throne
Thrust (of a vault), 6; see also Vault
Thucydides, 189
Thutmose, Pharaoh, 284
Tiberius, Emperor of Rome, 35
Tierceron, 150
Titian, 305
Toledo, capture of, 88; Cathedral, 3; tomb of Cardinal Portocarrero, 3
Tolls, 98
Tomb, sculpture, 306
Tombs, as altars, 15, 16, 17
Torcello, churches at, 26, f. p. 267, 267, 268
Toscanella, Church of S. Maria Maggiore, f. p. 42; Church of S. Pietro, f. p. 55
Toulouse, inquisition at, 123; S. Etienne, 181; S. Sernin, 160, 161, 181
Tours, 83, 89; Cathedral, 145 n.; windows in, 303; S. Martin, 145
Towers (of churches), 72, 76, 79, f. p. 87; development of, 77, f. p. 78, 78; flanking gates, 282, 287; origin of, 76; round, see Round towers

Towers of Gudea, Chapter Thirty-five, passim, 282-290
Towns, Twelfth Century, 113
Trade, see Commerce
Trade routes, mediæval, 132-140, 193; effect on church building, 134
Trajan, Emperor of Rome, 11, 35, 78
Transenna, 267
Transepts, 5, f. p. 42, f. p. 46, 69 (fig.), 267, 299; Chapter Four, passim, 30-42; Chapter Five, passim, 43-45; origin of, 30-41; purpose of, 41; symbolism, 164
Transjordania, house types, 237
Trastevere, Church of S. Maria, f. p. 27
Tre Fontana, Church of, 9
Treaty of Verdun, 87
Trebizond, 132, 135
Tree of Life, 300
Trent, Council of, 295
Tribal bond, Semitic, 20
Tribal law, Semitic, 20
Tribal religion, 20, 21
Trier, 249
Triforium, triforia, 26, 102 (fig.), f. p. 126, 149 (fig.); disappearance of, 202
Triglyphs, f. p. 235, 241; origin of, 242
Triple portals, f. p. 59; symbolism, 163
Triumphal Arch, 272; as magic symbol, 270, 272; origin of, 270-272
"Trojan Horse," 284
Troubadours, 303
Troy (ancient), 28, 171, 283, 287; "Divine Tower," 284
T-shaped basilica, f. p. 42
Tuscania, see Toscanella
Tutilo, of S. Gall, 103 n.
Tyler, Wat, revolt of, 196
Tympanum, 64; at Bourges Cathedral, frontis.
Tyre, 140, 247, 286; church in, 267; congestion in, 249

Universities, mediæval, 113
Ur of the Chaldees, 22, 282, 283
Ur-Nammu, 282, 283, 287
Urban population, growth of, 114; effect on temenoi, 249
Urban II, Pope, 138, 139, 145
Usury, its effects in Rome, 32, 35

Valerian, Emperor of Rome, 10
Vandals, 56, 57, 64, 74
Varangian route, 135-137
Van Eyck, 306
Vault, vaults, 6, 50, 51, 102 (fig.), 106-111, 147-151, 154-159; effects of use on design, 106; necessity of, 84, 89; origins

of, 89; see also Barrel vault, Gothic vaults, Groined vault, Half Barrel vault, Ribbed vault
Vault ribs in Flamboyant Gothic, 207
Vault thrusts, 106, 107, 147-150
Vaux-de-Cernay, Abbey, window of, 306
Vendôme, La Trinité, f. p. 206
Venice, 133, 134, 136, 140, 143, 194 n., 213; plague in, 188; S. Maria dei Miracoli, 221; S. Mark's church, 12, 134; palaces, 218
Venus, rites of, 10
Verona, 290
Versailles, chapel, 228, 230
Vézelay, monks of, 83; S. Madeleine, 104, f. p. 123, 302
Vienne, 74
Viffort, ribbed vault in, 157, 159
Vikings, see Northmen
Virgil, on capital at Caen, 302
Virgin Mary, the Blessed, 181-184; Renaissance conceptions of, 305, 306; as Theotokos, the Mother of God, 299
Visigoths, 56, 74; kings' votive crowns, 299, 300
Voices of the Cathedral, Chapter One, passim.
Voltaire, on Gothic art, 144
Voraburg, 172

Waddell, Helen, The Wandering Scholars, 103 n.
Walafrid Strabo, 292
Waldensians, 124
Ward, W. H., French Renaissance Architecture, 218, 219, 221
Washington, D. C., S. Alban's Cathedral, 12
Wat Tyler, 196
Water, human sacrifices to, 259, 260; magic power of, 252, 253; modern persistence in belief in, 263; ordeal by, 260-262; rituals, 259; rituals for blessing, 254, 255

Weather cock, 168
Werck, Alfred, Stained Glass, 180 n.
West Front, see Façades
Westlake, N. H. J., History of Design in Painted Glass, 180 n.
Westminster Abbey, see London
Weymouth, plague in, 188
Wilgeforte, legend of, and crucifixion, 296
William the Conqueror, King of England, iii, 160, 282
William de Nogaret, 127
William of Volpiano, 145
Wilmar, the Mason, 103 n.
Winchester Cathedral, 265; market cross, 98
Windows, Gothic, 151; Romanesque, 108; splayed, 62, 62 n.; symbolism, 167
Women, monastic fear of, 300
Women, segregation of, 26
Wood, in churches, 89; in Romanesque, 100, 104, 105, 154
Woolley, C. L., Ur of the Chaldees, 283 n.; Ur Excavations at Al-Ubaid, 283 n.
Worcester, 266
Word, The, as symbol, 163
Worms Cathedral, 76
Wren, Sir Christopher, 241
Wulfstan, S., 266
Wycliffe, 124

Xenophanes, 248
Xerxes, xv, 29, 261
XP, 30

"Yoke," as magic arch, 272
York, 131; Cathedral, 152, 265, 292

Zechariah, 276
Zikkurat, 288
Zindjirli, stronghold of, 282, 283, 286, 287, 289
Zosimus, 40